- 4 DEC 2013   28 Jan 19,
28/4/15   28/2/19
7 Jan 19

-5 SEP 2013

- 3 AUG 2016

- 3 OCT 2016

11/10/18

28/11/18

28/12 Return

OSIDGE
LIBRARY
020 8359 3920

PAG
3

A

PAG
25

Direct
Transp
Langua
Index
Map Legend.................... 287

Please return/renew this item by the
last date shown to avoid a charge.
Books may also be renewed by phone
and Internet. May not be renewed if
required by another reader.

www.libraries.barnet.gov.uk

BARNET
LONDON BOROU

D1348097

30131 05063191 7

LONDON BOROUGH OF BARNET

welcome to Naples, Pompeii & the Amalfi Coast

History & Art

Few parts of Europe would dare compare their cultural riches to those of Naples and its fabled surrounds. A former royal capital, Naples has been home to countless cultural deities, from painter Michelangelo Merisi da Caravaggio to sculptor Cosimo Fanzago and composer Alessandro Scarlatti. The region lays claim to Italy's largest opera house and royal palace, many of the country's finest paintings, sculptures and frescoes, and not to mention a large share of Graeco-Roman ruins. Let your imagination run wild at the temples at Paestum, on the chariot-grooved streets of Pompeii, or in the frescoed magnificence of Villa Oplontis. Compare the Gothic minimalism of Naples' Complesso Monumentale di San Lorenzo Maggiore to the outrageous rococo of its Chiesa di San Gregorio Armeno. From frescoes to marble carvings, the region's glut of artistic marvels will satiate the greediest cultural appetites.

Culinary Riches

Naples and its region are the country's culinary soul, home to Italy's best pizza, pasta, mozzarella, vegetables, citrus and seafood. It's like one never-ending feast; wood-fired pizza and potent espresso in Naples, long, lazy lunches at Cilento *agriturismi* (farm stays), *alici fritte* (fried sardines) on weathered Tyrrhenian islands and lavish pastries in chintzy Salerno *pasticcerie* (pastry shops). Even the simplest bite can be a revelation,

Naples, Pompeii and the Amalfi Coast is the Italy of your wildest and most lingering dreams: a rich, intense, hypnotic ragù of Arabesque street life, decadent palaces, pastel-hued villages and aria-worthy vistas.

(left) Harbour at Marina Grande (p113), Capri
(below) *Spaghetti alla vongole* (spaghetti with clams)

from salty, almond-flavoured *taralli* (round, savoury biscuits), to the sweet, fluffy ricotta inside a *sfogliatella* (ricotta-filled pastry). Should you scour the markets for seasonal produce? Tuck into *coniglio all'Ischitana* (Ischian-style rabbit) at a rustic island trattoria? Pick up some famous *colatura di alici* (anchovy essence) in Cetara? Or just kick back with a crisp local Falanghina as you debate who has the creamiest buffalo mozzarella – Caserta or Paestum? Whatever your choice, be certain that good food and wine are always just around the corner.

Natural Highs

Mother Nature went into overdrive in Campania, creating a thrilling jumble of rugged mountains, steaming fumaroles, and dazzling coastal grottoes. It's like one giant playground begging for a tackle, be it fast-paced and furious, or romantic and relaxed. Crank up the pulse rate exploring bat-filled grottoes at the Grotta di Castelcivita, cave diving off the Capri coast, or feeling the earth's subterranean wrath at the Solfatara Crater. If you need to bring it down a notch, the options are just as enticing, from horse-riding the slopes of Mt Vesuvius to sailing your way along the Amalfi Coast or simply stripping down and soaking at a thermal beach on Ischia. The options may be many, but there is one constant – a landscape that is beautiful, diverse, and just a little magic.

Naples, Pompeii & the Amalfi Coast

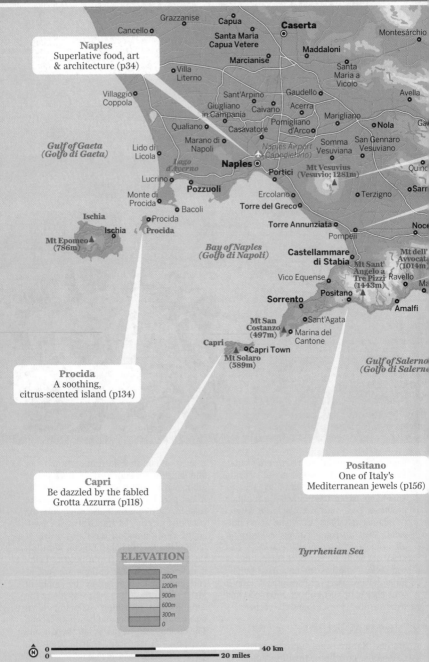

Naples
Superlative food, art & architecture (p34)

Procida
A soothing, citrus-scented island (p134)

Capri
Be dazzled by the fabled Grotta Azzurra (p118)

Positano
One of Italy's Mediterranean jewels (p156)

ELEVATION

1500m
1200m
900m
600m
300m
0

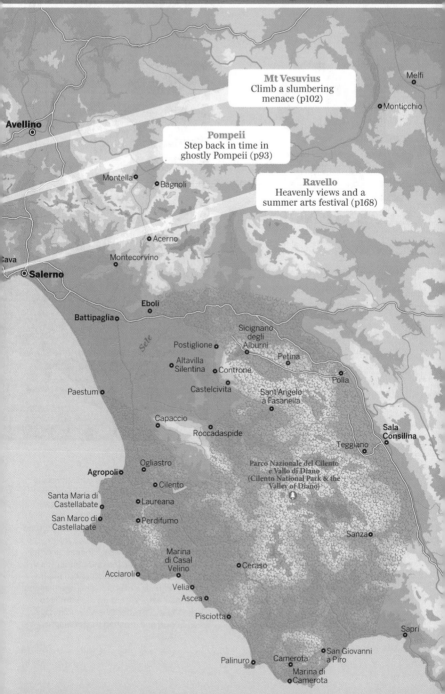

Mt Vesuvius
Climb a slumbering menace (p102)

Pompeii
Step back in time in ghostly Pompeii (p93)

Ravello
Heavenly views and a summer arts festival (p168)

Melfi

Monticchio

Avellino

Montella

Bagnoli

Acerno

Cava

Salerno

Montecorvino

Eboli

Battipaglia

Sele

Sicignano degli Alburni

Postiglione

Petina

Altavilla Silentina

Controne

Polla

Castelcivita

Sant'Angelo a Fasanella

Paestum

Capaccio

Roccadaspide

Sala Consilina

Teggiano

Ogliastro

Agropoli

Cilento

Parco Nazionale del Cilento e Vallo di Diano (Cilento National Park & the Valley of Diano)

Santa Maria di Castellabate

Laureana

San Marco di Castellabate

Perdifumo

Sanza

Marina di Casal Velino

Ceraso

Acciaroli

Velia

Ascea

Pisciotta

Sapri

Palinuro

Camerota

San Giovanni a Piro

Marina di Camerota

10
TOP
EXPERIENCES

Neapolitan Street Life

1 There's nothing like waking up to the sound of a Neapolitan street market, whether it's rough-and-ready Mercato di Porta Nolana (p47) or the city's oldest market, La Pignasecca (p54). A feast for the senses, it's as much akin to a North African bazaar as to a European market: fruit vendors raucously hawking their wares in Neapolitan dialect, swordfish heads casting sidelong glances at you across heaps of silvery sardines on ice, the irresistible perfume of crunchy *casareccio* (home-style) bread, and the just-baked *sfogliatelle* (ricotta-filled pastries). Mercato di Porta Nolana, Naples

Pompeii

2 Nothing piques human curiosity quite like a mass catastrophe and few can beat the ruins of Pompeii (p93), a once-thriving Roman town frozen for all-time in its 2000-year-old death throes. Wander Roman streets, the grassy, column-lined forum, the city brothel, the 5000-seat theatre and the frescoed Villa dei Misteri and ponder Pliny the Younger's terrifying account of the tragedy: 'Darkness came on again, again ashes, thick and heavy. We got up repeatedly to shake these off; otherwise we would have been buried and crushed by the weight'. Street in Pompeii

LONELY PLANET/GETTY IMAGES ©

LONELY PLANET/GETTY IMAGES ©

GLENN BEANLAND/GETTY IMAGES ©

Grotta Azzurra

3 Capri's craggy coast is studded with more than a dozen sea caves, most of them accessible and spectacular, but none as justifiably famous as the Grotta Azzurra (Blue Grotto; p193). Charted since antiquity, what makes this cave so spectacular is its magical, iridescent blue light. What's the secret, you ask? It's all in the refraction of sunlight through the water, which is reflected off the shimmering white sand. Visiting the cave is an experience in itself, on a little wooden rowboat complete with singing captain. Inside the Grotta Azzurra

Procida

4 Wind-swept and citrus-scented, tiny Procida (p134) oozes old-school southern Italian appeal. Faded gelato-hued houses crowd the marina as a first evocative introduction to an island where tourism has remained remarkably low-key – a tourist office only opened here in 2012. Narrow strung-with-washing lanes beckon strollers to the backstreets, secret swimming spots make for summertime bliss, and a handful of crumbling historic sights add a quiet sense of mystery. You may well eat some of the best fish of your trip here, served so fresh it's almost flapping. Marina Corricella, Procida

Ravello

5 Ravello (p168) exudes a tantalising sense of beauty, idle luxury and the past. Perched above the Amalfi Coast, the town bristles with sumptuous churches, palaces and villas. Among the latter is Villa Rufolo, its romantic gardens famously inspiring the German composer Wagner. In commemoration, a summer festival of classical music is held on its terrace, a fabulous event best booked ahead. Lyrical connections aside, Ravello's setting is sublime, framed by lush countryside. Villa Rufolo, Ravello

Positano

6 Pearl of the Amalfi Coast, Positano (p156) is scandalously stunning, a picture-perfect composition of pastel-coloured houses tumbling down towards a deep indigo sea. This ease with beauty also informs its skinny, pedestrian streets, lined with chic boutiques for fussy fashionistas. If fabulous food inspires you more than fine fabrics, swoon over seafood at the superb La Cambusa. Just don't forget neighbouring Praiano, a tranquil corner on this clamorous coast where locals, rather than tourists, fill the piazza benches and bars.

Amalfi Coast Trails

7 The charms of the Amalfi Coast (p140) stretch beyond the glittering baubles of the coastal towns. Venture inland and you find meandering footpaths that, prior to 1840, were the only way people got around on dry land. Orange groves, pine trees, wild orchids, and crumbling ruins flank the trails amid landscapes that shift and change according to the light and time of year. Yet, one thing remains constant: the breathtaking coastal views. If you are seeking something suitably divine, succumb to the Sentiero degli Dei, the 'Walk of the Gods', stippled with citrus and olive groves. Sentiero degli Dei (Walk of the Gods)

Museo Archeologico Nazionale

8 Naples' Museo Archeologico Nazionale (p49) is one of the world's most important archaeological museums. It's here that you'll find the breathtaking Toro Farnese (Farnese Bull), the largest sculptural group to have survived from antiquity. The epic piece keeps fine company, from detailed mosaics and glassware to frescoes that once adorned the region's elegant ancient villas. Of course, it wouldn't be a Roman affair without a little debauchery, waiting for you in the museum's infamous Gabinetto Segreto (Secret Chamber). Sculpture from Pompeii

Palazzo Reale di Capodimonte

9 It's just as well that Charles IV of Bourbon built big: his mother, Elisabetta Farnese, handed down one serious booty of art and antiquities. The blue bloods may have gone but the collection remains – a sumptuous, sprawling feast of epic canvases and tapestries, elegant sculptures, and dainty ceramics, with a splash of contemporary paintings and installations. Palazzo Reale di Capodimonte (p61) might be one of Italy's less-famous collections, but it's also one of its best, showcasing names like Raphael, Titian, Caravaggio, Masaccio and El Greco. Exterior of Palazzo Reale di Capodimonte

Mt Vesuvius

10 Guilty of decimating Pompeii and Herculaneum in AD 79, Mt Vesuvius (p102) looms over the Bay of Naples like a beautiful, silent menace. Though well-behaved since 1944, it remains mainland Europe's only active volcano, soaring a lofty 1281m above three million Neapolitans. Its slopes are part of the Parco Nazionale del Vesuvio, an area laced with soothing nature trails. But for the ultimate high, head to the summit, where you can peer into its mouth and scan the land from the Tyrrhenian Sea to the Apennine Mountains. Crater of Mt Vesuvius

need to know

Currency
» Euro (€)

Language
» Italian

When to Go

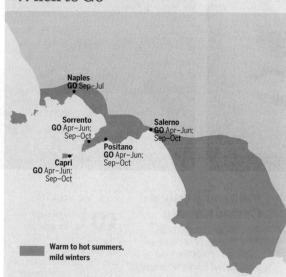

Naples
GO Sep–Jul

Sorrento
GO Apr–Jun;
Sep–Oct

Salerno
GO Apr–Jun;
Sep–Oct

Positano
GO Apr–Jun;
Sep–Oct

Capri
GO Apr–Jun;
Sep–Oct

Warm to hot summers,
mild winters

High Season
(Jul–Aug)

» Queues and crowds at big sights, beaches and on the road, especially August.

» Many restaurants and shops close in Naples in August.

» A good period for cultural events in tourist areas.

Shoulder
(Apr–Jun & Sep–Oct)

» Good deals on accommodation.

» Spring is best for festivals, flowers and local produce.

» June and September deliver summer heat without the August crowds.

Low Season
(Nov–Mar)

» Prices up to 30% lower than high season.

» Many sights, hotels and restaurants closed in coastal and mountainous areas.

» Christmas feasting and colourful Carnevale celebrations.

Your Daily Budget

Budget less than
€100

» Dorm bed: €15–25

» Double room in a budget hotel: €50–100

» Lunch and dinner of pizza and pasta: €15

» Excellent markets and delis for self-catering

Midrange
€100–200

» Double room in a hotel: €80–180

» Lunch and dinner in local restaurants: €25–50

Top end over
€200

» Double room in a four- or five-star hotel: €150–450

» Top restaurant dinner: €50–150

» Spa visit with treatment: €75

Money

» ATMs at Naples' Capodichino airport, major train stations and widely available in towns and cities. Credit cards accepted in most hotels and restaurants.

Visas

» Generally not required for stays of up to 90 days (or at all for EU nationals); some nationalities need a Schengen visa.

Mobile Phones

» European and Australian phones work; other phones should be set to roaming. Use a local SIM card for cheaper rates on local calls.

Accommodation

» Spans all options and budgets, from five-star luxury to B&Bs, hostels and *agriturismi* (farm stays). For information and listings, see the Accommodation chapter, p194.

Websites

» **Lonely Planet** (www. lonelyplanet.com/italy) Destination information, hotel bookings, traveller forum and more.

» **In Campania** (www. incampania.com) Campania tourist bureau website.

» **Napoli Unplugged** (www.napoliunplugged. com) Smart, updated website covering sights, events, news and practicalities.

» **Amalfi Coast Web** (www.amalficoastweb. com) Guide to services throughout the Amalfi Coast area.

» **Trenitalia** (www. trenitalia.com) Italian railways website.

Exchange Rates

Australia	A$1	€0.85
Canada	C$1	€0.81
Japan	¥100	€1.06
New Zealand	NZ$1	€0.65
UK	UK£1	€1.29
USA	US$1	€0.83

For current exchange rates see www.xe.com.

Important Numbers

Ambulance	☎118
Fire	☎115
Police	☎112/113
Country code	☎39
Directory assistance	☎1254
International access code	☎00
International reverse charge assistance	☎170

Arriving in Naples

» **Naples Capodichino Airport (NAP)**
Alibus (Airport Shuttle Bus) – €3 to Stazione Centrale and Molo Beverello (ferry terminal) every 20 to 30 minutes, 6.30am to 11.40pm
Taxi – €19 set fare to Piazza Municipio and Molo Beverello; journey time 20 to 30 minutes

» **Stazione Centrale, Naples**
Buses – €1.20 Route R4 to Piazza Municipio (beside Molo Beverello) every 9 to 14 minutes, 5.30am to midnight
Taxi – €10.50 set fare to Piazza Municipio and Molo Beverello; journey time 15 to 20 minutes

Driving Naples & the Amalfi Coast

Much of Naples' *centro storico* (historic centre) is off-limits to nonresident vehicles. In the rest of the city, anarchic traffic and illegal parking attendants demanding tips will quickly ruin your holiday. Nonresident vehicles are prohibited on Capri for much of the year, and driving is largely discouraged on Ischia and Procida. Peak season traffic can make driving along the Amalfi Coast less than relaxing, though having your own vehicle here means ultimate flexibility. Driving is ideal in the Cilento region, allowing you to discover out-of-the-way towns and beaches not well serviced by public transport. There are tolls on most motorways, payable by cash or credit card as you exit. For information on traffic conditions, tolls and driving distances, see www.autostrade.it. Headlights are compulsory day and night on all motorways.

first time

Everyone needs a helping hand when they visit a country for the first time. There are phrases to learn, customs to get used to and etiquette to understand. The following section will help demystify Naples, Pompeii and the Amalfi Coast so your first trip goes as smoothly as your fifth.

Language

Unlike in many other European countries, English is not widely spoken in Italy. Of course, in the main tourist centres you can get by, but in the countryside and off the tourist track you'll need to master a few basic phrases. This will improve your experience no end, especially when ordering in restaurants, some of which have no written menu. See the language section of this book for all the phrases you need to get by.

Booking Ahead

Reserving a room is essential during the high season and during key events (such as Easter and Christmas) when demand is usually high. Big-name restaurants and experiences such as an evening at the opera should also be booked ahead.

I would like to book...	Vorrei prenotare...
a single room	una camera singola
a double room	una camera doppia con letto matrimoniale
in the name of...	in nome di...
from... to... (date)	dal... al...
How much is it...?	Quanto costa...?
per night/per person	per la notte/per persona
Thank you (very much).	Grazie (mille).

What to Wear

Appearances matter in Italy. The concept of *la bella figura* (making a good impression) encapsulates the Italian obsession with looking good. In general, trousers (pants), jeans, shirts and polo shirts for men, and skirts or trousers for women, will serve you well in the city. Shorts, T-shirts and sandals are fine in summer and at the beach, but long sleeves are required for dining out. For the evening, think smart casual. A light sweater or waterproof jacket is useful in spring and autumn, and sturdy shoes are good for visiting archaeological sites. Dress modestly when visiting churches and religious sites, covering torso, shoulders and thighs.

What to Pack

» Passport (and a photocopy of it, kept separately)
» Credit cards
» Drivers licence
» Phrasebook
» Travel electricity adaptor
» Mobile (cell) phone charger
» Sunscreen
» Hat and sunglasses
» Waterproof jacket
» Comfortable shoes
» A stylish outfit
» Camera
» Money belt
» Earplugs
» A detailed driving map

Checklist

» Check the validity of your passport

» Check airline baggage restrictions

» Organise travel insurance (see p260)

» Make bookings (for sights, entertainment and accommodation)

» Inform your credit/ debit card company of your travel plans

» Check whether or not you can use your mobile (cell) phone

» Find out what you need to hire a car

Etiquette

Italy is a surprisingly formal society; the following tips will help you avoid any awkward moments.

» **Greetings**
Shake hands and say *buongiorno* (good day) or *buona sera* (good evening) to strangers; kiss both cheeks and say *come stai* (how are you) for friends. Use *lei* (you) in polite company; use *tu* (you) with friends and children. Only use first names if invited.

» **Asking for help**
Say *mi scusi* (excuse me) to attract attention; use *permesso* (permission) when you want to pass by in a crowded space.

» **Eating & Drinking**
When dining in an Italian home, bring wine or a small gift of *dolci* (sweets) from a local *pasticceria* (pastry shop) and dress well. Let your host lead when sitting and starting the meal. When dining out summon the waiter by saying *per favore* (please?).

» **Gestures**
Maintain eye contact during conversation.

Tipping

» **When to Tip**
Tipping is customary in restaurants, but optional elsewhere.

» **Taxis**
Optional, but most people round up to the nearest euro.

» **Restaurants**
Most restaurants have a *coperto* (cover charge; usually €1 to €2) and a *servizio* (service charge) of 10% to 15%. If service isn't included, consider a small tip.

» **Bars**
Italians often place a €0.10 or €0.20 coin on the bar when ordering coffee; if drinks are brought to your table, tip as if you're in a restaurant.

Money

Credit and debit cards can be used almost everywhere with the exception of some rural towns and villages. Visa and MasterCard are among the most widely recognised, but others like Cirrus and Maestro are also well covered. American Express is only accepted by some major chains and big hotels, and few places take Diners Club. Ask if bars and restaurants take cards before you order. Chip-and-pin is the norm for card transactions. ATMs are everywhere, but be aware of transaction fees. Some ATMs in Italy reject foreign cards. If this happens, try a few before assuming the problem is with your card. You can change travellers cheques at banks and post offices, although some readers have reported problems and hefty commissions. To reduce per-cheque charges get your cheques in large denominations.

if you like...

Food, Glorious Food

Campania's fertile fields, hillsides and turquoise sea are a giant larder, tended by proud farmers and fishermen. In this part of the country, traditions are fiercely guarded and eating well is a birthright. Tuck in!

Pizza Italy's most famous export is best sampled in its spiritual home, Naples (p34)

Markets Lip-smacking produce and electric street life collide at markets like **Porta Nolana** and **La Pignasecca** (p47 & p54)

Mozzarella di bufala Sink your teeth into Italy's silkiest cheese at dedicated spots like Inn Bufalita (p147)

Edivino A Capri gem, where homegrown produce and faultless hospitality make you feel like part of the family (p114)

Donna Rosa Every soupçon of fame is justified at this Amalfi Coast institution (p157)

Vinischia Savour local produce, vino and music at Ischia's appetite-piquing food and wine festival (p129)

Archaeological Treasures

Long before Rome was flaunting its Forum, Campania was basking in the glory of Magna Graecia, its coast graced by magnificent Hellenic temples and settlements. Millennia on, the region claims some of the world's finest Graeco-Roman mementos.

Museo Archeologico Nazionale An incomparable booty of ancient sculptures, mosaics, frescoes and decorative arts in the heart of Naples (p49)

Herculaneum Time stands still at this astoundingly well-preserved Roman town, complete with bathhouses, abodes, businesses, and furniture (p90)

Villa Oplontis Snoop around the reputed home of Emperor Nero's second wife, adorned with fabulous frescoes and a giant pool (p101)

Paestum Escape the hurly burly at these magical Greek temples, framed by fields and flowers (p182)

Villa Roma Antiquarium Envy how the other half lived at this luxe 1st-century abode, complete with private sauna (p172)

Il Vallone dei Mulino Ruins of ancient wheat mills deep in a central Sorrento gorge (p144)

Wild Beauty

Intense, dramatic and hypnotically beautiful, this corner of Italy seduces like few others. Grottoes shimmer in electric blue, cliffs plunge into milky-blue seas, and deep, dark forests harbour majestic caves. It's little wonder the Romans dubbed it *Campania Felix* (The Lucky Land).

Amalfi Coast More than just turquoise seas, the Amalfi Coast is laced with stunning, user-friendly walking trails (p140)

Parco Nazionale del Cilento An extraordinarily untamed wonderland of crystal-clear streams, rivers and tumbling waterfalls (p182)

Mt Vesuvius Mainland Europe's solo active volcano offers nature trails and on-a-cloud views from its time-bomb crater (p102)

Isole Faraglioni Capri's iconic limestone pinnacles rise from the sea like silent nymphs (p111)

Grotta di Matermania Faded mosaics adorn this giant cave, used by the Romans as a sacred shrine (p110)

Negombo Thermal pools, a private beach and beautiful botanical gardens put the luxe in alfresco downtime (p126)

GIOVANNI GUARINO/GETTY IMAGES ©

» Pizza margherita with buffalo mozzarella (p240)

Art

Frescoed chapels, canvas-slung palaces, art-pimped metro stations...Naples, Pompeii and the Amalfi Coast have no shortage of artistic highs. Whether you're after Warhol in a Bourbon palace, Caravaggio in a chapel, or William Kentridge on your commute, prepare to be inspired.

Palazzo Reale di Capodimonte From Botticelli and Caravaggio to poptastic Warhol, this palace-museum is home to art-world royalty (p55)

Museo del Novecento Twentieth-century southern Italian art in a hulking Neapolitan fortress (p67)

Naples Metro Let contemporary art transport you under the streets of Naples (p60)

Franco Senesi Two superb galleries dishing up edgy work from mostly Italian artists and sculptors (p156)

Museo Pinacoteca Provinciale From the Renaissance to the 20th century, Salerno's top art museum has you covered (p178)

Paolo Sandulli A defensive tower showcasing the work of a celebrity Amalfi Coast artist (p162)

Architecture

Campania bursts at the seams with architectural marvels, from elegant medieval monasteries to bombastic baroque churches, Industrial Age show-offs and the odd contemporary gem. Dive straight into a world of dizzying domes, sweeping staircases and pure built ambition.

Reggia di Caserta (Palazzo Reale di Caserta) An ambitious baroque palace with silver screen credentials (p44)

Galleria Umberto I This glorious arcade puts the cathedral in commerce (p51)

Cattedrale di Sant'Andrea Amalfi's zebra-stripe cathedral is a photogenic stunner (p164)

Palazzo dello Spagnuolo Not so much a staircase as an operatic tribute to the Neapolitan spirit (p68)

Auditorium Oscar Niemeyer A sinuous, striking structure that's causing controversial waves (p170)

Certosa di San Giacomo A 14th-century monastery oozing old-school Caprese style (p111)

Romantic Gardens

Italy's penchant for the 'outdoor room' has been going strong since Roman emperors landscaped their holiday villas. Blessed with sunshine, rich soil and heavenly vistas, Campania was always destined to house some of the country's best.

Ravello View the Amalfi Coast from the Belvedere of Infinity at **Villa Cimbrone** and swoon over classical tunes at **Villa Rufolo** (p170 & p169)

La Mortella An Ischian tropical paradise inspired by the gardens of Granada's Alhambra (p127)

Palazzo Reale di Caserta Caserta's royal gardens are the stuff of whimsical fairy tales (p44)

Villa Floridiana A villa, a tortoise-filled fountain and dreamy sea views define this romantic Neapolitan hideaway (p68)

Giardini di Augusto See what the Emperor saw in Augustus' former playground (p111)

Orto Medico, Ospedale degli Incurabili Seek out a secret cloister laced with healing herbs and trickling fountain (p43)

month by month

Top Events

1 **Settimana Santa**, March/April

2 **Maggio dei Monumenti**, May

3 **Napoli Teatro Festival Italia**, June & September

4 **Ravello Festival**, June to September

5 **Vinischia**, November

February

Short and accursed is how Italians describe February. It might still be chilly, but almond trees are starting to blossom and Carnevale season brightens things up with confetti, costumes and sugar-dusted treats.

 Carnevale
In the period leading up to Ash Wednesday, many southern Italian towns stage pre-Lenten carnivals. Kids don fancy costumes and throw *coriandoli* (coloured confetti), elaborate *carri* (floats) are paraded down the street, and everyone indulges one last time before Lent.

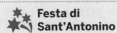 **Festa di Sant'Antonino**
Sorrento's patron saint is celebrated on 14 February with street stalls, fireworks, and musical processions through the *centro storico* (historic centre). It's also the perfect time to tuck into Sorrento's famous *torta di Sant'Antonio*; a chocolate and cream-filled tart.

March

The weather in March is capricious: sunny, rainy and windy all at once. The official start of Spring is 21 March, but things only really start to open up for the main season during Easter week.

 Settimana Santa
Processions and passion plays mark Easter Holy Week across the Campania region. On Good Friday and the Thursday preceding it, hooded penitents walk through the streets of Sorrento. On Procida, Good Friday sees wooden statues and life-size tableaux carted across the island.

May

The month of roses and early summer produce makes May a perfect time to travel, especially for walkers. The weather is warm but not too hot and prices are good value. It's also patron saint season.

 Festa di San Gennaro
Naples' patron saint day sees the faithful flock to the Duomo to see San Gennaro's blood liquefy. If it does, the city is deemed safe from volcanic catastrophe. Repeat performances take place on 19 September and 16 December.

 Maggio dei Monumenti
As the weather warms up, Naples puts on a mammoth, month-long program of art exhibitions, concerts, performances and tours in Naples. Many architectural and historical treasures usually off-limits to the public are open and free to visit.

June

The summer season kicks off in June. The temperature cranks up quickly, *lidis* (beaches) start to open in earnest and some of the big summer festivals commence. The Anniversary of the Republic, on 2 June, is a national holiday.

Napoli Teatro Festival Italia

Naples' theatre festival delivers top-quality home-grown and foreign theatre, performance art, and exhibitions over three weeks (www.napoliteatrofestival. it). Events take place across the city, from theatres to metro stations. A scaled-back edition of the festival takes place over six days in September.

Ravello Festival

Perched high above the Amalfi Coast, Ravello draws world-renowned artists during its summer-long festival (www.ravellofestival. com). Spanning everything from music and dance to film and art exhibitions, several events take place in the exquisite Villa Rufolo gardens from June to mid-September.

July

School is out and Italians everywhere are heading to the coast or mountains for their summer holidays. Prices and temperatures rise. The beaches are in full swing, as are several major music and cultural festivals.

Giffoni Film Festival

Europe's biggest children's film festival livens up the town of Giffoni Valle Piana, east of Salerno (www. giffonifilmfestival.it). Attracting children and teens from across the world, the 11-day event includes screenings, workshops and big-name guests such as Robert De Niro and Nicholas Cage.

Neapolis Festival

Southern Italy's largest contemporary music festival delivers 11 rocking days of top music acts (www.neapolis.it). Former festival acts include David Bowie, REM, The Cure, Patti Smith, Architecture in Helsinki and Massive Attack. Be sure to check the website for the current location.

Sagra del Tonno

Tiny Cetara plays host to this annual tuna festival, held over four days in late July or early August (www. prolococetara.it). Tuna dishes aside, you can taste-test the town's celebrated anchovies, made famous thanks to its *colatura di alici* (anchovy paste).

August

August in Campania is hot, expensive and crowded. Everyone is on holiday and while it may no longer be true that everything is shut, many businesses and restaurants do close for part of the month.

Ferragosto

After Christmas and Easter, Ferragosto is Italy's biggest holiday. While it now marks the Feast of the Assumption, even the ancient Romans honoured their pagan gods on Feriae Augusti. The beaches are super crowded, and Naples lets loose with particular fervour.

November

The advent of winter creeps down the peninsula in November, but there's still plenty going on, from the chestnut harvest to an island celebration of regional wine and produce.

Vinischia

Foodies and vinophiles flock to this four-day wine and food event, held on the island of Ischia (www.vinischia.it). Festival stalls showcase the best of the island's produce, from wine and cheese to olive oil and honey.

December

The days of alfresco living are at an end. Yet, despite the cooler days and longer nights, looming Christmas festivities warm things up with festive street lights, nativity scenes and Yuletide specialities.

Natale

The weeks preceding Christmas shine with religious events. Many churches set up nativity scenes known as *presepi*. People from across the country head to Naples to buy its famous *pastori* (nativity scene figurines or statues) on and around Via San Gregorio Armeno.

itineraries

Whatever your time frame, these itineraries provide a starting point for the trip of a lifetime. Want more inspiration? Head online to www.lonelyplanet. com/thorntree to chat with other travellers.

Twelve Days
Palazzi, Ruins & Islands

> Start with four action-packed days in **Naples**, taste-testing its famous pizza and espresso and swooning over its frescoed churches and *palazzi* (large buildings). On one of these days, consider a day trip to **Caserta**, home to a Unesco-lauded palace that upstages Versailles. From Naples, head west for two days in the Campi Flegrei, home to some of Italy's finest Graeco-Roman sights. In **Pozzuoli**, check out Italy's third-largest Roman amphitheatre, ancient market ruins, and the geological freakshow better known as the Solfatara Crater. Bathe like the Romans in **Lucrino**, see where Roman emperors soaked in **Baia**, and snoop around ancient Greek ruins in **Cuma**. On day seven, slow down the pace by catching a ferry across to **Procida**, where you can lose yourself in its stuck-in-time fishing villages, sleepy backstreets and secret beaches. Day nine sees you catching a ferry across to **Ischia**, the largest island in the Bay of Naples. Give yourself three days to explore its archaeology, botanical gardens, castle and wineries, and treat yourself at one of its thermal spas. Refreshed and restored, it's an easy ferry ride back to Naples on day 12.

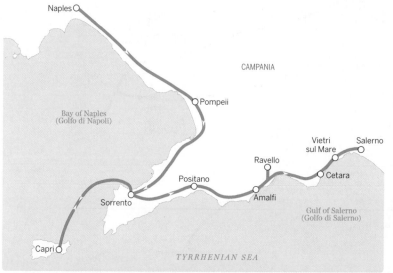

Two Weeks
A Coastal Affair

Start your sojourn with three days in **Naples**, indulging in its artistic, architectural and culinary riches. Make time for at least two of the city's impressive museums, explore its markets and catacombs, swoon over the *Christo velato* (Veiled Christ) sculpture in the Cappella Sansevero, and catch an aria at the majestic Teatro San Carlo. Spend day four turning back time at **Pompeii**, before evening cocktails in laid-back **Sorrento**. Spend the next day ambling Sorrento's streets, getting a crash course in craftsmanship at the Museo Correale and Museo Bottega della Tarsia Lignea, and finding peace in the cloisters of the Chiesa di San Francesco. Crank up the magic on day six by sailing across to **Capri**, giving yourself three days to fall madly in love with this fabled island. Glide into the dazzling Grotta Azzurra (Blue Grotto), ride up to Monte Solaro, and lose the hordes on side streets and bucolic walking trails.

On day nine, sail back to Sorrento and hit the hairpin turns and heavenly vistas of the Amalfi Coast. First stop: **Positano**. Check in for three nights, slipping on your Prada sandals and getting lost in its labyrinth of chic laneways. Sup on fresh seafood, hire your own boat, or tie up your hiking boots and get a natural high on the *Sentiero degli Dei* (Walk of the Gods). Spend day 12 in deeply historic **Amalfi**, exploring its sublime cathedral and cloisters before continuing to lofty **Ravello**, a long-time favourite haunt for composers, writers and Hollywood stars. Stay the night to soak up the town's understated elegance, and spend the following day swooning over its villas and uber-romantic gardens. If you can pull yourself away, continue east to upbeat Salerno, your final stop. On the way, drop into **Cetara** to sample its famous tuna and anchovies and into **Vietri sul Mare** to shop for local ceramics. Spend a full day in **Salerno**, diving into its medieval core to savour the city's fabulous seafood, pastries and street life. Come evening, join the locals for a spot of bar-hopping bonhomie – the *perfetto* end to your coastal affair.

Nine Days
The Cilento Trail

Start your adventure in the underrated city of **Salerno**. Its cathedral is widely lauded as Italy's most beautiful medieval church, and its engrossing multimedia Scuola Medica Salernitana Museo Virtuale tells the story of the city's medieval medical school, once one of Europe's most important. Head up to the Castello di Arechi for sweeping views, and to the revamped waterfront for a late-afternoon *passeggiata* (stroll). After dark, join the locals in the city's vibrant medieval heart for a little bar-hopping and *movida* (partying). On day two, bid Salerno *arrivederci* and head inland for three days in the rugged beauty of the **Parco Nazionale del Cilento e Vallo di Diano**, Italy's second largest national park and a Unesco World Heritage site. Base yourself at one of the park's *agriturismi* (farm stays) and explore the area's famous grottoes, namely the Grotta di Castelcivita and Grotta dell'Angelo. Make sure to spend a few hours in the medieval town of Postiglione – home to an 11th-century Norman castle – and a morning or afternoon in **Padula**, famous for its mammoth Carthusian monastery, the Certosa di San Lorenzo. Not far from the Certosa is the fabled Valle delle Orchidee (Valley of the Orchids), whose 70-plus varieties of springtime orchids create a spectacular blaze of colour. One of the national park's more curious sites is Roscigno Vecchia, a veritable ghost town abandoned early last century.

On day five, head back towards the coast to gasp at the mighty Greek temples of **Paestum**, the oldest of which dates back to the 6th century BC. Spend the evening and the following morning in **Agropoli**, wandering its atmospheric *centro storico* (historic centre) before heading south to **Santa Maria di Castellabate** for superlative seafood noshing. On day seven, head up to the beautiful medieval town of **Castellabate** and lose yourself in its shamelessly charming laneways, then spend the afternoon exploring the ancient ruins of **Velia**. End your Cilento adventure with a couple of lazy beach days in **Palinuro**, which, like Capri, lays claim to a dazzling Grotta Azzurra (Blue Grotto).

Eat & Drink Like a Local

When To Go

There's never a bad time to raise your fork in Campania. For specific details on food events, see p18 and specific destination chapters.

Spring (Mar–May)

Asparagus, artichokes and Easter specialities. Celebrate regional *vino* at Naples' Wine & The City (p77).

Summer (Jun–Aug)

Eggplants, peppers, tomatoes and Cetara's Sagra del Tonno (p173). Bite into *albicocche vesuviane* (Vesuvian apricots) and *pere mastantuono* (mastantuono pears).

Autumn (Sep–Oct)

Mushrooms, chestnuts, black truffles and *mele annurche* (annurche apples). Plough through pasta at Minori's Gustaminori (p172) food fest and taste-test island flavours at Ischia's Vinischia (p129).

Winter (Dec–Feb)

Christmas and Carnevale treats, plus turf staples like *zuppa di castagne e fagioli* (chestnut and bean soup). Dig into sausages by a bonfire at Sorrento's Sagra della Salsiccia e Ceppone (p147).

Naples, Pompeii and the Amalfi Coast are a culinary Valhalla, where produce and well-trained taste buds have created one of the world's most envied culinary landscapes. Whet your appetite with the following food trip essentials, then dig deeper on p239.

Food Experiences

So much produce, so many classics, so little time! Fine-tune your culinary radar with the following musts.

Meals of a Lifetime

» **Donna Rosa (p157), Positano** A Michelin-starred institution where honest home cooking gets an innovative twist.

» **Il Focolare (p130), Ischia** A carnivorous, Slow Food gem, where homegrown produce is put to delicious use.

» **Da Bruno (p81), Naples** What appears on the menu depends on what the fishing boats caught that morning. Classic, sophisticated flavours that are truly unforgettable.

» **Marina Grande (p166), Amalfi** Join the locals for fresh, fabulous seafood overlooking the beach.

Cheap Treats

» **Pane casareccio** Rustic, thick-crusted bread.

» **Pizza** Both wood-fired and *fritta* (deep fried).

» **Fritture** Deep-fried snacks including *crocchè* (potato croquettes), best bought from *frigittorie* (fried-food take-away outlets).

WHAT TO BOOK

Generally, all high-end and popular restaurants should be booked ahead, especially for Friday and Saturday evenings and Sunday lunch. In major tourist towns, always book restaurants in the summer high season and during Easter and Christmas. Cooking courses such as Sorrento Cooking School (p145), Mamma Agata (p170) and Gelateria David (p149) should also be booked ahead.

» **Sfogliatella** Cinnamon-scented ricotta pastries in *riccia* (filo) and *frolla* (shortcrust) varieties.

» **Gelato** The best Italian gelato uses seasonal ingredients and natural colours (no bright-green pistachio!).

Local Specialities

The Italian term for 'pride of place' is *campanilismo* but a more accurate word would be *formaggisimo*: loyalty to the local cheese. Each regional area boasts its own edible icons. The following are some of the best:

» **Naples** Italy's best pizza, *spaghetti alle vongole* (spaghetti with clams) and *pasta cacio e pepe* (pasta with caciocavallo cheese and pepper). Fill-up on *sartù* (rice timbale with cheese, vegetables and meat). Snack on *pizza fritta* (fried pizza dough stuffed with charcuterie, cheese and tomato) and *supplì di riso* (fried rice balls). Desserts include *pastiera napoletana* (a citrus-scented ricotta tart).

» **Caserta** Internationally renowned for its moreish *mozzarella di bufala* (buffalo-milk mozzarella).

» **Capri** Light *insalata caprese* (mozzarella, tomato and basil salad) and calorific *torta caprese* (almond and chocolate cake). Wash it down with *limoncello* (lemon liquer).

» **Ischia** Plunge into *spaghetti alla puttanesca* (spaghetti with olives, chilli, garlic and tomato sauce), *coniglio all'ischiatana* (rabbit with garlic, chilli, tomato, herbs and white wine), and aromatic *vino* from top local wineries Casa D'Ambra and Pietritorcia.

» **Minori** Taste-test the town's pasta, especially its fresh *scialatielli* (thick ribbons of pasta) and *'ndunderi*, ancient Roman percursors of gnocchi.

» **Cetara** Savour Italy's best anchovies with *spaghetti con alici e finocchietto selvatico* (spaghetti with anchovies and wild fennel) and *colatura di alici* (anchovy essence).

» **Salerno & the Cilento** Drizzle *Colline Salernitane DOP* extra virgin olive oil and devour buffalo-milk mozzarella from Paestum. Other notable Cilento cheeses include goat's milk *cacioricotta di capra* and cow's milk *caciocavallo podolico*.

How to Eat & Drink Like a Local

Now that your appetite is piqued, it's time for the technicalities of eating *alla campana* (Campania-style).

When to Eat

» **Colazione (Breakfast)** Often little more than a pre-work espresso with a *cornetto* (Italian croissant) or a *sfogliatella* (sweet ricotta-filled pastry).

» **Pranzo (Lunch)** Traditionally the main meal of the day, with many businesses closing for *la pausa* (afternoon break). Standard restaurant times are noon to 3pm, though locals don't lunch before 2pm.

» **Aperitivo** Popular in Naples, post-work drinks sees numerous bars offer tasty morsels for the price of a drink between 5pm and 8pm.

» **Cena (Dinner)** Traditionally lighter than lunch, though still a main meal. Standard restaurant hours are 7.30pm to 11pm (later in summer). Most locals don't dine before 8.30pm.

Choosing a Restaurant

» **Ristorante (Restaurant)** Formal service and refined dishes and wines make restaurants the obvious choice for special occasions.

» **Trattoria** A less formal version of a restaurant, with cheaper prices, more-relaxed service and classic regional specialities. Avoid places offering a 'tourist menu'.

» **Osteria** Historically a tavern focussed on wine, the modern version is an intimate trattoria or wine bar offering a handful of dishes.

» **Enoteca** Perfect for a little vino downtime, wine bars often serve snacks to accompany your tipple.

» **Agriturismo** A working farmhouse offering accommodation, as well as food made with farm-grown produce. Some offer farm activities.

» **Pizzeria** Great for a cheap feed and cold beer. The best pizzerias are often crowded: be patient.

» **Tavola Calda** Literally a 'hot table', these cafeteria-style options peddle cheap premade food like self-service pasta, roast meats and *pizza al taglio*.

Outdoor Activities

Coastal Grottoes
Glide into Campania's dazzling sea caves.

Amalfi Coast Hikes
See the fabled coast from God's POV.

Thermal Therapy
Loosen your knots at a soothing spa.

Solfatara Crater
Feel the fury at this hot-as-hell crater.

Mt Vesuvius
Scale the slopes of a sinister mountain.

Punta Campanella Marine Reserve
Dive down to meet some colourful characters.

Grotta di Castelcivita
Live out your speleological urges in Europe's oldest settlement.

Positano Cruising
Sail to a little-known archipelago for a sunset toast.

Best Time to Go
April to June Walk among wildflowers.
July & September Watersports and warm-water diving.

Naples and its surrounding region lay claim to some of Italy's most dramatic and breathtaking terrain. For outdoor aficionados, this means a long, satisfying list of possibilities, from diving off the Amalfi Coast to trekking in rugged, ancient Cilento woods. You can spend one day exploring the slopes of a volcano on horseback and the next sailing to your own private island beach.

Walking & Hiking
Lazy saunter or hardcore hike, Campania has you covered. In Naples, you can (literally) lose yourself in the sprawling Parco di Capodimonte (p65), spread across a high plateau overlooking the urban sprawl and bay. A former royal hunting ground, it's the city's largest patch of green, laced with palm-fringed lawns, quiet meadows, and soothing forest trails. For a truly elegant saunter, it's hard to beat the gardens of the Reggia di Caserta (p44), adorned with cascading water features and a romantic English Garden. For a walk on the wild side, however, head to Pozzuoli's **Solfatara Crater** (Map p74; ☏081 526 23 41; www.solfatara.it; Via Solfatara 161; admission €6; ◷8.30am to 1hr before sunset), where a walking trail circles a restless volcanic crater. Further west, crater-turned-lake Lago d'Averno (p76) offers an altogether more tranquil, bucolic circuit. On the other side of Naples, reaching the summit of Mt Vesuvius (p102) is easier than you may think, with regular shuttle buses connecting Ercolano-Scavi Circumvesuviana station to the summit carpark.

From here, it's a relatively easy 860m walk up to the summit, where your reward is a 360-degree panorama capturing Naples, its bay, and the distant Apennine mountains. The volcano is part of the Parco Nazionale del Vesuvio, a national park crisscrossed by nine *sentieri* (nature trails) of varying lengths and intensity. The most challenging and rewarding is the 6.7km-long '*Lungo la Strada Matrone*' ('Route 6'). Starting from Via Cifelli (2.5km north of Torre Annunziata Circumvesuviana station it heads up the volcano's southeastern slope to the summit. You'll find all nine routes explained at www.vesuviopark.it. For an altogether more relaxed exploration, Naples Trips & Tours (p103) runs horse-riding tours of the national park. The park itself is a rich natural oasis, home to hedgehogs, moles, stonemartens and foxes, as well as around 140 species of birds, including spotted woodpeckers, hawks and imperial ravens. Much to the surprise of many, both Capri and Ischia also offer some spectacular walks that will see you enjoying the islands away from the beach crowds. Across on the Amalfi Coast, the suitably named Walk of the Gods offers a very different experience of the area, passing through a sumptuous landscape of ancient vineyards, craggy cliff faces and verdant valleys. While this is the area's most famous and spectacular trail, it's only one of a network of well-marked paths. Local tourist offices can provide maps of the colour-coded routes. Southeast of the Amalfi Coast, the Parco Nazionale del Cilento & Vallo di Diano serves up relaxing walks and more challenging hikes, reliable guides and excellent maps. This remarkable wilderness area is home to circa around registered botanical species, as well as a number of rare birds, including the golden eagle and seacrow. The park's most famous feature, however, is an incredible series of caves. Among these are the Grotte di Castelcivita (p183) and Grotta dell'Angelo (p183), their Gothic-like stalagmites and stalactites yours to explore on daily speleological tours (tours of the Grotte di Castelcivita only run from March to September). For more information on hiking in the region, see Lonely Planet's dedicated *Hiking in Italy*. Online, www.parks.it offers useful information on the region's national parks.

Spa Therapy

The Bay of Naples has been celebrated for its thermal waters for thousands of years, seducing everyone from Roman emperors to frazzled celebrities. Easily reached on the Cumana train from Naples, the Terme Stufe di Nerone (p76) is one of the most famous thermal spas in the Campi Flegrei, complete with indoor and outdoor pools, terraced gardens, and saunas carved out of the region's trademark *tufo* rock. In the bay itself, Ischia is one of the world's richest, most diverse hydrothermal hotspots, with no less than 103 thermal springs, 67 fumaroles and 29 underground basins. Put its thermal offerings to good use at spa parks like Negombo (p126) and Giardini Poseidon (p128), both of which combine lush gardens with a booty of mineral pools, massage treatments and a private beach. Less luxurious but more historic is the Terme Cavascuro (p129), complete with old Roman baths and sweat-inducing grottoes.

HIKING TIPS

» Invest in comfortable lace-up walking shoes or sturdy boots.

» Pack a small daypack with an extra layer of clothing for if temperatures drop.

» Depending on the season, don't forget sunscreen, sunglasses and a hat.

» Pack a working compass!

» Take plenty of water, and some energy-stoking snacks.

» Invest in a good map with trails marked, particularly in the Parco Nazionale del Cilento.

» If planning a serious hike, let someone know the approximate duration and location.

TOP BEACHES

» **Baia di Ieranto** A spectacular beach at the tip of the Punta Penna peninsula south of Sorrento.

» **Il Sorgeto** (p130) Catch a water taxi to this toasty thermal beach on Ischia.

» **Spiaggia Marmelli** (p192) Retreat to a lush, soothing cove on the Cilento coast.

» **Spiaggia di Fornillo** (p156) Crystal-clear water awaits at this in-the-know alternative to Positano's main beach.

» **Santa Maria di Castellabate** (p190) Velvet-soft sand and powder-blue sea at a Cilento coast resort.

» **Spiaggia del Castello** (p76) Catch a boat to a petite beach set beneath a looming castle in the Campi Flegrei.

Beaches

Campania's aqua offerings are as varied as they are beautiful. While Naples itself offers metropolitan beaches, you're better off splashing about in the cleaner waters of the bay islands, or the Amalfi and Cilento coasts. As is the case in much of Italy, beaches in Campania are either private or public. Private beaches are especially prevalent at summertime hotspots like Capri, Ischia and the Amalfi Coast, offering everything from on-site restaurants and bars to *ombrellone* (beach umbrella) and *lettino* (sunbed) hire. Admission to these beaches is usually around €10. If you don't fancy paying for a place on the sand, you'll need to look for a *spiaggia libera* (free beach). Usually signposted, these often consist of crowded, narrow stretches of beach close to the nearest road access or sometimes right beside the private beach. Some (but not all) free beaches come with shower and toilet facilities.

Sailing

The region has a proud maritime tradition and you can readily hire a paddle boat or sleek sailing yacht on the bay islands as well as on the mainland coast. Sailors of all levels are catered for: experienced sailors can island hop around the Bay of Naples or along the Amalfi Coast on chartered yachts; weekend boaters can explore hidden coves in rented dinghies. This is especially ideal given that many of the region's best (and less crowded) swimming spots are only accessible by boat. Not that you need your own sails to reach *all* of Campania's coastal treasures. On Ischia, water taxis connect the village of Sant'Angelo to the thermal beach cove Il Sorgeto. On Capri, regular tours depart for the island's spectacular Grotta Azzurra (Blue Grotto), while across in Positano, boat tour options include sunset cruises to the Li Galli islands, former home of Rudolf Nureyev. Further west, boats depart from both Conca dei Marini and Amalfi for the ethereal **Grotta dello Smeraldo** (Emerald Grotto; admission €5; ☺9am-4pm Mar-Oct, 9am-3pm Nov-Feb). Amalfi's gilded maritime heritage comes to the fore every four years, when the town plays host to the **Regata delle Antiche Repubbliche Marinare** (Regatta of the Old Maritime Republics), an annual boat race between the once-mighty maritime republics of Amalfi, Venice, Genoa and Pisa. Amalfi's turn comes around again in 2016. Local tourist offices can provide information on tours and reputable boat hire companies.

Diving

Diving is a popular pursuit in Campania, and you'll have no trouble finding diving schools offering equipment hire, courses, and dives for all levels. Several diving schools are open most of the year, while others are open seasonally, typically from May to October. One of the region's best diving spots is the **Punta Campanella Marine Reserve**. Located at the tip of the Sorrento Peninsula, it's well known for its colourful marina fauna, small reefs and multicoloured seaweed. In general, try avoiding August, when much of Campania's coastline is besieged by holidaymakers and prices are at their highest. Information on diving schools and areas is available from local tourist offices and online at **Diveitaly** (www.diveitaly.com).

Travel with Children

Best Regions for Kids

Naples
Capital attractions: step back in time at Pompeii and Herculaneum, explore secret cisterns, passageways and ghoulish cemeteries below city streets, get experimental at a science museum, and sidle up to some geological freaks.

The Islands
Beach babes: seek your own perfect swimming cove on a private boat, slip inside an enchanted grotto, or pool-hop at a sprawling thermal spa resort.

Amalfi Coast
Surf and turf: chill out on a summertime boat trip, get splash-happy at a famous beach, hike high above the coastline, and take in a little history at a quirky paper museum.

Salerno & the Cilento
Wild and cultured: ponder ancient medicine and film plots, or simply go wild riding rivers, spotting wildlife and sorting out your stalactites from your stalagmites.

In Campania children are adored and welcomed. Encounters with hissing fissures, a dormant volcano or ancient skeletons should pique the interest of most young minds, though it's worth investing in a few children's history books to help along their imagination. On the downside, the region has few special amenities for junior travellers, and the combination of Naples' breathless pace, the Amalfi Coast's twisting coastal road, and the stroller-challenging cobbled stones at archaeological sites can prove unfriendly. With a bit of planning, you can expect some serious family fun.

Children's Highlights

If travelling with young ones, always ask at tourist offices about any family activities, festivals and events. Most museums and sights offer discounted entry for kids, although some discounts are for EU citizens only. For more information, see Lonely Planet's *Travel with Children*, the website www.italiakids.com, or the more general www.travelwithyourkids.com and www.familytravelnetwork.com.

Culture Vultures

» **MAV (Museo Archeologico Virtuale), Ercolano** Head back to AD 79 at this virtual reality museum. Holograms, videos and reconstructions bring the region's world-famous ruins back to life, making a real-life wander much more rewarding.

» **Città della Scienza, Bagnoli, Naples** Explore everything from magnetic fields to genetic code at this super-fun science museum. It's also home to a high-tech planetarium, where you can get the lowdown on the universe.

» **Museo Didattico della Scuola Medica Salernitana, Salerno** Inspire your little surgeon at this high-tech multimedia museum, dedicated to the wince-inducing marvels of medieval medicine. Do not try this at home!

Thrills & Spills

» **Solfatara Crater, Pozzuoli** Nothing quite excites like a geological hissy fit...and that's exactly what you'll get at this shallow volcanic crater.

» **Mt Vesuvius** Thrill the kids by peering into the mouth of this snoozing killer, or hit the saddle on a horse-riding trip on its forested slopes.

» **Negombo, Ischia** A splash-happy paradise, this thermal-springs park features 14 mineral pools and a thermal beach, plus massage and beauty treatments for frazzled guardians.

» **Grotta Azzurra, Capri** Forget Disney – when it comes to special effects, nothing comes close to Capri's Blue Grotto.

» **Hiking Trails, Amalfi Coast** Camera phones will click on the Amalfi Coast's walking trails, where exercise comes with beautiful Tyrrhenian views.

» **Parco Nazionale del Cilento e Vallo di Diano, Cilento** Get your kicks in myriad ways, from rafting down a river to exploring grottoes, or getting your hands dirty at a local *agriturismo* (farm stay).

Time Travel

» **Pompeii** Better than any history book, these ruins will have the kids snooping around ancient theatres, houses, shops, even a stadium.

» **Herculaneum** Smaller than Pompeii, Herculaneum is easier to visit in a shorter time. It's also better preserved, with carbonised furniture and interiors that bring the past to vivid life.

» **Napoli Sotterranea, Naples** It's a storybook scenario: you're led into a house, and then down a secret porthole into a magical labyrinth of ancient Graeco-Roman passageways and cisterns.

» **Catacomba di San Gennaro, Naples** More subterranean excitement awaits at this ancient burial ground, complete with mysterious-looking frescoes and a setting that looks straight out of *Raiders of the Lost Ark*.

» **Anfiteatro Flavio, Pozzuoli** Play out your own centurion battles at Italy's third-largest Roman amphitheatre. The area below the main arena is one of the country's best preserved.

» **Cimitero delle Fontanelle, Naples** It's Halloween every day at the ghoulish Fontanelle Cemetery, stacked with human skulls and bones. To appreciate its mystery, explore the site on a guided tour.

Planning

When to Go

The best time for families to visit Naples and around is May, June or September. The weather is warm and sunny, and the peak-season crowds of July and August are absent. If you're planning on beach time, July is a good bet. Colourful floats and costumes make Carnevale (February or March) another good choice, while the region's famous *presepi* (Christmas cribs) make December magical.

Where to Stay

In high season (summer), camping grounds are buzzing, and many offer activities for youngsters. Hostels and apartments are also a good bet for families, offering multibed rooms, guest kitchens and lounge facilities. *Agriturismo* (farm stays) offer plenty of space and perhaps a few furry friends.

Book accommodation in advance whenever possible. In hotels, some double rooms can't accommodate an extra bed for kids, so check ahead. If the child is small enough to share your bed, some hoteliers will let you do this for free. The website www.booking.com specifies the 'kid policy' for every hotel listed and what extra charges incurred.

Where to Eat

Most nosheries welcome kids, especially trattorias and pizzerias. If reserving a table, ask if they have a *seggiolone* (high chair). Children's menus are uncommon, though requesting a *mezzo piatto* (half plate) off the menu is usually fine.

Essentials

You can buy baby formula in powder or liquid form, as well as sterilising solutions, at pharmacies. Disposable nappies (diapers) are available at supermarkets and pharmacies. Fresh cow's milk is sold in cartons in supermarkets and in bars with a 'Latteria' sign. UHT milk is popular, and in many out-of-the-way areas , it's the only kind available.

Transport

Travelling with a stroller can be challenging. This is especially true in Naples, where buses are often crowded and some trains (including those on metro line 2) are higher than the platform. Transport operators offer free travel to children below the height of 1m. Most car-hire firms offer children's safety seats at a nominal cost, but should be booked ahead.

regions at a glance

Naples

Food ✓✓✓
History ✓✓✓
Museums ✓✓✓

Pizza and Pasta

When Italians all over the country tell you that *si mangia bene a Napoli* (one eats well in Naples) you know you're onto a good thing. Vying hard for Italy's culinary crown, the city's loud and lusty streets serve up some of the nation's most famous flavours: coffee, pizza, tomatoes, pasta, *sfogliatelle* (sweetened ricotta pastries), *babà* (rum-soaked sponge cake) and a panoply of seafood to be devoured every which way you can.

p34

Ancient Sites

Living in the shadow of Mt Vesuvius, the Neapolitans abide by the motto, *carpe diem* (seize the day). And why not? All around them, at Pompeii, Ercolano, Pozzuoli, Baia and Cuma, they are reminded that life is short and unpredictable. Even beneath the city you'll find reminders of long-lost lives, from ghostly Roman markets and theatres, to funerary frescoes and venerated skulls.

Museums & Galleries

Naples explodes with must-see museums and galleries, from heavyweights like the Museo Archeologico Nazionale, Palazzo di Capodimonte and Certosa e Museo di San Martino, to lesser-known gems like fashion repository Museo del Tessile e dell'Abbigliamento Elena Aldobrandini. It's like a never-ending hit of cultural highs: towering sculptures, brooding canvases, joyous frescoes, even a high-tech ode to Italy's grandest opera house.

The Islands

Spas ✓✓
Landscapes ✓✓✓
Food ✓✓✓

Thermal Spas

Ischia's thermal springs have been soothing weary muscles since ancient times. Find a little zen at a bubbling beach, soak in an old Roman bath, then get yourself wrapped and pummelled at a sprawling spa resort.

Island Feasts

Whether you're nibbling on *torta caprese* (almond and chocolate cake) on a Capri piazza, slow-cooked rabbit at a rustic Ischian trattoria, or just-caught fish on a Procida beach, prepare to savour some long-lasting culinary memories.

Superlative Scenery

From Capri's vertiginous cliffs and electric-blue grotto, to Ischia's luxe gardens and vine-clad hillsides, to Procida's peeling, pastel villages, beauty defines the details in the Bay of Naples. So aim your camera and make your social media peeps turn a deeper shade of green.

p106

Amalfi Coast

Scenery ✓✓✓
Activities ✓✓✓
Culture ✓✓

Coastal Perfection

Cloud-scraping cliffs, fishing villages, terraced vineyards, and turquoise Tyrrhenian waters – views come at you from all angles on Italy's most stunning and celebrated coastline.

Natural Highs

Above, below or at sea level, active types are spoilt rotten. Whether you fancy swimming or diving in crystal-clear seas, cove-hopping on a sailing boat or escaping the hordes on a lofty hiking trail, the Amalfi Coast will keep your heart rate up.

Art & Architecture

Cutting-edge sculpture in Positano, medieval cloisters in Amalfi, classical overtures in Ravello; beyond the gleaming yachts, crowded beaches and Gucci-clad eye candy awaits a small but precious booty of cultural riches.

p140

Salerno & the Cilento

Ruins ✓✓
Nature ✓✓✓
Food ✓✓

Greek Ruins

Long before the Romans took hold, Greek sandals stomped around this turf. Pay tribute to the power and elegance of *Magna Graecia* (Greater Greece) at the stoic temples of Paestum and the bucolic ruins of Velia.

Wild Places

Deep, dark woods, exhilarating rapids, and cathedral-like caves littered with early human history: the Parco Nazionale del Cilento and Vallo di Diano is one of the country's biggest, wildest natural playgrounds.

A Bountiful Larder

Luscious buffalo-milk mozzarella and peppery olive oil, perfect artichokes and velvety white figs, glistening seafood and plump pastries – Salerno and the Cilento have no shortage of lauded regional edibles.

p175

> **Every listing is recommended by our authors, and their favourite places are listed first**

> **Look out for these icons:**

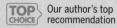 Our author's top recommendation

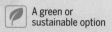 A green or sustainable option

 No payment required

See the Index for a full list of destinations covered in this book.

On the Road

Naples

POP 3,100,000

Best Places to Eat

» Palazzo Petrucci (p78)

» Da Bruno (p81)

» Ristorantino dell'Avvocato (p81)

» Pizzeria Starita (p83)

» Gay-odin (p79)

Best Places to Stay

» Casa D'Anna (p199)

» La Ciliegina Lifestyle Hotel (p197)

» Cerasiello B&B (p199)

» Hotel Piazza Bellini (p195)

Why Go?

Many visitors see Naples as little more than an unruly port-hole to destinations like Capri and the Amalfi Coast. Big mistake. Italy's third largest city is one of its oldest, most artistic and most delicious. Its *centro storico* (historic centre) is a Unesco World Heritage Site, its museums boast some of Europe's finest archaeology and art, and its swag of royal palaces and castles make Rome look positively provincial. Then there's the food: Naples is one of Italy's culinary heavyweights, serving up the country's best pizza, pasta and coffee.

Certainly, Naples can feel anarchic, tattered and unloved. But look beyond the grime and graffiti and you'll uncover a city of breathtaking frescoes, sculptures and panoramas, of bewitching street life, of spontaneous conversations and profound humanity. Welcome to Italy's most unlikely masterpiece.

Road Distance (KM)

	Naples	Pompeii	Ercolano	Vesuvius
Pompeii	24			
Ercolano	08	16		
Vesuvius	20	24	11	
Castellammare di Stabia	28	05	19	29

Accommodation

The *centro storico* is studded with churches and sights, artisan studios and student-packed bars. Seafront Santa Lucia delivers grand hotels, while Chiaia is best for fashionable shops and *aperitivo* bars. The laundry-strung Quartieri Spagnoli is within walking distance of all three neighbourhoods. For more information, see the Accommodation chapter (p194).

THREE PERFECT DAYS

Day 1 Cloisters, Classics & Evening Camparis

Start with a burst of colour in the cloister of the Basilica di Santa Chiara (p39) before ambling down Via Benedetto Croce and Via San Biagio dei Librai (Spaccanapoli) to explore their densely packed *palazzi* and churches. Relish Lanfranco's dome fresco at the duomo (p39) and a Caravaggio canvas at Pio Monte della Misericordia (p44). After lunch, don't miss the astounding Cristo velato (Veiled Christ) in the Cappella Sansevero (p38), then travel even further back in time at the Museo Archeologico Nazionale (p49). Round off the day with fine dining at Palazzo Petrucci (p78) and drinks on Piazza Bellini (p45).

Day 2 Produce, Art and Seaside Dolce Vita

Savour a morning stroll through La Pignasecca (p54) before viewing superlative art at the Palazzo Reale di Capodimonte (p61) or the Certosa e Museo di San Martino (p65). Either way, head down to the shore in the afternoon, taking a lazy stroll along the Lungomare (p59) and catching the sweeping views from atop the Castel dell'Ovo (p60). From here, it's an easy walk to Chiaia's chi-chi boutiques. Wardrobe revamped, sip and mingle with an *aperitivo* at Nais (p85) or Enoteca Belledonne (p85) before dinner at Ristorantino dell'Avvocato (p81) or Da Bruno (p81).

Day 3 Volcanic Views and Victims

Head into the suburbs and up Mt Vesuvius (p102) for dizzying views and a face-to-face with its deceptively peaceful crater. Back down the slope, walk the ghostly streets of ancient Pompeii (p93) or Herculaneum (p90) before heading back to town in time for a (pre-booked) performance at the Teatro San Carlo (p86).

Getting Around

Bus route R2 connects Stazione Centrale to Piazza Municipio (near the ferry terminal). Metro line 1 connects Vomero (Vanvitelli) to Via Toledo (Toledo) and Piazza Borsa (Università). Its extension (expected to open late 2013) will reach Piazza Municipio, Via Duomo and Stazione Centrale. Line 2 connects Stazione Centrale (Piazza Garibaldi) to the the *centro storico* (Piazza Cavour), Chiaia, Mergellina, Fuorigrotta and Pozzuoli. Funiculars reach Vomero from Via Toledo, Montesanto and Piazza Amedeo. Circumvesuviana trains reach Ercolano (Herculaneum) and Pompeii. Cumana trains go to Pozzuoli and Campi Flegrei.

DON'T MISS

Exploring Naples' subterranean otherworld of ancient aqueducts, shrines and catacombs. Among the best are the Catacomba di San Gennaro, the Cimitero delle Fontanelle, and the Complesso Monumentale di San Lorenzo.

Best Roman Ruins

» Ruins of Pompeii (p93)
» Ruins of Herculaneum (p90)
» Villa Oplontis (p101)
» Parco Archeologico di Baia (p73)
» Anfiteatro Flavio (p70)

Best Offbeat Sites

» Cimitero delle Fontanelle (p66)
» Catacomba di San Gaudioso (p67)
» Complesso Museale di Santa Maria delle Anime del Purgatorio ad Arco (p43)
» Casa e Chiesa di Santa Maria Francesca delle Cinque Piaghe (p54)
» Museo Nitsch (p55)

Naples Highlights

1 Fall for Giuseppe Sanmartino's superlative *Cristo velato* (Veiled Christ) in the **Cappella Sansevero** (p38).

2 Eye up ancient art and artifacts at the mighty **Museo Archeologico Nazionale** (p49).

3 Demand an encore at Italy's grandest opera house, **Teatro San Carlo** (p86).

4 Combine Caravaggio, Warhol and regal excess at the epic **Palazzo Reale di Capodimonte** (p61).

5 Explore a subterranean otherworld of ancient frescoes and burial sites at the lovingly restored **Catacombe di San Gennaro** (p66).

6 Admire lofty architecture, art and views at the hilltop **Certosa e Museo di San Martino** (p65).

7 Dive into Naples' liveliest, tastiest street market, the **Mercato di Porta Nolana** (p47).

8 Find solace in the majolica-tiled cloister of the **Basilica di Santa Chiara** (p39).

9 Drink, mingle and flirt the night away on bohemian **Piazza Bellini** (p45).

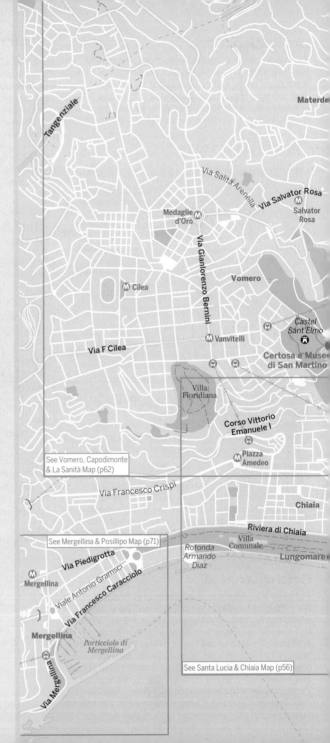

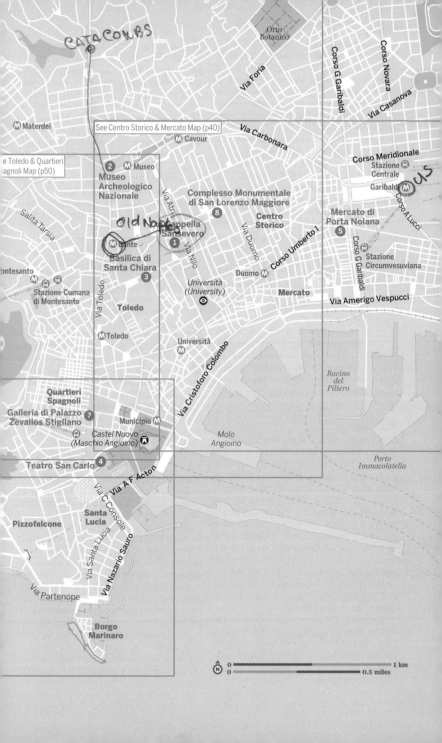

History

After founding nearby Cuma in the 8th century BC, the ancient Greeks settled the city in around 680 BC, calling it Parthenope. Under the Romans, the area became an ancient Miami of sorts: a sun-soaked spa region that drew the likes of Virgil. Dampening the bonhomie was Mt Vesuvius' unexpected eruption in AD 79.

Naples fell into Norman hands in 1139 before the French Angevins took control a century later, boosting the city's cred with the mighty Castel Nuovo. By the 16th century, Naples was under Spanish rule and riding high on Spain's colonial riches. By 1600, it was Europe's largest city and a burgeoning baroque beauty adorned by artists like Luca Giordano, Giuseppe de Ribera and Caravaggio.

Despite a devastating plague in 1656, Naples' ego soared under the Bourbons (1734–1860), with epic constructions such as the Teatro San Carlo and the Royal Palace in Caserta sealing the city's showcase reputation.

An ill-fated attempt at republican rule in 1799 was followed by a short stint under the French and a final period of Bourbon governance before nationalist rebel Giuseppe Garibaldi inspired the city to snip off the puppet strings and join a united Italy in 1860.

◉ Sights

CENTRO STORICO & MERCATO

Secret cloisters, cultish shrines and bellowing *pizzaioli* (pizza makers): the *centro storico* is a bewitching urban blend. Its three east–west *decumani* (main streets) follow the original street plan of ancient Neapolis. Most of the major sights are grouped around the busiest two of these classical thoroughfares: 'Spaccanapoli' (consisting of Via Benedetto Croce, Via San Biagio dei Librai and Via Vicaria Vecchia) and Via dei Tribunali. North of Via dei Tribunali, Via della Sapienza, Via Anticaglia and Via Santissimi Apostoli make up the quieter third *decumanus*.

Southeast of the *centro storico* await the shabby, frenetic streets of the Mercato district, a fast and filthy mix of cheap hotels, Sri Lankan spice shops and rough-and-ready markets, including the lip-smacking Mercato di Porta Nolana.

TOP CHOICE Cappella Sansevero CHAPEL

(Map p40; ☎081 551 84 70; www.museosansevero. it; Via de Sanctis 19; adult/reduced €7/5; ⊗10am-5.40pm Mon & Wed-Sat, 10am-1.10pm Sun; ⓂDante) It's in this Masonic-inspired chapel you'll find Giuseppe Sanmartino's incredible sculpture, *Cristo velato* (Veiled Christ), its marble veil so realistic that it's tempting to try to lift it and view Christ underneath. It's one of several artistic wonders, which also include Francesco Queirolo's sculpture *Disinganno* (Disillusion), Antonio Corradini's *Pudicizia* (Modesty) and riotously colourful frescoes by Francesco Maria Russo, the latter untouched since their creation in 1749.

Originally built around the end of the 16th century to house the tombs of the di Sangro family, the chapel was given its current baroque fit-out by Prince Raimondo di Sangro who, between 1749 and 1766, commissioned the finest artists to lavish the interior. In Queirolo's *Disinganno*, the man trying to untangle himself from a net represents Raimondo's father, Antonio, Duke of Torremaggiore. After the premature death of his wife, Antonio abandoned the young Raimondo, choosing instead a life of travel and hedonistic pleasures. Repentant in his later years, he returned to Naples and joined the priesthood, his attempt to free himself from sin represented in Queirolo's masterpiece.

Even more poignant is Antonio Corradini's *Pudicizia*, whose veiled female figure pays tribute to Raimondo's mother, Cecilia Gaetani d'Aquila d'Aragona. Raimondo was only 11 months old when she died, and the statue's lost gaze and broken plaque represent a life cruelly cut short.

The life of the chapel's original polychrome marble flooring was also cut short after a major collapse involving the chapel and the neighbouring Palazzo dei di Sangro in 1889. Designed by Francesco Celebrano, fragments of it survive in the passageway leading off from the chapel's right side. The passageway leads to a staircase, at the bottom of which you'll find two meticulously preserved human arterial systems – one of a man, the other of a woman. Debate still circles the models: Are the arterial systems real or reproductions? And if they are real, just how was such an incredible state of preservation achieved? More than two centuries on, the mystery surrounding the alchemist prince lives on.

TOP CHOICE Basilica di
Santa Chiara   CHURCH, MUSEUM
(Map p40; ☎081 1957 5915; www.monasterodisan
tachiara.eu; Via Benedetto Croce; nuns' cloisters
adult/reduced €5/3.50; ⊗basilica 7.30am-1pm &
4.30-8pm; cloisters & museum 9.30am-5.30pm
Mon-Sat, 10am-2.30pm Sun, last entry 30min before closing ; MⒹante) Vast, Gothic and cleverly
deceptive, this mighty basilica is actually a 20th-century recreation of Gagliardo
Primario's 14th-century original, severely
damaged in World War II. The pièce de résistance, however, is the basilica's adjoining
cloisters, lavished with wonderfully colourful 17th-century majolica tiles and frescoes.

While the Angevin porticoes date back to
the 14th century, the cloisters took on their
current look in the 18th century thanks to
the work of Domenico Antonio Vaccaro. The
walkways that divide the central garden of
lavender and citrus trees are lined with 72
ceramic-tiled octagonal columns connected
by benches. Painted by Donato e Giuseppe
Massa, the colourful tiles depict various rural
scenes, from hunting to vignettes of peasant
life. The four internal walls are covered with
17th-century frescoes of Franciscan tales.

Adjacent to the cloisters, a small and
elegant museum of mostly ecclesiastical
props also features the excavated ruins of a
1st-century spa complex, including a remarkably well-preserved *laconicum* (sauna).

Commissioned by Robert of Anjou for his
wife Sancia di Maiorca, the monastic complex was built to house 200 monks and the
tombs of the Angevin royal family. Dissed
as a 'stable' by Robert's ungrateful son
Charles of Anjou, the basilica itself received
a luscious baroque makeover by Domenico
Antonio Vaccaro, Gaetano Buonocore and
Giovanni Del Gaizo in the 18th century before taking a direct hit during an Allied air
raid on 4 August 1943. Its reconstruction was
completed in 1953. Features that did survive the fire include part of a 14th-century
fresco to the left of the main door and a
chapel containing the tombs of the Bourbon
kings from Ferdinand I to Francesco II.

TOP CHOICE Complesso
Monumentale di San
Lorenzo Maggiore   CHURCH, HISTORIC SITE
(Map p40; ☎081 211 08 60; www.sanlorenzomag
giorenapoli.it; Via dei Tribunali 316; church admission free, excavations & museum adult/reduced
€9/6; ⊗9.30am-5.30pm Mon-Sat, 9.30am-1pm

Sun; 🚌C55 to Via Duomo) Architecture and
history buffs shouldn't miss this richly layered religious complex, its breathtaking
basilica deemed one of Naples' finest medieval buildings. Aside from Ferdinando Sanfelice's petite facade, its baroque makeover
was stripped away last century revealing its
original austere Gothic elegance. Beneath it,
a sprawl of extraordinary ruins will transport you back two millennia.

Down here you can conjure up the Graeco-
Roman city as you walk past ancient bakeries, wineries and communal laundries.
At the far end of the *cardo* (road) there's a
cryptoporticus (covered market) with seven
barrel-vaulted rooms.

Back at current street level, the basilica
itself was commenced in 1270 by French architects, who built the apse. Local architects
took over the following century, recycling
ancient columns in the nave. Catherine of
Austria, who died in 1323, is buried here in
a beautiful mosaicked tomb. Legend has it
that this was where Boccaccio first fell for
Mary of Anjou, the inspiration for his character Fiammetta, while the poet Petrarch
called the adjoining convent home in 1345.

The religious complex is also home to the
Museo dell'Opera di San Lorenzo Maggiore
and its intriguing booty of local archaeological
finds, including Graeco-Roman sarcophagi,
ceramics and crockery from the digs below.
Other treasures include vivid 9th-century
ceramics, Angevin frescoes, paintings by
Giuseppe Marullo and Luigi Velpi, and camp
ecclesiastical drag for 16th-century bishops.

Duomo   CHURCH, RUIN, MUSEUM
(☎081 44 90 97; www.duomodinapoli.it; Via Duomo;
baptistry admission €1.50; ⊗cathedral, baptistry
& archaeological zone 8.30am-1pm & 3.30-7.30pm
Mon-Sat, 8.30am-1.30pm & 4.30-7.30pm Sun; 🚌C55
to Via Duomo) Whether you go for Giovanni
Lanfranco's fresco in the Cappella di San Gennaro (Chapel of St Janarius), the 4th-century
mosaics in the baptistry, or the thrice-annual
miracle of San Gennaro, don't miss Naples'
cathedral. Initiated by Charles I of Anjou in
1272 and consecrated in 1315, it was largely
destroyed in a 1456 earthquake, with copious
nips and tucks over the subsequent centuries.

Among these is the gleaming neo-Gothic
facade, only added in the late 19th-century.
Step inside and you'll immediately notice the
central nave's gilded coffered ceiling, studded
with late-Mannerist art. The high sections of

Centro Storico & Mercato

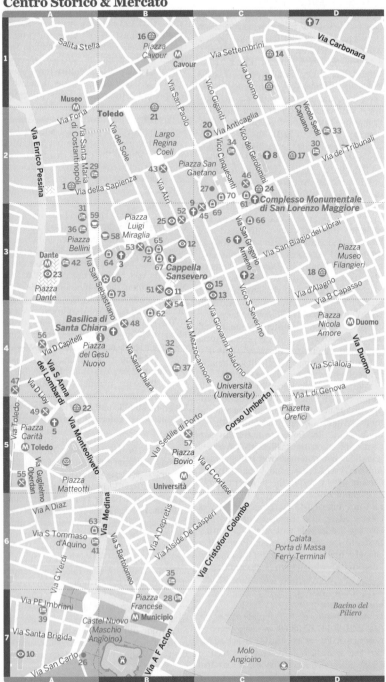

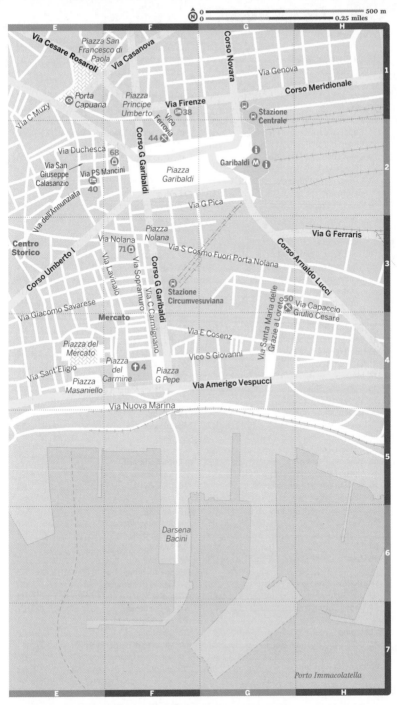

NAPLES

Via Cesare Rosaroli

Piazza San Francesco di Paola

Via Casanova

Corso Novara

Via Genova

Corso Meridionale

Porta Capuana

Piazza Principe Umberto

Via Firenze

38

Stazione Centrale

Via C Muzy

Vico Ferrovia

Via Duchesca

68

44

Corso G Garibaldi

Piazza Garibaldi

Garibaldi

Via San Giuseppe Calasanzio

Via PS Mancini

40

Via dell'Annunziata

Via G Pica

Via G Ferraris

Centro Storico

Piazza Nolana

Via Nolana

71

Via S Cosmo Fuori Porta Nolana

Corso Arnaldo Lucci

Corso Umberto I

Via Lavinaio

Via Sopramuro

Corso G Garibaldi

Stazione Circumvesuviana

50

Via Capaccio Giulio Cesare

Via Giacomo Savarese

Via C Carmignano

Mercato

Via E Cosenz

Via Santa Maria delle Grazie a Loreto

Piazza del Mercato

Piazza del Carmine

Vico S Giovanni

Via Sant'Eligio

4

Piazza G Pepe

Via Amerigo Vespucci

Piazza Masaniello

Via Nuova Marina

Darsena Bacini

Porto Immacolatella

Centro Storico & Mercato

the nave and the transept are the work of baroque overachiever Luca Giordano.

Off the left aisle, the 17th-century **Cappella di San Gennaro** (Chapel of St Januarius, also known as the Chapel of the Treasury) was designed by Giovanni Cola di Franco and completed in 1637. The most celebrated artists of the period worked on the chapel, creating one of the city's greatest baroque legacies. Highlights here include Giuseppe de Ribera's gripping canvas *St Gennaro Escaping the Furnace Unscathed* and Giovanni Lanfranco's dizzying dome fresco. Hidden away in a strongbox behind the altar is a 14th-century silver bust in which sit the skull of San Gennaro and the two phials that hold his miraculously liquefying blood.

The next chapel eastwards contains an urn with the saint's bones and a cupboard full of femurs, tibias and fibulas. Below the high altar is the **Cappella Carafa**, a Renaissance chapel built to house yet more of the saint's remains.

Off the north aisle sits one of Naples' oldest basilicas, dating to the 4th century. Incorporated into the main cathedral, the **Basilica di Santa Restituta** was subject to an almost complete makeover after the earthquake of 1688. Beyond this lurks the Duomo's **archaeological zone**, which showcases fascinating remains of Greek and Roman buildings and roads. Here, too, is the **baptistry**, the oldest in Western Europe, with its glittering 4th-century mosaics.

If you're intrigued by Naples' cultish love affair with San Gennaro, consider popping into the Duomo's adjacent **Museo del Tesoro di San Gennaro** (Map p40; www.museosan gennaro.com; Via Duomo 149; admission €7; ⊙9am-5.30pm daily Mar-Dec, 10am-5.30pm Thu-Tue Jan & Feb; ☐CS to Via Duomo), whose glittering collection of precious ex voto gifts includes bronze busts, silver ampullae, sumptuous paintings and a gilded 18th-century sedan chair used to shelter the saint's bust on rainy procession days.

Complesso Museale di Santa Maria delle Anime del Purgatorio ad Arco CHURCH

(Map p40; ☑081 551 95 47, 333 3832561; www.purga torioadarco.com; Via dei Tribunali 39; ⊙guided tours 10am-1pm Mon-Fri, 10am-5pm Sat, closed Sun; Ⓜ Dante) Consecrated in 1638, the engrossing *chiesa delle cape di morte* (the church of the skulls) sits on two levels. While the upper church boasts fine paintings – nominally Luca Giordano's *The Death of St Alessio* and Massimo Stanzione's *Madonna with the Souls of Purgatory* – the lower church is most famous as a hotspot for the worship of the *anime pezzentelle* (poor souls).

Between the 17th and early 19th centuries, the large, nameless grave at the centre of the floor received the remains of countless locals who could not afford to be buried in the church. Heaving with anonymous bones, the hypogeum became an epicentre for the cult of the *anime pezzentelle*, in which followers adopted skulls and prayed for their soul. It was hoped that once the soul reached heaven, it would offer graces and blessings as gratitude. Up to 60 masses were held here each day, and on All Souls' Day, queues leading into the underground vault would reach the Duomo, 450m away. Although burials on this site ceased soon after the declaration of the Edict of Saint-Cloud (a Napoleonic order banning burials within the city's borders), the wall shrines remained. The most famous of these belongs to 'Lucia' – a tiara-crowned skull named for a neon sign left at her shrine. According to legend, the skull was that of an 18th-century teenage bride, whose tragic death from tuberculosis saw her become the unofficial protector of young brides. To this day, you will find gifts of jewellery and bridal bouquets at her shrine, left by those who still believe in the cult.

Back upstairs, don't miss Dioniso Lazzari's sumptuous, Florentine-style inlaid marble work before slipping into the sacristy for a small but beautiful collection of devotional art and ecclesiastical robes. The church is sometimes used for evening cultural events – call ahead to see what might be coming up.

Ospedale degli Incurabili HISTORIC BUILDING

(Map p40; ☑339 5446243, 081 44 06 47; TBC; Via Maria Longo 50; €5 donation; ⊙90min guided tour 9am-2pm Sat, orto medico & Chiostro Santa Maria delle Grazie TBC ; Ⓜ Piazza Cavour) This 16th-century hospital and monastic complex is home to the 18th-century Farmacia Storica degli Incurabili, a breathtaking apothecary magically frozen in time. Divided into a glorious reception hall and a laboratory, its lavish walnut shelves are lined with decorative majolica vases, while Pietro Bardellino's epic ceiling painting portrays an episode from Homer's *Illiad*, in which Macaon is curing the wounded Menelaos. A more unusual but no less striking feature of the reception hall is a rococo inlay portraying an allegory of caesarean birth.

Despite its limited accessibility (by guided tour only; call or email ahead to confirm), the farmacia (pharmacy or apothecary) is well worth seeing. Some of Naples' finest baroque architects and artists worked on the site: Domenico Antonio Vaccaro styled the facade, Bartolomeo Vecchione designed the interior, and Gennaro di Fiore engraved the shelves, the latter also collaborating with Carlo Vanvitelli at the Reggia di Caserta (Palazzo Reale; www.reggiadicaserta.benicultur ali.it; Viale Douhet 22, Caserta; adult/concession €13.20/6.60; ⊘palace 8.30am-7pm Wed-Mon, Mostra Terrea Motus 9am-6pm Wed-Mon, park 8.30am-1hr before sunset Wed-Mon, Giardino Inglese 8.30am-2hr before sunset Wed-Mon Jun-Aug, reduced hrs rest of yr ; ☒Caserta). The majolica vases were painted by Lorenzo Salandra and Donato Massa (whose most famous tilework is found in the cloister of the Basilica di Santa Chiara, (p39)). Not surprisingly, the pharmacy is widely considered one of the city's finest examples of early 18th-century craftmanship.

The pharmacy shares the Cortile degli Incurabili (Courtyard of the Incurables) with the Museo delle Arti Sanitarie (Museum of the History of Medicine & Health; Map p40; Via Maria Longo 50, Ospedale degli Incurabili; admission free; ⊘9am-1.30pm Mon-Sat; Cavour, Museo), home to a wince-inducing collection of old surgical intruments and anatomical prints. The collection also includes an original *flagello della pesta*, a beak-like wooden mask worn during the city's infamous plagues.

Opposite the pharmacy, stairs lead up to the main hospital building, through which you can access the wonderfully tranquil Orto Medico (Medical Garden), lovingly adorned with medicinal plants and herbs. At its centre is a small fountain and a beautiful, 400-year-old camphor tree. Walk a little further and you'll stumble upon the smaller Chiostro Santa Maria delle Grazie, its lush tropical foliage framed by a frescoed, vaulted portico.

Chiesa del Gesù Nuovo   CHURCH

(☎081 551 86 13; Piazza del Gesù Nuovo; ⊘7am-1pm & 4.15-8pm; Ⓜ Dante) One of Naples' finest examples of Renaissance architecture, this 16th-century church actually sports the 15th-century, Giuseppe Valeriani–designed facade of Palazzo Sanseverino, converted to create the church. Inside, it's a baroque affair, with greats like Francesco Solimena, Luca Giordano and Cosimo Fanzago trans-

forming the barrel-vaulted interior into the frescoed wonder that you see today.

Countering the opulence is a small chapel dedicated to the much-loved local saint Giuseppe Moscati (1880–1927), a good doc who served the city's poor. Here walls heave with ex-votos (including golden syringes) and a recreation of the great man's study, complete with the armchair in which he died.

The church lies on the northern side of the beautiful Piazza del Gesù Nuovo, a favourite late-night hang-out for students and lefties. At its centre soars Giuseppe Genuino's lavish Guglia dell'Immacolata, built between 1747 and 1750. On 8 December, the feast of the Immacolata, firemen scramble up to the top to place a wreath of flowers at the Virgin Mary's feet.

Pio Monte della Misericordia   CHURCH, GALLERY

(☎081 44 69 44; www.piomontedellamisericordia. it; Via dei Tribunali 253; admission €6; ⊘9am-2pm Thu-Tue; ☒C55 to Via Duomo) The 1st floor of this octagonal, 17th-century church houses a small, satisfying collection of Renaissance and baroque art, including works by Francesco de Mura, Giuseppe de Ribera and Paul van Somer. Yet it's the painting above the main altar that steals the show: Caravaggio's masterpiece, *Le Sette Opere di Misericordia* (The Seven Acts of Mercy), considered by many to be the single most important painting in Naples.

Magnificently demonstrating the artist's chiaroscuro style, which had a revolutionary impact in Naples, the composition was considered unique in its ability to illustrate the various acts in one seamlessly choreographed scene. Also on display in the 1st-floor gallery is the *Declaratoria del 14 Ottobre 1607*, an original church document acknowledging payment of 400 ducats to Caravaggio for the masterpiece.

Port'Alba   STREET

(Via Port'Alba; Ⓜ Dante) A Mediterranean Diagon Alley, **Port'Alba** is an atmospheric porthole into the *centro storico*, best experienced on weekday afternoons. Crammed with bookshops and stalls, it's the place for leather-bound classics, a dog-eared Manzoni or retro postcards and magazines. The gate, which leads through to Piazza Dante, was opened in 1625 by Antonio Alvárez, the Spanish viceroy of Naples.

At the eastern end of Via Port'Alba, southbound Via San Sebastiano boasts the world's greatest concentration of musical-instrument shops, alongside 49th St in New York.

Piazza Bellini
PIAZZA

(Piazza Bellini; MDante) One of the best spots to chill with a spritz is this eclectic, bar-lined square. Featuring ruins from the city's 4th-century Greek city walls, it's a hot spot for bohemians and best experienced in the evening, when it heaves with uni students, left-leaning crowds and a healthy dose of flirtatious glances.

The piazza is also home to the roguish Mastiffs, the Napoli football club's hardcore supporter group. You'll find them arguing the finer points of goalkeeping outside their headquarters, between literary Intra Moenia (p85) and raffish Caffè Arabo.

Chiesa di San Pietro a Maiella
CHURCH

(Map p40; ☑081 45 90 08; Piazza Luigi Miraglia 25; ☺8am-noon; MDante) Dedicated to hermit Pietro del Morrone, who was promoted to Pope Celestine V in 1294, this church delivers a striking combo of Gothic restraint and baroque exuberance. The chapel to the left of the presbytery features 14th-century frescoes by Giovanni Barrile, while the nave is capped by 10 stunning ceiling paintings by baroque artist Mattia Preti.

Further baroque touches are provided by Cosimo Fanzago, designer of the marble altar, polychromatic balustrade and transept flooring, as well as Massimo Stanzione, whose *Madonna Appearing to Celestine V* hangs in one of the side chapels on the right. The Conservatorio di Musica San Pietro a Majella di Napoli – one of Italy's finest music schools – is housed in the adjoining convent.

FREE Cappella del Monte di Pietà
CHAPEL

(Map p40; ☑081 580 71 11; Via San Biagio dei Librai 114; ☺9am-7pm Sat, to 2pm Sun; ☐C55 to Via Duomo) This imposing 16th-century complex was originally home to the Pio Monte di Pietà, an organisation set up to issue interest-free loans to impoverished debtors. Its most impressive asset is the perfectly preserved Mannerist chapel and its four richly decorated side rooms. Flanking the entrance are two sculptures by Pietro Bernini, while above sits Michelangelo Naccherino's *Pietà*. Inside, striking 17th-century frescoes by Belisario Corenzio take the breath away.

Piazza San Domenico Maggiore
PIAZZA

(Piazza San Domenico Maggiore; MDante) Centre stage on this handsome square is the 18th-century **Guglia di San Domenico** (Map p40; Dante). The work of Cosimo Fanzago, Francesco Antonio Picchiatti and Domenico Antonio Vaccaro, it honours its namesake saint for ending the plague epidemic of 1656. Unfaithful Maria d'Avalos and her lover Don Fabrizio weren't quite as lucky – **Palazzo dei Di Sangro** (Piazza San Domenico 9) at No 9 is where Maria's jealous husband, Neapolitan musician Carlo Gesualdo, murdered the lovebirds in 1590.

More upbeat is the Gothic Chiesa di San Domenico Maggiore (p45), whose curious nave flanks the piazza's northern edge. See a face in the facade? You're not going crazy – it was an intentional add-on, created to liven the church's derrière once the piazza was created.

Chiesa di San Domenico Maggiore
CHURCH

(☑081 45 91 88; Piazza San Domenico Maggiore 8a; ☺8.30am-noon & 4-7pm Mon-Sat, 9am-1pm & 4.30-7.15pm Sun; MDante) Completed in 1324 on the orders of Charles I of Anjou, this was the royal church of the Angevins. Of the few 14th-century remnants surviving this church's countless makeovers, the frescoes by Pietro Cavallini in the Cappella Brancaccio take the cake. The sacristy is equally noteworthy, featuring a beautiful ceiling fresco by Francesco Solimena and 45 coffins of Aragon princes and other nobles.

In the Cappellone del Crocifisso, the 13th-century *Crocifisso tra La Vergine e San Giovanni* is said to have spoken to St Thomas Aquinas, asking him: '*Bene scripsisti di me, Thoma; quam recipies a me pro tu labore mercedem?*' ('You've written good things about me, Thomas, what will you get in return?') – '*Domine, non aliam nisi te*' ('Nothing if not you, O Lord'), Thomas replied diplomatically. Curiously enough, the first bishop of New York, Richard Luke Concanen (1747–1810), is also buried here.

Via San Gregorio Armeno
STREET

Naples is famous for its traditional *presepi* (nativity scenes) and this narrow street is where many Italians come to buy their Christmas crib figurines. Connecting Spaccanapoli with Via dei Tribunali, the *decumanus maior* (main road) of ancient Neapolis, its clutter of shops and workshops sell everything from doting donkeys to kitsch celebrity caricatures.

At No 8 you'll find the workshop of **Giuseppe Ferrigno** (Map p40; Via San Gregorio

Armeno 8; [train]CS to Via Duomo), whose terracotta figurines are the most famous on the strip.

Chiesa e Chiostro di
San Gregorio Armeno   CHURCH, MONASTERY

(Map p40; [phone]081 420 63 85; Via San Gregorio Armeno 44; ☉church 9.30am-noon daily, cloisters 9.30am-noon Mon-Fri, 9.30am-12.45pm & 3-5pm Sat & Sun; [train]C55 to Via Duomo) Overstatement knows no bounds at this richly ornamented 16th-century monastic complex, its church featuring lavish wood and papier-mâché choir stalls, a sumptuous altar by Dionisio Lazzari, and Luca Giordano's masterpiece fresco *The Embarkation, Journey and Arrival of the Armenia Nuns with the Relics of St Gregory*. Accessible by a gate on Vicolo Giuseppe Maffei are the complex's superb cloisters.

Giordano's famous fresco recounts the 13th-century exile of nuns fleeing persecution in Constantinople. Once in Naples, the holy escapees set up this monastic complex, naming it after the Bishop of Armenia, San Gregorio, whose earthly remains they were carrying with them. More famously, though, they also kept the relics and dried blood of Santa Patrizia (St Patricia), who, having escaped from Constantinople, died in Naples sometime between the 4th and 8th centuries. Patricia's powdered blood is said to liquefy every Tuesday, unlike that of Naples' patron saint, San Gennaro, who can only manage it three times a year.

Sublimely peaceful, the cloisters feature a whimsical baroque fountain embellished with masks, dolphins and sea horses, and two exquisite statues portraying Christ and the Samaritan by Matteo Bottigliero. At the southern end is the convent's old bakery, which is still adorned with old cooking utensils. Close by is the *Cappella della Madonna dell'Idria*. Adorned with painting by baroque artist Paolo De Matteis, the chapel is the only surviving remnant of the original medieval convent.

From the cloisters one can enter the beautifully decorated coro delle monache ('nuns' choir stall), which look down on the church nave and altar. If you're lucky, you might catch a glimpse of the choir's 612-year-old wooden nativity scene, usually hidden away in wooden cabinet on the southern wall. Either way, take note of the discreet windows lining the oval cupola above the choir stall. These belong to a secret second choir stall, hidden away so that even ill, bedridden nuns could attend mass.

Piazzetta Nilo   PIAZZA

(Via Nilo, Piazzetta Nilo; [M]Dante) You'll stumble across two local deities in this dusty little square. First up is ancient-Egyptian river god Nilo, whose marble sculpture Statua del Nilo was erected by the city's Alexandrian merchants, who lived in the area during Roman times. Questions shroud the Statua del Nilo, which mysteriously disappeared when the Egyptian expats moved out, before turning up headless in the 15th century. Renamed *Il Corpo di Napoli* (The Body of Naples), its great bearded bonce was added in the 18th century.

Opposite the statue, on the wall outside Bar Nilo, is the tongue-in-cheek Maradona shrine (Map p40), dedicated to Argentine football player and ex-Napoli deity Diego Armando Maradona.

Stuck to an epic poem written in Maradona's honour is a small, black hair – 'Kapel Original of Maradona' reads the English label, a direct translation of the Italian *Capello originale di Maradona*. The small container is full of genuine Maradona tears...and shame on anyone who suggests it's only water.

Napoli Sotterranea   TOUR

(Underground Naples; Map p40; [phone]081 29 69 44; www.napolisotterranea.org; Piazza San Gaetano 68; tours adult/reduced €9.30/6; ☉English tours 10am, noon, 2pm, 4pm & 6pm Mon-Fri, extra tours Thu, Sat & Sun; [train]C55 to Via Duomo) This evocative guided tour leads you 40m below street level to explore Naples' ancient labyrinth of aqueducts, passages and cisterns.

The passages were originally hewn by the Greeks to extract tufa stone used in construction and to channel water from Mt Vesuvius. Extended by the Romans, the network of conduits and cisterns was more recently used as an air-raid shelter in WWII. Part of the tour takes place by candlelight via extremely narrow passages – not suitable for expanded girths!

Basilica di San Paolo Maggiore   CHURCH

([phone]081 45 40 48; Piazza San Gaetano 76; ☉9am-7pm Mon-Sat; [train]C55 to Via Duomo) Despite dating to the 8th century, this glorious basilica was almost entirely rebuilt at the end of the 16th century. Its huge, gold-stuccoed interior features paintings by Massimo Stanzione and Paolo De Matteis, and a striking geometric floor by Nicola Tammaro. Top billing, however, goes to the sumptuous sacristy, lavished with luminous frescoes by baroquemeister Francesco Solimena.

Built in 1603, the double staircase adorning the basilica's main facade is the work of Francesco Grimaldi. Much older are the two columns flanking the entrance, taken from the Roman temple to Castor and Pollux that stood on the site.

Mercato di Porta Nolana   MARKET
(Porta Nolana; ☺8am-6pm Mon-Sat, to 2pm Sun; ☐R2 to Corso Umberto I) Bellies rumble greedily at this colourful street market, one of the city's best. The market's namesake is medieval city gate **Porta Nolana**, which stands at the head of Via Sopramuro. Its two cylindrical towers, optimistically named Faith and Hope, support an arch decorated with a bas-relief of Ferdinand I of Aragon on horseback.

Below and beyond it, the *mercato* is an intoxicating place, where bellowing fishmongers and *frutti vendoli* (greengrocers) collide with fragrant delis, bakeries, and a growing number of ethnic food shops. Expect to find anything from buxom tomatoes and mozzarella to crunchy *casareccio* bread, cheap luggage and bootleg '80s compilation CDs.

Chiesa di Sant'Angelo a Nilo   CHURCH
(☑081 420 12 22; Vico Donnaromita 15; ☺8.30am-1pm & 4.30-6.30pm Mon-Sat, 8.30am-1pm Sun; ☒Dante) This modest 14th-century church contains one of the first great art works to grace the Neapolitan Renaissance – the majestic tomb of Cardinal Brancaccio, the church's founder. Although considered a part of Naples' artistic heritage, the sarcophagus was actually sculpted in Pisa by Donatello, Michelozzo and Pagno di Lapo Partigiani. Taking a year to complete, the sculptured marvel was shipped to Naples in 1427.

**Complesso Monumentale
dei Girolamini**   CHURCH, GALLERY
(Map p40; ☑081 44 91 39; Via Duomo 142; ☺church 9.30am-noon Mon-Sat, 9.30am-2pm Sun, cloister & art gallery 10am-12.30pm Sat; ☐C55 to Via Duomo) The richly baroque **Chiesa dei Girolamini** features two facades; the more-imposing 18th-century option can be admired from Piazza dei Girolamini on Via dei Tribunali. The real highlights, however, are next door in the 17th-century convent. The first is the beautiful main **cloister**, complete with faded majolica tiles. The second is the upstairs **art gallery**, featuring local greats like Luca Giordano, Battista Caracciolo and Giuseppe de Ribera.

MADRE   MUSEUM
(Museo d'Arte Contemporanea Donnaregina; Map p40; ☑081 1931 3016; www.museomadre.it; Via Settembrini 79; adult/reduced €3.50/1.50, free Mon; ☺10.30am-7.30pm Mon & Wed-Sat, to 11pm Sun; ☐C55 to Via Duomo, ☒Piazza Cavour) At the time of research, the future of Naples' once-wonderful contemporary art museum was undecided. Its 'Historical Collection' of modern painting, photography, sculpture and installations from greats such as Mario Merz, Damien Hirst and Olafur Eliasson was closed indefinitely, with only its specially commissioned, 1st-floor installations on display. Inspired by Naples, these installations include works by Francesco Clemente, Anish Kapoor, Rebecca Horn, and Jeff Koons.

Check the museum website for updates.

Museo Diocesano di Napoli   MUSEUM
(Map p40; ☑081 557 13 65; www.museodioc esanonapoli.it; Largo Donnaregina, Chiesa di Santa Maria Donnaregina Nuova; adult/reduced €5/4; ☺9.30am-4.30pm Mon & Wed-Sat, 9.30am-2pm Sun; ☒Piazza Cavour) Splendid baroque architecture meets religiously themed art at the revamped Chiesa di Santa Maria Donnaregina Nuova. Now known as the Diocesan Museum of Naples, its collection spans Renaissance triptychs and 19th-century wooden sculptures, to works from baroque masters including Luca Giordano, Fabrizio Santafede and Andrea Vaccaro.

Collection highlights include Giordano's final canvases, which hang on either side of the church's main altar, Paolo De Matteis' *San Sebastiano Curato dalle Pie Donne* (St Sebastian Attended to by the Pious Women) and a young Francesco Solimena's fresco *Il Miracolo delle Rose di San Francesco* (The Miracle of the Roses of St Francis), above the church's presbytery.

On weekends in April and May, the museum usually hosts **classical music concerts** by the Nuova Orchestra Alessandro Scarlatti (www.nuovaorchestrascarlatti.it). Tickets ($14) can be purchased at the museum. Check the museum or orchestra websites for programme details.

Museo di Filangieri   MUSEUM
(Map p40; ☑081 203 175, 081 749 93 05; http://fi langieri.sbapsaena.campaniabeniculturali.it; Via Duomo 288; ☐C55 to Via Duomo) Only accessible by phoning ahead (check the website for changes), this wonderfully kooky museum houses everything from Asian and European armour to ancient pottery and sumptuous

paintings spanning the 15th to the 19th centuries. Much of the collection belonged to 19th-century prince Gaetano Filangieri, whose private, walnut-panelled *biblioteca* (library) afforded him commanding views of the building's showpiece *Sala Agata* (Agatha Hall). At the time of research, future prices and opening times had not been confirmed. Contact the museum or tourist office for updates.

It's in this hall that you'll find many of the museum's highlights, among them Luca della Robbia's delicate sculpture *Testa di fanciullo imberbe* (Head of a Beardless Boy), Adriaen Hendriex van Ostade's humourous painting *Interno di taverna* (Inside a Tavern), and Giuseppe de Ribera's deeply psychological canvas *Santa Maria Egiziaca* (St Mary of Egypt).

The museum building itself dates back to the late 15th century, its design heavily influenced by the architecture of Renaissance Florence. Incredibly, the widening of Via Duomo in the 1880s saw the palazzo completely demolished and rebuilt 20m further back.

Santissima Annunziata CHURCH, HISTORIC SITE

(☑081 254 26 08; Via dell'Annunziata 34; ☉8am-noon & 5.30-7.30pm Mon-Sat, 7.30am-1pm Sun, former orphanage 9am-6pm Mon-Sat, crypt 8am-noon & 5.30-7.30pm Mon-Sat, 7.30am-1pm Sun; ◻R2 to Corso Umberto I) The most engrossing site at this 14th-century religious complex is its infamous **ruota** (wheel), set in the orphanage wall to the left of the basilica. As late as the 1980s, unwanted children were placed in a hollow in the wheel. On the other side of the wall sat a nun ready to take the baby, wash it in the adjacent basin and record its time of entry. Older children were sometimes forced into it, subjecting them to serious injury.

The basilica itself was significantly restructured by Luigi Vanvitelli and his son Carlo after a devastating fire in 1757 (the soaring 67m-high cupola is one of their additions). Luckily, the 1580 **sacristy** (to the right of the nave) survived the blaze. Here, exquisitely carved wooden armoires by Girolamo D'Auria and Salvatore Caccavello depict New Testament scenes, while vault frescoes by Belisario Corenzio take care of Old Testament tales. If the sacristy is closed, seek out the sacristan and politely request to see it.

Another fire survivor is the wooden *mamma chiatta* (chubby mother), a sculp-

ture of the Virgin Mary in the third chapel to the left of the nave. Its image was once reproduced on the leaden medals worn by the children left at the former orphanage.

Continue through into the building's main courtyard. If the first door on the right-hand wall is open, step inside and sneak through the red curtains on your left. Your reward will be Carlo Vanvitelli's extraordinary, round, vaulted **crypt**, complete with six altars. The main altar features a statue of *Madonna and Child* by Domenico Gagini, set against stucco work by Giuseppe Sanmartino, creator of the incredible *Cristo Velato* inside the Cappella Sansevero.

T293 GALLERY

(Map p40; www.t293.it; Via dei Tribunali 293; ☉noon-7pm Tue-Fri; ◻C55 to Via Duomo) Sneaky T293 is a fantastic surprise for lovers of contemporary art. Hidden away up an anonymous stairwell, it has a knack for thought-provoking shows which feature some of the world's most exciting artists (think Henrik Olai Kaarstein, Damien Roach and Martin Soto Climent). Check the website for current exhibition details.

Chiesa di Santa Maria del Carmine CHURCH

(Map p40; ☑081 20 11 96; Piazza del Carmine; ☉6.30am-noon Mon, Tue & Thu-Sat, 6.30am-1.30pm Wed, 6.30pm-2pm Sun; ◻R2 to Corso Giuseppe Garibaldi) Its 17th-century *campanile* (bell tower) is Naples' tallest and this iconic church is home to a famously nimble crucifix. Now hanging in a tabernacle beneath the church's main arch, the cross reputedly dodged a cannonball fired at the church in 1439, during the war between Alfonso of Aragon and Robert of Anjou. Equally miraculous is the 13th-century Byzantine icon of the *Madonna della Bruna*, held behind the main altar, and famously celebrated with fireworks each 16 July.

Indeed, the much-loved Chiesa di Santa Maria del Carmine is shrouded in legend. According to Neapolitan folklore, when Conrad (Corradino) of Swabia was charged with attempting to depose Charles I of Anjou in 1268, his mother, Elisabetta di Baviera, desperately tried to collect the money required to free her son. Alas, the money arrived too late, Conrad lost his head and his grief-stricken mamma handed the cash to the church (on the condition that the Carmelite brothers prayed for him every day). They agreed, the church went up and a monument to Conrad still remains in the transept.

Just northwest of the church and Piazza del Carmine, the **Piazza del Mercato** has an even more macabre past. The starting point for the deadly plague of 1656, it was here that over 200 supporters of the ill-fated Parthenopean Republic of 1799 were systematically executed.

TOLEDO & QUARTIERI SPAGNOLI

Constructed by Spanish viceroy Don Pedro de Toledo in the 16th century, *palazzo*-flanked Via Toledo (also known as Via Roma) is Naples' veritable high street and a popular strip for an evening *passeggiata* (stroll). Capped by buzzing Piazza Trento e Trieste at its southern end, it becomes Via Enrico Pessina further north, skimming past Piazza Dante and the Museo Archeologico Nazionale on its way towards Capodimonte.

Directly west of Via Toledo lie the razor-thin streets of the Quartieri Spagnoli (Spanish Quarter), originally built to house Don Pedro's Spanish troops. Low on actual sights, its washing-strung streets harbour hidden delights, from raucous trattorias and progressive cultural hang-outs, to the unmissable Pignasecca market. With an eye on your bag, dive in for a serve of pure *Napoli popolana* (working-class Naples).

TOP CHOICE **Museo Archeologico Nazionale**   MUSEUM

(Map p50; ☎081 44 01 66; www.museoarcheologiconazionale.campaniabeniculturali.it; Piazza Museo Nazionale 19; admission €6.50; ☺9am-7.30pm Wed-Mon; Ⓜ Museo, Piazza Cavour) Boasting many of the best mosaics and frescoes from Pompeii and Herculaneum, as well as priceless classical sculptures like the mighty *Toro Farnese* (Farnese Bull), the National Archaeological Museum is utterly unmissable. Before tackling the four floors of galleries, consider investing €12 on the *National Archaeological Museum of Naples*, published by Electa, or, to concentrate on the highlights, €5 for an audioguide in English.

Originally a cavalry barracks, the museum was established by the Bourbon king Charles VII in the late 18th century to house the rich collection of antiquities he had inherited from his mother, Elisabetta Farnese.

While the basement houses the Borgia collection of Egyptian relics and epigraphs, the ground-floor Farnese collection of colossal Greek and Roman sculptures include the *Toro Farnese* (Farnese Bull) in Room XVI and the muscle-bound *Ercole* (Her-

cules) in Room XI. Sculpted in the early 3rd century AD and noted in the writings of Pliny, the *Toro Farnese*, probably a Roman copy of a Greek original, depicts the death of Dirce, Queen of Thebes. According to Greek mythology she was tied to a wild bull by Zeto and Amphion as punishment for her treatment of their mother Antiope, the first wife of King Lykos of Thebes. Carved from a single colossal block of marble, the sculpture was discovered in 1545 near the Baths of Caracalla in Rome and was restored by Michelangelo, before eventually being shipped to Naples in 1787.

Ercole was discovered in the same Roman dig and like the *Toro Farnese* remained in Rome until 1787. Originally without legs, *Ercole* had a new pair made for him by Guglielmo della Porta. In fact, the story goes that the Farnese were so impressed with della Porta's work that they refused to reinstate the original legs when they were subsequently found. The Bourbons, however, had no such qualms and later attached the originals in their rightful place. You can see the della Porta legs displayed on the wall behind *Ercole*.

If you're short on time, take in both these masterpieces before heading straight to the mezzanine floor, home to an exquisite collection of Pompeian mosaics. Of the series taken from the Casa del Fauno, it is *La battaglia di Alessandro Contro Dario* (The Battle of Alexander Against Darius) in Room LXI that stands out. The best-known depiction of Alexander the Great, the 20-sq-metre mosaic was probably made by Alexandrian craftsmen working in Italy around the end of the 2nd century BC. In room LIX, look out for the amusing *Scene di commedia: musici ambulanti* (Comedy Scene: Street Musicians), which portrays a motley group of roving performers. Other outstanding mosaics include one of a feline killing a duck in Room LX and a study of Nile animals in Room LXIII.

Beyond the mosaics, the **Gabinetto Segreto** (Secret Chamber) contains a small but much-studied collection of ancient erotica. Guarding the entrance is a marble statue of a lascivious-looking Pan draped over a very coy Daphne. Pan is then caught in the act, this time with a nanny goat, in the collection's most famous piece – a small and surprisingly sophisticated statue taken from the Villa dei Papiri in Herculaneum. There is also a series of nine paintings depicting

Toledo & Quartieri Spagnoli

NAPLES

0 — 200 m
0 — 0.1 miles

Via R Imbriani

Via Salvator Rosa

Museo Archeologico Nazionale

M Museo

Via Foria

Piazza Museo Nazionale

Via Santa Maria di Costantinopoli

Via dei Sole

Piazza Mazzini

Vico Lungo Pontecorvo

Salita Pontecorvo

Salita Tarsia

5

Via G Brombeis

Via Bellini

Via Enrico Pessina

Piazza Luigi Miraglia

Piazza Bellini

Corso Vittorio Emanuele I

Via Ventaglieri

Piazza Tarsia

Vico S Domenico Soriano

M Dante

Piazza Dante

Via San Sebastiano

Piazza Olivella

Piazza Montesanto

Via Montesanto

Via D Capitelli

Montesanto M

Via Porta Medina

Via S Anna dei Lombardi

Via Toledo

Piazza del Gesù Nuovo

Funicolare di Montesanto

Stazione Cumana di Montesanto

Via Pignatelli

Via Pignasecca

11

Piazza Monteoliveto

Via Pasquale Scura

Via S Liborio

Via Formale

Toledo

Via Monteoliveto

Via Donnalbina

2

Piazza Carità

Via G Simonelli

M Toledo

Vico P Galluppi

Via C Battisti

15

Via Concezione a Montecalvario

Piazza Matteotti

Quartieri Spagnoli

Via A Diaz

Vico Figurella a Montecalvario

7

17

3 10

9

Via De Deo

12 16

Vico Giardinetto

Via S Giacomo

Via Medina

6 1

Vico della Tofa

Via Toledo

Via G Verdi

Via S Bartolomeo

Piazzetta Cariati

8

Municipio M

Funicolare Centrale

14

Via Santa Brigida

Emanuele III

Via Santa Caterina da Siena

4

Funicolare Station

Castel Nuovo (Maschio Angioino)

Vico Sergente Maggiore

13

Parco Castello

Toledo & Quartieri Spagnoli

NAPLES SIGHTS

erotic positions – a menu of sorts for brothel clients.

Originally the royal library, the enormous **Sala Meridiana** (Great Hall of the Sundial) on the 1st floor is home to the *Farnese Atlante*, a statue of Atlas carrying a globe on his shoulders, as well as various paintings from the Farnese collection. Look up and you'll find Pietro Bardellino's riotously colourful 1781 fresco depicting the *Triumph of Ferdinand IV of Bourbon and Marie Caroline of Austria*.

The rest of the 1st floor is largely devoted to fascinating discoveries from Pompeii, Herculaneum, Boscoreale, Stabiae and Cuma. Among them are breathtakingly vivid, mythologically themed wall frescoes from the Villa di Agrippa Postumus and the Casa di Meleagro, as well as a pair of gladiator's helmets, ceramics and glassware – even eggcups. Rooms LXXXVI and LXXXVII house an extraordinary collection of vases of mixed origins, many carefully reassembled from fragments. Also on this floor are various engraved coppers and Greek funerary vases.

If you are set on seeing particular museum collections, it's worth calling ahead to ensure the galleries you want to see are open; unfortunately, staff shortages often mean that sections of the museum close for part of the day.

Galleria di Palazzo
Zevallos Stigliano GALLERY
(☏081 42 50 11; www.palazzozevallos.com; Via Toledo 185; adult/reduced €4/3; ⊙10am-6pm Tue-

Fri & Sun, 10am-8pm Sat; ☐R2 to Piazza Trieste e Trento) While the 19th-century stucco detailing and frescoes of the 17th-century Palazzo Zevallos Stigliano are delightful, the protagonist here is Caravaggio's final masterpiece, *The Martyrdom of St Ursula* (1610). Completed weeks before the artist's lonely death, it depicts the brutal scene of a vengeful king of the Huns piercing the heart of his unwilling virgin bride-to-be, Ursula.

Positioned behind the dying martyr is a haunted Caravaggio, an eerie premonition of his own impending fate. The tumultuous history of both the artist and the painting is documented in the free, highly informative audioguide. Caravaggio's canvas is the centrepiece of the palazzo's small **art gallery**, its other works of note including a fascinating pictorial map of 17th-century Naples by Alessandro Baratta and 18th- and 19th-century landscape paintings by Anton Smink Pitloo and Gaspar van Wittel. The latter artist is the father of celebrated architect Luigi Vanvitelli

Galleria Umberto I ARCHITECTURE
(Map p40; Via San Carlo; ☐R2 to Via San Carlo) Paging Milan's Galleria Vittorio Emanuele, Naples' most-famous 19th-century arcade is a breathtaking pairing of richly adorned neo-Renaissance fronts and a delicate glass ceiling capped by a lofty, 56m dome. Complete with a sumptuous marble floor, the *galleria* is at its most spectacular at night, when it becomes a surreal setting for impromptu soccer games.

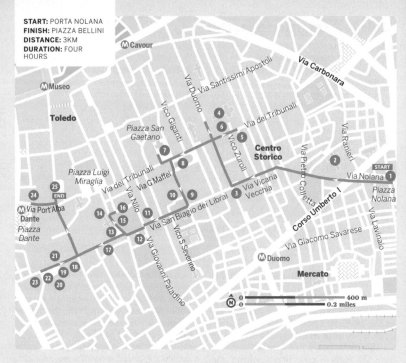

START: PORTA NOLANA
FINISH: PIAZZA BELLINI
DISTANCE: 3KM
DURATION: FOUR HOURS

Walking Tour
Centro Storico: A World Heritage Wander

❯ Bustling for over 2000 years, Naples' *centro storico* (historic centre) is a rumbling mass of contradictions. Hyperactive streets sit atop silent ruins, crumbling facades mask mighty baroque interiors, and cultish shrines flank hedonistic bars. No other part of the city intrigues or intoxicates so intensely, and none offers such a density of artistic and architectural treasures.

Begin your walk at the 15th-century city gate of ❶ **Porta Nolana**, its exterior wall featuring a marble relief of Ferdinand I; illegitimate son of Alfonso V of Aragon who was also king of Naples between 1458 to 1494. On the other side of the gate is a 17th-century bust of San Gaetano. These days, Porta Nolana is better known as the gateway to the Mercato di Porta Nolana, whose booty of bakeries, fishmongers, butchers, delis and grocers make for an appetising morning saunter.

After exploring the market's colours and scents, head west along Via Nolana. Cross Corso Umberto I, head right into Via Egiziaca

a Forcella and then right again into Via dell'Annunziata. A little way down on your right you'll see the ❷ **Santissima Annunziata**, famous for its orphanage and *ruota*, the wooden wheel where babies were once abandoned. Head back to Via Egiziaca a Forcella and turn right into it. After crossing Via Pietro Colletta, follow the street as it veers left and merges into Via Vicaria Vecchia. Where it meets the busy cross street, Via Duomo, stands one of Naples' oldest churches, the ❸ **Basilica di San Giorgio Maggiore**. Built by St Severus in the 4th century but thoroughly restyled by Cosimo Fanzago in the mid-17th century, its original Palaeo-Christian apse is now part of the main entrance. Two blocks northwest up Via Duomo soars Naples' cathedral, the ❹ **Duomo**. It is here that thousands gather every May, September and December to witness San Gennaro's coagulated blood miraculously liquefy.

Double back down Via Duomo until you meet Via dei Tribunali. Known to the Romans as the *decumanus maior*, this street runs parallel to the *decumanus inferior*, aka Spaccanapoli, aka Via San Biagio dei Librai. Before heading right into the very heart of the *centro storico*, quickly nip left to admire Caravaggio's masterpiece *Le Sette Opere di Misericordia* (The Seven Acts of Mercy) in the ⑤ **Pio Monte della Misericordia**. Before you retrace your steps to Via Duomo, have a quick look at the ⑥ **Guglia di San Gennaro** in the small square opposite the church. Dating back to 1636, with stonework by Cosimo Fanzago and a bronze statue by Tommaso Montani, the obelisk is a soaring '*grazie*' to San Gennaro for protecting Naples from the 1631 eruption of Mt Vesuvius.

After you've crossed Via Duomo make for Piazza San Gaetano, about 150m down on the right. The tiny square where the Roman forum once stood is now dominated by the imposing ⑦ **Basilica di San Paolo Maggiore**, whose sumptuous baroque sacristy is one of the city's hidden delights. Opposite the piazza, is the ⑧ **Complesso Monumentale di San Lorenzo Maggiore**, its stark but beautiful Gothic basilica sitting atop Roman *scavi* (excavations). Head underground for a peek before heading down ⑨ **Via San Gregorio Armeno**. In December people come from all over Italy to visit the shops that line this street. They specialise in the *presepi* (nativity scenes) that no traditional Italian house is without at Christmas. Along this street you'll also find the ⑩ **Chiesa e Chiostro di San Gregorio Armeno**, famous for its extravagant rococo interior and weekly miracle – the blood of Santa Patrizia is said to liquefy here every Tuesday.

At the end of the road you hit Via San Biagio dei Librai. Turn right and after about 250m you'll be on ⑪ **Piazzetta Nilo**, home to the Statua del Nilo, an ancient statue depicting Nilus, the ancient Greek god of the River Nile. Less imposing is the altar to footballer Maradona on the wall opposite the statue. Further down on the left, the ⑫ **Chiesa di Sant'Angelo a Nilo** is home to an exquisite tomb whose transitional style features both Gothic and Renaissance influences. From here it's only a few steps to handsome ⑬ **Piazza San Domenico Maggiore**, location of the imposing ⑭ **Chiesa di San Domenico Maggiore**. It was in this church that a crucifix reputedly spoke to St Thomas Aquinas; the theologian taught in the adjoining monastery. At No 9 stands the notorious ⑮ **Palazzo dei Di Sangro**, where on 16 October 1590, nobleman and composer Carlo Gesualdo brutally murdered his cousin-wife,

Maria d'Avalos, and her lover, Fabrizo Carafa, after catching them *in flagrante*. Suspicious of d'Avalos' unfaithfulness, the crafty Gesualdo had tricked his wife into thinking that he was out of town on a hunting trip. Around the corner from the palazzo is Via Francesco deSanctis, where you'll find the not-to-be-missed ⑯ **Cappella Sansevero**. A jewel of a chapel, it's home to the mesmerising *Cristo velato* (Veiled Christ) sculpture. The Venetian sculptor Antonio Canova famously said that he'd have given 10 years of his life to be its creator.

Back on Via San Biagio dei Librai, the road becomes Via Benedetto Croce. On the left, at No 45, stands ⑰ **Palazzo Carafa della Spina**, designed by Domenico Fontana in the late 16th century and revamped in the first half of the 18th century. Its baroque *portone* (entrance) is one of Naples' finest, complete with balcony-supporting satyrs and the Carafa family's coat of arms. Flanking the entrance are two marble sea monsters, their open mouths once used to extinguish torches. Further west is the ⑱ **Basilica di Santa Chiara**, a testament to the skill of Naples' restoration experts after it was almost completely destroyed by WWII bombs. Savour a little silence in the basilica's adjacent majolica-tiled cloisters, then spill into ⑲ **Piazza del Gesù Nuovo**, home to much nightly revelry and, at No 14, ⑳ **Libreria Dante & Descartes**, an erudite bookshop popular with writers and intellectuals. Dominating the piazza's northern side is the richly decorated ㉑ **Chiesa del Gesù Nuovo**, while at its centre is the ㉒ **Guglia dell'Immacolata**, created between 1747 and 1750; the gilded copper statue of the Virgin Mary was added in 1753. Cinephiles may recognise the central balcony of ㉓ **Palazzo Pandola**, at No 33, from the closing scene of Vittorio De Sica's *Matrimonio all'italiana* (Marriage Italian Style), a comedy starring Sophia Loren and Marcello Mastroianni. Backtrack from the square to the first intersection and turn left along Via San Sebastiano, packed with musical-instrument vendors. At the next intersection on your left, book-lined Via Port'Alba leads down to ㉔ **Port'Alba**, a city gate built in 1625 which leads into Piazza Dante.

Double back the way you came, turn left back into Via San Sebastiano, and a block to your right is ㉕ **Piazza Bellini**. The perfect place to end your saunter is in one of the piazza's cafes – just don't forget to inspect the remains of the 4th century BC Greek city walls under the square.

Accademia di Belle Arti GALLERY

(Map p40; ☑081 44 18 87; www.accademiadinapoli.
it; Via Santa Maria di Costantinopoli 107, entry from
Via Bellini; admission free; ⊙10am-1.30pm Tue-
Sat, 2-6pm Fri; MDante) The 2nd-floor gallery
at Naples' esteemed Academy of Fine Arts
houses an important collection of 19th- and
20th-century Neapolitan work, many by
former academy alumni, including water-
colourist Giacinti Gigante and sculptor
Vincenzo Gemito. That so many of Gemito's
busts were created in 1874 is not a coincidence – he frantically chipped away to pay
his way out of military service.

The building itself was once the convent of
San Giovanni Battista delle Monache. Built
in the 17th century, it was given a thorough
makeover in 1864 by architect Enrico
Alvino, who gave the structure a neoclassical facade, a grand staircase and two noble
lions to guard the main entrance.

La Pignasecca MARKET

(Map p50; Via Pignasecca; ⊙8am-1pm; MToledo)
Naples' oldest street market is a multi-
sensory escapade into a world of wriggling
seafood, drool-inducing delis and clued-up
casalinghe (housewives) on the hunt for perfect produce. Shop for local cheeses and vino
at Antiche Delizie and scour the streetside
stalls for everything from discounted perfume and linen to Neapolitan hip-hop CDs
and dirt-cheap designer bags and threads.

Piazza Dante PIAZZA

(Map p40; MDante) On hot summer evenings,
Piazza Dante turns into a communal living room, packed with entire families who
stroll, eat, smoke, play cards, chase balloons,
and whinge about the in-laws.

Dominating the eastern flank of the
square is the enormous facade of the Con-
vitto Nazionale, the pièce de résistance of
Luigi Vanvitelli's spectacular 18th-century
square. Dedicated to the Bourbon king
Charles VII, its central protagonist is now a
sand-blasted marble Dante looking out over
Via Toledo.

Below it all, the Dante metro station
doubles as a cutting-edge art space, with
installations from some art-world heavy-
weights. As you head down on the escalator,
look up and catch Joseph Kosuth's Queste
Cose Visibili (These Visible Things) above
you. Eye-squintingly huge and neon, it's an
epic quotation from Dante's Il Convivio.
Along the wall at the bottom of the escalator you'll find artist Jannis Kounellis's rene-
gade train tracks running over abandoned
shoes. Right behind you, above the second
set of escalators, sits Intermediterraneo,
Michelangelo Pistoletto's giant mirror map
of the Mediterranean Sea.

Chiesa di Sant'Anna dei Lombardi CHURCH

(Map p40; ☑081 551 33 33; Piazza Monteoliveto;
⊙9am-1pm & 4-6pm; MToledo) Dubbed a veritable museum of Renaissance art, this magnificent church is testament to the close
links that once existed between the Neapolitan Aragonese and the Florentine Medici
dynasty. One particular highlight is Guido
Mazzoni's spectacular Pietà. Dating to 1492,
the terracotta ensemble is made up of eight
life-size terracotta figures surrounding the
lifeless body of Christ.

Originally the figures were painted, but
even without colour they still make quite
an impression. The sacristy is a work of
art in itself. The walls are lined with glori-
ously inlaid wood panels by Giovanni da Ve-
rona, while the ceiling is covered by Giorgio
Vasari's 16th-century frescoes that depict the
Allegories and Symbols of Faith.

Across Via Monteoliveto from the church
is the 16th-century Palazzo Gravina (Map
p40; Via Monteoliveto 3), the seat of Naples University's architecture faculty.

Casa e Chiesa di Santa Maria Francesca delle Cinque Piaghe CHURCH, HISTORIC SITE

(Map p50; ☑081 42 50 11; Vico Tre Re a Toledo 13;
⊙church 7am-noon, apartment 9am-noon, also
4.30-7.30pm on the 6th of every month; MToledo)
The very essence of Naples' cultish brand of
Catholicism, this holy sanctuary was once
the stomping ground of stigmatic and mystic
Santa Maria Francesca delle Cinque Piaghe,
the city's only canonised woman. It is also
home to her miraculous wooden chair, a
particular hit with infertile believers, who sit
down on it in the hope of falling pregnant.
(Those after a blessing can request one
from the Daughters of Santa Maria Francesca, who run the place.)

The holy furniture piece inhabits the
saint's meticulously preserved 18th-century
apartment. Here, the walls heave with
modern baby trinkets and vivid 18th- and
19th-century paintings depicting fantastical holy healings – ex voti offered by those
whose prayers have been answered. Other
household objects include the stigmatic's
blood-stained clothes, her bed and pillow,
her self-flagellation cords and a rare, hand-

painted *spinetta* (spinet or harpsichord) from 1682.

The apartment is positioned above a tiny chapel famed for its beautiful 18th-century Neapolitan liturgical art, including glass-eyed holy statues. Particularly rare is the statue of the *Divina Pastora* (Divine Shepherdess) on the left side of the nave. The only sculpture of its kind in Naples, it features an unusual depiction of the Virgin Mary reclined and wearing a shepherdess' hat that has its roots in 18th-century Spain. To the left of the nave, a statue of Santa Maria Francesca contains the holy local's bones.

Museo Nitsch   MUSEUM

(Map p50; ☑081 564 16 55; www.museonitsch.org; Vico Lungo Pontecorvo 29d; adult/reduced €10/5; ⊙10am-7pm Mon-Fri, 10am-2pm Sat; ⓂDante) In 1974, experimental Austrian artist Hermann Nitsch was invited to perform one of his 'actions' (a bloody, ritualistic art performance) in Naples, leading to his immediate arrest and deportation from Italy. Not one for the squeamish or easily offended, this savvy museum and cultural centre documents the now revered artist's intriguing, symbolic, confronting works through photographs, video, painting and props.

Set in a converted power station with superb views from its rooftop, the centre also hosts regular cultural events, such as avant-garde film screenings.

[FREE] Largo Baracche   GALLERY

(Map p50; ☑393 3641664; www.largobaracche. org; Piazza Baracche; ⊙by appointment; ⓂToledo) From ancient ruin to WWII air-raid shelter to subterranean art gallery, underground Largo Baracche was set up to support young, talented, emerging local artists. Check the website for upcoming exhibitions, and don't forget to ask the guys to turn off the lights – it's the only way you'll catch the glow-in-the-dark murals by Neapolitan street artists cyop&kaf (www.cyopekaf.org).

SANTA LUCIA & CHIAIA

At its southern end, Via Toledo spills into lavish Santa Lucia, whose grandiose residents include the sweeping Piazza del Plebiscito, art-lined Palazzo Reale, the velvety Teatro San Carlo and, further east, one-time Angevin stronghold Castel Nuovo (Maschio Angioino). Directly south of Castel Nuovo, ferries for Capri, Ischia, Procida and Sorrento dock at Molo Beverello, while further south-west diners seated at candlelit tables tuck into seafood at harbourside Borgo Marinaro.

Soaring above Via Santa Lucia is Monte Echia and the Pizzofalcone district, inhabited since the 7th century BC and a little-known warren of dark streets, macabre votive shrines and knockout views.

Further west, Chiaia is Naples' epicentre of 'posh', home to fashion-obsessed Via Calabritto, former Rothschild address Villa Pignatelli and the city's chicest bars.

[TOP CHOICE] Palazzo Reale   MUSEUM, PALACE

(Royal Palace; Map p56; ☑081 40 04 54; Piazza del Plebiscito; adult/reduced €4/3; ⊙9am-7pm Thu-Tue; ☐R2 to Piazza Trieste e Trento) Envisaged as a 16th-century monument to Spanish glory (Naples was under Spanish rule at the time), the magnificent Palazzo Reale is home to the Museo del Palazzo Reale, a rich and eclectic collection of baroque and neoclassical furnishings, porcelain, tapestries, statues and paintings, spread across the palace's royal apartments.

Among the many highlights is the restored Teatrino di Corte, a lavish private theatre created by Ferdinando Fuga in 1768 to celebrate the marriage of Ferdinand IV and Marie Caroline of Austria. Incredibly, Angelo Viva's statues of Apollo and the Muses set along the walls are made of papier mâché.

Snigger smugly in Sala (Room) XII, where the 16th-century canvas *Gli esattori delle imposte* (The Tax Collectors) by Dutch artist Marinus Claesz Van Roymerswaele confirms that attitudes to tax collectors have changed little in 500 years.

The next room, Sala XIII, used to be Joachim Murat's study in the 19th century but was used as a snack bar by Allied troops in WWII. Meanwhile, what looks like a waterwheel in Sala XXIII is actually a nifty rotating reading desk made for Marie Caroline by Giovanni Uldrich in the 18th century.

The Cappella Reale (Royal Chapel) houses a colossal 18th-century *presepe*. Impressively detailed, its cast of wise men, busty peasants and munching mules was crafted by a series of celebrated Neapolitan artists including Giuseppe Sanmartino, creator of the incredible *Cristo velato* (Veiled Christ) that is housed in the Cappella Sansevero (p38).

Extending out from Sala IX, the once-impressive hanging gardens are still closed for restoration, although they are sometimes opened for the Maggio dei Monumenti (p77). Otherwise, head to the picture-perfect garden

Santa Lucia & Chiaia

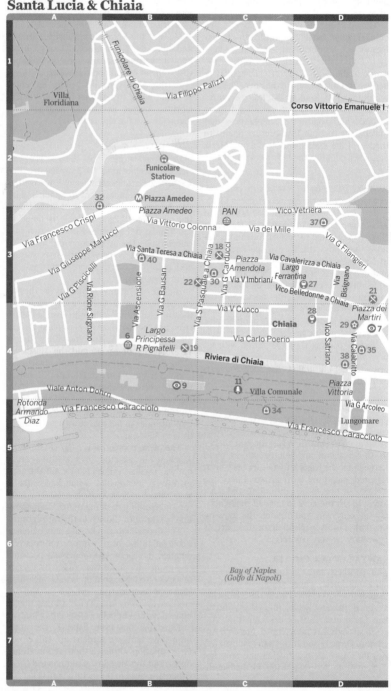

Villa
Floridiana

Funicolare di Chiaia

Via Filippo Palizzi

Corso Vittorio Emanuele I

Funicolare
Station

32

M Piazza Amedeo

Piazza Amedeo

PAN

Vico Vetriera

Via Vittorio Colonna

Via dei Mille

37

Via Francesco Crispi

Via Giuseppe Martucci

Via G Piscicelli

Via Rione Sirignano

Via Santa Teresa a Chiaia

40

Via Ascensione

Via G Bausan

18

Via S Pasquale a Chiaia

22

30

Via G Carducci

Piazza
Amendola

Via V Imbriani

Via Cavalerizza a Chiaia

Largo
Ferrantina

27

Vico Belledonne a Chiaia

Via G Filangieri

Via Bisignano

21

Piazza dei
Martiri

Via V Cuoco

28

29

7

Chiaia

6

Largo
Principessa
R Pignatelli

19

Via Carlo Poerio

Vico Satriano

Via Calabritto

Via G Arcoleo

38

35

Riviera di Chiaia

Viale Anton Dohrn

9

11

Villa Comunale

Piazza
Vittoria

Rotonda
Armando
Diaz

Via Francesco Caracciolo

34

Lungomare

Via Francesco Caracciolo

Bay of Naples
(Golfo di Napoli)

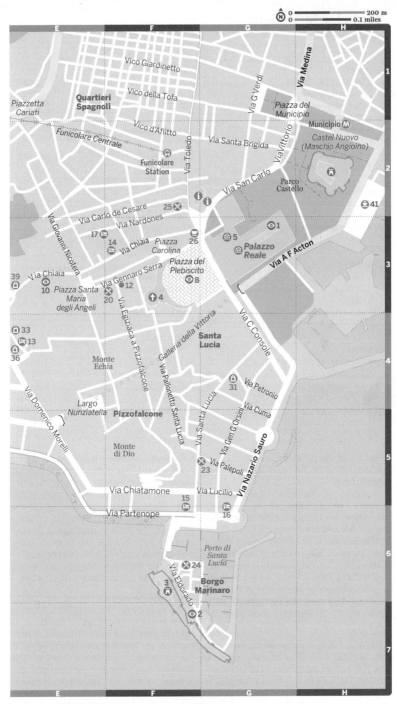

Santa Lucia & Chiaia

to the left of the palace's main ground-floor entrance. Entry is free and there are bay views to boot.

Designed by Domenico Fontana and completed two long centuries later in 1841, the palace also houses the **Biblioteca Nazionale** (National Library; Map p56; ☏081 781 92 31; www.bnnonline.it; Piazza del Plebiscito, Palazzo Reale; admission free; ☺8.30am-7.15pm Mon-Fri, 8.30am-1.15pm Sat, papyri exhibition closes 1pm; ☐R2 to Piazza Trieste e Trento), which includes at least 2000 papyri discovered at Herculaneum and fragments of a 5th-century Coptic Bible. Entry to the library requires photo ID.

Memus MUSEUM
(Museum & Historical Archive of the Teatro San Carlo; Map p56; www.memus.org; Piazza del Plebiscito, Palazzo Reale; adult/reduced €10/5; ☺10am-5pm Mon, Tue, Thu & Fri, to 7pm Sat & Sun; ☐R2 to Piazza Trieste e Trento) Located inside the Pal-

azzo Reale (purchase tickets at the palace ticket booth), this state-of-the-art museum documents the history of Europe's oldest working opera house, the Teatro San Carlo (p86). The collection combines historic costumes, sketches, instruments and memorabilia with interactive, multimedia displays allowing you to relive the theatre's music and stage design. To delve deeper into the archive, hit the computers upstairs. Admission includes Palazzo Reale ticket holders.

Piazza del Plebiscito PIAZZA
(Map p56; Piazza del Plebiscito; ☐R2 to Piazza Trieste e Trento) For Continental grandeur, it's hard to beat Piazza del Plebiscito. Whichever way you look, the view is impressive. To the northwest, vine-covered slopes lead up to Castel Sant'Elmo and the Certosa di San Martino; to the east, the pink-hued Palazzo Reale shows off its oldest facade. And to the

west stands Pietro Banchini's neoclassical facsimile of Rome's Pantheon, the **Chiesa di San Francesco di Paola** (Map p56; ☎081 74 51 33; Piazza del Plebiscito; ☺8.30am-noon & 4-7pm).

A later addition to the columned colonnade of Joachim Murat's original 1809 piazza design, the church was commissioned by Ferdinand I in 1817 to celebrate the restoration of his kingdom after the Napoleonic interlude. Standing guard outside are Antonio Canova's statue of a galloping King Charles VII of the Bourbons and Antonio Calí's rendering of Charles' son Ferdinand I.

At its northern end, Piazza Plebiscito spills onto Piazza Trieste e Trento , the city's buzzing heart and home to its most glamorous cafe, Caffé Gambrinus (p84) – a fabulous spot to slip on those shades, join the poseurs and eye up the passing parade.

Castel Nuovo   CASTLE, MUSEUM

(☎081 795 58 77; Piazza Municipio; admission €5; ☺9am-7pm Mon-Sat, last entry 6pm) Known as the Maschio Angioino (Angevin Keep) by the locals, this hulking 13th-century castle is one of Naples' most striking icons. It's also home to the **Museo Civico** (Civic Museum), whose collection include frescoes, paintings and sculptures spanning the 14th to the 20th centuries.

The castle's bio stretches back to Charles I of Anjou, who upon taking over Naples and the Swabians' Sicilian kingdom, found himself in control not only of his new southern Italian acquisitions, but also of possessions in Tuscany, northern Italy and Provence (France). It made sense to base the new dynasty in Naples, rather than Palermo in Sicily, and Charles launched an ambitious construction program to expand the port and city walls. His plans included converting a Franciscan convent into the castle that still stands in Piazza Municipio.

Christened the Castrum Novum (New Castle) to distinguish it from the older Castel dell'Ovo and Castel Capuano, it was completed in 1282, becoming a popular hang-out for the leading intellectuals and artists of the day – Giotto repaid his royal hosts by painting much of the interior. Of the original structure, however, only the Cappella Palatina remains; the rest is the result of Aragonese renovations two centuries later, as well as a meticulous restoration effort prior to WWII.

The two-storey Renaissance triumphal arch at the entrance – the **Torre della Guardia** – commemorates the victorious entry of Alfonso I of Aragon into Naples in 1443,

while the stark stone **Sala dei Baroni** (Hall of the Barons) is named after the barons slaughtered here in 1486 for plotting against King Ferdinand I of Aragon. Its striking ribbed vault fuses ancient Roman and Spanish late-Gothic influences.

Only fragments of Giotto's frescoes remain in the **Cappella Palatina**, on the splays of the Gothic windows. Above the chapel's elegant Renaissance doorway is a beautiful Catalan-style rose window. To the left of the chapel, the glass-floored **Sala dell'Armeria** (Armoury Hall) showcases Roman ruins discovered during restoration works on the Sala dei Baroni. Among the finds are the remains of a private swimming pool, as well as skeletons dating to the medieval period.

All this forms part of the museum, spread across several halls on three floors. The 14th- and 15th-century frescoes and sculptures on the ground floor are of the most interest.

The other two floors mostly display paintings, either by Neapolitan artists, or with Naples or Campania as subjects, covering the 17th to the early 20th centuries. Worth seeking out is Guglielmo Monaco's 15th-century bronze door, complete with a cannonball embedded in it.

Lungomare   STREET, PARK, AQUARIUM

(seafront; Via Francesco Caracciolo; ☐154 to Piazza Vittoria) When you need a break from Naples' hyperactive tendencies, take a deep breath on its recently pedestrianised seafront strip. Stretching 2.5km along Via Partenope and Via Francesco Carrociolo, its views are nothing short of exquisite, taking in the bay, Mt Vesuvius, two castles and Vomero's Liberty-style villas. It's particularly romantic at dusk, when Capri and the volcano take on a soft orange hue.

Separating the Lungomare from Riviera di Chiaia is the **Villa Comunale** (Map p56; Piazza Vittoria; ☺7am-midnight; ☐C25 to Riviera di Chiaia), a long, leafy park designed by Luigi Vanvitelli for private Bourbon frolicking. Its bountiful booty of fountains include the Fontana delle Paperelle (Duck Fountain), which replaced the famous Toro Farnese after its transferral to the Museo Archeologico Nazionale in 1825.

The park is also home to the take-it-or-leave-it **Stazione Zoologica** (Aquario; Map p56; ☎081 583 32 63; www.szn.it; Viale Aquario 1; adult/child €1.50/1; ☺9am-6pm Tue-Sat, 9am-7.30pm Sun; ☐C25 to Riviera di Chiaia), Europe's oldest aquarium. Housed in a stately

ART IN TRANSIT

Underground art means just that in Naples, with many of the city's metro stations designed or decorated by A-list artists, both homegrown and foreign. You'll find Mario Merz's blue neon digits at Vanvitelli; a witty Fiat installation by Perino & Vele at Salvator Rosa; and Technicolor wall drawings by Sol LeWitt at Materdei. And that's before we mention the snapshots by heavyweight Italian photographers at Museo; or Jannis Kounellis' eerie shoe installation at Dante.

Most of the city's 'Art Stations' are on Line 1, which is currently being extended. Its newest stations – Università and Toledo – are arguably its best yet.

'It kid' industrial-designer Karim Rashid is the force behind Università, a playful, candy-coloured ode to the digital age. White tiles clad the station entrance, each one printed with a word created in the last century. In the station itself you'll find lenticular icons that change perspective and colour, a sculpture reflecting the nodes and synapses of the brain, platform steps pimped with abstracted portraits of Dante and Beatrice, even platform walls adorned with glowing, 'animated' artwork (stare persistently).

No less breathtaking is Toledo station, its lobby featuring ruins from an Aragonese fortress and a spectacular wall mosaic by conceptual artist William Kentridge. Depicted in the latter is a medley of Neapolitan icons, from San Gennaro and a *pizzaiolo* (pizza maker) to the Museo Archeologico Nazionale's famous sculpture *Farnese Atlante*. Another Kentridge mural hovers above the escalators (it's said that the cat represents the artist himself).

Toledo station reaches a depth of 50m below sea level, a fact not lost on the station's colour scheme, which goes from ochre (representing Naples' tufo stone) to a dazzling blue as one descends. It's here, 'below the sea' that you'll find a spectacular, mosaic porthole, streaming down light from the sky above. The porthole's light installation is by artist Bob Wilson, whose wave-motif concourse panels 'move' as you hurry past them.

At the time of research, **MetroNapoli** (www.metro.na.it) was running free one-hour tours (usually in Italian) of Museo, Dante and Università stations on Tuesdays at 10am, with tours departing from the Museo station atrium (check the website for updates). Alternatively, read about each art station on the MetroNapoli website and explore at your own pace...all for the price of a metro ticket.

neoclassical building designed by Adolf von Hildebrandt, its tired-looking tanks are home to 200 species of marine flora and fauna from the city's bay.

FREE **Castel dell'Ovo** CASTLE
(Map p56; ☏081 240 00 55; Borgo Marinaro; ⊙9am-6pm Mon-Sat, to 2pm Sun; ⛟154 to Via Santa Lucia) Built by the Normans in the 12th century, Naples' oldest castle owes its name (Castle of the Egg) to Virgil. The Roman scribe reputedly buried an egg on the site where the castle now stands, warning that when the egg breaks, the castle (and Naples) will fall. Thankfully, both are still standing, and walking up to the castle's ramparts will reward you with a breathtaking panorama.

Used by the Swabians, Angevins and Alfonso of Aragon, who modified it to suit his military needs, the castle sits on the rocky, restaurant-lined 'island' of **Borgo Marinaro** (Map p56; ⛟C25 to Via Partenope). According to legend, the heartbroken siren Partenope washed ashore after failing to seduce Ulysses with her song. It's also where the Greeks first settled the city in the 7th century BC, calling the island Megaris. Its commanding position wasn't wasted on the Roman general Lucullus, either, who had his villa here long before the castle hit the skyline. Views aside, the castle now also hosts regular art exhibitions.

Museo Pignatelli MUSEUM
(Map p56; ☏081 761 23 56; http://museopign atelli.campaniabeniculturali.it; Riviera di Chiaia 200; adult/reduced €2/1; ⊙8.30am-2pm Wed-Mon, last entry 1pm; ⛟C24 to Riviera di Chiaia) When Ferdinand Acton, a minister at the court of King Ferdinand IV (1759–1825), asked Pietro Valente to design Villa Pignatelli in 1826, Valente whipped up this striking Pompeiian lookalike. Now the Museo Pignatelli, its aristocratic collection includes sumptuous furniture, decorative arts, royal hunting

whips, as well as paintings and busts from the Banco di Napoli's extensive art collection.

Bought and extended by the Rothschilds in 1841, the villa became home to the Duke of Monteleone, Diego Aragona Pignatelli Cortes, in 1867, before his granddaughter Rosina Pignatelli donated it (and its treasures) to the state. Permanent collection highlights include a fine collection of local and foreign porcelain in the Salotto Verde (Green Room), and a leather-lined smoking room. You'll find the Banco di Napoli's treasures in the basement, its collection of mainly 17th- to 19th-century Neapolitan works including Francesco Solimena's masterpiece painting *Agar e l'angelo* (Hagar and the Angel; 1695–99). The first floor hosts around three temporary exhibitions annually – a recent show focussed on vintage Japanese photography.

The adjoining **Museo delle Carrozze** contains a collection of 19th- and 20th-century carriages but remains closed indefinitely.

Tunnel Borbonico   TOUR
(Bourbon Tunnel; Map p56; ✆081 764 58 08; www. tunnelborbonico.info; Vico del Grottone 4; €10; ⊗ guided tours 10am, noon, 3.30pm & 5.30pm; ⛟R2 to Piazza Trieste e Trento) Run by the Borbonica Sotterranea cultural association, this atmospheric tour will have you snooping around what was designed as an escape tunnel for the Bourbon royal family. Tours can be booked on the association's website.

Via Chiaia   STREET
(Map p56; ⛟R2 to Piazza Trieste e Trento) Join the perma-tanned for a spot of window shopping on this popular pedestrianised strip. Linking Piazza Trieste e Trento with Piazza dei Martiri, it's a particular hit with evening *flâneurs*, not to mention home to 16th-century **Palazzo Cellamare** at No 149. Built as a summer residence for Giovan Francesco Carafa, it would go on to host numerous Bourbon royal guests, among them Goethe and Casanova.

Towards the street's western end, what looks like a triumphal arch is in fact a bridge built in 1636 to connect the hills of Pizzofalcone and Mortella. Past the bridge, turn right into blue-ribbon Via Gaetano Filangieri and continue up to Via dei Mille, where sharply garbed locals and shops mix it with flouncy Stile Liberty (Italian Art Nouveau) architecture.

Piazza dei Martiri   PIAZZA
(Map p56; ⛟C24 to Piazza dei Martiri) If Chiaia is Naples' drawing room, then Piazza dei Martiri is its chaise longue. The square's centrepiece is Enrico Alvino's 19th-century monument to Neapolitan martyrs, with four lions representing the anti-Bourbon uprisings of 1799, 1820, 1848 and 1860. At No 30 is **Palazzo Calabritto**, designed by Luigi Vanvitelli, best known for creating Caserta's epic Palazzo Reale.

Great names of the fashion variety abound around the corner on exclusive Via Calabritto, among them legendary local tailor Finamore (p79). On the piazza itself is book and music store Feltrinelli (p89), where locals head to browse, exchange flirtatious glances and guzzle espresso at the in-store cafe.

VOMERO, CAPODIMONTE & LA SANITÀ

All roads might lead to Rome, but three Neapolitan funiculars lead to Vomero, a hilltop neighbourhood where quasi-anarchy is replaced with mild-mannered *professori*, Liberty villas and the stunning Certosa di San Martino.

Northeast of Vomero, former royal hunting ground Capodimonte boasts its own cultural jewel in Palazzo Reale di Capodimonte, where names like Caravaggio, Botticelli and Warhol grace its regal rooms.

In stark contrast, the rough-and-tumble Sanità district (squeezed between Via Foria and Via Santa Teresa degli Scalzi directly south of Capodimonte) is a strangely bewitching mix of *bassi* (one-room, ground-floor houses), baroque staircases and ancient catacombs. To many, this is Naples at its earthiest and most authentic, a fact not lost on its growing number of resident artists and bohemians. It's also the birthplace of Italian comic legend Totò (at Via Santa Maria Antesaecula 109, to be precise!).

🔺TOP CHOICE **Palazzo Reale di Capodimonte**   PALACE, MUSEUM, PARK
(Map p62; ✆081 749 91 11; www.polomusealenapoli. beniculturali.it/museo_cp/museo_cp.html; Parco di Capodimonte; adult/reduced €7.50/3.75; ⊗museum 8.30am-7.30pm Thu-Tue, last entry 6pm; park 7.45am-1hr before sunset; ⛟R4 to Via Miano) This colossal palace took more than a century to build. Originally planned as a hunting lodge for Charles VII of Bourbon, the king's plans just kept getting grander. By its completion in 1759, Naples had a new palazzo. Official residence of Joseph Bonaparte and Joachim Murat during the decade of French rule (1806–15), it's now home to the **Museo**

Vomero, Capodimonte & La Sanità

NAPLES

Cimitero delle Fontanelle ⊙

Piazza Fontanelle alla Sanità

Materdei

Via R Imbriani

Via delle Fontanelle

Via B Caracciolo

Tangenziale

Monte Donzelli Ⓜ

Via F Verrotti

Medaglie d'Oro Ⓜ

Via Giotto

Via E Suarez

Piazza F Celebrano

Via Salvator Rosa

Salvator Rosa Ⓜ

Piazza dell'Immacolata

Piazza Leonardo

Via G Sagrera

Via T da Canzano

Via G Paisiello

Piazza degli Artisti 🔒26

Via Luca Giordano

Ⓜ Cilea

Via G Gianlorenzo Bernini

Viale Michelangelo

Vico Cacciottoli

Viale Raffaello

Vico dei Monte

13 🏛

Piazzetta Trinità alla Cesarea

Corso Vittorio Emanuele I

Funicolare di Montesanto

Vomero

24🍴

Via Tito Angelini

Via F Cilea

Via Solimene

Via A Scarlatti

Vanvitelli

Piazza Vanvitelli

Ⓜ16🍴

14🍴

17🍴 15🍴

21 🏛

Via Domenico Cimarosa

Funicolare Station

🍴Piazza Fuga 🏛Funicolare Station

Funicolare Station

Castel Sant'Elmo 🏰 🏛

Certosa e Museo di San Martino

Parco Lamaro

Villa Floridiana

Corso Vittorio Emanuele I

Parco Elena

7🍴 Viale Privato Diaz

🏛 4

Parco Ameno

11 🏛

Funicolare Station

22 ✪

Ⓜ Piazza Amedeo

Via dei Mille

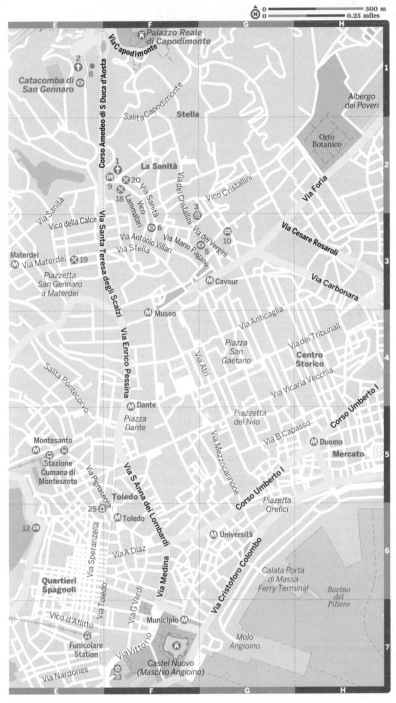

0 500 m
0 0.25 miles

Palazzo Reale
di Capodimonte

Via Capodimonte

Catacomba di
San Gennaro

Albergo
dei Poveri

Corso Amedeo di S Duca d'Aosta

Salita Capodimonte

Stella

Orto
Botanico

Via Foria

La Sanità

Via Santa Teresa degli Scalzi

Via Sanità

Vico della Calce

Via dei Cristallini

Via Santa

Vico Cristallini

Via Cesare Rosaroli

Materdei

Via Materdei

19

Vico
Lammatari

6

Via Antonio Villari

Via Mario Pagano

Via dei Vergini

Via Cristallini

10

Via Stella

Via Carbonara

Piazzetta
San Gennaro
a Materdei

Cavour

Museo

Via Anticaglia

Via dei Tribunali

Salita Pontecorvo

Via Enrico Pessina

Via Atri

Piazza
San
Gaetano

Centro
Storico

Via Vicaria Vecchia

Dante

Piazza
Dante

Piazzetta
del Nilo

Via B Capasso

Corso Umberto I

Montesanto

Stazione
Cumana di
Montesanto

Via Pignasecca

Via S Anna dei Lombardi

Via Mezzocannone

Duomo

Mercato

12

25

Toledo

Toledo

Corso Umberto I

Via A Diaz

Università

Piazzetta
Orefici

Quartieri
Spagnoli

Via Speranzella

Via Toledo

Via Medina

Via Cristoforo Colombo

Calata Porta
di Massa
Ferry Terminal

Bacino
del
Piliero

Vico d'Aflitto

Via G Verdi

Funicolare
Station

Municipio

Via Nardones

Via Vittorio

Castel Nuovo
(Maschio Angioino)

Molo
Angioino

23

Vomero, Capodimonte & La Sanità

Nazionale di Capodimonte and its superlative art collection.

With much of the collection inherited by Charles from his mother Elisabetta Farnese, the museum's extensive booty is spread over three floors and 160 rooms. The 1st floor is dominated by the Galleria Farnese and the Appartamento Reale (Royal Apartment); the 2nd floor contains the Galleria delle Arti a Napoli; while the top floor is dedicated to modern art.

To do the whole museum in one day is impossible – you'd need at least two to start getting to grips with the place. For most people, though, a full morning is sufficient for a shortened best-of tour, and forking out €5 for the insightful audioguide is a worthy investment.

First-floor highlights include family portraits of the Farnese by Raphael and Titian in room 2 and Masaccio's celebrated *Crocifissione* (Crucifixion; 1426) in Room 3. Botticelli's *Madonna col Bambino e due angeli* (Madonna with Baby and Angels; Room 6), Bellini's *Trasfigurazione* (Transfiguration; Room 8) and Parmigianino's *Antea* (Room 12) are all must-see pieces, while Joachim

Beukelaer's voluptuous 16th-century market scenes will whet your appetite in Room 18. In Room 20, a glum-looking Hercules is torn between a stern-looking Virtue and a fun-loving Vice in Annibale Carracci's 16th-century painting *Ercole al bivio* (Hercules at the Crossroads).

The Galleria delle Cose Rare (Gallery of Rare Objects) is home to Cardinal Alessandro Farnese's gold-embossed, blue majolica table service. The nifty centrepiece depicting Diana the huntress can be used as a goblet by taking off the stag's detachable head.

A study in regal excess, the 1st-floor Appartamento Reale (Royal Apartment) occupies rooms 31 to 60. Sumptuous rooms positively heave with valuable Capodimonte porcelain, heavy curtains and shiny inlaid marble. The Salottino di Porcellana (Room 52) is an extraordinary example of 18th-century chinoiserie, its walls and ceiling crawling with whimsically themed porcelain 'stucco'. The Appartamento Reale is also home to Volaire's *Eruzione del Vesuvio dal Ponte Maddalena* (Eruption of Vesuvius from the Bridge of Maddalena).

The 2nd floor is packed to its elegant rafters with works produced in Naples between the 13th and 18th centuries. The first room you come to, however, is lined with a series of epic 16th-century Belgian tapestries depicting episodes from the Battle of Pavia. Simone Martini's work *San Ludovico di Tolosa* (1317) is brilliantly displayed in Room 66. Considered the museum's finest example of 14th-century art, Martini's golden work portrays the canonisation of Ludovico, brother of King Robert of Anjou.

The piece that many come to Capodimonte to see, *Flagellazione* (Flagellation; 1607–10) hangs in reverential solitude in Room 78, at the end of a long corridor. Caravaggio's arresting image of Jesus about to be flogged was originally painted for the de Franchis family chapel in the Chiesa di San Domenico Maggiore. And, like his other great Neapolitan work *Le sette opere di misericordia* (The Seven Acts of Mercy), its intensity and revolutionary depiction of light were to have a huge influence on his contemporaries.

The 28 rooms that remain on the 2nd floor contain works by Ribera, Giordano, Solimena and Stanzione. Admittedly, your attention span may be seriously waining by this stage. If so, simply pop into the small gallery of modern art on the 3rd floor to see Andy Warhol's poptastic Mt Vesuvius before taking in Giuseppe de Ribera's *San Girolamo e l'angelo* (St Jerome and the Angel) back on the 2nd floor (Room 90). This floor also houses works from the Gabinetto Disegni e Stampe (Drawing and Print Room), including several sketches by Michelangelo and Raphael.

Mercifully, the Giovanni Antonio Medrano–designed palace is set in the rambling, 130-hectare **Parco di Capodimonte** (admission free; ⏱9am-1hr before sunset; 🚌R4 to Via Miano), its lakes, wood, and various 18th-century buildings (including former royal porcelain workshop Palazzo Porcellane) a soothing antidote for any cultural OD.

🔝 **Certosa e Museo di San Martino** MUSEUM, MONASTERY
(Map p62; 📞848 80 02 88; http://museosanmartino.campaniabeniculturali.it; Largo San Martino 5; adult/reduced €6/3; ⏱8.30am-7.30pm Thu-Tue, last entry 6pm; Montesanto to Morghen, Ⓜ Vanvitelli) Originally built by Charles of Anjou in 1325, this former Carthisian monastery hilltop has been decorated, adorned and altered over the centuries by some of the greats of Italian art and architecture, most importantly Giovanni Antonio Dosio in the 16th century and baroque master Cosimo Fanzago a century later. Today, it's a superb repository of Neapolitan artistry, all of it wisely collected by its resident monks.

The monastery's **church** and the rooms that flank it contain a feast of frescoes and paintings by some of Naples' greatest 17th-century artists. In the *pronaos* (a small room flanked by three walls and a row of columns), Micco Spadaro's frescoes of Carthusian persecution seem to defy perspective as figures sit with their legs hanging over nonexistent edges. Elsewhere throughout the church you'll discover works by Francesco Solimena, Massimo Stanzione, Giuseppe de Ribera, Luca Giordano and Battista Caracciolo. Especially noteworthy is the sascristy, adorned with extraordinarily detailed 16th-century marquetry (inlaid wood) and carvings.

Adjacent to the church, the **Chiostro dei Procuratori** is the smaller of the monastery's two cloisters. A grand corridor on the left leads to the larger **Chiostro Grande** (Great Cloister), considered one of Italy's finest. Originally designed by Giovanni Antonio Dosio in the late 16th century and added to by Fanzago, it's a sublime composition of Tuscan-Doric porticoes, garden and marble statues. The sinister skulls mounted on the balustrade were a light-hearted reminder to the monks of their own mortality.

Just off the Chiostro dei Procuratori is the **Sezione Navale**, whose two exhibition halls focus on the history of the Bourbon navy from 1734 to 1860. The collection features a series of detailed scale models of late-18th- and 19th-century warships used by the former royals, as well as original navy weaponry. The true highlight, however, is the small collection of original royal barges, among them a gilded, canopied number used by Charles VII and a beautifully carved 18th-century gift to Ferdinand IV from Turkish sultan Selim III.

One of the many museum highlights is the **Sezione Presepiale**, which houses a whimsical collection of rare Neapolitan *presepi* carved in the 18th and 19th centuries. These range from the minuscule – a nativity scene in an ornately decorated eggshell – to the colossal Cuciniello creation, which covers one wall of what used to be the monastery's kitchen. Angels fly down to a richly detailed landscape of rocky houses, shepherds and local merrymakers, all made out of wood, cork, papier-mâché and terracotta.

The **Quarto del Priore** in the southern wing houses the bulk of the picture collection, as well as one of the museum's most famous pieces, Pietro Bernini's tender *La vergine col bambino e San Giovannino* (Madonna and Child with the Infant John the Baptist).

A pictorial history of Naples is told in the section **Immagini e Memorie di Napoli** (Images and Memories of Naples). Here you'll find portraits of historic characters (Don Pedro de Toledo in Room 33, Maria Carolina di Borbone in Room 43); antique maps, including a 35-panel copper map in Room 45; and rooms dedicated to major historical events such as the Revolt of the Masaniello (Room 36) and the plague (Room 37). Room 32 boasts the beautiful Tavola Strozzi (Strozzi Table), whose fabled depiction of 15th-century maritime Naples is one of the city's most celebrated historical records.

It's worth noting that some of the exhibitions may close down for some part of the day, so it's a good idea to phone ahead and check if you're especially keen on seeing a particular part of the museum.

TOP CHOICE **Cimitero delle Fontanelle** CEMETERY
(Map p62; ☑081 744 37 14; Piazza Fontanelle alla Sanità 154; ☺10am-5pm Thu-Tue; ☐C51) Currently holding an estimated eight million human bones, the ghoulish Fontanelle Cemetery was first used during the plague of 1656, before becoming the city's main burial site during the cholera epidemic of 1837. At the end of the 19th century it became a cult spot for the worship of the dead, which saw locals adopting skulls and praying for their souls.

Dubbed the *culto delle anime pezzentelle* (cult of the poor souls), the practice took hold here after Father Gaetano Barbati began cleaning and cataloguing the abandoned skeletal remains in 1872. Devotees joined him, adopting the anonymous skulls, building little *scarabattole* (cabinets) to encase them in, and praying for their souls. It was hoped that once a soul was released from purgatory, it would bestow blessings in gratitude. No doubt Father Gaetano would have turned in his grave when, in 1969, the Archbishop of Naples banned the practice, condemning it as 'fetishistic'. Decades later, the cemetery remains a powerful testament to the melding of the sacred and the profane in Neapolitan spirituality.

Of the countless bodies laid to rest here, only the two lying in coffins in the left-hand nave have been identified: Count Filippo Carafa and his mummified wife, Donna Margherita Petrucci. According to legend, poor Margherita died choking on a *gnocco* (a gnocchi), hence her somewhat panicked expression. The left-hand nave is also home to the cemetery's mysterious 'sweating' skull, Donna Concetta. To the faithful, the skull was the resident fortune teller, responding in the affirmative by sweating, and in the negative by not. Exactly how Donna Concetta performs her 'trick' remains a mystery.

While you can visit the the cemetery independently, the lack of information makes joining a guided tour such as those organised by the Cooperativa Sociale Onlus 'La Paranza' (p67) much more rewarding. Avoid guides offering tours at the entrance.

TOP CHOICE **Catacomba di San Gennaro** CATACOMB
(Map p62; ☑081 744 37 14; www.catacombedinapoli.it; Via di Capodimonte 13; adult/reduced €8/5, incl entry to Catacomba di San Gaudioso; ☺1hr tours every hr 10am-5pm Mon-Sat, to 1pm Sun; ☐R4 to Via Capodimonte) Recently extended thanks to an ongoing, community-based restoration project, Naples' oldest and most sacred catacomb became a Christian pilgrimage site when San Gennaro's body was interred here in the 5th century. It's an evocative otherworld of tombs, corridors and broad vestibules, its treasures including 2nd-century Christian frescoes, 5th-century mosaics and the oldest known portrait of San Gennaro.

You'll find three types of tombs in here, each reflecting a different social class. The wealthy opted for the open-room *cubiculum*, originally guarded by gates and adorned with colourful wall frescoes. One *cubiculum* to the left of the entrance features an especially beautiful funerary fresco of a mother, father and child. In actual fact, you're looking at three layers of frescoes, one commissioned for each death. The smaller, rectangular wall niches, known as *loculum*, were the domain of the middle classes, while the *forme* (floor tombs) were reserved for the poor.

Further ahead you'll stumble upon the so-called *basilica minore* (minor basilica), home to the tombs of San Gennaro and 5th-century Archbishop of Naples, Giovanni I. Sometime between 413 and 431, Giovanni I accompanied the martyr's remains from Pozzuoli to Naples, burying them here before Lombard prince Sico I of Benevento snatched them in the 9th century. The *basilica minore* also harbours fragments of a fresco depicting Naples' first bishop, Sant'Aspreno. The city's bishops were buried in this catacomb until the 11th century.

Close to the basilica minore is a 3rd-century tomb whose Pompeiian-hued artwork employs both Christian and pagan elements. In the image of three women building a castle, the figures represent the three virtues, while the castle symbolises the Church.

The catacomb's recently opened lower level is even older, dating back to the 2nd century and speckled with typically pagan motifs like fruit and animals. The painting on the side of San Gennaro's tomb – depicting the saint with Mt Vesuvius and Mt Somma on his shoulders – is the first known image of San Gennaro as the protector of Naples. Also on the lower level is the Basilica di Agrippino, named in honour of Sant'Agrippino. The sixth bishop of Naples, Agrippino was also the first Christian to be buried in the catacomb, back in the 3rd century.

Tours of the catacomb are run by the **Cooperativa Sociale Onlus 'La Paranza'** (Map p62; ☑081 744 37 14; www.catacombedinapoli.it; Via Capodimonte 13; ⊙info point 10am-5pm; ☐R4 to Via Capodimonte), whose ticket office is to the left of the **Chiesa di Madre di Buon Consiglio** (Map p62; ☑081 741 00 06; Via Capodimonte 13; ⊙8am-12.30pm & 5-7pm Mon-Sat, 9am-1pm & 5-7pm Sun), a snack-sized replica of St Peter's in Rome completed in 1960. The co-operative also runs a fascinating walking tour called Il Miglio Sacro (The Holy Mile), which explores the neighbouring Sanità district. It must be pre-booked; see their website for details.

Basilica Santa Maria della Sanità & Catacomba di San Gaudioso
CHURCH, CATACOMB

(Map p62; (☑081 544 13 05; www.catacombedinapoli.it; Piazza Sanità 14; basilica free, catacomb adult/reduced €8/5, incl entry to Catacomba di San Gennaro; ⊙basilica 9am-1.30pm daily, 50-minute catacomb tours 10am, 11am, noon, 1pm daily; ⊠Piazza Cavour, Museo) While we love the baroque paintings by Andrea Vaccaro and Luca Giordano – not to mention the two contemporary sculptures by Riccardo Dalisi – it's the atmospheric catacomb beneath this 17th-century basilica that makes it unforgettable. Entered through the 5th-century **Cappella di San Gaudioso**, which lurks below

the high altar, its damp walls reveal a rather macabre method of medieval burial.

Firstly, bodies would be stored in the arched wall niches, where the *sciacciamorti* (literally 'corpse squashers') would poke them to release all blood and bodily fluids. Once dried out, the body would be buried, while the skull would be cemented to the wall and set over a fresco of the dearly departed. The skull set above a frescoed body depicted with paintbrushes and a ruler belonged to 16th-century mannerist painter Giovanni Balducci. The Florentine artist had struck a deal with the Dominicans – in return for decorating their catacomb free of charge, they would allow him to be buried here (considered a priviledge at the time). Remnants of Balducci's frescoes remain, though much better preserved is the so-called *Trionfo della croce* (Triumph of the Cross) mosaic. Created in the 5th or 6th century, its earthy tones and unusually large lambs suggest that the artist hailed from Africa. The African connection continues with the catacomb's namesake, San Gaudioso, a North African bishop who died in Naples in AD 452 and was buried on this site.

In the Cappella di San Gaudioso itself, scan the walls for an intensely colourful 9th-century fresco of the Madonna and Child flanked by St Gregory and St Marciano. Recently restored, the image was discovered in the 1990s beneath a known 19th-century fresco.

Castel Sant'Elmo
CASTLE, MUSEUM

(☑081 578 40 30; www.polomusealenapoli.beniculturali.it; Via Tito Angelini 22; adult/reduced €5/2.50; ⊙castle 8.30am-7.30pm Wed-Mon, last entry 6.30pm, museum 9am-6pm on the hour Wed-Mon; ⊠Vanvitelli, Montesanto to Morghen) This star-shaped castle was originally a church dedicated to St Erasmus. Some 400 years later, in 1349, Robert of Anjou turned it into a castle before Spanish viceroy Don Pedro de Toledo had it further fortified in 1538. Used as a military prison until the 1970s, it's now famed for its jaw-dropping panorama, and the **Museo del Novecento**, dedicated to 20th-century Neapolitan art.

The museum's collection of painting and sculpture documents major influences in the local art scene, including Futurism and the Nuclear Art movement. Standout works include Eugenio Viti's sensual *La schiena* (The Back) in Room 7, Raffaele Lippi's unnerving *Le quattro giornate di Napoli* (The Four Days of Naples) in Room 9, and

SIGHTSEE FOR LESS

If you're planning to blitz the sights, the **Campania artecard** (☑800 60 06 01; www.campaniartecard.it) is an excellent investment. A cumulative ticket that covers museum admission and transport, it comes in various forms. The Naples and Campi Flegrei three-day **ticket** (adult/reduced €16/10) gives free admission to three participating sites, a 50% discount on others and free transport in Naples and the Campi Flegrei. Other options range from €12 to €30 and cover sites as far afield as Pompeii and Paestum. Buy the card online, at Stazione Centrale, or at particpating sites and museums.

Salvatore Cotugno's striking, untitled sculpture of a bound, wrapped, muted figure in Room 17. The latter strangely echoes Giuseppe Sanmartino's astounding *Cristo velato* (Veiled Christ), in the Cappella Sansevero (p38).

FREE **Museo Nazionale della Ceramica Duca di Martina** MUSEUM, GARDENS (National Museum of Ceramics; Map p62; ☑081 578 84 18; http://floridiana.spmn.campaniabeni culturali.it; Via Domenico Cimarosa 77; ⊗museum 8.30am-2pm, last entry 1.15pm, gardens 8.30am-1hr before sunset; MVanvitelli) The National Museum of Cermaics houses a beautiful, 6000-piece collection, with priceless Chinese Ming (1368–1644) ceramics and Japanese Edo (1615–1867) vases on the lower floor, lively Renaissance majolica on the midde floor, and more European ceramics (including some sumptuous Meissen pieces) on the top floor. You'll also find a smattering of paintings from greats such as Francesco Solimena, Francesco De Mura and Vincenzo Camuccini.

The museum's home is the stately **Villa Floridiana** (Via Domenico Cimarosa 77; admission free; ⊗8.30am-1hr before sunset; Vanvitelli), a not-so-modest gift from King Ferdinand I to his second wife, the Duchess of Floridia. Its lush, manicured gardens are worth the trip alone, with dreamy bay and city views, and a pretty little fountain sprinkled with tortoises.

Palazzo dello Spagnuolo ARCHITECTURE (Map p62; Via dei Vergini 19; MPiazza Cavour, Museo) In baroque-rich Naples, even staircases

can be an event and the masterpiece gracing the courtyard of this *palazzo* is one of its most showstopping. Designed by Ferdinando Sanfelice and dating from 1738, its double-ramped, five-arched flights were put to good use in film classics like Luigi Zampa's *Processo alla città* (A City Stands Still) and Vittorio De Sica's *Giudizio universale* (Judgement Day).

Believe it or not, horses once used the stairs, providing door-to-door service for lazy cavaliers.

If Sanfelice's sweeping architectural statement will leave you stair-crazy, a quick walk north will lead you to his debut effort inside the **Palazzo Sanfelice** (Map p62; Via della Sanità 2; Cavour). Upon its completion in 1726 the double-ramped diva became the talk of the town, and from then on there was no stopping Sanfelice, who perfected his dramatic staircase design in various *palazzi* across the city.

While neither of these two buildings is technically open to the public, the porter should let you through if you ask nicely. Porters generally work office hours, so avoid the early afternoon if you want to find someone there.

Museo del Tessile e dell'Abbigliamento Elena Aldobrandini MUSEUM (Map p50; ☑081 497 61 04; www.fondazionemon dragone.it; Piazzetta Mondragone 18, Fondazione Mondragone Napoli ; admission free; ⊗9.30am-6pm Mon-Fri; ☑Centrale to Corso Vittorio Emanuele) Despite the lack of information accompanying the exhibitions, this petite textile and fashion museum is a gem. Swoon over a beautiful selection of mid-20th-century gowns, including creations by late Neapolitan fashion great Emilio Schuberth, dubbed 'tailor of the stars' and mentor to Valentino. Capri's equally famous designer Livio De Simone is also showcased, alongside vintage millinery, gloves, ecclesiastical garb and reproductions of 16th and 17th-century garments.

One of the more unusual exhibits features reproductions of the fashion worn in painter Diego Velázquez's 17th-century masterpiece *Las Meninas* (The Maids of Honour). The museum is tucked away inside the Fondazione Mondragone, established as a 'retreat for noble matrons and virgins' in the mid-17th century.

Chiesa San Giovanni a Carbonara CHURCH (Map p40; ☑081 29 58 73; Via Carbonara 5; ⊗9am-5.30pm Mon-Sat; MPiazza Cavour, Museo) Sumptuous sculpture make this Gothic church worth a detour. Andrea de Firenze, Tuscan sculptors and northern-Italian artists collaborated on the Gothic-Renaissance mausoleum of King Ladislas, soaring 18m behind the main altar. Behind it, the circular Cappella Caracciole del Sole uplifts with its colourful 15th-century frescoes and Leonardo da Besozzo's tomb for Giovanni Caracciolo, the ambitious lover of King Ladislas' sister Queen Joan II of Naples.

Caracciolo's increasing political power led the queen to plot his demise and in 1432 he was stabbed to death in the nearby Castel Capuano.

Other important works include the Cappella Caracciolo di Vico (renowned for showcasing early-16th-century Roman style in southern Italy), the *Monumento Miroballo* by Tommaso Malvito and Jacopo dell Pila and the colourful 14th-century Cappella Somma, complete with mannerist frescoes and an exquisite 16th-century altar executed by Annibale Caccarello and Giovan Domenico d'Auria. The 18th-century double-flight staircase leading up to the church itself is the work of baroque great Ferdinando Sanfelice.

The church derives its name from its location, on the former site of an Angevin *carbonarius* (waste disposal and incineration site).

Laboratorio Oste   MUSEUM, GALLERY
(Map p62; ☑081 44 44 45; www.facebook.com/LaboratorioOste; Via dei Cristallini 138; ☉usually 9am-6pm Mon-Fri; MPiazzaCavour, Museo) The late Annibale Oste was one of Naples' most celebrated sculptors and designers and his workshop is now a small gallery/archive showcasing some of his works, including whimsical light sculptures, vases, and fantastical furniture pieces spanning 2001 to 2010. The venue, charming in itself, is now lovingly run by his artist children, Mariasole and Vincenzo, the latter's striking contemporary jewellery also on display (and for sale).

Deemed a visionary by his peers, Annibale Oste breathed a sense of energy and playfulness into materials as diverse as bronze, steel, wood, alabaster and glass. His use of fibreglass in the 1970s was lauded as pioneering, and his creations – which include a storage unit that evokes a deliciously giant chocolate block – are an extraordinary symphony of textures, shapes and colours. Interestingly, the building's courtyard was once used for staging plays, with the workshop's office used as a changing room by local actors. Among them was a young Totò, who

NAPLES SIGHTS

THE CAPTAIN'S CURSE

Of the many macabre tales crawling around the Cimitero delle Fontanelle (p66), none intrigues quite like that of *il Capitano* (The Captain); the centre skull at the base of the cemetery's three Calvary crosses.

According to legend, a pious young woman from La Sanità adopted the skull, a common practice in Naples until the late 1960s. As incongruous as it seems, the Cimitero delle Fontanelle doubled as a lover's lane for lovebirds with nowhere else to go. This was not lost on the woman's less-than-pious boyfriend, who convinced her to lose her virginity at the site.

Pensive and nervous, the young woman approached the Captain, asking the skull to bless their relationship and grant them a happy marriage. Not one for superstitious beliefs, the boyfriend began mocking her and the Captain, poking the skull's eye socket and daring it to turn up at their wedding. Adding insult to injury, his took his lover's virginity then and there.

Fast forward to the couple's wedding banquet, where a stranger enters wearing an eye patch and old-fashioned officer's uniform. No less cocky than at the cemetery that fateful day, the young groom corners the guest as he is leaving, demanding to know who had invited him. The officer turns around, smiles, and replies 'You did... at the Fontanelle' before opening his coat to reveal a full skeleton that immediately crumbles to the floor.

Not surprisingly, the shock killed both the groom and his bride, whose final resting place suitably remains a mystery. While some say that the couple's remains lie in the Cimitero delle Fontanelle, others believe that a funerary fresco of a couple in the Catacomba di San Gaudioso (p67) indicates their place of eternal regret.

would go on to become one of Italy's greatest comic film stars.

If you plan on visiting, it's always a good idea to email or call ahead to ensure that someone is there to let you in.

MERGELLINA & POSILLIPO

Located at the western end of the now-pedestrianised Lungomare, Mergellina exudes an air of faded grandeur with its Liberty *palazzi* and slightly scruffy seafront. Kitsch marina chalets sell gelato to lovestruck teens, while, close by, hydrofoils head out to the islands.

Further west, on the headland dividing the Bay of Naples from the Bay of Pozzuoli, Posillipo is a verdant, blue-ribbon neighbourhood of sprawling villas, secret swimming coves and the urban oasis of Parco Virgiliano.

Porticciolo   HARBOUR
(Map p71; Via Francesco Caracciolo; MMergellina) Once home to the area's fishing fleet, Mergellina's marina is now a crowd-pulling combo of anchored yachts and kitsch Neapolitan chalets, neon-lit seaside gelaterie and bars. Pick up an ice-cream brioche at Chalet Ciro Mergellina and soak up the postcard view of the *castello* (castle) and volcano.

From here, opt for a lazy *passeggiata* (stroll) eastward along the car-free *lungomare* (seafront; p59); or, if you don't mind the incline, head southwest along Via Posillipo for enchanting vistas of the bay, the city and lushly gardened villas.

Parco Vergiliano   PARK, ARCHAEOLOGICAL SITE
(Map p71; ☑081 66 93 90; Salita dell Grotta 20; ☺9am-6pm; MMergellina) Head up the steep steps at this off-the-radar park and you'll find yourself peering into the world's longest Roman tunnel. A 700m-long affair, it once linked Naples to Pozzuoli. At the top of the steps lies the tomb of Virgil, who died in Brindisi in 19 BC. Legend has it that the Roman poet's remains were carted to Naples and buried in this Augustan-era vault.

Also buried in the park is the 19th-century poet Giacomo Leopardi.

Parco Virgiliano   PARK
(Map p74; Viale Virgilio; ☺7am-1am late June-Sep, 7am-midnight May-late Jun, 7am-9pm rest of year; ☐140 to Via Posillipo) Perched high above the shimmering sea on the westernmost tip of posh Posillipo hill, this much-loved park is the place to kick back on a terrace and soak up the views; from Capri to the south, and

Nisida, Procida and Ischia to the southwest, to the Bay of Pozzuoli and Bagnoli to the west. Trendy Posillipo market takes place outside the main gates on Thursday between 9am and 2pm.

History buffs may know that the tiny island of Nisida is where Brutus reputedly conspired against his over-achieving nemesis Julius Caesar.

CAMPI FLEGREI

Stretching west of Posillipo Hill to the Tyrrhenian Sea, the oft-overlooked Campi Flegrei (Phlegrean Fields) counterbalances its ugly urban sprawl with steamy active craters, lush volcanic hillsides and priceless ancient ruins. While its Greek settlements are Italy's oldest, its Monte Nuovo is Europe's youngest mountain. Gateway to the region is the port town of Pozzuoli, home to archaeological must-sees and handy for ferries to Ischia and Procida.

POZZUOLI & SURROUNDS

Founded around 530 BC by political exiles from the Aegean island of Samos, Pozzuoli (ancient Dikaiarchia) came into its own under the Romans, who in 194 BC colonised it, renamed it Puteoli (Little Wells), and turned it into a major port. It was here that St Paul is said to have landed in AD 61, that San Gennaro was beheaded and that screen goddess Sophia Loren spent her childhood. A bout of bradyseism (the slow upward and downward movement of the earth's crust) saw Pozzuoli's seabed rise 1.85m between 1982 and 1984, rendering its harbour too shallow for large vessels.

Indeed, geological curiosities surround the town, from the sizzling Solfatara Crater (p72) 1.2km to the east, to novice mountain Monte Nuovo 3km to the west.

[TOP CHOICE] Anfiteatro Flavio   RUIN
(☑081 526 60 07; Via Terracciano 75; adult/reduced €4/2; ☺varies, usually 9am-1hr before sunset Wed-Mon; ☒Cumana to Pozzuoli, MPozzuoli) In its heyday, Italy's third-largest amphitheatre could hold over 20,000 bloodthirsty spectators, who would pour in to cheer on mock naval battles (yes, the stadium was occasionally flooded for fun), and indulge in a little *schadenfreude* as lions chased those captive Christians. Planned by Nero and completed by Vespasian (AD 69–79), the ancient stadium's best-preserved remains lie under the main arena.

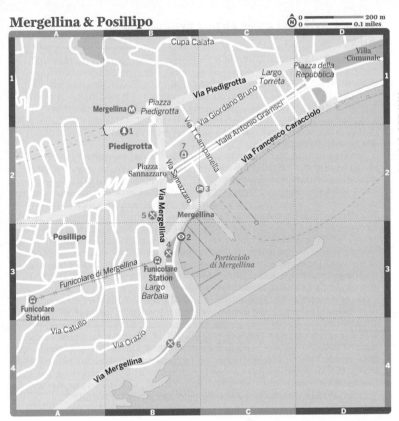

Wander among the fallen columns and get your head around the complex mechanics involved in hoisting the caged wild beasts up to their waiting victims through the overhead 'skylights'. In AD 305 seven Christian martyrs were thrown to the animals by the emperor Diocletian. They survived, only to be later beheaded. One of the seven was San Gennaro, the patron saint of Naples.

Opening times can be fickle, so consider calling ahead.

Rione Terra　　　　　HISTORIC SITE, RUIN
(☑848 80 02 88; Largo Sedile di Porto; adult/concession €4/2; ⊙vary; ℝCumana to Pozzuoli; MPozzuoli) Rione Terra is Pozzuoli's oldest quarter and its ancient acropolis. Beneath the current cluster of 17th-century buildings lies an archaeological treasure trove of roads, shops and even a brothel dating back to the days when Pozzuoli was the ancient port of Puteoli. More often closed than open, call the Pozzuoli tourist office for updates.

Mergellina & Posillipo

If you are lucky enough to explore the ruins, you'll find yourself walking down the *decumanus maximus* – check out ancient taverns, peer into millers' shops (complete with intact grindstones) and decipher

RICCARDO DALISI & THE ART OF BENEVOLENCE

From his *Dedicate a Klee* sculptures at Salvator Rosa metro station to his quirky light sculptures at La Stanza del Gusto, the art of Riccardo Dalisi (born 1931) has become iconic within contemporary Naples. Dubbing himself '*Il designer del opera buffa*' (the designer of humorous creations), Dalisi turns scrap metal and junk into lively, whimsical sculptures that radiate a fantastical, childlike sensibility – from 'dancing' cans with top hats to '*amorous*' *caffettiere* (percolators). Indeed, the Neapolitan *caffettiera* – an elongated version of the standard Italian model – is one of Dalisi's trademark motifs, an obsession that began after Italian design company Alessi commissioned him to design one for its 1979 catalogue.

Despite a string of other famous commissions for the likes of Zanotta, Fiat and Bisazza, Dalisi has always eschewed diva demands, preferring humility, humanity and a social conscience. Graduating as an architect in 1957, he first achieved fame as a pioneer of Italy's anti-design movement in the 1960s, which decried consumerist thinking in design in favour of individuality, spontaneity and an acknowledgement of every person's creative potential. By the 1970s, the artist was running *design povero* (poor design) workshops for underprivileged Neapolitan youth, teaching them how to turn scrap metal into works of art. His more recent collaboration with locals from the rough-and-ready Sanità district reached fruition with the birth of the **Iron Angels** (☎331 8860287; www.ironangels.it), an artisan co-op based inside a deconsecrated neighbourhood church. Offering work and hope to youth otherwise vulnerable to criminal careers, the group's recycled creations adorn a number of locations, including the ancient Catacomba di San Gennaro (p66).

As you'd expect, a visit to Dalisi's own **studio** (Map p62; ☎081 68 14 05; studiodalisi@libero.it; Calata San Francesco 59; admission free; ⊙9am-2pm Mon-Fri, call ahead; ⊟C28 to Via Aniello Falcone) is a wonderful experience, its collection of rooms packed to the rafters with charismatic prototypes, works-in-progress and roll upon roll of Dalisi's own paintings and illustrations (the recycling theme continues here, with Dalisi only using pre-used paper, much of which comes from schools). The gentle *maestro* also offers free three-, four- or five-day workshops (book a week ahead), though it's worth considering that Dalisi does not speak English. And while all visitors are welcome at the studio, don't forget to call ahead and book a time with Dalisi's assistant, Carla Rabuffetti, first.

graffiti written by the poet Catallus in a dingy slaves' cell. Archaeologists made the startling find after volcanic activity in the 1970s forced a mass evacuation of the quarter. Above ground, Pozzuoli's 16th-century duomo is built around an ancient Capitolium, itself lavishly restructured by Lucius Cocceius in the Augustan age.

Solfatara Crater   VOLCANO

(☎081 526 23 41; www.solfatara.it; Via Solfatara 161; adult/reduced €7/4.50; ⊙8.30am-1hr before sunset; ⓂPozzuoli, then 900m walk north along Via Solfatara) Unnerving and surreal, this steamy crater was called Foro Vulcani (home of the god of fire) by the Romans. At the far end of the crater you can see the Stufe, two ancient grottos excavated at the end of the 19th century to create two brick *sudatoria* (sweat rooms). Christened Purgatory and Hell, they both reach temperatures of up to 90°C.

The crater's acrid steam, bubbling mud and sulphurous water have been lauded for their curative qualities for thousands of years. If the thought of reaching the crater on foot sounds like purgatory, catch any city bus heading uphill from Pozzuoli metro station and ask the driver to let you off at Solfatara.

Tempio di Serapide   RUIN

(Temple of Serapis; Via Serapide; ⓇCumana to Pozzuoli, ⓂPozzuoli) Badly damaged by centuries of seismic bradyseism and occasionally flooded by sea water, this sunken square just east of the port wasn't a temple at all but rather an ancient *macellum* (town market). Named after a statue of the Egyptian god Serapis found here in 1750, its ancient toilets (at either side of the eastern apse) are considered works of historical ingenuity.

Mercato del Pesce di Pozzuoli   MARKET

(Pozzuoli Fish Market; Map p74; Via Nicola Fasano; ⊙7.30am-1.30pm Tue-Sun; ⓇCumana to Pozzuoli, ⓂPozzuoli) Pozzuoli's atmospheric fish market is just the spot for an appetising morning stroll. Good weather brings in the best catches, with local staples including *pesce azzurro (mackeral), pesce bandiera* (sailfish), *seppie* (squid), *polipi* (octopus), *alici* (anchovies) and *gamberoni* (giant prawns). The second of the two aisles is a mouth-watering spectacle of robust salami and *salsiccie* (sausages), plump cheeses, local fruits and vegetables, and crunchy *casareccio* (home-style) bread.

Peckish? Stock up for an impromptu picnic on nearby Monte Nuovo (p73). The market is an easy 300m walk northwest of the ancient market ruins of the **Tempio di Serapide** (Map p74; Via Serapide; ☒Cumana to Pozzuoli, Pozzuoli).

Monte Nuovo   PARK
(New Mountain; Map p74; ☎081 804 14 62; Via Virgilio; ◔9am-1hr before sunset Mon-Sun, 9am-1pm Sun; ☒Cumana to Arco Felice) At 8pm on 29 September 1538, a crack appeared in the earth near the ancient Roman settlement of Tripergole, violently spewing out a concoction of pumice, fire and smoke over six days. By the end of the week, Pozzuoli had a new 134m-tall neighbour. Today, Europe's newest mountain is a lush and peaceful nature reserve, its shady sea-view slopes the perfect spot for a picnic.

The mountain's 'conception' actually goes back to the early 1530s, when an unusual level of seismic activity began rattling the area. It was at this time that locals also noticed a dramatic uplift of the land between Lago d'Averno, Monte Barbaro and the sea, a shift that displaced the coast by several hundred metres. Little did they know that under them a Monte Nuovo was rehearsing for its grand debut.

Città della Scienza   MUSEUM
(Science City; Map p74; ☎081 242 00 24; www.cittadellascienza.it; Via Coroglio 104; adult/reduced €7.50/5.50; ◔9am-5pm Tue-Sat, 10am-7pm Sun, also open 9am-5pm Mon Mar-May, closed late Jul–mid-Sep; ☒Cumana to Bagnoli, then, ☒C1 or R7) Part of a long-term redevelopment of the Bagnoli steelworks area, 5km southeast of central Pozzuoli, the huge and interactive Città della Scienza takes the 'geek' out of science. It's a particular hit with kids, who can get clued up on physics at the science gym, walk through constellations in the high-tech planetarium (€3) or just go plain silly pressing lots of funky buttons.

LUCRINO, BAIA & BACOLI

This string of towns spreads west from Pozzuoli along a built-up and inspiring coastal road. First up is Lucrino, where you'll find peaceful Lago d'Averno (the mythical entrance to hell) and a famous thermal spa centre. A further 3km southwest, Baia takes its name from Baios, a shipmate of Ulysses who died and was buried here. A glamorous Roman holiday resort with a sordid reputation, much of the ancient town is now under water (bradyseism again), though evocative ruins and a recently expanded archaeological museum help kickstart the imagination. A further 4km south is the sleepy fishing town of Bacoli, home to the magical Piscina Mirabilis.

TOP CHOICE ⬦ Parco Archeologico di Baia   RUIN
(Map p74; ☎081 868 75 92; Via Sella di Baia; adult/reduced €4/2 Sat & Sun, free Tue-Fri, ; ◔9am-1hr before sunset Tue-Sun; ☒Cumana to Fusaro, then walk 900m or, ☒EAV BUS to Baia) In Roman times, these 1st century BC ruins were part of a

NAPLES SIGHTS

A SCANDALOUS ADDRESS

Few buildings fire up the local gossipmongers like Posillipo's seaside **Palazzo Donn'Anna** (Largo Donn'Anna 9; ☒140 to Via Posillipo). Incomplete, semiderelict yet strangely beautiful, it takes its name from Anna Carafa, for whom it was built as a wedding present from her husband, Ramiro Guzman, the Spanish viceroy of Naples. When Guzman hotfooted it back to Spain in 1644 he left his wife heartbroken in Naples. She died shortly afterwards and architectural whiz-kid Cosimo Fanzago gave up the project. The grand-yet-forlorn heap sits on the site of an older villa, La Sirena (The Mermaid), reputed setting for Queen Joan's scandalous sex orgies and crimes of passion (rumour has it that fickle Joan dumped her lovers straight into the sea). Exactly which Queen Joan is up for debate. Some believe her royal nastiness was Joan I (1326–82), daughter of Charles, Duke of Calabria, whose list of alleged wicked deeds includes knocking off her husband. Others place their bets on Joan II (1373–1435), sister of King Ladislao, whose appetite for men remains the stuff of licentious legend. Palazzo Donn'Anna is not open to the public.

Campi Flegrei

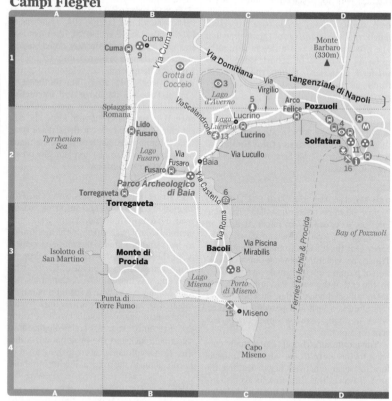

sprawling palace and spa complex. Emperors would entertain themselves and their guests in a series of lavishly decorated thermal baths that descended to the sea. Among the surviving snippets are exquisite floor mosaics, a beautifully stuccoed *balneum* (bathroom), an outdoor theatre and the impressive Tempio di Mercurio, its oculus-punctured dome predating Rome's Pantheon.

The dome once covered a *frigidarium* (cold-water pool), located approximately 7m below the current water level. It would have been a glorious sight, its walls covered in marble and its dome glittering with mosaics.

At the time of research, weekend visitors to the site were required to pre-purchase their tickets at the Museo Archeologico dei Campi Flegrei (p74). It's worth calling ahead to confirm any changes. To get here on public transport, catch the Cumana train to Fusaro station and walk 150m north to Via Fusaro. From here, the site is a 900m walk east along Via Fusaro. Alternatively, from Via Fusaro, you can catch a Miseno-bound EAVBUS bus, which run roughly every 30 minutes Monday to Saturday and every hour on Sunday to the site, and on to Bacoli, home of the Piscina Mirabilis (p76).

Museo Archeologico
dei Campi Flegrei   MUSEUM, CASTLE

(Archaeological Museum of the Campi Flegrei; Map p74; ☑081 523 37 97; http://museoarcheologicocampiflegrei.campaniabeniculturali.it; Via Castello 39; admission €4 Sat & Sun, free Tue-Fri; ⊙varies, usually 9am-1pm Tue-Sun; ☐EAV BUS to Baia) One of Naples' lesser-known gems, the Archaeological Museum of the Campi Flegrei delivers local ancient treasures without the crowds. Among the highlights is a bewitching nymphaeum, dredged up from underwater Baiae and skilfully reassembled. Monuments consecrated to the nymphs, nymphaeums were a popular spot to tie the proverbial knot.

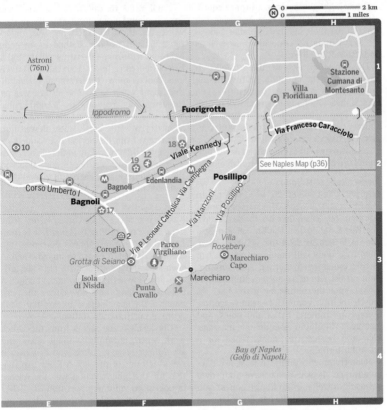

Campi Flegrei

◎ Top Sights

Parco Archeologico di Baia B2

◎ Sights

1	Anfiteatro Flavio	D2
2	Città della Scienza	F3
3	Lago d'Averno	C1
4	Mercato del Pesce di Pozzuoli	D2
5	Monte Nuovo	C1
6	Museo Archeologico dei Campi Flegrei	C2
7	Parco Virgiliano	F3
8	Piscina Mirabilis	C3
9	Scavi Archeologici di Cuma	B1
10	Solfatara Crater	E2
11	Tempio di Serapide	D2

⊕ Activities, Courses & Tours

12	Edenlandia	F2
13	Terme Stufe di Nerone	C2

⊗ Eating

14	Da Cicciotto	F3
15	Da Giona	C4
16	Exytus Caffè	D2

⊕ Entertainment

17	Arenile Reload	F2
18	Stadio San Paolo	F2
19	Teatro Palapartenope	F2

⊜ Shopping

Cartolibreria '900 .... (see 11)

Other highlights include a bronze equestrian statue of the Emperor Domitian (altered to resemble his more popular successor Nerva upon his deposition), as well as finds from Rione Terra.

The museum sits in the Castello di Baia, built in the late 15th century by the Aragonese as a defence against possible French invasion. Later enlarged by Spanish viceroy Don Pedro de Toledo, it served as a military orphanage for most of the 20th century. The bay views are sublime.

It's always worth calling ahead as the museum's opening times are notoriously fickle.

Terme Stufe di Nerone
SPA

(Map p74; ☑081 868 80 06; www.termestufedin erone.it; Via Stufe di Nerone 37; admission incl massage from €50; ☺8am-11pm Tue, Thu & Fri, to 8pm Mon, Wed & Sat, to 3pm Sun Sep-Jun, 8am-8pm Mon-Sat, to 3pm Sun Jul & Aug; ⓡCumana to Lucrino) Your body will thank you after a trip to this much-loved thermal spa complex. Built on the site of an ancient Roman prototype (spot the remnants in the bar), its muscle-melting combo of steamy grottos, therapeutic mineral baths and pools, and massage (40-minute essential-oils massage, €35) and beauty treatments make for a blissful interlude.

Book treatments online at least two days in advance. If you don't have your own swimsuit, towel and flip-flops (thongs), you can purchase them at the bar. From Lucrino train station, walk 500m southwest along Via Miliscola before turning right into Via Stufe di Nerone. The entrance is 200m ahead. If you have your own wheels, on-site parking costs €2.50 for cars and €2 for scooters.

Piscina Mirabilis
RUIN

(Marvellous Pool; Map p74; ☑081 523 59 68; Via Piscina Mirabilis; ☺varies; ⓡCumana to Fusaro, then, ⓤEAV BUS to Bacoli)

You'll need to call ahead to visit the world's largest Roman cistern, but it's well worth the effort to experience this underrated ancient wonder. Bathed in an eerie light and featuring 48 soaring pillars and a barrel-vaulted ceiling, the so-called 'Marvellous Pool' is more 'subterranean cathedral' that 'giant water tank'. The cistern was an Augustan-era creation, its 12,600 cubic metre water supply serving the military fleet at nearby Miseno. Fresh water flowed into the cistern from the Serino river aqueduct, which was then raised up to the terrace with hydraulic engines, exiting through doors in the central nave. Engineers still marvel at its sophistication.

Lago d'Averno
LAKE, RUIN

(Lake Averno; Map p74; Via Lucrino Averno; ⓡCumana to Lucrino) In Virgil's *Aeneid,* it is from Lago d'Averno that Aeneas descends into the underworld. It's hard to imagine hell in such a soothing setting, with old vineyards and citrus groves lining this ancient crater. A popular walking track now circles the perimeter of the lake, located an easy 1km walk north of Lucrino train station.

The lake's name stems from the Greek work άορνος, meaning 'without birds', and according to legend, birds who flew over it would fall out of the sky. A likely explanation for this phenomenon was the release of poisonous volcanic gases from the lake's fumaroles. Yet, while it may have been unlucky for feathered critters, Lago d'Averno proved useful to Roman general Marcus Vipsanius Agrippa, who in 37 BC linked it to nearby Lago Lucrino and the sea, turning hell's portal into a strategic naval dockyard. The battleships may have gone, but the lakeside ruins of the **Tempio di Apollo** (Temple of Apollo) remain. Built during the reign of Hadrian in the 2nd century AD, this thermal complex once boasted a domed roof almost

---

A CHOICE DIP

Right below the Castello di Baia sits the wonderful Spiaggia del Castello (Castle Beach). A sandy double-sided affair, it's only accessible by **boat** (☑338 169 34 48; one-way ticket €2.50, Sat, Sun & Aug €4; ☺8.30am-7pm Jun-Aug, to 6pm late Apr-May & early-mid Sep) from a nearby jetty. To reach the jetty, catch the EAV bus to Baia and get off outside the FIART factory just south of town. Walk a further 250m south and turn left into the driveway beside the green gate at the curve. At the end sit the car park and white-coloured jetty, where you can hire a sundeck (€5/6 weekdays/weekends) or umbrella (€5) for stylish waterside sunning. Avoid the weekend summer crowds by coming earlier in the week.

the size of the Pantheon's in Rome. Alas, only four great arched windows survive.

CUMA

Founded in the 8th century BC by Greek colonists from the island of Euboea, Cumae exerted a powerful sway on the ancient imagination. Today its ruins are among the region's most evocative, overlooking lush Mediterranean flora and the Tyrrhenian Sea.

Scavi Archeologici di Cuma RUIN
(Map p74; ☑081 854 30 60; Via Montecuma; admission €4; ⊘9am to 1hr before sunset, last entry 1hr before close; ®Cumana to Fusaro, then, ☐EAV BUS to Cuma) Dating back to the 8th-century BC, Cuma was the first Greek settlement on the Italian mainland. Its ruins are shrouded in ancient mythology: the Antro della Sibilla Cumana (Cave of the Cumaean Sibyl) is where the oracle reputedly passed on messages from Apollo.

The poet Virgil, probably inspired by a visit to the cave himself, writes of Aeneas coming here to seek the sibyl, who directs him to Hades (the underworld), entered from nearby Lago d'Averno. More prosaic are recent studies that maintain that the 130m-long trapezoidal tunnel was actually built as part of Cuma's defence system.

Even more fantastical is the Tempio di Apollo (Temple of Apollo), built on the site where Daedalus is said to have flown in Italy. According to Greek mythology, Daedalus and his son Icarus took to the skies to escape King Minos in Crete. En route Icarus flew too close to the sun and plunged to his death as his wax-and-feather wings melted from the heat. At the top of the ancient acropolis stand the ruins of Tempio di Giove (Temple of Jupiter). Dating back to the 5th century BC, it was later converted into a Christian basilica, of which the remains of the altar and the circular baptismal font are visible.

From the Fusaro Cumana station, walk 150m north to Via Fusaro, from where Cuma-bound EAVBUS buses run roughly every 30 minutes Monday to Saturday and every hour on Sunday.

FUORIGROTTA

Wedged between Naples and the Campi Flegrei, suburban Fuorigrotta district is home to several entertainment venues, including the city's iconic fun park.

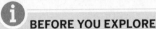

BEFORE YOU EXPLORE

Before exploring the Campi Flegrei, it's worth stopping at the helpful **tourist office** (☑081 526 66 39; www.infocampi flegrei.it; Largo Matteotti 1a; ⊘9am-3pm Mon-Fri; ®Cumana to Pozzuoli, Pozzuoli) in Pozzuoli to pick up tourist information and maps of the area. An easy five-minute walk downhill from the metro station, the tourist office also sells the good-value €4 cumulative ticket, which covers the Museo Archeologico dei Campi Flegrei, the Parco Archeologico di Baia, and the Scavi Archeologici di Cuma.

Also useful is bookshop **Cartoli-breria '900** (Map p74; ☑081 526 13 63; Via Pergolesi 38c/d; ⊘9am-1pm & 4-8pm Mon-Sat; ®Cumana to Pozzuoli, Pozzuoli), which stocks great books and information on the area and has internet access (€1 per hr).

Edenlandia AMUSEMENT PARK
(Map p74; ☑081 239 40 90; www.edenlandia.it; Viale Kennedy 76; adult/child under 1.1m €3/free, per ride from €2, unlimited-rides ticket €12; ⊘varies, see website; ®Cumana to Edenlandia) Fabulously kitsch and loads of fun, Naples' major amusement park boasts a plethora of attractions, including dodgem cars, a fairy-tale castle, a 3D cinema and a flight simulator. The €3 admission covers the 3D cinema, variety show and children's theatre.

✪ Festivals & Events

Festa di San Gennaro RELIGIOUS
The faithful flock to the duomo to witness the miraculous liquefaction of San Gennaro's blood on the Saturday before the first Sunday in May. Repeat performances take place on 19 September and 16 December.

Maggio dei Monumenti CULTURAL
A month-long cultural feast, with a bounty of concerts, performances, exhibitions, guided tours and other events across the city; takes place throughout May.

Wine & The City GASTRONOMIC
(www.wineandthecity.it) A four-day celebration of regional *vino*, with free wine tastings and cultural events in shops across Chiaia and the *centro storico*; May.

Napoli Teatro Festival THEATRE
(www.napoliteatrofestival.it) Three weeks of local and international theatre and performance art, staged in conventional and unconventional venues across the city; June. A shorter, six-day edition takes place in September.

Napoli Film Festival FILM
(www.napolifilmfestival.com) Six days of local and international flicks and celluloid chat; varies.

Madonna del Carmine RELIGIOUS
Pilgrims and fireworks on Piazza del Mercato, in honour of the Chiesa di Santa Maria del Carmine's miraculous Madonna; 16 July.

✖ Eating

Naples is one of Italy's gastronomic darlings, and the bonus of a bayside setting makes for some seriously memorable meals. While white linen, candlelight and €50 bills are readily available, some of the best bites await in the city's spit-and-sawdust trattorias, where three courses and house wine can cost under €15. Even cheaper is Naples' plethora of top-notch pizzerias and *friggitorie* (fried-food kiosks). On the downside, many eateries close for two weeks in August, so call ahead if visiting then.

CENTRO STORICO & MERCATO

TOP CHOICE **Palazzo Petrucci** CAMPANIAN €€€
(Map p40; ☏081 552 40 68; www.palazzopetrucci.it; Piazza San Domenico Maggiore 4; 5-course degustation menu €50; ◷lunch Tue-Sun, dinner Mon-Sat; ⓂDante) Progressive Petrucci is a breath of fresh air, exciting palates with mostly successful new-school creations like raw prawn and mozzarella 'lasagne' or poached-egg onion soup. Knowledgeable, polished service and a fine-dining air make it a perfect spot to celebrate something special. For an inspired culinary journey, opt for the good-value degustation menu.

Pizzeria Gino Sorbillo PIZZA €
(Map p40; ☏081 44 66 43; www.accademiadelapizza.it; Via dei Tribunali 32; pizzas from €2.50; ◷Mon-Sat; ⓂDante) Debate may rage about whether Gino Sorbillo's pizzas are *the* best in town, but that doesn't stop the clamouring crowds. We specify Gino because there are two other Sorbillo pizzerias on the same block, all from one family of 21 pizza-making siblings. Gino's pizzas are gigantic, tasty and best followed by a velvety *semifreddo*, made fresh by renowned *pasticceria* Scaturchio

(p80). We're addicted to the chocolate and *torroncino* (almond nougat) combo.

Done, check out the converted condom vending machine in the basement, now dispensing Neapolitan lucky charms. It's one of several in-house works by artistic duo Ulderico & Ognissanti.

La Stanza del Gusto OSTERIA, ITALIAN €€
(Map p40; ☏081 40 15 78; www.lastanzadelgusto.com; Via Costantinopoli 100; lunch special €13, degustation menus €35-65; ◷11am-midnight Sat, lunch only Sun ; ⓂDante) Focussed on top-quality ingredients and artisinal producers, 'The Taste Room' offers a trendy ground-floor 'cheese bar', a more-formal restaurant upstairs, and a small basement provedore selling deli treats and wines. Frankly, the degustation menus aren't great value, with hit-and-miss 'modern Italian' dishes and patchy service. The 'cheese room', however, is utterly *perfetto* for get-in-the-know cheese, *salumi* (sliced cured meats) and vino sessions.

Campagnola CAMPANIAN €€
(Map p40; ☏081 45 90 34; Via dei Tribunali 47; meals €18; ◷closed Tue; ⓂDante) A change of ownership has breathed new life into this old stalwart. Spruced up with local art and friendly, young waitstaff, its soul-coaxing grub includes some lip-licking pasta dishes, including a killer *genovese* (pasta with a slow-cooked lamb, tomato and onion ragù), and a wonderfully refreshing spaghetti *olive e caperi* (with olives and capers). The rum-soaked babà is exceptional.

La Masardona PIZZA FRITTA €
(Map p40; Via Capaccio Giulio Cesare 27; pizza fritta small/regular from €2.50/4; ◷ 7am-3.30pm Tue, Wed & Fri-Sun, to 10.30pm Sat; ⓂGaribaldi) Naples' iconic pizza fritta – deep-fried pizza dough stuffed with pork *ciccioli* (dried lard cubes), salami, ham, smoked provola, ricotta, tomato – is best savoured at this no-frills, cult-status joint. Most regulars order it *senza ricotta* (without ricotta), and wash it down with sweet marsala wine. There's an escarole, olives and provola cheese version, and both come in a snack-size version, called *batti l'occhio*.

Di Matteo SNACKS, PIZZA €
(Map p40; ☏081 45 52 62; Via dei Tribunali 94; snacks €0.50, pizzas from €2.50; ◷9am-midnight Mon-Sat; ◻C55 to Via Duomo) Di Matteo's golden *crocchè* (potato croquettes) are like a culinary cuddle. In fact, the little street stall at this no-frills pizzeria sells some of the city's best fried

SARTORIAL NAPLES

Milan may be the hyped-up face of Italian style, but Naples is its heart and soul. The city's bespoke tailors are legendary and once drew the likes of early-20th-century Italian king Emmanuel III to their needles and threads.

The key to this success is traditional, handmade production, superlative fabrics and minute attention to detail and form. Suitwise, the look is more brat pack than power broker – slim-fit flexible cut, natural and unengineered shoulders (great for gesticulating), high-set armholes and the signature *barchetta* (little boat) breast pocket.

A classic Neapolitan shirt will often feature fine Italian, Swiss or Irish cottons, hand-stitched collar, yoke and sleeve, hand-sewn buttonholes and gathered pleating at the shoulder.

While most of the boutiques offer prêt-à-porter threads and accessories (including ready-made suits), creating a shirt or suit from scratch will usually involve a couple of fittings and anything from three to eight weeks. Finished items can be shipped overseas.

Credit card at the ready, hit these needle-savvy icons for a Neapolitan revamp:

Anna Matuozzo (Map p71; 081 66 38 74; www.annamatuozzo.it; Viale Antonio Gramsci 26; Mergellina) The softly spoken Signora Matuozzo was once the apprentice of Mariano Rubinacci. Now the *signora* and her daughters are famed for their bespoke shirts, which feature mother-of-pearl buttons and vintage hand stitching. Silk ties in luscious tones complete the elegant look. Fittings must be booked.

Cilento (Map p40; 081 551 33 63; www.cilento1780.com; Via Medina 61-63; R2 to Piazza Municipio) In business since 1780, Cilento is as much a heritage site as it is a gentlemen's atelier, with 18th- and 19th-century family garments on display, and its own charming little textile museum next door (open on request). Bespoke suits aside, their seven-fold silk ties are also highly prized. Other temptations include handsome handmade shoes, ready-to-wear Cilento polo shirts, men's and women's bags, hard-to-find fragrances, and scarves.

Finamore (Map p56; 081 246 18 27; www.finamore.it; Via Calabritto 16; C25 to Riviera di Chiaia) Ready-to-wear and bespoke hand-sewn shirts in delectable shades such as royal blue, pastel pink and citrus green. There are ties and scarves to match.

Mariano Rubinacci (Map p56; www.marianorubinacci.net; Via Filangieri 26; Piazza Amedeo) Beautiful, lightweight and precisely fitting suits from the granddaddy of Neapolitan tailoring. Former clients include Neapolitan film director Vittorio de Sica.

Marinella (Map p56; www.marinellanapoli.it; Via Riviera di Chiaia 287; C25 to Riviera di Chiaia) One-time favourite of Luchino Visconti and Aristotle Onassis, this is *the* place for prêt-à-porter and made-to-measure ties. Match them with an irresistible selection of luxury accessories, including shoes, shirts, sweaters and vintage colognes.

---

snacks, from *pizza fritta* to nourishing *arancini* (fried rice balls). If you're after a sit-down feed, head inside for trademark sallow lighting, surly waiters, and lip-smacking pizzas, best washed down with a cold bottled beer.

TOP CHOICE Gay-odin   CHOCOLATE €
(Map p40; 081 551 07 94; www.gay-odin.it; Via Benedetto Croce 61; ice cream from €1.70; 9am-8.15pm Sun-Thu, to 11.30pm Fri & Sat; Dante) Not so much a chocolatier as an institution, Gay-odin concocts some of the city's finest cocoa creations, including oh-so-Neapolitan chocolate 'cozze' (mussels). For a punch to the palate, try the chocolate-coated coffee beans or the fiery *peperoncino-cioccolato* (chilli-chocolate) combo. This branch also sells Gay-odin's sublime ice cream; they produce the city's best non-sorbet flavours.

Timpani & Tempura   CAMPANIAN, DELI €
(Map p40; www.timpanietempura.it; Vico della Quercia 17; timbali dishes €9; deli 9.30am-7.30pm Tue-Sat, to 3.30pm Mon & Sun, lunch from 12.30pm; Dante) Aside from stocking gorgeous regional cheeses, wines, pasta, jams and other pantry must-haves, this tiny Slow Food deli serves comforting *timbali* – baked pasta tortes originating in 18th-century Neapolitan court cuisine. Varieties include *paccheri in piedi* (ricotta, fior di latte cheese and San Marzano tomato) and the hearty *sartù* (rice, peas, meat balls, provola cheese and chicken livers).

Scaturchio
PASTICCERIA €

(Map p40; ☑081 551 70 31; Piazza San Domenico Maggiore 19; pastries from €1.50; ⊙7.20am-8.40pm; ⓂDante) In a city infamous for belt-busting temptations, this piazza-side *pasticceria* enjoys cult status. While you'll find all the local classics (including a particularly luscious *babà*), the star attraction is the *ministeriale*. A dark-chocolate medallion invented in the 19th century, the ingredients of its liqueur-laced ganache filling are a closely guarded secret.

Trattoria Mangia e Bevi
CAMPANIAN €

(Map p40; ☑081 552 95 46; Via Sedile di Porto 92; meals €7; ⊙lunch Mon-Fri; ⓂUniversità) Utterly unmissable, this loud and lively trattoria sees everyone from pierced students to be-spectacled *professori* squeeze around the communal tables for brilliant home cooking at rock-bottom prices. Scan the daily-changing menu, jot down your choices and prepare yourself for gems such as grilled *provola* cheese, juicy *salsiccia* (pork sausage) and *peperoncino*-spiked *friarielli* (local broccoli).

The *casareccio* bread is crunchy perfection and best washed down with a plastic cup of vino.

Angelo Carbone
PASTICCERIA €

(Map p40; ☑081 45 78 21; Largo Regina Coeli 4-8; pastries from €1; ⊙7am-8pm; ⓂPiazza Cavour, Museo) Off the tourist trail but well on the radar of locals, this chintzy bar-pasticceria-*rosticceria* makes one seriously buttery *sfogliatella* (sweet ricotta-filled pastries), not to mention a heavenly *pasticcino crema e amarena* (a short-pastry bun filled with cherries and custard). Savoury options include satisfying *panini* (€2.50) and there's alfresco seating beside the frescoed porticos of the Chiesa Santa Maria Regina Coeli opposite.

Attanasio
SNACKS €

(Map p40; ☑081 28 56 75; Vico Ferrovia 1-4; snacks from €1.10; ⊙6.30am-7.30pm Tue-Sun; ⓂGaribaldi) So you thought a *sfogliatella* from Pintauro was crispy perfection? Bite into the piping-hot ricotta filling at this retro pastry pedlar and prepare to reassess. But why stop there with so many trays of fresh, plump treats on show, from creamy *cannolli siciliani* to a runny, rummy *babà*. Savoury fiends shouldn't pass up the hearty *pasticcino rustico*, stuffed with *provola* cheese, ricotta and salami.

Pizzeria Vesi
PIZZA €

(Map p40; ☑081 29 99 95; Via dei Tribunali 388; pizzas from €3; ⊙noon-5pm & 7pm-1am; ⓂDante) If Gino Sorbillo is closed, this popular pizzeria makes for a handy back-up plan. The pizzas are more than decent and there's warm-weather alfresco seating for voyeuristic noshing.

TOLEDO & QUARTIERI SPAGNOLI

Trattoria San Ferdinando
CAMPANIAN €€

(Map p56; ☑081 42 19 64; www.trattoriasanferdinando.net; Via Nardones 117; meals €30; ⊙lunch Mon-Sat, dinner Wed-Fri; ◻R2 to Piazza Trieste e Trento) Hung with theatre posters and playbills, saffron-hued San Ferdinando pulls in well-spoken theatre types and intellectuals. For a Neapolitan taste trip, ask for a run-down of the day's antipasti and choose your favourites for an *antipasto misto* (mixed antipasto). Seafood standouts include a delicate *seppia ripieno* (stuffed squid), while the homemade desserts make for a satisfying dénouement.

Il Garum
ITALIAN €€

(Map p40; ☑081 542 32 28; Piazza Monteoliveto 2A; meals €35; ⊙lunch & dinner; ⓂToledo) Rustic yet genteel, softly lit Il Garum is a sound spot for delicately flavoured, revamped classics. Stand out dishes include rigatoni with shredded courgettes (zucchini) and mussels, and an exquisite grilled calamari stuffed with seasonal vegetables and cheese. Just leave room for desserts like *torta di ricotta e pera* (ricotta and pear cake), all proudly made on-site.

Kukai
JAPANESE €€

(Map p50; ☑081 41 19 05; www.kukai.it; Via Carlo de Cesare 52; meals €30; ◻R2 to Piazza Trieste e Trento) Sick of spaghetti? Then join the urban-savvy for fresh, real-deal Japanese nosh that a Tokyoite couldn't fault. The clued-up sushi list includes well-executed sashimi, *uramaki* and *temaki,* while warming options including crisp tempura, teppanayki and soothing noodles. Wash it down with sake or a Sapporo, and finish off with the cultish *maccha keki* (chocolated-crusted green-tea ricotta flan).

Antiche Delizie
DELI €

(Map p50; ☑081 551 30 88; Via Pasquale Scura 14; ⊙8am-8pm Mon-Sat; ⓂMontesanto) Hanging hams, succulent salami and the best mozzarella in town: this legendary deli is the perfect picnic pit stop. If it's Friday, don't miss the heavenly *caprignetti* (goat's cheese stuffed with herbs). Otherwise, taste test the *provolone del Monaco* (a cheese seasoned in wine cellars), pick up some *prêt-à-manger* antipasto or furnish the cellar with a bottle of local Greco del Tufo.

Fantasia Gelati
GELATERIA €

(Map p40; ☎081 551 12 12; Via Toledo 381; gelato from €2; ⊗7.30am-midnight; Ⓜ Toledo) Many hardcore gelato aficionados swear that Gay-odin (p79) does better cream-based flavours, but they'll also tell you that when it comes to fruit-flavoured sorbets, no one comes close to this place. Make up your own mind with a serve of the dangerously dense *cuore nero* (dark chocolate). The *gelato caldo* (hot gelato) flavours aren't actually warm – just creamier. There's another handy branch in Vomero.

Hosteria Toledo
CAMPANIAN €€

(Map p50; ☎081 42 12 57; www.hosteriatoledo.it; Vico Giardinetto 78; meals €26; ⊗lunch daily, dinner Wed-Mon; Ⓜ Toledo) Hung with nostalgic Nea-politan photos and framed banknotes, this warm, welcoming nook in the Quartieri Spag-noli keeps both locals and out-of-towners purring with its reliable Campanian clas-sics. Tuck into soothing pasta e *fagioli con le cozze* (pasta with beans and mussels), succulent *gamberini alla griglia* (grilled prawns) or *contorni* (sides) like smoky, pepper-spiked *zucchini alla griglia* (grilled zucchini).

Pintauro
PASTICCERIA €

(Map p50; ☎348 7781645; Via Toledo 275; sfoglia-telle €2; ⊗8am-2pm & 2.30-8pm Mon-Sat, 9am-2pm Sun Sep-May; ☒R2 to Piazza Trieste e Trento) Another local institution (even the owner looks like Sofia Loren's long-lost cousin), cinnamon-scented Pintauro sells perfect *sfogliatelle* to shopped-out locals. But don't stop there; it makes a mean *babà* to boot.

Tavola Calda Da Angelone
CAMPANIAN €

(Map p40; Via Guglielmo Oberdan; meals €7; ⊗lunch Mon-Sat; Ⓜ Toledo) This in-the-know, cafeteria-style lunch spot serves dirt-cheap Neapoli-tan grub to a democratic mix of tie-clad bu-reaucrats and working-class families. Head upstairs to the chintzy dining room, grab a seat, and wait for the waiter to rattle off tried-and-tested specials like *gatò di patate* (potato, cheese and salami torte) and orec-chiette pasta with provola, ricotta and to-mato sauce.

SANTA LUCIA & CHIAIA

TOP CHOICE Ristorantino dell'Avvocato
CAMPANIAN €€

(Map p56; ☎081 032 00 47; www.ilristorantinodel lavvocato.it; Via Santa Lucia 115-117; degustation menu €40; ⊗lunch daily, dinner Tue-Sat; ☒154 to Via Santa Lucia) This elegant-yet-welcoming restaurant has quickly won the respect of Neapolitan gastronomes. Apple of their eye is affable head chef and owner Raffaele Car-dillo, whose passion for his region's culinary heritage merges with a knack for subtle, refreshing twists – think gnocchi with fresh mussels, clams, crumbed pistachio, lemon, ginger and garlic.

The degustation menu is good value, while the vino-versed staff will happily guide you towards the perfect Italian drop. Book ahead Thursday to Saturday.

TOP CHOICE Da Bruno
ITALIAN €€€

(Map p56; ☎081 251 24 11; Riviera di Chiaia 213-214; meals €45; ⊗Tue-Sun; ☒C25 to Riviera di Chiaia) Discerning palates flock here for sublimely fresh seafood, a 250-strong wine list and im-peccable service. Tease the taste buds with the *antipasto misto*, which might include a delicate salad of octopus, potato and toma-to, then swoon over gems like the specialty *granseola con vermicelli* (crab with vermi-celli pasta). The homemade tiramisu makes for an unforgettable epilogue.

Trattoria Castel dell'Ovo
SEAFOOD €€

(Map p56; ☎081 764 63 52; Via Lucalliana 28; meals €35; ⊗lunch & dinner Fri-Wed, closed Sun dinner Nov-Apr; ☒154 to Via Santa Lucia) While locals dismiss many of the bigger restaurants on Borgo Marinaro as tourist traps, they adore this cheaper, third-generation bolthole. Sit beside bobbing boats and tuck into surf staples like *zuppa di pesce* (fish soup), *al-ici fritte* (fried anchovies) and *insalata di polipo* (octopus salad with fresh tomato). Consider booking ahead (same day usually suffices), and bring cash as credit cards are not accepted.

Da Ettore
CAMPANIAN €€

(Map p56; ☎081 764 35 78; Via Gennaro Serra 39; meals €25; ⊗lunch daily, dinner Tue-Sat; ☒R2 to Piazza Trieste e Trento) This homely, eight-table trattoria has an epic reputation. Scan the walls for famous fans like comedy great Totò, and a framed passage from crime writer Massimo Siviero, who mentions Et-tore in one of his tales. Casting the spell are solid regional dishes like the signature

SECRET ARTISAN STUDIOS

Down dark streets, behind unmarked doors, in unsuspecting courtyards, artisan studios litter the *centro storico*. In these secret bolt-holes, some of Naples' most intriguing artists celebrate, reinterpret and sometimes subvert Neapolitan traditions – think meticulously crafted nativity statues to pop portraits of a scooter-riding holy family. Dive into the city's idiosyncratic arts scene at the following locations:

» **Laboratorio Scarabattola** (Map p40; www.lascarabattola.it; ☺by prior appointment only, 11am-2pm & 4-6pm Mon-Fri, 11am-2pm Sat; Dante) On the opposite side of the same courtyard, this two-level workshop is where a charming team of siblings (and relatives) fire, paint and sew meticulously detailed *presepe*- (nativity-) style sculptures for their shop La Scarabattola. Melding 18th-century techniques with a modern sensibility, their attention to detail has won them worldwide acclaim. To sneak a peak, you'll need to request a visit at their nearby showroom, La Scarabattola (p87).

» **Lisa Weber Laboratorio di Ceramica** (Map p40; ☑334 8410039; Via Giovanni Paladino 4; ☺11am-1.30pm & 5-7pm Tue-Fri, 11am-1.30pm Sat, 5-7pm Mon, closed Sun & Aug; Dante) This is the earthy workshop of Swiss-expat ceramicist Lisa Weber, whose creations span playfully translucent candle holders and Pompeii-esque terracotta vases and jugs, to whimsical teasets and lamps.

» **Zhao** (Map p40; ☑329 3469011; Via Atri 31; ☺varies; Dante) In a tiny studio opened with a giant 18th-century key, sculptor and painter Salvatore Vitagliano takes fragments of ancient terracotta figurines and completes them, creating simple yet striking works that literally fuse old and new. This theme of 'temporal collision' extends to his Neapolitan playing cards, handpainted onto metro tickets. Call two days ahead to visit, though it's worth noting that Salvatore doesn't speak English.

» **Officina D'Arti Grafiche di Carmine Cervone** (Map p40; ☑081 29 54 83; carmine.cervone@libero.it; Via Anticaglia 12; ☺9.30am-2pm & 3-6.30pm Mon-Sat; Cavour) Lovers of print and typography shouldn't miss Carmine's one-of-a-kind printing workshop, crammed with rare vintage machinery, including a late-19th-century linotype machine. That Carmine speaks little English never detracts from the young gun's passion for his craft and his love of showing it off. Indeed, he often collaborates with artists, producing limited-edition prints, lithographs and books. Best of all, he can even design and print you a one-of-a-kind business card or invitations (allow two days) if you fancy your own take-home memento.

pasta patata e provola (pasta with potato and provola cheese). Book two days ahead for Sunday lunch.

Antica Osteria Da Tonino   ITALIAN €€
(Map p56; ☑081 42 15 33; Via Santa Teresa a Chiaia 47; meals €18; ☺lunch daily, dinner Fri & Sat; MPiazza Amedeo) Quick-witted octogenarian Tonino (nicknamed JR by his wife) is still going strong, just like his heirloom *osteria*. At the front, time-pressed *signore* pick up their takeaway orders, while at the few packed tables, Rubinacci suits, old-timers and the odd Nobel Prize winner (Dario Fo ate here) tuck into simple homecooking like *rigatoni ragù e ricotta* (rigatoni in a meat and ricotta sauce).

Moccia   PASTICCERIA €
(Map p56; ☑081 41 13 48; Via San Pasquale a Chiaia 21-22; pastries from €0.70; ☺Wed-Mon; ☐C24

to Riviera di Chiaia) With gleaming displays of dainty strawberry tartlets, liqueur-soaked *babà* and creamy gelato (try a watermelon and peach combo), no one is safe at this pastry *pasticceria* – blow-waved matriarchs, peckish professionals or waif-thin Chiaia princesses. The almond *caprese* is the best in town, and best washed down with a potent espresso.

L.U.I.S.E.   DELI €
(Map p56; ☑081 41 77 35; Piazza dei Martiri 68; snacks from €1.20, meals €15; ☺7.30am-8.30pm Mon-Sat, 8.30am-3.30pm Sun; ☐C24 to Piazza dei Martiri) A chic little deli that's a gourmand's playpen, L.U.I.S.E. peddles everything from plump local cheeses to homemade foodstuffs and bottles of luscious wine. In the back room, lunching nine-to-fivers tuck into warming *parmigiana di melanzane* (au-

bergine parmigiana), risottos and gnocchi. Busy travellers can take away, with freshly fried *pizza fritta*, crisp *arancini* and sugar-dusted *pasticcini crema amarena* (pastries filled with cherry cream).

VOMERO, CAPODIMONTE & LA SANITÀ

Pizzeria Starita
PIZZA €

(Map p62; ☏081 557 46 82; Via Materdei 28; pizzas from €3.50; ⊗Tue-Sun; ⓂMaterdei) The giant fork and ladle hanging on the wall at this cultish pizzeria were used by Sophia Loren in *L'Oro di Napoli,* and the kitchen made the *pizze fritte* sold by the actress in the film. While the 60-plus pizza varieties include a tasty *fiorilli e zucchini* (zucchini, zucchini flowers and *provola*), our allegiance remains to its classic marinara.

Antica Cantina di Sica
CAMPANIAN €€

(Map p62; ☏081 556 75 20; Via Gianlorenzo Bernini 17; meals €30; ⊗Tue-Sun; ⓂVanvitelli) This genteel gastronomic hideaway is true to classic regional fare made with salutary attention to detail. The generous antipasto is an inspiring introduction (think tender tripe in fragrant tomato sauce and buttery *parmigiana di melanzana*), while the *frittura mista* (mixed fried seafood) stays crispy to the last bite. The homemade desserts (try the velvety *cassata napoletana*) are equally inspired.

[TOP CHOICE] Friggitoria Vomero
SNACKS €

(Map p62; ☏081 578 31 30; Via Cimarosa 44; snacks from €0.20; ⊗9.30am-2.30pm & 5-9.30pm Mon-Fri, 9.30am-2.30pm & 5-11pm Sat; ☐Centrale to Fuga) The stuff of legend, this spartan snack bar makes some of the city's finest *fritture* (deep-fried snacks). Crunch away on deep-fried aubergines, potatoes and *zeppole* (doughnuts), *frittatine di maccheroni* (fried pasta and egg) and *supplì di riso* (rice balls). Located opposite the funicular, it's a handy pit stop before legging it to the Certosa di San Martino.

Donna Teresa
ITALIAN €

(Map p62; ☏081 556 70 70; Via Michele Kerbaker 58; meals €14; ⊗Mon-Sat; ⓂVanvitelli) This swing-a-cat-sized dining room – there are only nine tables – has an epic reputation for solid home cooking. Mamma Teresa's photo looks on approvingly as regulars tuck into simple classics like *pasta provola e melanzane* (pasta with *provola* cheese and aubergines) and *salsicce al sugo* (sausages with tomato sauce). The menu is limited, changes daily and pulls in the hordes, so go early.

Tarallificio Esposito
SNACKS

(Map p62; Via Sanità 129; snacks from €0.40; ⊗6am-8.30pm Mon-Sat, 8am-3pm Sun; ⓂPiazza Cavour, Museo) Made with pepper, almonds and pork fat, oven-baked *taralli mandorlati* (savoury almond biscuits) are dangerously addictive and readily available at this heirloom Sanità bakery. But don't stop at the classic, with moreish variations including buttery *taralli* (crunchy, ring-shaped biscuits) with *friarielli* (Neapolitan broccoletti), *olio* (olive oil) and lemon glaze. For a more substantial feed, fill up on the scrumptious focaccia.

Mario Gallucci
CHOCOLATE €

(Map p62; www.cioccolatonapoli.com; Vico Lammatari 38; ⊗8.30am-1pm & 2-6.30pm Mon-Fri, 8.30am-1pm Sat; ⓂPiazza Cavour, Museo) Hidden away down a Sanità side street, this vintage chocolatier has been compromising waistlines since 1890. Aside from a wicked selection of dark, milk and white chocolate pralines and truffles, you can pick up very Neapolitan edible souvenirs like giant chocolate lemons and a chocolate *caffettiera* (coffee percolator), complete with edible *tazze* (cups).

Fantasia Gelati
GELATERIA €

(Map p62; ☏081 578 83 83; Piazza Vanvitelli 22; gelato from €2; ⊗7am-1am Mon-Fri, to 2am Sat, to 1.30am Sun; ⓂVanvitelli) This branch of Naples' king of gelato serves fresh, seasonal, icy perfection to Vomero's middle-class gluttons. Do not deprive your taste buds!

MERGELLINA & POSILLIPO

[TOP CHOICE] Da Cicciotto
SEAFOOD €€

(Map p74; ☏081 575 11 65; Calata Ponticello a Marechiaro 32; meals €40; ⊗daily; ☐140 to Via Posillipo) Perched on a cliff in the fishing village of Marechiaro, low-key yet elegant Cicciotto is a seasoned charmer. Edible highlights include a sublime carpaccio antipasto (thin slices of raw seafood drizzled with lemon juice and olive oil), lightly battered courgette flowers stuffed with ricotta and a *pacchetti* pasta dish served with local crab and cherry tomatoes.

Desserts such as *crostata* (tart) with lemon cream, wild strawberries and Chantilly cream are equally mesmerising. Book ahead.

Don Salvatore
CAMPANIAN €€

(Map p71; ☑081 68 18 17; www.donsalvatore.it; Via Mergellina 4a; meals €40; ☉Thu-Tue; ☐140 to Via Mergellina) The key to happiness? Balmy nights, sea breezes and impeccable seafood. You're guaranteed at least the last two at this stylish veteran, with its *dolce vita* terrace and softly lit interior. Here, culinary clichés make way for inspired gems such as *cecinielle* (fried fish patties), comforting *minestra in brodo* (thick noodle broth) and *seppie con uva passa* (baby squid with pine nuts and raisins).

Di Girolamo Giuseppe
BAKERY, PIZZA €

(Map p71; ☑081 66 44 98; Via Mergellina 55e; pizza al taglio from €1.50, pasta from €3; ☉8am-3pm & 5-11pm; ⓂMergellina) A lovable bakery-snack bar with tasty eat-and-go grub; pop in for superb *pizza al taglio* (pizza by the slice), with combos including pumpkin, tomato, basil and olives. Other winners include *pizza fritta*, focaccia, just-like-mamma-made *pasta al forno* and tray upon tray of luscious, gleaming *crostate*.

Chalet Ciro Mergellina
GELATERIA €

(Map p71; ☑081 66 99 28; www.chaletciro.it; Via Mergellina 31; pastries from €1.50, gelato brioche €4; ☉7am-2am Thu-Tue; ⓂMergellina) This iconic seaside chalet sells everything from coffee and pastries to crêpes, but the reason to head here is for *brioche con gelato*, a sweetened bun stuffed with delectable ice cream and topped with a dollop of *panna* (cream). Pay inside, choose your flavours at the street-side counter, and then kill the cals with a bayside saunter.

CAMPI FLEGREI

Da Giona
SEAFOOD €€

(Map p74; ☑081 523 46 59; www.dagiona.it; Via Dragonara 6, Miseno; meals €35; ☉lunch & dinner May-Oct, lunch only Nov-Apr; ⓂCumana) Right on a sandy beach with views of Procida and Ischia, this retro, sun-bleached restaurant enjoys cult status in Naples (book ahead on weekends). The seafood dishes are simple, fresh and lingering, from the *antipasto misto* (which might include fried courgettes and prawns, marinated carpaccio and octopus salad) to an unforgettable *spaghetti alle vongole* (spaghetti with clams).

If the weather's on your side, request a table on the raffish deck (or right on the sand) and while away the hours with a local Falanghina. To get here, take the train from Cumana to Fusaro, then the EAV bus to Miseno.

Exytus Caffè
CAFE €

(Map p74; ☑081 526 70 90; Corso della Repubblica 126, Pozzuoli; cornetto €0.80; ☉7.30am-2am; ⓇCumana to Pozzuoli, ⓂPozzuoli) It might just be a tiny hole-in-the-wall (OK, technically, there are two holes in the wall), but Exytus is a street cafe with a big reputation. Join the curbside crowd for espresso with perfect *schiuma zuccherata* (sugared froth), best enjoyed with a brilliant *cornetto* (croissant); we have a major crush on the *crema e amarena* (custard and cherry) combo.

🍷 Drinking & Entertainment

Neapolitans aren't big drinkers and in the *centro storico*, many people simply buy a bottle of beer from the nearest bar and hang out on the streets. Here, bar hot spots include Piazza Bellini, Via Cisterno dell'Olio, and Piazza del Gesù Nuovo, where a high concentration of students, artists and bohemians lend a energetic, live-and-let-live vibe. Those after fashion-conscious prosecco sessions should sashay straight to Chiaia's sleek bars, famed for their evening aperitivo spreads (gourmet nibbles for the price of a drink, nightly from around 6.30pm to 9.30pm). Popular strips include Via Ferrigni, Via Bisignano and Vicolo Belledonne a Chiaia.

Although Naples is no London, Milan or Sydney on the entertainment front, it does offer some top after-dark options, from opera and ballet, to thought-provoking theatre and cultured classical ensembles. To see what's on, scan daily papers like *Corriere del Mezzogiorno* or *La Repubblica* (Naples edition), click onto www.napoliunplugged.com, or ask at the tourist office. In smaller venues you can usually buy your ticket at the door; for bigger events try the box office inside Feltrinelli (Map p56).

Cafes & Bars

Caffè Gambrinus
CAFE

(Map p56; ☑081 41 75 82; www.grancaffegambrinus.com; Via Chiaia 12; ☉7am-1am Sun-Thu, to 2am Fri, to 3am Sat; ☐R2 to Piazza Trieste e Trento) Grand, chandeliered Gambrinus is Naples' oldest and most venerable cafe. Oscar Wilde knocked back a few here and Mussolini had some of the rooms shut down to keep out left-wing intellectuals. Sure, the prices may be steeper, but the pre-dinner aperitivo nibbles are decent and sipping a spritz while soaking up elegant Piazza Triesto e Trento is a moment worth savouring.

TO MARKET, TO MARKET

Porta Nolana and La Pignasecca are only two of Naples' loud and legendary markets. Stock up on cheap shoes, designer fakes and the odd vintage gem at the following favourites.

» **Bancarelle a San Pasquale** (Map p56; Via San Pasquale a Chiaia, Via Imbriani & Via Carducci; ⊗8am-2pm Mon-Wed, Fri & Sat, closed Aug; ⊠C25 to Riviera di Chiaia) Hit the stalls on Via Imbriani for hip threads, sarongs and avant-garde jewellery. The section between Via Carducci and Via San Pasquale is great for fish, spices, fruit and vegetables. Don't haggle.

» **Fiera Antiquaria Napoletana** (Map p56; Villa Comunale; ⊗8am-2pm last 2 weekends of month, closed Aug; ⊠C25 to Riviera di Chiaia) This waterfront antiques market sells vintage silverware, jewellery, furniture, paintings, prints and wonderful, overpriced junk.

» **La Duchessa** (Map p40; Via San Giuseppe Calasanzio and surrounding streets; ⊗8am-2pm Mon-Sat, closed Aug; ⊠R2 to Piazza Garibaldi) Gritty, multi-ethnic and obscenely cheap; head here for bargain denim, shoes, knickers, make-up and bootleg DVDs. Serious music buffs head in early to hunt for original, recent-release CDs and the odd hard-to-find special edition for as little as €3.

» **Mercatino di Antignano** (Map p62; Piazza degli Artisti; ⊗8am-1pm Mon-Sat, closed Aug; Medaglie D'Oro) Up high in Vomero, this place is popular for bags, jewellery, linen, kitchenware, shoes, and new and end-of-season clothing.

» **Mercatino di Posillipo** Not the cheapest market, but the best for quality goods. Top buys include genuine designer labels (although the D&G and Louis Vuitton bags are fakes), women's swimwear, underwear and linen. It's only the African vendors who don't mind a haggle.

» **Mercato di Poggioreale** (Via Nuova Poggioreale; ⊗8am-1pm Fri-Mon, closed Aug; ⊠No 1 to Via Nuova Poggioreale) Set in the city's old slaughterhouse, this hugely popular market has 40 shoe stalls alone selling designer overstock and no-frills everyday brands. Equally fab are the cheap casual wear, suits, colourful rolls of fabrics and kitchenware.

Nea CAFE, GALLERY, BAR
(Map p40; www.neartgallery.it; Via Constantinopoli 53; ⊗9am-7pm Mon-Wed, to late Thu-Sun; ☎; MDante) Aptly skirting bohemian Piazza Bellini, this whitewashed art gallery features its own candlelit cafe-bar, with alfresco seating at the bottom of a baroque staircase. Eye-up exhibitions of mostly 20th-century Italian and foreign art, then kick back with caffé or a Spritzer. Check Nea's Facebook page for upcoming readings, live music gigs or DJ sets.

Enoteca Belledonne BAR
(Map p56; ☎081 40 31 62; www.enotecabelledonne.com; Vico Belledonne a Chiaia 18; ⊗10am-1.30pm & 5pm-late Tue-Sat, 7pm-midnight Mon & Sun; ☎; ⊠C24 to Riviera di Chiaia) Exposed-brick walls and bottle-lined shelves set a cosy scene at Naples' best-loved wine bar – just look for the evening crowd spilling out onto the street. Swill, sip and eavesdrop over a list of well-chosen, mostly Italian wines, as well as a grazing menu that includes *salumi* and cheeses (€12), crostini (€5) and bruschette (€6).

Nàis BAR
(Map p56; Via Ferrigni 29; ⊗6.30pm-1am Sun-Thu, to 3am Fri & Sat; ⊠C24 to Riviera di Chiaia) Of all the aperitivo bars lining Via Ferrigni, Nàis is definitely our favourite. Tacky, club-inspired decor is ditched for a warm, tasteful, convivial air, with friendly bartenders, comfy suede banquettes and a book-lined shelf. Order a glass of vino, pick at the decent aperitivo spread, and eye-up the candy crowd.

Intra Moenia CAFE
(Map p40; ☎081 29 07 20; Piazza Bellini 70; ⊗10am-2am ; ☎; MDante) Despite the sloppy service, this free-thinking cafe–bookshop-publishing house located on Piazza Bellini is a good spot for chilling out. Browse limited-edition books on Neapolitan culture, pick up a vintage-style postcard, or simply slip on that beret, sip a *prosecco* and act the intellectual. The house wine costs €4 a glass and there's a range of salads, snacks and classic Neapolitan grub for peckish bohemians.

Fonoteca
CAFE, BAR

(Map p62; www.fonoteca.net; Via Morghen 31, C/F; ☺noon-1am Mon-Thu, to 2am Fri & Sat, 6.30pm-1.30am Sun; Ⓜ Vanvitelli) Sip, groove and read away at hip Fonoteca, a hybrid music store/cafe/bar. Hunt for CDs spanning electronica and classic rock to jazz, blues and world, flick through art and music-themed tomes, or head straight to the slick back bar for *caffè*, cocktails and edibles like bruschetta and salads. You can even surf the internet (€2.50 an hour).

Live Music & Nightclubs

Associazione Scarlatti
CLASSICAL MUSIC

(Map p56; ☎081 40 60 11; www.associazionescarlatti.it; Piazza dei Martiri 58; ☐C24 to Piazza dei Martiri) Naples' premier classical-music association organises an annual program of chamber-music concerts in venues across the city, including Teatro San Carlo and Castel Sant'Elmo. Local talent mixes it with foreign guests, which have included the Amsterdam Baroque Orchestra, St Petersburg's Mariinsky Theatre Orchestra and Belgian composer Philippe Herreweghe.

Centro di Musica Antica
Pietà de' Turchini
CLASSICAL MUSIC

(Map p62; ☎081 40 23 95; www.turchini.it; Via Santa Caterina da Siena 38; ☐Centrale to Corso Vittorio Emanuele) Classical-music buffs are in for a treat at this beautiful deconsecrated church. Home to the historic Orchestra Cappella della Pietà dei Turchini, it's an evocative setting for concerts of mostly 17th- to 19th-century Neapolitan works. Tickets cost about €10, and upcoming concerts are listed on the venue's website.

Galleria 19
CLUB

(Map p40; www.galleria19.it; Via San Sebastiano 19; ☺Tue-Sun; Ⓜ Dante) Set in a long, cavernous cellar scattered with chesterfields and industrial lamps, this cool and edgy club draws a uni crowd early in the week and 20/30- somethings with its Friday and Saturday electronica sessions. It's also home to one of the city's best mixologists, Gianluca Morziello, famed for his Cucumber Slumber. At the time of research, plans were under way to also open the space as a daytime cafe/bar.

Arenile Reload
CLUB, LIVE MUSIC

(Map p74; www.arenilereload.com; Via Coroglio 14b; ☺daily Apr-Sep weather permitting; ☐Cumana to Bagnoli) The biggest of Naples' beachside clubs, head in for poolside cocktails, see-and-be-seen *aperitivo* sessions, live bands and dancing under the stars. The club is a short walk south of Bagnoli station on the Cumana rail line.

Teatro Palapartenope
LIVE MUSIC

(Map p74; ☎081 570 00 08; www.palapartenope.it; Via Barbagallo 115; ☺box office 9am-1pm & 2-5.30pm Mon-Fri, 9am-12.45pm Sat; ☐Cumana to Edenlandia) Located in suburban Fuorigrotta, west of central Naples, the architecturally uninspiring Palapartenope is the biggest indoor concert venue in town. A 6000-plus seating capacity sets the scene for big-name Italian and international acts, which have included everyone from local crooner Pino Daniele to vintage icons Lou Reed and Spandau Ballet.

Opera, Ballet & Theatre

TOP CHOICE Teatro San Carlo
OPERA, BALLET

(Map p62; ☎box office 081 797 23 31, guided tours 081 553 45 65, special Sunday tour 081 797 24 68; www.teatrosancarlo.it; Via San Carlo 98; performances from €15; guided tour adult/reduced €5/3, special Sunday tour €15 incl aperitivo drink; ☺box office 10am-7pm Mon-Sat, 10am-3.30pm Sun, guided tours 10am-4pm Mon-Sat, special tour 11am & 12.30pm Sun; ☐R2 to Piazza Treiste e Trento) A night at Italy's biggest and oldest opera house is a magical experience. Although the original 1737 theatre burnt down in 1816, Antonio Niccolini's 19th-century reconstruction is pure Old World opulence. Dazzling after a €76 million restoration, its six gilded levels of boxes and pitch-perfect acoustics set an unforgettable scene for world-class opera, ballet and contemporary symphony. Just as well – Neapolitan audiences are notoriously demanding.

The opera season here runs from January to December, with a midseason break in the summer. Reckon on €50 for a place in the sixth tier, €100 for a seat in the stalls, or – if you're under 30 and can prove it, €30 for a place in a side box. Ballet tickets range from €35 to €90, with €25 tickets for under 30s. Tickets to one-off events can start as low as €15 – check the website for details. Be aware that not all shows take place on the main stage, with other venues including the smaller Teatrino di Corte in neighbouring Palazzo Reale (p55).

If you're not catching a show, you can still soak up the building's beauty on a guided tour. The special Sunday tours (book ahead) include performing actors and one *aperi-*

tivo drink. The adjoining Palazzo Reale is also home to the theatre's new multimedia museum, Memus (p58).

Galleria Toledo
THEATRE

(Map p50; ☑081 42 50 37; www.galleriatoledo.org; Via Concezione a Montecalvario 34; ☺box office 6-7.30pm Tue-Sat; ⓂToledo) If it's cutting edge, independent or experimental, chances are it's playing at this cult-status theatre, tucked away in the Quartieri Spagnoli. Gigs span both local and global plays and live music, with the odd offbeat arthouse flick thrown in for good measure. Phone bookings are taken (including at weekends), with ticket pick-up at the box office 30 minutes prior to the performance.

Sport

TOP CHOICE Stadio San Paolo
FOOTBALL

(Map p74; Piazzale Vincenzo Tecchio; ⓂNapoli Campi Flegrei) Naples' football team Napoli is the third-most supported in Italy after Juventus and Milan, and watching them play in the country's third-largest stadium is a highly charged rush. The season runs from late August to late May, with seats costing between €20 and €100. Book tickets from tobacconists, **Azzurro Service** (☑081 593 40 01; www.azzurroservice.net; Via Francesco Galeota 19; ☺9am-1pm & 3.30-7pm Mon-Fri, also Sat & Sun on match days; Napoli Campi Flegrei) or **Box Office** (Map p40; ☑081 551 91 88; www.boxofficenapoli.it; Galleria Umberto I 17; ☺9.30am-8pm Mon-Fri, 9.30am-1.30pm & 4.30-8pm Sat; ☐R2 to Piazza Trieste e Trento) and don't forget your photo ID. On match days, tickets are also available at the stadium itself.

🛍 Shopping

Shopping in Naples is a highly idiosyncratic experience, dominated by specialist, family-heirloom businesses. For Neapolitan tailors and high-end labels, hit Chiaia's Via Calabritto, Via dei Mille and Via Gaetano Filangieri. For antiques, explore Via Domenico Morelli in Chiaia and Via Costantinopoli in the *centro storico*. Also in the *centro storico*, hit up-and-coming Vico San Domenico Maggiore for interesting little shops selling everything from vintage threads to organic soaps. For the ultimate Neapolitan shopping experience, however, explore the legendary markets, home to everything from dirt-cheap kinky knickers, frocks and shoes, to pots and pans. Many shops close for two weeks in August.

CENTRO STORICO & MERCATO

Scriptura
LEATHER GOODS

(Map p40; Via San Sebastiano 22; ☺ 3-8pm Mon, 10.30am-8pm Tue-Sat; ⓂDante) Family-run Scriptura crafts beautiful, soft leather goods using top-shelf Tuscan leather. Its range includes handbags, satchels, wallets, belts and leather-bound notebooks, with styles and colours covering both the classic and the contemporary. Best of all, prices are reasonable, with bags starting from €36 and wallets from €30.

Kiphy
BEAUTY

(Map p40; ☑393 8703280; www.kiphy.it; Vico San Domenico Maggiore 3; ☺10.30am-2pm & 3-7pm Tue-Sat, closed Sat Jun-Aug; ⓂDante) Named after a fabled ancient Egyptian perfume, this funky shop-workshop sells pure, handmade slabs of soap that look as beautiful as they smell. Lined up under low-slung lights, varieties include a refreshing orange-and-cinnamon blend. The freshly made shampoos, creams and oils use organic, fair-trade ingredients and can be personally tailored. Best of all, products are gorgeously packaged, reasonably priced and made with love.

La Scarabattola
ARTS & CRAFTS

(Map p40; ☑081 29 17 35; www.lascarabattola.it; Via dei Tribunali 50; ☺10am-6pm Mon-Sat; ☐C55 to Via Duomo) Not only have La Scarabattola's handmade sculptures of *magi* (wise men), devils and Neapolitan folk figures featured in top exhibitions (including the Venice Biennale), their fans include Spanish royalty. Figurines aside, their sleek, contemporary ceramic creations (think Pulcinella-inspired place-card holders) make for some urbane souvenirs. Ask nicely and you might just get to see the masters in action at their nearby workshop.

Ars Neapolitana
ARTS & CRAFTS

(Map p40; ☑392 537 71 16; Via dei Tribunali 303; ☺10am-6.30pm Mon-Fri, to 3pm Sat, also open 10am-6.30pm Sat & Sun late Oct-early Jan; ☐C55 to Via Duomo) Guglielmo Muoio sold his first *pastore* (nativity scene figurine) at age 13. A decade on, the talented artisan has even exhibited at the European Parliament in Strasbourg. Pop into his little workshop-showroom and you'll probably find him sculpting or painting one of his impressively detailed terracotta saints, angels or 18th-century folkloric characters.

Colonnese
PRINTS, BOOKS

(Map p40; www.colonnese.it; Via San Pietro a Maiella 32-33; MDante) Neighbouring one of Italy's most esteemed music conservatories, this erudite bookshop fills with the sound of practising musicians. While most of its new and vintage-edition titles are in Italian, you'll also find quality original and reproduction Neapolitan prints from the 17th and 18th centuries. Ask to see the collectable postcards from the late 19th and early 20th centuries, kept behind the counter.

Elia's Vintage
FASHION

(Map p40; 081 29 15 89; www.eliasvintage.it; Vicoletto San Domenico; MDante) Revamp your wardrobe at this eccentric fashion bolt-hole, where vintage threads and accessories mix it with boho-chic one-offs designed and handsewn by Angela and her costume-designer sister-in-law, Antonella. Expect anything from lusciously knitted scarves to ruffled felt necklaces and bags made from rockabilly beer caps. Even the jewellery pouches are whipped up using vintage fabric scraps.

Salvatore Malinconico
FASHION

(Map p40; 331 4909562; Vico San Domenico Maggiore 19; 10am-8pm Mon-Sat; MDante) Young designer Salvatore Malinconico transforms old threads and vintage fabrics into edgy, architecturally inspired frocks and jackets. Choose from a small selection of ready-to-wear creations – think slinky black cocktail dresses pimped with coloured side panels – or let Salvatore sew-up something fabulous from scratch. A dress can take as little as three hours to create, but ring ahead for an appointment.

Charcuterie
FOOD & DRINK

(Map p40; 081 551 69 81; Via Benedetto Croce 43; 9am-8pm Mon-Sat, to 2.30pm Sun; MDante) Even the doors heave with gourmet grub at this jam-packed little deli. Fill your bags with everything from pasta, macaroons and *grappa* (Italian pomace brandy), to lemon-flavoured olive oil and chocolate-coated figs.

Limonè
FOOD & DRINK

(Map p40; 081 29 94 29; www.limoncellodinapoli. it; Piazza San Gaetano 72; C55 to Via Duomo) For a taste of Napoli long after you've gone home, stock up on a few bottles of Limonè's organic, homemade *limoncello* (lemon liqueur). Ask nicely and you might get a sip for free. Other take-home treats include lemon pasta, lemon-infused grappa and a refreshing *crema di melone* (melon liqueur).

TOLEDO & QUARTIERI SPAGNOLI

Talarico
ARTS & CRAFTS

(Map p50; 081 40 77 23; www.mariotalarico.it; Vico Due Porte a Toledo 4b; 8am-8pm Mon-Sat; MToledo) Mario Talarico and his nephews have turned the humble umbrella into a work of art. Sought after by international heads of state, each piece is a one-off, complete with mother-of-pearl buttons, a horn tip and a handle made from a single tree branch. While top-of-the-range pieces can fetch up to €300, there are more-affordable options that will keep the budget-conscious singing in the rain.

Napolimania
SOUVENIRS

(Map p50; 081 41 41 20; www.napolimania.com; Via Toledo 312; MToledo) This offbeat shrine to local pop culture is the place for plastic Totò statues, Neapolitan 'survival kits', and jocks and tops with witty local slang.

SANTA LUCIA & CHIAIA

Bowinkel
PRINTS

(Map p56; 081 764 07 39; www.bowinkel.it; Via Santa Lucia 25; 154 to Via Santa Lucia) The city's finest vintage prints, photographs, watercolour paintings and classic frames. If you can't find what you're looking for here, check out its sister branch at Piazza dei Martiri 24 (081 764 43 44). Erudite owner Umberto speaks a smattering of English and will arrange shipments abroad.

Contemporastudio
JEWELLERY

(Map p56; 081 247 99 37; www.asadventrella. it; Via Francesco Crispi 50; 10am-1.30pm & 4-7.30pm Mon-Fri, 10am-1.30pm Sat; MPiazza Amedeo) A concrete-clad gallery stocking funky, experimental jewellery from Neapolitan Asad Ventrella: necklaces made of solid-silver *penne rigate* (penne pasta shapes), fat double-faced rings in titanium and aluminium and sharp-looking cufflinks for style-savvy gents.

Livio De Simone
FASHION

(Map p56; 081 764 38 27; Via Domenico Morelli 15; C24 to Piazza dei Martiri) The late Livio De Simone put Capri on the catwalk, dressing the likes of Audrey Hepburn and Jackie O in his bold, colourful creations. Inspired by the island, summer and the sea, his daughter, Benedetta, keeps the vision alive with the label's distinctive hand- and block-printed *robe chemesiers* (shirt dresses), frocks, suits, coats, and matching bags and shoes.

Tramontano
LEATHER GOODS

(Map p56; ☑081 41 48 37; www.tramontano.it; Via Chiaia 143-144; ☐C24 to Piazza dei Martiri) With fans including Woody Allen, Tramontano has an epic rep for exquisitely crafted Neapolitan leather goods, from butter-soft wallets to glam handbags and preppy-cool satchels. Famously each Christmas, a new model bag is released, inspired by a classic song...such as Patti Smith's 'Kimberley'.

Feltrinelli
BOOKS, MUSIC

(Map p56; ☑081 240 54 11; www.lafeltrinelli.it; Piazza dei Martiri 23; ☺10am-9pm Mon-Fri, to 11pm Sat, 10am-2pm & 4-10pm Sun; ☐C24 to Piazza dei Martiri) Pick up anything from Italian music CDs and DVDs to novels and coffee-table tomes at this three-level book and music mega store, complete with cafe and box office. There's a fair-sized English-language section in the basement.

Verdegrano
CERAMICS

(Map p56; ☑081 40 17 54; Via Santa Teresa a Chiaia 17; ☺10.30am-1pm & 5-7.30pm Tue-Sat, closed Mon morning Oct–late May, closed Sat afternoon late May-Sep; Ⓜ Piazza Amedeo) Give your *casa* that Mediterranean look with exquisitely patterned, hand-painted porcelain pots, vases, plates and decorative items. Prices are reasonable and there are some easy-to-pack smaller pieces for the trip home.

VOMERO, CAPODIMONTE & LA SANITÀ
De Paola Cameos
JEWELLERY

(Map p62; ☑081 578 29 10; Via Annibale Caccavello 67; ☺9am-8pm Mon-Sat, to 2pm Sun; ☐Centrale to Fuga) Head here for a beautiful range of finely carved cameos as well as coral necklaces, earrings, pendants and bracelets. Designs range from vintage to modern and there's no pressure to buy.

ℹ Information

Emergencies
Ambulance (☑118)
Loreto-Mare Hospital (Ospedale Loreto-Mare; ☑081 20 10 33; Via Amerigo Vespucci 26)
Police (☑113, 112)
Police Station (Questura; ☑081 794 11 11; Via Medina 75) Has an office for foreigners.To report a stolen car, call 113.

Tourist information
Tourist Information Office Piazza del Gesù Nuovo (Piazza del Gesù Nuovo 7; ☺9am-7pm Mon-Sat, 9am-2pm Sun); Stazione Centrale (p263); Via San Carlo (p263)

ℹ Getting There & Away

AIRPORT Capodichino (NAP; ☑081 789 61 11; www.gesac.it), 7km northeast of the city centre, is southern Italy's main airport, linking Naples with most Italian and several European cities, as well as New York. Budget carrier Easyjet operates several routes to/from Capodichino, including London, Paris-Orly, Berlin and Geneva.

TRAIN Naples is southern Italy's rail hub and on the main Milan–Palermo line, with good connects to other Italian cities and towns.

National rail company Trenitalia (p266) runs regular services to Rome (2nd class €10.50 to €43, 70 minutes to three hours, up to 30 daily).

BOAT Fast ferries and hydrofoils for Capri, Ischia, Procida and Sorrento depart from Molo Beverello in front of Castel Nuovo; hydrofoils for Capri, Ischia and Procida also sail from Mergellina.

Ferries for Sicily, the Aeolian Islands and Sardinia sail from Molo Angioino (right beside Molo Beverello) and neighbouring Calata Porta di Massa.

See the Transport chapter for a list of ferry companies.

BUS Most national and international buses leave from Piazza Garibaldi.

Regional bus services are operated by numerous companies, the most useful of which is **SITA** (☑089 405 145; www.sitabus.it). Connections from Naples include Amalfi, Positano and Salerno. You can purchase SITA tickets and catch buses either from Porto Immacolatella, near Molo Angioino, or from Via Galileo Ferraris, near Stazione Centrale.

CAR Naples is on the north–south Autostrada del Sole, the A1 (north to Rome and Milan) and the A3 (south to Salerno and Reggio di Calabria).

ℹ Getting Around

CITY BUSES Airport shuttle Alibus (p265) connects the airport to Piazza Garibaldi (Stazione Centrale) and Molo Beverello (€3, 45 minutes, every 20 to 30 minutes).

ANM (p267) buses serve the city and its periphery. Many routes pass through Piazza Garibaldi, outside Stazione Centrale. This is where you'll find the ANM information kiosk. See the Transport chapter for useful routes.

CITY TRAINS Metronapoli (p60) operates three metro lines. Line 1 (yellow) and Line 2 (blue) are the most useful. Line 2 runs from Gianturco to Garibaldi (Stazione Centrale) and on to Pozzuoli. Line 1 currently begins at Piazza Bovia (Università), running north along Via Toledo and on to Vomero and the northern suburbs. Scheduled for completion in late 2013, its extension will also see stops at Piazza Municipio, Via Duomo and Stazione Centrale. Before this time, lines 1 and 2 only interchange at Museo (Line 1) / Cavour (Line 2). Tickets (also valid on city buses, funiculars and trams) can be purchased at kiosks, tobacconists or from automated ticket machines at metro stations.

Circumvesuviana (p270) operates frequent services to Sorrento (€4, 70 minutes) via Ercolano (€2.10, 20 minutes), Pompeii (€2.80, 40 minutes) and other towns along the coast, departing from Stazione Circumvesuviana.

The Ferrovia Cumana (p270) and the Circumflegrea, based at Stazione Cumana di Montesanto on Piazza Montesanto, 500m southwest of Piazza Dante, operate services to Pozzuoli (€1.20, every 25 minutes) and other Campi Flegrei towns beyond.

CITY FUNICULARS Three services connect central Naples to Vomero, while a fourth connects Mergellina to Posillipo.

TAXI Official fares to the airport are as follows: €23 from a seafront hotel or from Mergellina hydrofoil terminal; €19 from Piazza del Municipio or Molo Beverello ferry terminal; and €15.50 from Stazione Centrale.

Book a taxi by calling any one of the following companies:

» **Consortaxi** ☑081 22 22

» **Consorzio Taxi Napoli** ☑081 88 88

» **Radio Taxi Napoli** ☑081 556 44 44

» **Radio Taxi La Partenope** ☑081 01 01

BOAT Suspended indefinitely, Metro del Mare usually connects Bacoli and Pozzuoli to Naples and from there has services to Sorrento, Positano and Amalfi.

From Easter to October Amalfi, Positano, Salerno, Capri, Naples and Sorrento are connected by ferry or hydrofoil.

CITY TRAMS Two lines run along the waterfront. Line 1 connects Mercato di Poggioreale to Piazza Garibaldi, Molo Beverello (ferry terminal), and Piazza Vittoria in Chiaia.

BAY OF NAPLES

Buried for centuries beneath metres of volcanic debris, Naples' archaeological sites are among the best-preserved and most-spectacular Roman ruins in existence. And it's here, in the dense urban sprawl stretching from Naples to Castellammare, that you'll find Italy's blockbuster finest: Pompeii and Herculaneum, as well as a host of lesser-known jewels, from salubrious ancient villas to the country's biggest vintage clothes market.

While Pompeii, Herculaneum and Oplontis are within easy walking distance of

stations on the Naples–Sorrento Circumvesuviana train line, Stabiae and Boscoreale both require a bit more searching around.

As for Mt Vesuvius, it's an easy bus trip from Pompeii or Ercolano.

⊙ Sights

TOP CHOICE **Ruins of Herculaneum** RUIN

(☑081 732 43 38; www.pompeiisites.org; Corso Resina 6, Ercolano; adult/reduced €11/5.50, combined ticket incl Pompeii, Oplontis, Stabiae & Boscoreale €20/10; ⊙8.30am-7.30pm Apr-Oct, to 5pm Nov-Mar, last entry 90min before closing; ⊞Circumvesuviana to Ercolano-Scavi) Unfairly upstaged by Pompeii's ancient offerings, the Ruins of Herculaneum have a wealth of archaeological finds, from ancient advertisements and stylish mosaics, to carbonised furniture and terror-struck skeletons. Indeed, this superbly conserved Roman fishing town of 4000 inhabitants is smaller and easier to navigate than Pompeii, and can be explored with a map and **audioguide** (€6.50, €10 for two).

From the site's main gateway on Corso Resina, head down the wide boulevard, where you'll find the ticket office on the left. Pick up a free map and guide booklet here, and then follow the boulevard right to the actual entrance into the ruins themselves.

Herculaneum's fate runs parallel to that of Pompeii. Destroyed by an earthquake in AD 62, the AD 79 eruption of Mt Vesuvius saw it submerged in a 16m-thick sea of mud that essentially fossilised the city. This meant that even delicate items, such as furniture and clothing, were discovered remarkably well preserved. Tragically, the inhabitants didn't fare so well; thousands of people tried to escape by boat but were suffocated by the volcano's poisonous gases. Indeed, what appears to be a moat around the town is in fact the ancient shoreline. It was here in 1980 that archaeologists discovered some 300 skeletons, the remains of a crowd that had fled to the beach only to be overcome by the terrible heat of clouds surging down from Vesuvius.

The town itself was rediscovered in 1709 and amateur excavations were carried out intermittently until 1874, with many finds being carted off to Naples to decorate the houses of the well-to-do or to end up in museums. Serious archaeological work began again in 1927 and continues to this day, although with much of the ancient site buried beneath modern Ercolano it's slow going. Indeed,

Herculaneum

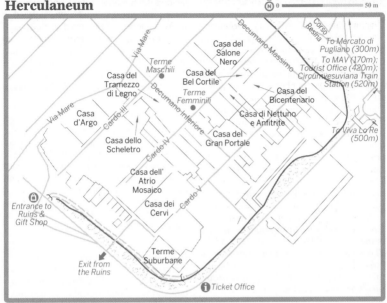

note that at any given time some houses will invariably be shut for restoration; at the time of writing these included the Terme Suburbane and the Casa dell'Atrio a Mosaico.

Casa d'Argo & Casa dello Scheletro

As you begin your exploration northeast along Cardo III you'll stumble across Casa d'Argo (Argus House). This noble pad would originally have opened onto Cardo II (as yet unearthed). Onto its porticoed, palm-treed garden open a *triclinium* (dining room) and other residential rooms. Across the street sits the Casa dello Scheletro (House of the Skeleton), a modestly sized house boasting five styles of mosaic flooring, including a design of white arrows at the entrance to guide the most disorientated of guests. In the internal courtyard, don't miss the skylight, complete with the remnants of an ancient security grill. Of the house's mythically themed wall mosaics, only the faded ones are originals; the others now reside in the Museo Archeologico Nazionale (p49).

Terme Maschili

Just across the Decumano Inferiore (one of ancient Herculaneum's main streets), the Terme Maschili (Male Baths) were the men's section of the Terme del Foro (Forum Baths). Note the ancient latrine to the left of the entrance before you step into the *apodyterium* (changing room), complete with bench for waiting patrons and a nifty wall shelf for sandal and toga storage. While those after a bracing soak would pop into the *frigidarium* (cold bath) to the left, the less stoic headed straight into the *tepadarium* (tepid bath) to the right. The sunken mosaic floor here is testament to the seismic activity preceding Mt Vesuvius's catastrophic eruption. Beyond this room lies the *caldarium* (hot bath), as well as an exercise area.

Decumano Massimo

At the end of Cardo III, turn right into the Decumano Massimo. This ancient high street is lined with shops; fragments of advertisements still adorn the walls, such as that to the right of the Casa del Salone Nero. This ancient consumer information listed everything from from the weight of goods to their price.

Further east along Decumano Massimo, a crucifix found in an upstairs room of the Casa del Bicentenario (Bicentenary House) provides possible evidence of a Christian presence in pre-Vesuvius Herculaneum.

Casa del Bel Cortile & Casa di Nettuno e Anfitrite

Turning into Cardo IV from Decumano Massimo, you'll hit the Casa del Bel Cortile (House of the Beautiful Courtyard). Inside lie three of the 300 skeletons discovered on the ancient shore by archaeologists in 1980. Almost two millennia later, it's still a poignant sight to see the assumed mother, father and young child huddled together in the last, terrifying moments of their lives.

Next door awaits the Casa di Nettuno e Anfitrite (House of Neptune and Amfitrite), an aristocratic pad taking its name from the mosaic in the *nymphaeum* (fountain and bath). The warm colours in which the sea god and his nymph bride are depicted hint at how lavish the original interior must once have been.

A quick walk further southwest along Cardo IV leads you to the women's section of the Terme del Foro, the Terme Femminili. Though smaller than its male equivalent, it boasts finer floor mosaics – note the beautifully executed naked figure of Triton in the *apodyterium* (changing room).

Casa del Tramezzo di Legno

Across the Decumano Inferiore is the Case del Tramezzo di Legno (House of the Wooden Partition), which unusually features two atria. It's likely that the atria belonged to two separate houses merged together in the 1st century AD. Predictably, the most famous relic here is a wonderfully well-preserved wooden screen, separating the atrium from the *tablinum*, where the owner talked business with his clients. The second room off the left side of the atrium features the remains of an ancient bed.

Casa dell'Atrio a Mosaico

Further southwest on Cardio IV, ancient mansion Casa dell'Atrio a Mosaico (House of the Mosaic Atrium) harbours extensive floor mosaics, although time and nature have left the floor buckled and uneven. Particularly noteworthy is the black-and-white chessboard mosaic in the atrium.

Backtrack up Cardo IV and turn right at Decumano Inferiore. Here you'll find the Casa del Gran Portale (House of the Large Portal), named after the elegant brick Corinthian columns that flank its main entrance. Step inside to admire some well-preserved wall paintings.

Casa dei Cervi

Accessible from Cardo V, the Casa dei Cervi (House of the Stags) is an imposing example of a Roman noble family's house which, before the volcanic mud slide, boasted a seafront address. Constructed around a central courtyard, the two-storey villa contains murals and some beautiful still-life paintings. Waiting for you in the courtyard is a diminutive pair of marble deer assailed by dogs, and an engaging statue of a drunken, peeing Hercules.

Terme Suburbane

Marking the site's southernmost tip is the 1st-century AD Terme Suburbane (Suburban Baths), one of the best preserved bath complexes in existence, with deep pools, stucco friezes and bas-reliefs looking down upon marble seats and floors. This is also one of the best places to observe the soaring volcanic deposits that literally smothered the ancient coastline.

Getting There & Away

If you're travelling to the *scavi* (ruins) by Circumvesuviana train (€2.10 from Naples or Sorrento), get off at Ercolano-Scavi station and walk 500m downhill to the ruins – follow the signs for the *scavi* down the main street, Via IV Novembre. En route you'll pass the **tourist office** (Via IV Novembre 82; ⊗8am-6pm Mon-Sat; ⓡCircumvesuviana to Ercolano-Scavi) on your right.

MAV   MUSEUM
(Museo Archeologico Virtuale; ☑081 1980 6511; www.museomav.com; Via IV Novembre 44; adult/reduced €7.50/6, optional 3D documentary €4; ⊗9.30am-5.30pm Tue-Sun, last entry 4.30pm; ⓡCircumvesuviana to Ercolano-Scavi) Using high-tech holograms and computer-generated footage, this 'virtual archaeological museum' brings ruins like Pompei's forum and Capri's Villa Jovis back to virtual life. Especially fun for kids, it's a useful place to comprehend just how impressive those crumbling columns once were. The museum is on the main street linking Ercolano-Scavi train station to the Ruins of Herculaneum.

Mercato di Pugliano   MARKET
(Via Pugliano; ⊗9am-1pm Mon-Sat; ⓡCircumvesuviana to Ercolano-Scavi) Straddling Via Pugliano in the heart of Ercolano, Italy's largest pre-loved clothing market peddles everything from stock-standard junk to fabulous offbeat finds (killer cocktail dresses, vinyl-LP handbags and the odd military jacket). One of the best shops is **Old Star** (Via Pugliano 60; ⊗8am-1pm Mon-Sun; ⓡCircumvesuviana to Ercolano-Scavi); ask politely and

you may be shown the rare stock upstairs, often borrowed by international designers for study and inspiration.

Look out for the vintage Moschino and Fendi, ornate 1970s Indian fashion, and top-quality cashmere sweaters. From the Circumvesuviana Ercolano-Scavi station, walk downhill 400m to Prima Traversa Mercato. Turn right into it and you'll stumble onto Via Pugliano 200m later.

TOP
CHOICE **Ruins of Pompeii**   RUIN

(☑081 857 53 47; www.pompeiisites.org; entrances at Porta Marina & Piazza Anfiteatro; adult/reduced €11/5.50, combined ticket incl Herculaneum, Oplontis, Stabiae & Boscoreale €20/10; ⊙8.30am-7.30pm Apr-Oct, 8.30am-5pm Nov-Mar, last entry 90min before closing) The ruins of Pompeii are priceless. Much of the site's value lies in the fact that it wasn't simply blown away by Vesuvius in AD 79, rather it was buried under a layer of *lapilli* (burning fragments of pumice stone). The result is a remarkably well-preserved slice of ancient life, where visitors can walk down Roman streets and snoop around millennia-old abodes and businesses (including a brothel).

As terrible as the eruption was, it could have been worse. Seventeen years earlier Pompeii (Pompei in Italian) had been devastated by an earthquake and much of the 20,000-strong population had been evacuated. Many had not returned by the time Vesuvius blew, but 2000 men, women and children perished nevertheless.

The origins of Pompeii are uncertain, but it seems likely that it was founded in the 7th century BC by the Campanian Oscans. Over the next seven centuries the city fell to the Greeks and the Samnites before becoming a Roman colony in 80 BC.

After its catastrophic demise, Pompeii receded from the public eye until 1594, when the architect Domenico Fontana stumbled across the ruins while digging a canal. Exploration proper didn't begin until 1748, however. Of Pompeii's original 66 hectares, 44 have now been excavated. Of course that doesn't mean you'll have unhindered access to every inch of the Unesco-listed site – expect to come across areas cordoned off for no apparent reason, a noticeable lack of clear signs and the odd stray dog. Audio-guides are a sensible investment and a good guidebook will also help – try the €10 *Pompeii* published by Electa Napoli.

At the time of writing, the Casa dei Vettii was closed for restoration. The Terme Suburbane, just outside the city walls, are visitable on weekends subject to prior booking at www.arethusa.net. It's here that you'll find the erotic frescoes that scandalised the Vatican when they were revealed in 2001. The saucy panels decorate the changing rooms of what was once a private baths complex.

Porta Marina

The site's main entrance is at Porta Marina, the most impressive of the seven gates that punctuated the ancient town walls. A busy passageway now as it was then, it originally connected the town with the nearby harbour, hence the gateway's name. Immediately on the right as you enter the gate is the 1st century BC Tempio di Venere (Temple of Venus), formerly one of the town's most opulent temples.

The Forum

Continuing northeast along Via Marina you'll hit the grassy *foro* (forum). Flanked by limestone columns, this was the ancient city's main piazza and the buildings

---

POMPEII TOURS

You'll almost certainly be approached by a guide outside the ticket office. Authorised guides wear identification tags. Reputable tour operators include the following:

» **Yellow Sudmarine** (☑329 101 03 28; www.yellowsudmarine.com)

» **Torres Travel** (☑081 856 78 02; www.torrestravel.it)

Expect to pay around €100 for a two-hour tour, whether you're alone, in a couple or in a group of up to 25 people.

For more information, contact the town's tourist office at **Porta Marina** (☑081 536 32 93; www.pompeiturismo.it; Piazza Porta Marina Inferiore 12; ⊙8am-3.45pm Mon-Sat) or in **central Pompeii** (☑081 850 72 55; Via Sacra 1; ⊙8am-3.30pm Mon-Fri, 8.30am-2pm Sat, closed Sun all year).

Pompeii

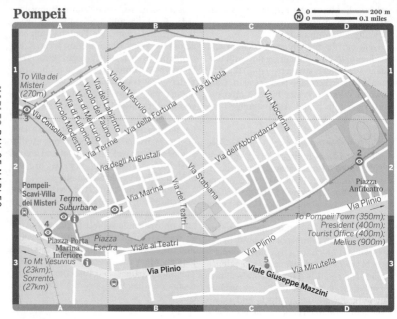

Pompeii

⦿ Sights
1 Basilica	B2
2 Piazza Anfiteatro Entrance & Ticket Office	D2
3 Porta Ercolano	A1
4 Porta Marina Entrance & Ticket Office	A3

⦿ Activities, Courses & Tours
5 Torres Travel	C3

surrounding it are testament to its role as the city's hub of civic, commercial, political and religious activity.

At its southwestern end sit the remains of the **basilica**, the 2nd century BC seat of the city's law courts and exchange. Their semicircular apses would later influence the design of early Christian churches. Opposite the basilica, the **Tempio di Apollo** (Temple of Apollo) is the oldest and most important of Pompeii's religious buildings. Most of what you see today, including the striking columned portico, dates to the 2nd century BC, although fragments remain of an earlier version dating to the 6th century BC.

At the forum's northern end is the **Tempio di Giove** (Temple of Jupiter), which has

one of two flanking triumphal arches remaining, and the **Granai del Foro** (Forum Granary), now used to store hundreds of amphorae and a number of body casts that were made in the late 19th century by pouring plaster into the hollows left by disintegrated bodies. The **macellum** nearby was once the city's main meat and fish market.

Lupanare
From the market head northeast along Via degli Augustali to Vicolo del Lupanare. Halfway down this narrow alley is the Lupanare, the city's only dedicated brothel. A tiny two-storey building with five rooms on each floor, its collection of raunchy frescoes was a menu of sorts for its randy clientele.

Teatro Grande
Heading back south, Vicolo del Lupanare becomes Via dei Teatri. At the end you'll find the verdant Foro Triangolare, which would originally have overlooked the sea and the River Sarno. The main attraction here was, and still is, the 2nd century BC Teatro Grande, a 5000-seat theatre carved into the lava mass on which Pompeii was originally built. Behind the stage, the porticoed Quadriportico dei Teatri was initially used for the

(Continued on page 101)

Historic Naples & The Amalfi Coast

Ancient Wonders »
Tragedy in Pompeii »
The Baroque »

Temple of Apollo, Pompeii

KEN WELSH/GETTY IMAGES ©

Ancient Wonders

Southern Italy is a sun-drenched repository of ancient art and architecture, from Unesco World Heritage temples and cities to lesser-known archaeological gems. If you've ever longed to turn back time, this is the place to do it.

Pompeii

1 Priceless Pompeii (p93) channels ancient life like no other site. See the world through a gladiator's eyes at the anfiteatro, peek into cubicles of wild lust at the Lupanare and ponder the very last moments of life in the Orto dei Fuggiaschi.

Herculaneum

2 A bite-sized Pompeii, Herculaneum (p90) is even better preserved than its rival. This is the place to delve into the details, from shop props, advertisements and carbonised furniture, to mosaics and even an ancient security grill.

Campi Flegrei

3 The Phlegrean Fields simmer with history. Seek out the sibyl in Cuma (p77), ponder ancient booty at the Museo Archeologico dei Campi Flegrei (p74) or simply spare a thought for martyrs at the Anfiteatro Flavio (p70).

Paestum

4 Great Greek temples never go out of vogue and the wonders at Paestum (p182) are among the greatest outside Greece. With its oldest structures stretching back to the 6th century BC, the place makes Rome's Colosseum feel positively modern.

Subterranean Naples

5 Eerie aqueducts, mysterious crypts and silent streets: beneath Naples lurks a wonderland of Graeco-Roman ruins. For a taste, head below the Complesso Monumentale di San Lorenzo Maggiore (p39) or follow the leader on a Napoli Sotterranea (p46) tour.

Clockwise from top left
1. Columns in Pompeii 2. Mosaic, Terme del Foro, Herculaneum 3. Anfiteatro Flavio, Pozzuoli

MARTIN MOOS/GETTY IMAGES ©

LONELY PLANET/GETTY IMAGES ©

Tragedy in Pompeii

24 August AD 79
8am Buildings including the **Terme Suburbane** **1** and the **foro** **2** are still undergoing repair after an earthquake in AD 63 caused significant damage to the city. Despite violent earth tremors overnight, residents have little idea of the catastrophe that lies ahead.

Midday Peckish locals pour into the **Thermopolium di Vetutius Placidus** **3**. The lustful slip into the **Lupanare** **4**, and gladiators practise for the evening's planned games at the **anfiteatro** **5**. A massive boom heralds the eruption. Shocked onlookers witness a dark cloud of volcanic matter shoot some 14km above the crater.

3pm–5pm Lapilli (burning pumice stone) rains down on Pompeii. Terrified locals begin to flee; others take shelter. Within two hours, the plume is 25km high and the sky has darkened. Roofs collapse under the weight of the debris, burying those inside.

25 August AD 79
Midnight Mudflows bury the town of Herculaneum. Lapilli and ash continue to rain down on Pompeii, bursting through buildings and suffocating those taking refuge within.

4am–8am Ash and gas avalanches hit Herculaneum. Subsequent surges smother Pompeii, killing all remaining residents, including those in the **Orto dei Fuggiaschi** **6**. The volcanic 'blanket' will safeguard frescoed treasures like the **Casa del Menandro** **7** and **Villa dei Misteri** **8** for almost two millennia.

Terme Suburbane
The *laconicum* (sauna), *caldarium* (hot bath) and large, heated swimming pool weren't the only sources of heat here; scan the walls of this suburban bathhouse for some of the city's raunchiest frescoes.

Villa di Diomede
Casa Ve
Casa del Poeta Tragico
Porta Ercolano
Casa Fa
Basilica
Tempio di Apollo
Porta Marina
1
2
8
Terme del Foro
Macellum
Teatro Grande
Quadriportico dei Teatri
Porta di Stabia
Teatro Piccolo

Foro
An ancient Times Square of sorts, the forum sits at the intersection of Pompeii's main streets and was closed to traffic in the 1st century AD. The plinths on the southern edge featured statues of the imperial family.

TOP TIPS
» **Visit** in the afternoon
» **Allow** three hours
» **Wear** comfortable shoes and a hat
» **Bring** drinking water
» **Don't** use flash photography

Villa dei Misteri
Home to the world-famous *Dionysiac Frieze* fresco. Other highlights at this villa include *trompe l'oeil* wall decorations in the *cubiculum* (bedroom) and Egyptian-themed artwork in the *tablinum* (reception).

Lupanare
The prostitutes at this brothel were often slaves of Greek or Asian origin. Mattresses once covered the stone beds and the names engraved in the walls are possibly those of the workers and their clients.

Thermopolium di Vetutius Placidus
The counter at this ancient snack bar once held urns filled with hot food. The *lararium* (household shrine) on the back wall depicts Dionysus (the god of wine) and Mercury (the god of profit and commerce).

Eyewitness Account
Pliny the Younger (AD 61–c 112) gives a gripping, first-hand account of the catastrophe in his letters to Tacitus (AD 56–117).

Porta del Vesuvio

Porta di Nola

Casa della Venere in Conchiglia

Porta di Sarno

Grande Palestra

Tempio di Iside

Casa del Menandro
This dwelling most likely belonged to the family of Poppaea Sabina, Nero's second wife. A room to the left of the atrium features Trojan War paintings and a polychrome mosaic of pygmies rowing down the Nile.

Orto dei Fuggiaschi
The Garden of the Fugitives showcases the plaster moulds of 13 locals seeking refuge during Vesuvius' eruption – the largest number of victims found in any one area. The huddled bodies make for a moving scene.

Anfiteatro
Magistrates, local senators and the games' sponsors and organisers enjoyed front-row seating at this veteran amphitheatre, home to gladiatorial battles and the odd riot. The parapet circling the stadium featured paintings of combat, victory celebrations and hunting scenes.

The Baroque

Innately extravagant, effusive and loud, Naples found its soul mate in the baroque. As a booming metropolis, Naples was hungry for big, bold and bombastic – the baroque ensured it got it.

Cappella di San Gennaro

1 Every patron saint deserves a little attention, and Naples' San Gennaro gets plenty in the chapel (p43) that houses his liquefying blood. From Cosimo Fanzago's sculptures to Giovanni Lanfranco's 'Paradise' fresco, it's a spiritual tour de force.

Church, Certosa di San Martino

2 The Carthusian monks at this charterhouse (p65) commissioned the baroque's finest to pimp their church. Their prayers were answered with luscious sculptures, canvases, and inlaid stone and wood.

Reggia di Caserta

3 Four courtyards, 1000-plus rooms, two dozen state apartments, a library, theatre and one of Europe's most ambitious landscaped gardens; Caserta's Unesco-listed royal palace (p44) made sure the baroque went out with a very loud bang.

Cappella Sansevero

4 Incredibly, Francesco Maria Russo's vivid vault fresco has remained untouched since its debut in 1749. Then again, the di Sangro family chapel (p38) is not short of jaw-dropping revelations, among them Giuseppe Sanmartino's *Cristo velato* sculpture.

Farmacia Storica dell'Ospedale degli Incurabili

5 Diva of Italian drugstores, the Farmacia Storica dell'Ospedale degli Incurabili (p43) is the country's most faithfully preserved 18th-century pharmacy, not to mention a high-inducing feast of walnut cabinets, majolica ceramics and brooding oil brushstrokes.

From top
1. Frescoes, Cappella di San Gennaro, Naples
2. Courtyard, Certosa di San Martino, Naples

(Continued from page 94)

audience to stroll between acts, and later as a barracks for gladiators. Next door, the **Teatro Piccolo** (also known as the Odeion) was once an indoor theatre renowned for its acoustics, while the pre-RomanTempio di Iside (Temple of Isis) was a popular place of cult worship.

Terme Stabiane & Casa della Venere in Conchiglia

As it shoots eastward, Via Marina becomes Via dell'Abbondanza (Street of Abundance). Lined with ancient shops, this was the city's main thoroughfare and where you'll find the Terme Stabiane, a typical 2nd century BC bath complex. Entering from the vestibule, bathers would stop off in the vaulted *apodyterium* before passing through to the *tepidarium* and *caldarium*. Particularly impressive is the stuccoed vault in the men's changing room, complete with whimsical images of *putti* (winged babies) and nymphs.

Towards the northeastern end of Via dell'Abbondanza, Casa della Venere in Conchiglia (House of the Venus Marina) has recovered well from the WWII bomb that damaged it in 1943. Although unexceptional from the outside, it houses a gorgeous peristyle (a colonnade-fringed courtyard) that looks onto a small, manicured garden. And it's here in the garden that you'll find the striking Venus fresco after which the house is named.

Anfiteatro

Just southeast of the Casa della Venere in Conchiglia, gladiatorial battles thrilled up to 20,000 spectators at the grassy anfiteatro. Built in 70 BC, it's the oldest known Roman amphitheatre in existence. Over the way, lithe ancients kept fit at the **Grande Palestra**, an athletics field with an impressive portico dating to the Augustan period. At its centre lie the remains of a swimming pool.

NAPLES POMPEII

WORTH A TRIP

VINTAGE VILLAS

Buried beneath the unappealing streets of Torre Annunziata, **Oplontis** was once a blue-ribbon seafront suburb under the administrative control of Pompeii. First discovered in the 18th century, only two of its houses have been unearthed, and only one, Villa Poppaea, is open to the public. This villa is a magnificent example of an *otium* villa (a residential building used for rest and recreation), thought to have belonged to Sabina Poppaea, Nero's second wife. Particularly outstanding are the richly coloured 1st-century wall paintings in the *triclinium* (dining room) and *calidarium* (hot bathroom) in the west wing. Marking the villa's eastern border is a garden with an envy-inducing swimming pool (17m by 61m). The villa is a straightforward 300m walk from Torre Annunziate Circumvesuviana train station.

South of Oplontis, **Stabiae** stood on the slopes of the Varano hill overlooking what was then the sea and is now modern Castellammare di Stabia. Here at Stabiae you can visit two villas: the 1st century BC Villa Arianna and the larger Villa San Marco, said to measure more than 11,000 sq metres. Neither is in mint condition, but the frescoes in Villa Arianna suggest that it must once have been quite something. Both are accessible by bus from Via Nocera Circumvesuviana station.

Some 3km north of Pompeii, the archaeological site of **Boscoreale** consists of a rustic country villa dating back to the 1st century BC, and a fascinating antiquarium showcasing artefacts from Pompeii, Herculaneum and the surround region. Among the more unsual items on display are shreds of Roman fabric, egg shells from Pompeii, and a carbonised loaf of bread. At the time of writing, getting here involved a 2km walk from Pompeii-Scavi-Villa dei Misteri Circumvesuviana station. Contact the Pompeii tourist office for further details.

Opening times are standard: 8.30am to 7.30pm (last entry 6pm), April to October, and 8.30am to 5pm (last entry 3.30pm), November to March. All three sites are covered by a single **ticket** (adult/reduced €5.50/2.75). The sites are also covered by a five-sites cumulative ticket (adult/reduced €20/10), which also includes Pompei and Herculaneum.

Casa del Fauno

From the Grande Palestra, backtrack along Via dell'Abbondanza and turn right into Via Stabiana to view some of Pompeii's grandest houses. Turn left into Via della Fortuna and then right down Via del Labirinto to get to Vicolo del Mercurio and the entrance to Casa del Fauno (House of the Faun), Pompeii's largest private house. Covering an entire *insula* (city block) and boasting two atria at its front end (humbler homes had only one), it is named after the delicate bronze statue in the *impluvium* (rain tank). It was here that early excavators found Pompeii's greatest mosaics, most of which are now housed in Naples' Museo Archeologico Nazionale (p49). Valuable on-site remainders include a beautiful, geometrically patterned marble floor.

A couple of blocks away, the **Casa del Poeta Tragico** (House of the Tragic Poet) features one of the world's first 'Beware of the Dog' (*Cave Canem*) warnings. To the north, the **Casa dei Vettii** on Via di Mercurio is home to a famous depiction of Priapus whose oversized phallus balances on a pair of scales...much to the anxiety of many a male observer.

Villa dei Misteri

From the Casa del Fauna, follow the road west and turn right into Via Consolare, which takes you out of the town through **Porta Ercolano**. Continue past **Villa di Diomede** and you'll come to the 90-room Villa dei Misteri, one of the most complete structures left standing in Pompeii. The

dionysiac frieze, the most important fresco still on site, spans the walls of the large dining room. One of the largest paintings from the ancient world, it depicts the initiation of a bride-to-be into the cult of Dionysus, the Greek god of wine. A farm for much of its life, the villa's own vino-making area is still visible at the northern end.

If travelling to the *scavi* (ruins) by Circumvesuviana train (€2.80 from Naples, €2.10 from Sorrento), alight at Pompeii-Scavi-Villa dei Misteri station, located beside the main entrance at Porta Marina. Signs direct those arriving by car from the A3 to the *scavi*.

Mt Vesuvius　　　　　　　　　VOLCANO
(www.parconazionaledelvesuvio.it; adult/reduced €8/5; ◷9am-6pm Jul & Aug, to 5pm Apr-Jun & Sep, to 4pm Mar & Oct, to 3pm Nov-Feb, ticket office closes 1hr before the crater) Since exploding into history in AD 79, Vesuvius has blown its top more than 30 times. The most devastating of these was in 1631, and the most recent in 1944. What redeems this lofty menace is the spectacular panorama from its **crater** – a breathtaking panorama that takes in sprawling city, sparkling islands, and the Monti Picentini, part of the Apennine mountains. Unbeknown to many, admission includes a free guided walk halfway around the crater. You'll find the guides at the entrance gate; ignore any requests for tips as they're obliged to guide you for free.

Whether arriving by bus or car, the end of the road is the summit car park and the ticket office. From here, a relatively easy 860m path leads up to the summit (allow 35 minutes), best tackled in trainers and with a sweater in tow (it can be chilly up top, even in summer). When the weather is bad the summit path is shut and bus departures are suspended.

The mountain itself was once higher than it currently stands, claiming a single summit rising to about 3000m rather than the 1281m of today. Its violent outburst in AD 79 not only drowned Pompeii in pumice and pushed the coastline back several kilometres but also destroyed much of the mountain top, creating a huge caldera and two new peaks.

Mt Vesuvius itself is the focal point of the **Parco Nazionale del Vesuvio** (Vesuvius National Park; www.parconazionaledelvesuvio.it), which offers nine interesting nature walks around the volcano. A map of the trails is available from the ticket office, with a free,

---

ⓘ PREPARING FOR POMPEII

If visiting Pompeii's ruins in summer, bring a hat, sun block and plenty of water. If you've got small children, try to visit in the early morning or late afternoon when the sun's not too hot. Unfortunately, there's not much you can do about the uneven surfaces, which are a challenge for strollers. To do justice to the place, allow at least three or four hours, longer if you want to go into detail. And don't forget to bring a passport or ID card to claim discounts or to hire an audioguide.

Mt Vesuvius

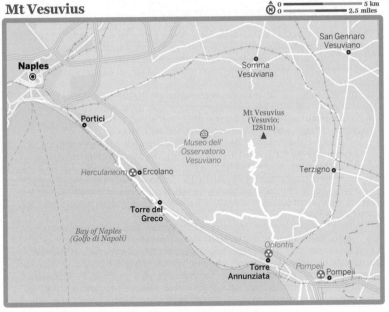

smaller version available on the website. Alternatively, **Naples Trips & Tours** (☑349 7155270; www.naplestripsandtours.com) runs a daily horseriding tour of the park (weather permitting). The tour, which costs €50 and runs for three to four hours, includes transfers to/from Naples or Ercolano-Scavi Circumvesuviana station, helmet, saddle, guide and (most importantly) coffee.

About halfway up the hill, the **Museo dell'Osservatorio Vesuviano** (Museum of the Vesuvian Observatory; ☑081 610 84 83; www.ov.ingv.it; admission free; ☉10am-2pm Sat & Sun) tells the history of 2000 years of Vesuvius-watching.

The easiest way to reach Mt Vesuvius is to get a bus from Ercolano up to the crater car park. **Vesuvio Express** (☑081 739 36 66; www.vesuvioexpress.it; Piazzale Stazione Circumvesuviana, Ercolano) operates buses every 40 minutes from 9.30am to 4pm daily. Buses depart from Piazzale Stazione Circumvesuviana, right outside Ercolano-Scavi station on the Circumvesuviana train line. The journey time is twenty minutes each way and return tickets (which include entry to the volcano summit) are €18.

If travelling by car, exit the A3 at Ercolano Portico and follow signs for the Parco Nazionale del Vesuvio.

✕ Eating

TOP CHOICE **President**   CAMPANIAN €€
(☑081 850 72 45; www.ristorantepresident.it; Piazza Schettini 12; meals €40; ☉closed Mon & dinner Sun Nov-Mar, closed 2 weeks Jan; 🖪FS to Pompei, 🖪Circumvesuviana to Pompei Scavi - Villa dei Misteri) With its dripping chandeliers, Bacharach melodies and breathtakingly gracious service, the President feels like a private dining room in an Audrey Hepburn film. Conducting the charm is owner Paolo Gramaglia, whose passion for local produce is only matched by the menu's creative brilliance, best savoured with a degustation menu (€40 to €70).

Let your tastebuds swoon over wonders like aubergine *millefoglie* with Cetara anchovies, mozzarella *filante* (melted mozzarella) and grated tarallo biscuit presented like a wrapped-up *caramella* (lolly). A word of warning: if you plan on catching a *treno regionale* (regional train) back to Naples from nearby Pompei station (a closer, more convenient option than the Pompei Scavi - Villa dei Misteri station on the Circumvesuviana train line), check train times on www.trenitalia.com first as the last service from Pompei can depart as early as 9.40pm.

THE ART OF THE NEAPOLITAN PRESEPE

Christmas nativity cribs may not be exclusive to Naples, but none match the artistic brilliance of the *presepe napoletano* (Neapolitan nativity crib). What sets the local version apart is its incredible attention to detail, from the life-like miniature *prosciutti* (hams) in the tavern to the lavishly costumed *pastori* (crib figurines or sculptures) adorning the newborn Christ.

While the origin of Christmas cribs stretches back to the early centuries of Christianity, Naples' homegrown *presepi* have their roots in 1535. It was in this year that a much-loved local priest by the name of Gaetano da Thiene ditched tradition, dressing his crib characters in Neapolitan garb instead of traditional biblical robes.

Da Thiene's crib makeover ignited a passion that would reach its zenith with the 18th century *presepe del Settecento* (crib of the 1700s). This often-epic crib was quite a departure from its humbler DIY sibling, the *presepe popolare* (common crib). While the setting of the *presepe popolare* was often dark, gloomy and subterranean, with only the nativity brightly illuminated (symbolising the light of salvation), its baroque spin-off was set in bucolic, sunlit European landscapes, its hues reflecting the palettes of the era's great artists.

Despite their differing scale and composition, both versions shared the same rich symbolism, from the tavern as a representation of sin to the stream or fountain as a symbol of purification. In the *presepe del Settecento*, the nativity itself was often set among the ruins of a pagan temple, reflecting both Christianity's triumph over paganism and a fascination with the century's archaeological discoveries, among them Pompeii.

For the nobility and the bourgeoisie of 18th-century Naples, the *presepe* allowed a convenient marriage of faith and ego, the crib becoming as much a symbol of wealth and good taste as a meditation on the Christmas miracle. The finest sculptors were commissioned and the finest fabrics used. Even the royals got involved: Charles III of Bourbon consulted the esteemed *presepe* expert, Dominican monk Padre Rocco, on the creation of his 5000-*pastore* spectacular, still on show at the Palazzo Reale (p55). Yet even this pales in comparison to the epic crib showcased at the Certosa e Museo di San Martino (p65), considered the world's greatest.

Centuries on, the legacy continues, with *presepe* and *pastore* peddlers dotted across the city. Sadly, many of these now sell mass-produced reproductions, with only a few workshops or studios completely handcrafting their *pastori* the old-fashioned way. Among the latter are Ars Neapolitana (p87) and La Scarabattola (p87), who share the honour with Sorrelle Corcione, Fratelli Sinno, and further out in suburban Torre del Greco, veteran *presepe* maestro, Salvatore Giordano.

These artisans remain true to the *presepe*'s golden age. Each *pastore*'s bust is molded from fine-grain clay on a damp wooden block called *il morto* (literally, 'the dead man'), commencing with the chest, then the neck and finally the head. After the basic bust is formed and aired for an hour, work begins on sculpting the details, from the neck muscles and nose to wrinkles. Tradition insists that the *pastore*'s bodily features reflect those of the past, hence the prevalence of missing teeth, warts, and goiters. Interestingly, some Neapolitans still wittily refer to the 'aesthetically challenged' as '*curiuso comm'a nu'pastore*' (as ugly as a crib figurine).

Once completed, the bust is fired in a kiln for eight hours before the character is given glass eyes and painted using either acrylic paint or traditional oil paint. The bust is then attached to the rest of the body (hemp thread wrapped around a metal skeleton) and – last but not least – adorned with an intricate, handmade costume.

TOP CHOICE **Viva Lo Re** CAMPANIAN €€
(☑081 739 02 07; www.vivalore.it; Corso Resina 261, Ercolano; meals €30; ☺Tue-Sat, lunch only Sun, closed Aug; ☒Circumvesuviana to Ercolano-Scavi) Set on the so-called *Miglio d'oro* (Golden Mile) – a once-glorious stretch of road graced by 18th-century villas – Viva Lo Re (Long Live the King) is a stylish, inviting haven, where vintage prints and bookshelves meet a superb wine list, gracious staff and

some of the best revamped regional cooking around.

Start on a high note with the artful antipasto, whose row of 'tastings' may include a *polpettina di baccalà* (salted cod patty), *crocchetta di taleggio con porcino* (taleggio and porcini croquette) and a ricotta-filled courgette flower. Topping it all off are some delectable desserts, like a heavenly strawberry tartlet.

Melius   DELI €
(☎081 850 25 98; Via Lepanto 156-160; ⊗8am-2pm & 4.30-8.30pm Mon-Sat, 8am-2pm Sun; ☒FS to Pompei) Beef up the larder (or picnic hamper) at this luscious gourmet deli, where local delicacies include fresh *mozzarella di bufala*, Graniano pasta, *sopressata Cilentana* (smoked salami from Cilento), citrusy Amalfi Coast marmalades and *liquore alla mela annurca*, a liqueur made using Annurca apples. For a self-catered treat, pick up some fragrant bread, a bottle of local Falanghina and some ready edibles; the peppery marinated aubergines and *pizza di scarole* (escarole pie) are equally divine.

❶ Getting There & Away

TRAIN Circumvesuviana (p270) operates frequent trains between Naples' Stazione Circumvesuviana (connected to Stazione Centrale) and Sorrento, stopping at Ercolano (€2.10 from Naples or Sorrento) and Pompeii (€2.80 from Naples, €2.10 from Sorrento). Alight at Ercolano-Scavi station for the Ruins of Herculanemum and Pompei Scavi–Villa dei Misteri station for the Ruins of Pompeii.

Regional trains connect central Pompei to Naples' Stazione Centrale.

BUS SITA (☎089 405 145; www.sitabus.it) buses for Pompeii depart every 30 minutes from Naples (€2.80), beside the central train station (Stazione Centrale). From Ercolano, Vesuvio Express (p103) operates buses every 40 minutes between 9.30am and 4pm (€18, including entry to the summit) to Mt Vesuvius.

CAR From Naples, the A3 runs southeast along the Bay of Naples. To reach the Ruins of Herculaneum, exit at Ercolano Portico and follow the signs to car parks near the site. Use the same exit for Mt Vesuvius, following the signs for the Parco Nazionale del Vesuvio. For Pompeii, use the Pompeii exit and follow signs to Pompei Scavi. Car parks (about €7 all day) are clearly marked and vigorously touted.

The Islands

Best Places to Eat

» Edivino (p115)
» Il Focolare (p130)
» Il Geranio (p115)
» Caracale (p138)

Best Places to Stay

» Hotel Villa Eva (p200)
» Mezzatorre Resort & Spa (p202)
» Hotel Semiramis (p202)
» Hotel La Vigna (p203)

Why Go?

Tossed like so many colourful dice into this beautiful velvet-blue bay, the islands here are justifiably famous and sought out. They are tantalisingly different as well. Procida, Ischia and Capri vary not just in ambience and landscape, but also in their sights, activities and size. Picturesque Procida is the smallest island of the trio: tiny, tranquil and unspoiled, and possible to explore in just a few hours. The fashionable flip-side is Capri, with its celebrity circuit of experiences, sights and shops; plan your day (and your footwear!) with care, especially if you're hoping to hike. Ischia is the largest island, so get your priorities straight beforehand: natural spas, botanical gardens, hidden coves and exceptional dining are a taster of what's on offer. If that all sounds too challenging, make a bee line for the beaches – they are the Bay of Naples' best.

Road Distance (KM)

	Capri	Procida	Ischia	Sorrento	Pozzuoli
Procida	47				
Ischia	33	09			
Sorrento	18	68	51		
Pozzuoli	32	12	20	32	
Naples	33	25	32	28	20

Getting Around

Unless you travel by helicopter, ferries are the only way to go if you are visiting the islands Procida, Ischia and Capri in the Bay of Naples. Note that ferries departing from Positano and Amalfi operate solely from Easter to September. At other times of the year, you will have to catch the ferry or hydrofoil from Naples or Sorrento. All three islands have an excellent public transport infrastructure and also provide scope for hiking and cycling.

THREE PERFECT DAYS

Day 1: Simple pleasures on Procida

Escape the clamour and crowds of Naples and enjoy a day of tranquillity a short ferry hop away on this picturesque, unspoilt island. After a gentle stroll in the *centro storico* (historic centre), pull up a chair at lovely Marina Corricella for a simple meal of fresh seafood overlooking the fishing boats. Take an afternoon boat trip around the island's evocative hidden coves.

Day 2: Ischia's gardens, shops & spas

Plan on an early arrival in Ischia, then head for the botanical gardens of La Mortella for a wander along the shady cool pathways surrounded by exotic plants. Lunch should be spent near the beach at scenic Sant'Angelo. In the afternoon, catch a water taxi to Terme Cavascuro, the island's oldest natural spa, for an afternoon of restorative self-pampering. Round off the day poking around the eclectic mix of shops on Via Roma, within walking distance of the ferry pier.

Day 3: Capri's natural beauty & glamour

Turn up before the day trippers descend and join the local who's who brigade at the emblematic square La Piazzetta. Leave the surrounding sophisticated strut of shops behind as you head towards the nearby Giardini di Augusto terraced gardens and some of the best views in Capri. Pick a terraced restaurant overlooking the water then enjoy the beauty of the island's trails with either a country amble or a more demanding hike.

Accommodation

In Capri you can stay in celeb-style luxury, a stylish B&B or somewhere comfortable, modern and in the midrange bracket. Ischia and Procida have a wider price range, but all three are firmly seasonal, with most hotels closed from around November to Easter. For more information, see the Accommodation chapter.

DON'T MISS

Getting away from the tourists, particularly on Ischia and Capri, and particularly in midsummer. Duck down side streets, hike the interior, hire a boat, rent a bike....just go and explore.

Best Views

» Monte Solaro (Capri; p111)

» Villa Jovis (Capri; p110)

» Marina Corricella (Procida; p135)

» Monte Epomeo (Ischia; p129)

Best Swimming Spots

» Punta Carena (Capri; p113)

» Spiaggia di Chiaia (Procida; p136)

» Punta Caruso (Ischia; p130)

» Grotta Azzurra (Capri; p118)

Resources

» **Capri Online** (www.caprionline.it) Has information about all aspects of Capri.

» **Ischia Online** (www.ischiaonline.it) A good all-round website.

» **Isola di Procida** (www.isoladiprocida.it) Includes an accommodation booking service.

» **Anacapri Life** (www.anacapri-life.com) Has news and information about Anacapri.

» **Ischia and Procida Islands Tourist Office** (www.infoischiaprocida.it) The local tourist office website.

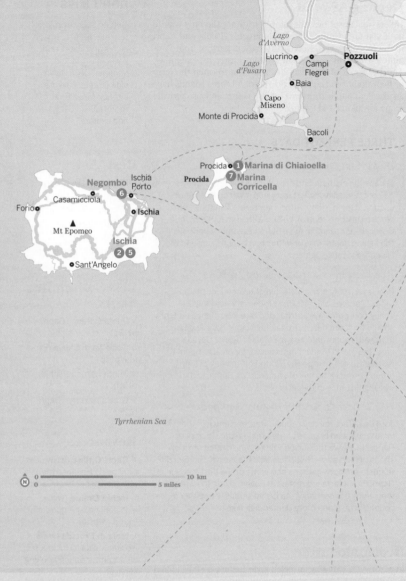

Lago d'Averno

Lucrino

Campi Flegrei

Pozzuoli

Lago d'Fusaro

Baia

Capo Miseno

Monte di Procida

Bacoli

Procida ❶ **Marina di Chiaioella**

Procida ❼ **Marina Corricella**

Negombo

Ischia Porto ❻

Forio

Casamicciola

❶ **Ischia**

Mt Epomeo

Ischia ❷ ❺

Sant'Angelo

Tyrrhenian Sea

0 ——— 10 km
0 ——— 5 miles

The Islands Highlights

❶ Have a lazy lunch at a seafood restaurant overlooking the bay at Procida's **Marina di Chiaiolella** (p136)

❷ Hire a scooter in **Ischia** (p122) and discover the hidden charms of the island

❸ Take the chairlift to the top of **Monte Solaro** (p111), the highest point on Capri

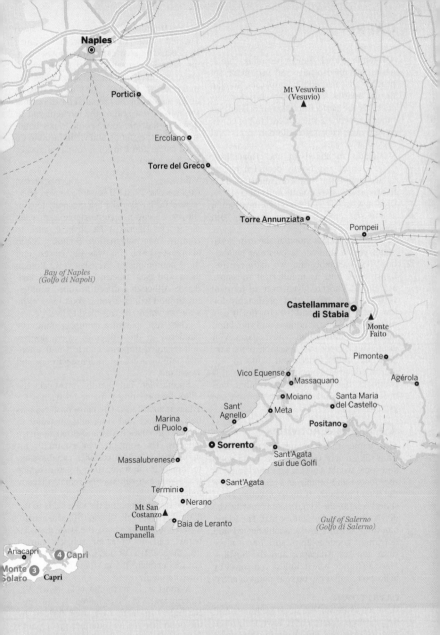

Naples

Portici

Mt Vesuvius
(Vesuvio)

Ercolano

Torre del Greco

Torre Annunziata

Pompeii

*Bay of Naples
(Golfo di Napoli)*

Castellammare
di Stabia

Monte
Faito

Pimonte

Agérola

Vico Equense

Massaquano

Moiano

Santa Maria
del Castello

Sant'
Agnello

Meta

Marina
di Puolo

Positano

Sorrento

Sant'Agata
sui due Golfi

Massalubrense

Sant'Agata

Termini

Nerano

Mt San
Costanzo

Baia de Leranto

*Gulf of Salerno
(Golfo di Salerno)*

Punta
Campanella

Anacapri

④ Capri

Monte ③
Solaro

Capri

④ Treat yourself to a drink
in **La Piazzetta** (p118), the
centre of cafe life on Capri

⑤ Flop back on one of the
pristine sandy stretches in
Ischia (p130)

⑥ Indulge in a soothing dip
and massage at spa park
Negombo (p126)

⑦ Hang out with the
fishermen in the pastel-hued
village of **Marina Corricella**
(p135)

CAPRI

POP 12,130

A legendary idyll: Capri's beguiling combination of fabled beauty and hedonistic appeal has charmed Roman emperors, Russian revolutionaries and showbiz stars for decades. It's the perfect microcosm of Mediterranean appeal – a smooth cocktail of chichi piazzas and cool cafes, Roman ruins and rugged seascapes.

Already inhabited in the Palaeolithic period, Capri was briefly occupied by the Greeks before the Emperor Augustus made it his private playground and Tiberius retired here in AD 27. Its modern incarnation as a tourist centre dates from the early 20th century.

It's also a hugely popular day-trip destination and a summer favourite of holidaying VIPs. Inevitably, the two main centres, Capri Town and its uphill rival Anacapri, are almost entirely given over to tourism with the high prices that predictably follow. But explore beyond the effortlessly cool cafes and designer boutiques, and you'll find that Capri retains an unspoiled charm, with grand villas, overgrown vegetable plots, sunbleached peeling stucco and banks of brilliantly coloured bougainvillea. All of this overlooks the deep blue water that laps unseen into secluded coves and mysterious grottoes.

◎ Sights & Activities

The name Capri comes, appropriately, from the ancient Greek *kaprie* (wild goat) and some would say that you need to be as sure footed and nimble as a goat to explore the island properly. If time (or your pair of shoes) is tight, the island's sights may be visited by funicular, bus and/or taxi. The island has three distinct areas: sophisticated and downright good-looking Capri Town; more rural, low-key Anacapri; and the bustling Marina Grande which, unless you travel by helicopter, is likely to be your point of entry.

CAPRI TOWN

With its whitewashed stone buildings and tiny, car-free streets, Capri Town feels more film set than real life. A diminutive model of upmarket Mediterranean chic, it's a pristine mix of luxury hotels, expensive bars, fancy restaurants and designer boutiques. In summer the centre swells with crowds of camera-wielding day trippers and gangs of the glossy rich.

Piazza Umberto I   PIAZZA

Located beneath the clock tower and framed by see-and-be-seen cafes, this showy, open-air salon is central to your Capri experience, especially in the evening when the main activity in these parts is dressing up and hanging out. Be prepared for the cost of these front row seats – the moment you sit down for a drink, you're going to pay handsomely for the grandstand views (around €6 for a coffee and €16 for a couple of glasses of white wine).

Villa Jovis   HISTORIC BUILDING

(Jupiter's Villa; ☑081 837 06 34; Via Amaiuri; adult/reduced €2/1; ⊗9am–1hr before sunset) East of the town centre, a comfortable 2km walk along Via Tiberio, Villa Jovis is sure to capture your imagination. Standing 354m above sea level, this was the largest and most sumptuous of the island's 12 Roman villas and was Tiberius' main Capri residence. Although reduced to ruins, wandering around will give you a good idea of the scale on which Tiberius liked to live.

This vast pleasure complex famously pandered to the emperor's saucy desires, and included imperial quarters and extensive bathing areas set in dense gardens and woodland.

Spectacular but hardly practical, the villa's location posed major headaches for Tiberius' architects. The main problem was how to collect and store enough water to supply the villa's baths and 3000-sq-metre gardens. The solution they eventually hit upon was to build a complex canal system to transport rainwater to four giant storage tanks; you can still spy the remains clearly today.

The stairway behind the villa leads to the 330m-high Salto di Tiberio (Tiberius' Leap), a sheer cliff from where, the story goes, Tiberius had out-of-favour subjects hurled into the sea. True or not, the stunning views are real enough; if you suffer from vertigo, tread carefully.

A short walk from the villa, down Via Tiberio and Via Matermània, is the Arco Naturale – a huge rock arch formed by the pounding sea and another great photo opportunity.

Chiesa di Santo Stefano   CHURCH

(Piazza Umberto I; ⊗8am-8pm) Overlooking Piazza Umberto I, this baroque 17th-century church boasts a well-preserved marble floor (taken from Villa Jovis) and a statue of San

Costanzo, Capri's patron saint. Note the pair of languidly reclining patricians in the chapel to the south of the main altar, who seem to mirror some of the mildly debauched folk in the cafes outside. Beside the northern chapel is a reliquary with a saintly bone that reputedly saved Capri from the plague in the 19th century.

FREE Certosa di San Giacomo   MONASTERY
(☑081 837 62 18; Viale Certosa 40; ⊙9am-2pm Tue-Sun) This picturesque monastery is generally considered to be the finest remaining example of Caprese architecture and today houses a school, library, temporary exhibition space and a museum with some evocative 17th-century paintings. Be sure to look at the two cloisters which have a real sense of faded glory (the smaller dates to the 14th century, the larger to the 16th century).

The history is a harrowing one: it became the stronghold of the island's powerful Carthusian fraternity and was viciously attacked during Saracen pirate raids in the 16th century. A century later, monks retreated here to avoid the plague and were rewarded by an irate public (who they should have been tending), who tossed corpses over the walls. There are some soothing 17th-century frescoes in the church, which should hopefully serve as an antidote as you contemplate the monastery's dark past.

To reach here take Via Vittorio Emanuele, to the east of Piazza Umberto 1, which meanders down to the monastery.

FREE Giardini di Augusto   GARDENS
(Gardens of Augustus; ⊙dawn-dusk) Get away from the Capri crowds by heading southwest from the Certosa di San Giacomo monastery where, at the end of Via G Matteotti, you'll come across the unexpected green oasis of the colourful Giardini di Augusto. Founded by the Emperor Augustus, you should spend a few minutes contemplating the breathtaking view from here: gaze ahead to the Isole Faraglioni and the three dramatic limestone pinnacles that rise vertically out of the sea.

Measuring 109m, 81m and 104m respectively, the pinnacles are home to a rare blue lizard that was once thought to be unique to the Faraglioni but has since been found on the Sicilian coast. While a picture of the lizards from here is sadly beyond the capacity of even the most sophisticated camera lens, a photo from here should still impress the folks back home. From the gardens, pretty

Via Krupp winds down a bend to Marina Piccola, past a bust of Lenin overlooking the road from a nearby platform; no one seems to know who placed it here, or why.

ANACAPRI & AROUND

Traditionally Capri Town's more subdued neighbour, Anacapri is no stranger to tourism. The focus is largely limited to Villa San Michele di Axel Munthe and the souvenir stores on the main streets. Delve further though and you'll discover that Anacapri is still, at heart, the laid-back, rural village that it's always been.

Villa San Michele
di Axel Munthe   HISTORIC BUILDING
(☑081 837 14 01; Via Axel Munthe; adult/reduced €5/free; ⊙9am-6pm) The former home of self-aggrandising Swedish doctor Axel Munthe, San Michele di Axel Munthe should be included on every visitor's itinerary. Built on the site of the ruins of a Roman villa, the gardens make a beautiful setting for a tranquil stroll, with pathways flanked by immaculate flowerbeds. There are also superb views from here, plus some fine photo props in the form of Roman sculptures.

If you are here between July and September, you may be able to catch one of the classical concerts that take place in the gardens. Check the Axel Munthe Foundation website for the current program and reservation information.

TOP CHOICE Seggiovia del
Monte Solaro   MOUNTAIN
(☑081 837 14 28; single/return €7.50/10; ⊙9.30am-5pm) A fast and painless way to reach Capri's highest peak, the Seggiovia del Monte Solaro chairlift whisks you to the top of the mountain in a tranquil, beautiful ride of just 12 minutes. The views from the top are outstanding – on a clear day, you can see the entire Bay of Naples, the Amalfi Coast and the islands of Ischia and Procida.

If all that camera clicking has worked up an appetite, there's a cafeteria here that serves snacks, drinks and ice creams.

Casa Rossa   MUSEUM
(☑081 838 21 93; Via Guiseppe Orlandi 78, Anacapri; admission €3; ⊙10am-1.30pm & 5.30pm-8pm) The striking Moroccan-style 'Red House' was built by an American colonel, John Clay MacKown, in 1876. Constructed around a 16th-century defensive tower, the building houses an eclectic collection

Capri

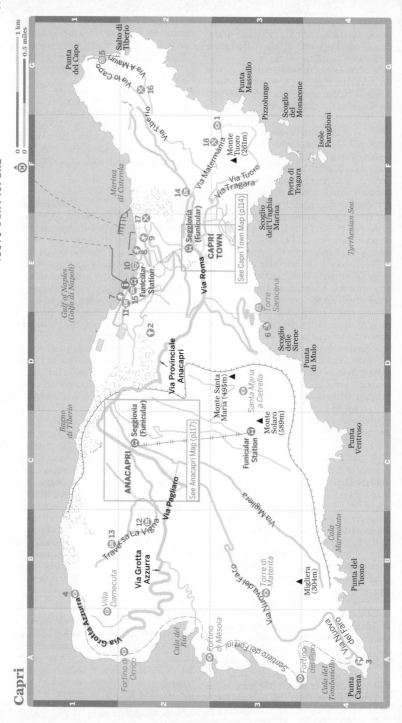

0   1 km
0   0.5 miles

Punta del Capo
Salto di Tiberio
Via A Maiuri
Via lo Capo
16
Via Tiberio
18
1
Monte Tuoro (261m)
Via Tuoro
Via Tragara
Punta Massullo
Pizzolungo
Scoglio del Monacone
Isole Faraglioni
Marina di Caterola
14
17
9
8
10
Seggiovia (Funicular)
CAPRI TOWN
Via Matermania
Via Roma
See Capri Town Map (p114)
Porto di Tragara
Scoglio dell'Unghia Marina
Tyrrhenian Sea
Gulf of Naples (Golfo di Napoli)
7
11
15
Funicular Station
2
Via Provinciale Anacapri
Torre Saracena
Scoglio delle Sirene
6
Punta di Mulo
Bagno di Tiberio
Monte Santa Maria (495m)
Santa Maria a Cetrella
Monte Solaro (589m)
Seggiovia (Funicular)
ANACAPRI
See Anacapri Map (p117)
Funicular Station
Via Pagliaro
Via Migliera
Punta Ventroso
Cala Marmolata
13
12
Via Grotta Azzurra
Traversa La Vigna
Via Nuova del Faro
Torre di Materita
Migliera (304m)
Punta del Tuono
Villa Damecuta
4
Via Grotta Azzurra
Fortino di Orrico
Cala del Rio
Sentiero dei Fortini
Fortino di Mesola
Fortino del Pino
Cala del Tombosiello
Punta Carena
3
Via Nuova del Faro

Capri

of 19th-century paintings, including some evocative scenes of Capri by Gonsalvo Carelli (1818–1900), and by French painter Eduard Alexandre Sain, who really captures the spirit of 19th century Capri in spirited works such as the 'Wedding in Capri'.

The museum also houses a colossal 1st century Roman statue discovered during excavations of the Blue Grotto in the early 19th century.

Chiesa di San Michele CHURCH
(Piazza San Nicola; adult/reduced €2/free; ◷9.30am-7pm) If you appreciate the colour, intricate patterns and historical tradition of antique majolica tiles, check out this stunning church. The glorious octagonal 18th-century majolica-tiled floor vividly depicts Adam and Eve along with a bizarre animal menagerie, including a unicorn, bull, several goats and an elephant.

Faro LIGHTHOUSE
(Punta Carena) Rising above Punta Carena, Capri's rugged southwesterly point, is the *faro*, Italy's second-tallest and most powerful lighthouse. The rocks nearby are a great place to swim in the summer with lots of rocks to dive (safely) from and clear turquoise water.

If this sounds like something you'd take the plunge and do, then hop on the bus that runs from the centre of Anacapri every 20 minutes to the *faro* in summer (if you are a real chill seeker, it runs every 40 minutes in winter).

MARINA GRANDE
Capri's main port is a shabbily attractive place and very Italian, with little evidence of the cosmopolitan glitz that awaits up the hill. If you're desperate for a swim, there's a 200m-long pebble beach to the west of the port.

Chiesa di San Costanzo CHURCH
(Via Marina Grande) This is the island's oldest church and the only real sight around the marina. Dating from the 5th century, this whitewashed *chiesa* is dedicated to the island's patron saint, who settled on the island after escaping a vicious storm en route from Constantinople to Rome. Its original incarnation was built over an earlier Roman construction, although the Byzantine version you see today is the result of a 10th-century makeover.

Sercomar DIVING
(✆081 837 87 81; www.capriseaservice.com; Via Colombo 64; ◷closed Nov; ⓓ) Offering various diving packages, costing from €100 for a single dive (maximum of three people) to €150 for an individual dive and €350 for a four-session beginner's course. They also organise children's snorkelling classes from €35 for 30 minutes (12 years or over).

Banana Sport BOAT HIRE
(✆081 837 51 88; 2hrs rental €75, day €175; ◷Jun-Sep) Located on the eastern edge of the waterfront, Banana Sport hires out five-person motorised dinghies, allowing you to explore the island's more secluded coves and grottoes. You can also visit the popular swimming spot **Bagno di Tiberio**, a small inlet west of Marina Grande. It's said that Tiberius once swam here, although he wouldn't have had to pay €8.50 to access the private beach as you will.

Capri Whales BOAT HIRE
(✆081 837 58 33; www.capriwhales.it; Marina Grande 17; 2hrs rental, €90; ◷May-Oct; ⓓ) These

Capri Town

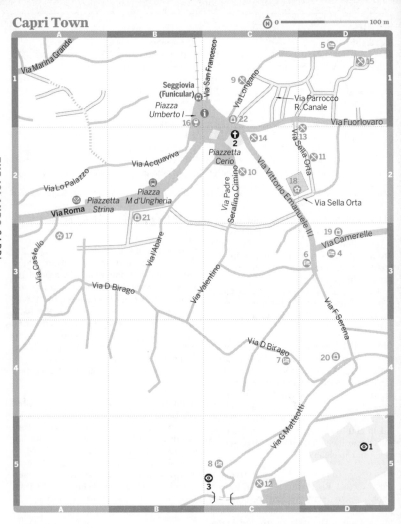

dinghies are well equipped for families, with coolers, snorkelling gear, floats and water toys.

MARINA PICCOLA

Little more than a series of private bathing facilities, Marina Piccola is on the southern side of the island, directly south of Marina Grande. A short bus ride from Capri Town, or a downhill 15-minute walk, it has a 50m-long public pebble beach hemmed in by the **Scoglio delle Sirene** (Rock of the Sirens) at the western end and the **Torre Saracena** (Saracen Tower) at the other. The swim-

ming's not great but the two rocks rising out of the water about 10m offshore make excellent diving boards.

Bagni Lo Scoglio delle Sirene   CANOEING
(☑081 837 02 21; ☺Jun-Sep) You can hire canoes at a couple of places along the beach here, including this reliable outfit which charges around €15 per hour for a double canoe or €8 for a single.

✗ Eating

Traditional Italian food served in traditional Italian trattorias is what you'll find on Capri.

Capri Town

THE ISLANDS CAPRI

Prices are high but drop noticeably the further you get from Capri Town.

The island's culinary gift to the world is *insalata caprese*, a salad of fresh tomatoes, basil and mozzarella drizzled with olive oil. Look out for *caprese* cheese, a cross between mozzarella and ricotta, and *ravioli caprese*, ravioli stuffed with *caprese* cheese and herbs.

Many restaurants, like the hotels, close over winter.

CAPRI TOWN & AROUND

TOP CHOICE **Edivino** CAMPANIAN €€
(☎081 837 83 64; Via Sella Orta; meals €20; ☺Fri-Wed, dinner only Jun-Sep) Look hard for the faint sign; this place is a well-kept secret. Step inside the front door and you land squarely in what resembles a traditional sitting room, the only hint that this is a restaurant are the tantalising aromas and the distant tinkle of glasses. The food changes daily, according to whatever is fresh from the garden or market.

Some tables are outside amid lemon trees, while other seating is spread throughout a couple of more homey rooms, decorated with antiques, family pics and a fireplace.

Il Geranio SEAFOOD €€€
(☎081 837 06 16; www.geraniocapri.com; Via G Matteotti 8; meals €50; ☺Apr-Oct) Time to pop the question, celebrate that anniversary or quell those pre-departure blues? The terrace here has stunning views over the pine trees to the sea and beyond, to the extraordinary Faraglioni di Capri rocks. Seafood is the speciality, particularly the salt baked fish. Other good choices include octopus salad and linguini with saffron and mussels. Dress to impress: it's that kind of place.

Al Grottino CAMPANIAN €€
(☎081 837 05 84; Via Longano 27; meals from €30; ☺Apr-Oct) Two minutes' walk from La Piazzetta down a narrow alley, you can expect a queue here. A real old timer, dating from 1937, Al Grottino was a renowned VIP dining spot in the '50s and '60s (check out the photos in the window – hang on – how did Jerry Springer wind up here!).

It continues to lure locals and visitors with traditional Neapolitan dishes like *ravioli al ragú* (ravioli in a meat and garlic sauce) and specials like *cocotte* (handmade pasta with mixed seafood served in a paella-like pan). The small dining space is reassuringly traditional, right down to the decorative chianti bottles.

L'Approdo CAMPANIAN €€
(☎081 837 89 90; www.approdocapri.com; Piazzeta Ferraro 8, Marina Grande; pizzas from €4, meals €25) If you have arrived on the ferry with an appetite, head here; a three-minute walk to the left from where you disembark. You can easily fill up on the superb antipasti spread (€15) and the pizzas are also tasty and varied – try the *sfilatino* with ricotta, ham and mozzarella.

Seafood is pricier but the fish is as fresh as the day's catch, and includes spiny lobster grill and seafood risotto. There are picturesque views of the colourful fishing boats and nets from the sprawling outdoor terrace, with little to remind you of Capri's fabled glitz up the hill.

La Capannina
TRATTORIA €€€

(📞081 837 07 32; Via le Botteghe 12; meals €50; ☉mid-Mar–Oct) Dating back to the 1930s, this is the island's most famous traditional trattoria and a long-time favourite on the celebrity circuit. Set up to look like a Hollywood version of a rustic eatery – pink tablecloths, pink roses, hanging copper pots and carved wooden chairs – it serves a classic island menu of comfort food.

Popular dishes include high-quality seafood pasta, *ravioli caprese*, grilled meat and fresh fish, as well as the speciality, *linguine al sugo di scorfano* (flat ribbons of pasta with scorpion fish). Reservations are highly recommended.

La Savardina da Edouardo
CAMPANIAN €€

(📞081 837 63 00; Via lo Capo 8; meals €30; ☉Mar-Oct) You'll build up a hearty appetite as you stroll up to this laid-back restaurant in the Capri countryside. But as you collapse on the open-air terrace under the lemon trees and look out to Ischia in the hazy distance, you'll appreciate the effort. Family run, the food is great, too. Dishes are made with local produce and are unapologetically simple. For proof, try the grilled mozzarella with lemon leaves, followed by succulent lamb chops or one of the ravioli dishes.

Scialapopola
TRATTORIA €€

(📞081 837 90 54; Via Gradoni Sopramonte 6-8; meals from €25) Tucked up a side street, this is a welcoming place jauntily decorated with strings of peppers and tambourines hung with ribbons. The menu includes such homespun classics as *pasta e ceci con noci* (pasta with chickpeas and nuts), as well as some international-style surprises, like vegetable couscous. They have a bustling take away counter that also dishes up pizza.

Le Grottelle
CAMPANIAN €€

(📞081 837 57 19; Via Arco Naturale 13; meals around €28; ☉Apr-Oct) This is a great place to impress your partner. Not so much for the food, which is decent enough – think simple pasta dishes followed by grilled fish, chicken or rabbit – but for its atmospheric setting. About 150m from the Arco Naturale. It's got two dining areas, one set in a cave, the other, more appealing, on a terrace perched above a wooded hillside that slopes dramatically down to the sea.

Trattoria da Giovanni a Gradola
TRATTORIA €

(Grotta Azzurra; meals €18; ☉Apr-Oct) This laidback, sand-between-your-toes trattoria is just beyond the swish bathing facilities at the Grotta Azzurra. The setting is lovely for a summer lunch, with basic wooden tables on a narrow terrace overlooking the deep blue sea. Menu stalwarts include *parmigiana di melanzane* (baked aubergine with tomato and Parmesan), fried fish and *pasta e fagioli* (pasta and bean stew).

Raffaele Buonacore
SNACKS €

(📞081 837 78 26; Via Vittorio Emanuele III 35; snacks €2-4.50; ☉Mar-Oct; 👶) Ideal for a quick fill-up, this popular snack bar does a roaring trade in savoury and sweet treats, including frittatas, *panini* (sandwiches), pastries, waffles and ice cream. Hard to beat, though, are the delicious *sfogliatelle* (cinnamon-infused ricotta in a puff-pastry shell) and the featherlight speciality *caprilu al limone* (lemon and almond cakes) for just €0.90.

Donna Rachele
TRATTORIA €€

(📞081 837 53 87; www.donnarachele.com; Via Padre Serafino Cimmino 2; pizza from €6, meals €25) Tucked away in a corner, this place has a traditional trattoria atmosphere, with small rooms, tiled pictures and walls lined with bottles. There are a couple of tables on the outside terraces. Vegetarians will do well with the antipasti choices like grilled artichokes, sautéed spinach, and white beans, while the seafood lovers will enjoy specialities on the main menu like *moscardini* (octopus baked in a pizza-like-crust) and traditional Neapolitan fish soup.

ANACAPRI & AROUND

La Rondinella
ITALIAN €€

(📞081 837 12 23; Via Guiseppe Orlandi 295; meals €28; ☉Fri-Mon) La Rondinella has a relaxed, rural feel and remains one of Anacapri's most consistently good restaurants; apparently Graham Greene had a favourite corner table here. The menu features a number of Italian classics such as *saltimbocca alla Romana* (veal slices with ham and sage).

For something different, try chef Michele's *linguine alla ciammura*, a delicious pasta dish with a creamy white sauce of anchovies, garlic and parsley. Top it all off with a slice of *torta di mandorle* (chocolate and almond tart).

Anacapri

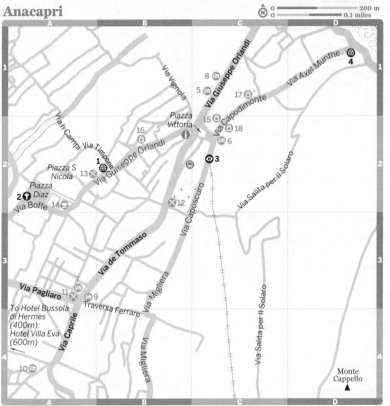

Anacapri

⊚ Sights

🛏 Sleeping

⊗ Eating

☕ Drinking

🛍 Shopping

Le Arcate   CAMPANIAN **€€**
(☎081 837 33 25; Via de Tommaso 24; meals €30)
This is the restaurant that the locals recommend – and frequent. An unpretentious place with hanging baskets of ivy, sunny yellow tablecloths and well-aged terracotta tiles, it specialises in delicious *primi* (first courses) and pizzas. A real show stopper is the *risotto con polpa di granchio, rughetta*

THE ISLANDS CAPRI

DON'T MISS

GROTTA AZZURA

Capri's single most famous attraction is the **Grotto Azzura** (Blue Grotto; adult/reduced €12.50/free; ⊙9am–5pm; 🚹), a stunning sea cave illuminated by an other-worldly blue light.

Long known to local fishermen, it was rediscovered by two Germans – writer Augustus Kopisch and painter Ernst Fries – in 1826. Subsequent research, however, revealed that Emperor Tiberius had built a quay in the cave around AD 30, complete with a *nymphaeum*. You can still see the carved Roman landing stage towards the rear of the cave.

Measuring 54m by 30m and rising to a height of 15m, the grotto is said to have sunk by up to 20m in prehistoric times, blocking every opening except the 1.3m-high entrance. And this is the key to the magical blue light. Sunlight enters through a small underwater aperture and is refracted through the water; this, combined with the reflection of the light off the white sandy seafloor, produces the vivid blue effect to which the cave owes its name.

The easiest way to visit is to take a boat tour from Marina Grande. A return trip will cost €18.50, comprising a return motorboat to the cave, the rowing boat into the cave itself and admission fee; allow a good hour. The singing 'captains' are included in the price, so don't feel any obligation if they push for a tip.

The grotto is closed if the sea is too choppy and swimming in the cave is forbidden, although you can swim outside the entrance – get a bus to Grotta Azzurra, take the stairs down to the right and dive off the small concrete platform.

e scaglie di parmigiano (risotto with crab meat, rocket and shavings of Parmesan).

Trattoria Il Solitario　　　　TRATTORIA €
(☑081 837 13 82; Via Giuseppe Orlandi 96; pizzas from €4.50, meals around €20; ⊙Apr-Oct; 🚹) This is the nearest you will get to being invited into someone's home. Tables are set in a small backyard with lemon trees and children's toys in the corner, and the whole ambience is one of unhurried holiday time.

The unremarkable menu lists the usual island fare – pasta and seafood, grilled meat and pizzas – but the helpings are large and the quality high. The pizzas include a vast *pizza bianche* choice, which is handy if you're tiring of tomatoes.

🍷 Drinking & Entertainment

Capri's nightlife is a showy business. The main activity is dressing up and hanging out, ideally at one of the four cafes on La Piazzetta (Piazza Umberto 1). Aside from the cafes, the nightlife here is fairly staid, with surprisingly few nightclubs, given the penchant for the locals to glitz up and strut their stuff.

Bar Pulalli　　　　WINE BAR
(☑081 837 41 08; Piazza Umberto 1, Capri Town; ⊙noon-3pm & 7pm-midnight Wed-Mon) Grab a table on the outside terrace to discreetly check out the classy crowd in the piazza

below. Choose from an excellent selection of wines from all over Italy (Sicily, Sardinia, Puglia, and Basilicata), ranging from a reasonable €12 to the triple-hiccup price of €250 a bottle. Order an accompanying plate of cheese and salami (€12), or the grilled prawns (€15), but just don't toss the shells into those fancy hair dos below!

Taverna Anema e Core　　　　CLUB
(☑081 837 64 61; www.anemaecore.com; Via Sella Orta 39E, Capri Town; ⊙Apr-Oct) Lying beyond a humble exterior is one of the island's most famous nightspots, Taverna Anema e Core, run by the charismatic Guido Lembo. This smooth and sophisticated bar-cum-nightclub attracts an appealing mixture of super chic and casually dressed punters, here for the relaxed atmosphere and regular live music, including unwaveringly authentic Neapolitan guitar strumming and singing.

Guarrancino　　　　LIVE MUSIC
(☑081 837 05 14; Via Castello 7, Capri Town; ⊙Apr-Oct) Located under the arches, this place dates back to 1972, when brothers Brun and Gianni Lembo started playing the songs they learned from their father, the original owner. Today you can warble along with the best of them during a lively sing-song show that sounds naff but has a heady good-time holiday atmosphere.

Caffè Michelangelo CAFE

(Via Giuseppe Orlandi 138, Anacapri) It's not that flashy but the position of the delightful Caffè Michelangelo, on a street flanked by tasteful shops and located near two lovely piazzas, makes it a perfect spot for indulging in a little people-watching-cum-cocktail time. Large cushioned chairs and a raised terrace add to the kick-back appeal.

Shopping

Boasting more designer boutiques per square metre than almost anywhere else on earth, Capri's shopping scene is conservative and expensive. Along the town's two main strips, Via Vittorio Emanuele III and Via Camarelle, you'll find most of the fashion big guns as well as a number of jewellery and shoe shops. If you are looking for souvenirs or gourmet goodies, lemons reign supreme, pictured on everything from T-shirts to tea cloths. The island is famous for its perfume and *limoncello*. The former smells like lemons and the latter tastes like sweet lemon vodka.

TOP CHOICE Pop Gallery CERAMICS

(☑081 978 05 13; Via Capodimonte 24, Anacapri; ☺Apr-Oct) Grown weary of the ubiquitous lemon motif? Then this cutting-edge showroom will delight and inspire with its modern sculptures and objets d'art by Italian artists. The faux abalone pieces are particularly ingenious, as are the sculpted heads with their bad-hair-day sea sponge bouffant hairdos in vivid colours sculpted by Paolo Sandulli. You can also visit his workshop in Praiano.

La Parissienne FASHION

(☑081 837 02 83; www.laparisiennecapri.it; Piazza Umberto 1, 7, Capri Town) First opened in 1906 (yes, that is not a misprint!), and best known for introducing Capri pants in the 1960s – famously worn by Audrey Hepburn – who bought them from here, La Parissienne can run you up a made-to-measure pair within a day. They also sell off-the-hook Capri pants (from €200).

Apparently Clark Gable was another Hollywood star who favoured the fashions

THE ISLANDS CAPRI

CELEBRITY ISLAND

A byword for Mediterranean chic, Capri has long enjoyed a reputation as a celebrity haunt.

The first big name to decamp here was Emperor Tiberius in AD 27. A man of sadistic sexual perversions – at least if the Roman author Suetonius is to be believed – he had 12 villas built on the island, including the vast Villa Jovis. He also left deep scars and until modern times, his name was equated with evil by the islanders. When the Swedish doctor Axel Munthe first began picking about the Roman ruins on the island in the early 20th century and built his villa on the site of a Tiberian palace, locals would observe that it was all 'roba di Tiberio' – Tiberius' stuff.

But more than Tiberius' capers, it was the discovery of the Grotta Azzurra in 1826 that paved the way for Capri's celebrity invasion. As news of the spectacular cave spread, so artists, intellectuals, industrialists and writers began to visit, attracted by the island's isolated beauty and, in some cases, the availability of the local lads. An early habitué, Alfred Krupp, the German industrialist and arms manufacturer, was involved in a gay scandal, while author Norman Douglas and French count Jacques Fersen set all manner of tongues wagging.

The island also proved an escape for Russian revolutionaries. In 1905 the author Maxim Gorky moved to Capri after failing to topple the Russian Tsar, and five years later Lenin stopped by for a visit.

In the course of the early 20th century, the Chilean poet Pablo Neruda and German author Thomas Mann visited regularly, British writers Compton Mackenzie and Graham Greene lived here for extended periods and Britain's wartime singer Gracie Fields retired here.

More recently, singer Mariah Carey bought a holiday villa here, Liz Hurley was seen shopping for a wedding dress and Leonardo di Caprio was spotted sipping a coffee at a pavement cafe. It's Hollywood stars like this who help keep Capri's reputation alive and its overworked paparazzi in business.

FOUR GREAT CAPRI WALKS

Surprisingly, for such a small place, Capri offers some memorable hiking. A network of well-maintained paths weaves its way across the island, leading through areas that even in the height of summer are all but deserted. The following are four of the most popular and best known walks; the tourist office can provide you with maps.

Arco Naturale To Punta Dell'arcera

» Distance 1.2km
» Duration 1¼ hours

This walk starts at the Arco Naturale, a curious eroded limestone arch which was part of a large grotto. At the end of Via Matermània, backtrack to Le Grottelle (p116) restaurant and take the nearby set of stairs. About halfway down you'll pass the Grotta di Matermània, a giant natural cave used by the Romans as a *nymphaeum* (shrine to the water nymph). You can still see traces of the mosaic wall decorated with shells. At the bottom, continue down the path as it follows the coastline south. The striking flat-roofed red villa you see on your left, on the Punta Massullo promontory, is Villa Malaparte, the former holiday home of Tuscan writer Curzio Malaparte (1898–1957). The sea views become increasingly impressive as the path continues westward around the lower wooded slopes of Monte Tuoro. A few hundred metres further along and you will arrive at a staircase on your right, which leads up to the Belvedere di Tragara and some stunning views of the Isole Faraglioni.

Anacapri To Monte Solaro

» Distance 2km
» Duration two hours

Rising 589m above Anacapri, Monte Solaro (p111) is Capri's highest point. To get to the top you can either take the *seggiovia* (chairlift) from Piazza Vittoria or you can walk. To do the latter, take Via Axel Munthe and turn right up Via Salita per il Solaro. Follow the steep trail until you come to the pass known as La Crocetta, marked by a distinctive iron crucifix. Here the path divides: go right for the summit and its spectacular views over the Bay of Naples and the Amalfi Coast, or go left for the valley of Cetrella and the hermitage of Santa Maria a Cetrella (generally open on Saturday afternoon until sunset). If you don't fancy the walk up, do what many people do and take the chairlift up and walk down.

Anacapri To Belvedere Di Migliera

» Distance 2km
» Duration 45 minutes

A lovely, relaxing walk, this leads out to the Belvedere di Migliera, a panoramic platform with spectacular sea views. The route couldn't be simpler: from Piazza Vittoria take Via Caposcuro and carry on straight along its continuation, Via Migliera. Along the way you'll pass fruit orchards, vineyards and small patches of woodland. Once at the Belvedere you can return to Anacapri via the Torre di Materita or, if you've still got the legs, continue up Monte Solaro. Note, however, that this tough walk is graded medium-difficult by the Club Alpino Italiano (CAI; Italian Alpine Club).

Carena To Punta Dell'arcera, The Sentiero Dei Fortini

» Distance 5.2km
» Duration three hours

Snaking its way along the island's oft-overlooked western coast, the Sentiero dei Fortini (Path of the Small Forts) is a wonderful, if somewhat arduous walk that takes you from Punta Carena, the island's southwestern point, up to Punta dell'Arcera near the Grotta Azzurra (p118) in the north. Named after the three coastal forts (Pino, Mésola and Orrico) along the way, it passes through some of Capri's most unspoiled countryside.

here, particularly the Bermuda shorts, which (believe it or not) were considered quite raffish in their day.

Limoncello di Capri
DRINK

(☎081 837 29 27; Via Capodimonte 27, Anacapri) Don't be put off by the gaudy yellow display; this historic shop stocks some of the island's best *limoncello*. In fact, it was here that the drink was first concocted (or at least that is the claim). Apparently, the grandmother of current owner Vivica made the tot as an after-dinner treat for the guests in her small guesthouse.

Nowadays, the shop produces some 70,000 bottles each year, as well as lemon and orange chocolates (recommended), lemon marmalade and lemon honey. They also sell a tasty lemon sorbet (€2) which is two per cent alcohol.

Carthusia I Profumi di Capri
PERFUME

(☎081 837 03 68; Via F Serena 28, Capri Town) Allegedly, Capri's famous floral perfume was discovered in 1380 by the Prior of the Certosa di San Giacomo. Caught unawares by a royal visit, he arranged a floral display of the island's most beautiful flowers for the queen. Three days later, he went to change the water in the vase only to discover that it had acquired a mysterious floral odour. This became the base of the perfume that's now sold at this smart laboratory outlet.

Capri Naturale
FASHION

(☎081 837 47 19; Via Capodimonte 15, Anacapri; ☺Apr-Oct) One of the better shops along touristy Via Capodimonte, Capri Naturale sells a limited range of women's fashions. Expect whisper-thin linen frocks in delphinium blue or dip-dyed lavender and a small selection of handmade sandals. Everything is made locally and prices are reasonable, all things considered.

Da Costanzo
SHOES

(☎081 837 80 77; Via Roma 49, Capri Town; ☺Mar-Nov) In 1959 Clarke Gable stopped off at this tiny, unpretentious shoe shop on the main street to get himself a pair of handmade leather sandals (to go with the Bermuda shorts he picked up earlier at the famous La Parissienne). The shop's still going, selling a bewildering range of colourful styles to a mixed crowd of passers-by and shoe aficionados. Prices start at around €90, which is a small investment for gleaning a piece of Hollywood history.

Capri Watch
WATCHES

(☎081 837 71 48; www.capricapri.com; Via Camerelle 21, Capri Town) The stunning selection of watches here are made by local watchmaker, Silvio Staiano. The prices start surprisingly low, around €40 for a relatively straightforward time piece, spiralling up to several zeros worth of precious and semiprecious bejewelled little numbers.

Elegantia
FASHION

(Via Giuseppe Orlandi 75, Anacapri) Always fancied yourself flouncing around in one of those sherbet yellow, baby pink or powder blue coloured floppy hats? Then this is the place to pick one up (€15). The owner can also run up copies of clothing, and do alterations and repairs.

ℹ Information

Tourist Offices

Capri Tourism (www.capritourism.com) **Anacapri** (☎081 837 15 24; www.capritourism.com; Via Giuseppe Orlandi 59; ☺8.30am-8.30pm); **Capri Town** (☎081 837 06 86; www.capritourism.com; Piazza Umberto I; ☺8.30am-8.30pm); **Marina Grande** (☎081 837 06 34; www.capritourism.com; Quayside; ☺9am-1pm & 3.30-6.45pm).

ℹ Getting There & Away

Unless you're prepared to pay €1300 for a helicopter transfer from Naples' Capodichino Airport, you'll arrive in Capri by boat.

Sam Helicopter (☎0828 35 41 55; www.capri-helicopters.com)

Boat

The two major ferry routes to Capri are from Naples and (more seasonally) Sorrento, although there are also connections with Ischia and the Amalfi Coast (Amalfi, Positano and Salerno).

Caremar (☎081 837 07 00; www.caremar.it) operates ferries to/from Naples and Capri (€12, 1¼ hours, seven daily) and hydrofoils to/from Sorrento (€13, 25 minutes, four daily).

Gescab (☎081 807 18 12; www.gescab.it) runs hydrofoils to/from Sorrento and Capri (€15, 20 minutes, 18 daily).

Navigazione Libera del Golfo (☎081 552 07 63; www.navlib.it) operates up to eight daily hydrofoils to/from Naples and Capri (€18.70, 45 minutes).

SNAV (☎081 837 75 77; www.snav.com) operates up to 13 daily hydrofoils to/from Naples and Capri (€18, 45 minutes).

For more information on ferries to the island, see the Transport section (p266) in the Survival Guide.

THE ISLANDS CAPRI

GETTING YOUR BEARINGS

All hydrofoils and ferries arrive at Marina Grande, the island's transport hub. From here, the quickest way up to Capri Town is by funicular, but there are also buses and more costly taxis. On foot, it's a tough 2.3km climb along Via Marina Grande. At the top, turn left (east) at the junction with Via Roma for the centre of town or right (west) for Via Provinciale di Anacapri, which eventually becomes Via Giuseppe Orlandi as it leads up to Anacapri.

Pint-sized Piazza Umberto I is the focal point of Capri Town. A short hop to the east, Via Vittorio Emanuele leads down to the main shopping street, Via Camerelle.

Up the hill in Anacapri, buses and taxis drop you off in Piazza Vittoria, from where Via Giuseppe Orlandi, the main strip, runs southwest and Via Capodimonte heads up to Villa San Michele di Axel Munthe.

ⓘ Getting Around

Bus

Sippic (📞081 837 04 20; Via Roma, Bus Station, Capri; €1.80) runs regular buses to/from Marina Grande, Anacapri and Marina Piccola. It also operates buses from Marina Grande to Anacapri and from Marina Piccola to Anacapri.

Staiano Autotrasporti (📞081 837 24 22; Via Tommaso, Bus Station, Anacapri; €1.80) buses serve the Grotta Azzurra and Faro of Punta Carena.

Scooter Hire

Ciro dei Motorini (📞081 837 80 18; www.capriscooter.com; Via Marina Grande 55, Marina Grande; per hr/day €15/60) If you're looking to hire a scooter at Marina Grande, stop here.

Rent A Scooter (📞081 837 38 88; Piazza Barile 20, Anacapri; per hr/day €15/65)

Funicular

Funicular (€1.80; ⊙6.30am-12.30am) The first challenge facing visitors is how to get from Marina Grande to Capri Town. The most enjoyable transport is the funicular, if only for the evocative en route views over the lemon groves and surrounding countryside.

Ischia

POP 62,027

The volcanic outcrop of Ischia is the most developed and largest of the islands in the Bay of Naples. It is an intriguing concoction of sprawling spa towns, buried necropolises, rheumatic Germans and spectacular scenery, with forests, vineyards and picturesque small towns. Ischia only attracts a fraction of the day trippers that head for Capri from Naples in the summer. Perhaps someone should tell them that the beaches are a lot better here.

Most visitors head straight for the north-coast towns of Ischia Porto, Ischia Ponte, Casamicciola Terme, Forio and Lacco Ameno. Of these, Ischia Porto boasts the best bars, Casamicciola the worst traffic and Ischia Ponte and Lacco Ameno the most appeal.

On the calmer south coast, the car-free perfection of Sant'Angelo offers a languid blend of a cosy harbour, sunning cats and nearby bubbling beaches. In between the coasts lies a less-trodden landscape of dense chestnut forests, loomed over by Monte Epomeo, Ischia's highest peak.

The island was an important stop on the trade route from Greece to northern Italy in the 8th century but has since seen its fair share of disaster. The 1301 eruption of the now-extinct (and unfortunately named) Monte Arso forced the locals to flee to the mainland where they remained for four years. Five centuries later, in 1883, an earthquake killed more than 1700 people and razed the burgeoning spa town of Casamicciola to the ground. To this day, the town's name signifies 'total destruction' in the Italian vernacular.

◉ Sights & Activities

A narrow coastal band of development rings the thickly forested and mainly vertiginous slopes of the island's heartland. This is not the place for verdant open meadows and rambling walks, although there are excellent guided geological hikes available. Land is at a premium in Ischia and the main circular highway can get clogged with traffic in the height of summer. This, combined with the penchant the local youth have for overtaking on blind corners and the environmental impact of just too many cars, means that you may want to consider riding the excellent network of buses or hopping in a taxi to get around. For more information, see p133.

ISCHIA PORTO & ISCHIA PONTE

Although technically two separate towns, Ischia Porto and Ischia Ponte are bookends to one long, sinuous sprawl of pastel-coloured buildings, sprawling terrace bars and restaurants, and palm-fringed shops and hotels.

The ferry port itself was a crater lake, opened up to sea at the request of Spanish King Ferdinand II in 1854. While the story goes that he couldn't stand the stench of the lake, his request was more likely inspired by the prospect of increasing shipping tax revenue. Whatever the reason, it was a great idea, and now the harbour is fringed by a string of restaurants serving fresh seafood. Head further east and you'll hit the heart-stealing **Spiaggia dei Pescatori** (Fishermen's Beach), a compelling scene of brightly painted fishing boats, bronzed flesh, lurid beach umbrellas and mothers on balconies calling in their chubby kids (or husbands) for lunch.

Chiesa di San Pietro CHURCH
(cnr Corso Vittoria Colonna & Via Gigante, Ischia Porto; ⊙8am-12.30pm & 4-7.30pm) Check out this church's 18th-century baroque extravaganza, with its fetching convex facade, semicircular chapels and elevated terrace popular with flirty teens and gossipy *signore* (women). Grab an ice cream from the nearest gelateria and absorb the *dolce vita* atmosphere.

Santa Maria della Scala CHURCH
(Via Luigi Mazzella, Ischia Ponte; ⊙8am-12.30pm & 4.30-8pm) A striking 15th-century watchtower, Torre del Mare, now serves as the bell tower to Ischia's cathedral. The current church, designed by Antonio Massinetti and completed in 1751, stands on the site of two older churches, one built in the 13th century and the other in the 17th century. Step inside its peeling interior and you'll find the original 14th-century baptismal font, a Romanesque wooden crucifix and a wistful 18th-century canvas by Giacinto Diano.

Museo del Mare MUSEUM
(☎081 98 11 24; Via Giovanni da Procida 2, Ischia Ponte; adult/reduced €4/free; ⊙10.30am-12.30pm & 3-7pm Mar-Jan; ⛴) If you are an old salt at heart (or have a penchant for model ships), don't miss Ischia's maritime museum with its lovingly documented exhibits. Objects include cult ex-votos (offerings to the saints)

from sailors to saints, ancient urns, beautifully crafted model ships and revealing photographs of island life in the 20th century, including the arrival of Ischia's very first American car in 1958 – you can just imagine what a celebratory occasion that must have been.

LACCO AMENO

In the 1950s and 1960s, French starlets and European royalty came to play at the legendary Terme Regina Isabella spa resort. The stars may have gone but one local icon remains, sprouting out of the sea: the iconic **Il Fungo** (The Mushroom) is a 10m volcanic rock formation spat out by Monte Epomeo thousands of years ago.

According to legend, the body of the martyr Restituta was washed ashore on nearby San Montano Beach in the 4th century on a boat steered from Tunisia by a seaworthy angel. Her subsequent cult spread from North Africa to Italy and is historically associated with the expulsion of Catholics from North Africa by the king of the Vandals, Genseric.

Every May, residents re-enact her arrival on the beach.

Area Archeologica di Santa Restituta ARCHAEOLOGICAL SITE
(☎081 98 05 38; Piazza Restituta; admission €3; ⊙9.30am-12.30pm & 5-7pm Mon-Sat, 9.30am-12.30pm Sun) Beneath the pretty-in-pink **Chiesa di Santa Restituta** church, rebuilt after the 1883 earthquake, be sure to visit the **Area Archeologica**. Excavations undertaken between 1951 and 1974 have uncovered parts of an ancient Greek kiln, Roman temple and street, 4th-century burial amphorae and an early Christian basilica. Rows of cabinets display other ancient objects, from Roman bracelets and votive gifts to a 3300-year-old stove from Procida.

The ground-floor collection goes back to the future, with exquisite 17th-century *pastori* (nativity scene figurines), colourful 18th-century ceramics, high camp clerical garb and the 18th-century wooden statue of Santa Restituta still used in the annual procession in the Bay of San Montano. You can borrow an informative, handwritten guide to the excavations from the ticket desk.

Museo Archeologico di Pithecusae MUSEUM
(☎081 99 61 83; www.pithecusae.it; Corso Angelo Rizzoli 210, Lacco Ameno; admission includes Museo Angelo Rizzoli €5; ⊙9.30am-1pm & 3-6.30pm Tue-Sun) Housed in the elegant Villa Arbusto, former home of local celeb Angelo Rizzoli,

Ischia

the Museo Archeologico di Pithecusae enjoys a heady historical location, overlooking Monte Vico, site of the ancient settlement and acropolis of Pithecusae. The museum has a fascinating collection of important finds from the island's Hellenic settlement, ranging from imported earthenware to parts of the acropolis itself.

A highlight is the legendary 7th-century BC Nestor's Cup in Sala (Room) II bearing one of the oldest known Greek inscriptions, which appropriately celebrates the wine of Is-

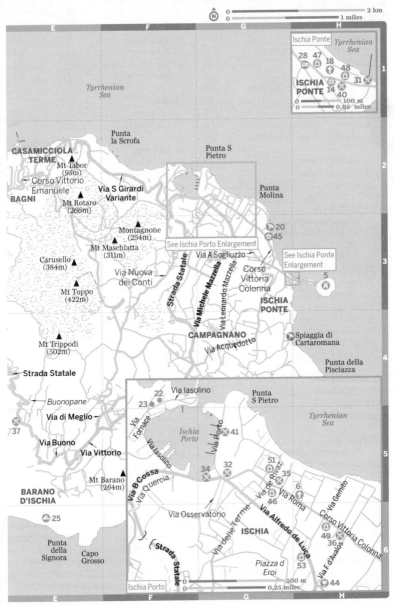

chia. The space also encompasses the Museo Angelo Rizzoli.

Museo Angelo Rizzoli MUSEUM
(☎081 99 61 83; www.pithecusae.it; Corso Angelo Rizzoli 210, Lacco Ameno; admission includes Museo Archeologico di Pithecusae €5; ☺9.30am-1pm & 3-6.30pm Tue-Sun; ⁂) As a frivolous sidekick to all that archaeology, this small, entertaining museum pays homage to the man who turned humble little Lacco into a celebrity hotspot in the 1950s. Cool paparazzi shots

Ischia

and clippings of a Hitchcock-esque Rizzoli and his famous pals decorate rooms, that once played host to the likes of Gina Lollabrigida, Grace Kelly and Federico Fellini.

Equally striking are the villa's gardens, complete with lemon trees, fountain, a children's playground and star-worthy views towards the Campi Flegrei.

Negombo   SPA

(☏081 98 61 52; www.negombo.it; Baia di San Montano, Lacco Ameno; admission all day €30, from 1pm €25, from 3.30pm €17; ◎8.30am-7pm Apr-Oct) This is the place to come for a dose of pampering. Part spa resort, part botani-

cal wonderland, with more than 500 exotic plant species, the Negombo's combination of Zen-like thermal pools, hammam, contemporary sculpture and private beach on San Montano Bay tends to draw a younger crowd than many other Ischian spa spots.

There's a Japanese labyrinth pool for weary feet, a decent *tavola calda* (snack bar), and a full range of massage and beauty treatments. Those arriving by car or scooter can park all day on site (car €4, scooter €2.50). For a free dip in the bay, follow the signs to the spiaggia (beach) out the front of Negombo.

CASTELLO ARAGONESE

Head for the elegant 15th-century Ponte Aragonese, which connects the town to **Castello Aragonese** (Castle D'Aragona; 📞081 99 28 34; Rocca del Castello, Ischia Ponte; adult/reduced €10/6; ⏰9am-7pm; 🚻), a sprawling, magnificent castle perched high and mighty on a rocky islet. While Syracusan tyrant Gerone I built the site's first fortress in 474 BC, the bulk of the current state dates from the 1400s, when King Alfonso of Aragon gave the older Angevin fortress a thorough makeover, building the fortified bastions, current causeway and access ramp cut into the rock.

Further up lie the sunbaked, stuccoed ruins of the 14th-century Cattedrale dell'Assunta, which collapsed under British cannon fire in 1809. The 11th-century crypt below features snippets of 14th-century frescoes inspired by Giotto. Better preserved is the 18th-century Chiesa dell'Immacolata, with its Greek-cross plan and dome studded with curved tympanum windows. Commissioned by the adjoining Convento delle Clarisse (Convent for Clarisse nuns), it was left in its minimalist state after building funds ran out. When the nuns' own lives expired, they were left to decompose sitting upright on stone chairs in the macabre Cimitero delle Monache Clarisse, as a grisly reminder of mortality.

Carry on until you reach the elegant, hexagonal Chiesa di San Pietro a Pantaniello and sombre Carcere Borbonico, the one-time prison for leading figures of the Risorgimento (the 19th-century Italian unification movement), such as Poerio, Pironti, Nusco and Settembrini. Don't miss the Museo delle Torture, a small museum of medieval torture instruments, or the 15th-century tall tunnel. While you are strolling around, you may want to counteract all that darkness surrounding the castle's history with a touch of fairytale romance: in the 1500s, the castle was home to Vittoria Colonna, a poet-princess who married Ferrante d'Avalos here before becoming closely linked with Michelangelo. The great artist wrote romantic poetry dedicated to Vittoria and sent her a painting, the *Crucifixion*, for her private chapel.

FORIO & THE WEST COAST

The largest town on the island, and apparently the favoured destination of Tennessee Williams and Truman Capote in the 1950s, Forio is home to some of the best restaurants on Ischia, as well as good beaches and a couple of stunning botanical gardens.

Chiesa di Santa Maria del Soccorso   CHURCH

(Via Soccorso 1, Forio; ⏰10am-sunset) This dazzling white church located on the western edge of town was originally part of a 14th-century Augustinian monastery; its side chapel and dome were added in 1791 and 1854 respectively, the latter rebuilt after the 1883 earthquake. The 18th-century mismatched majolica tiles adorning the semicircular staircase out the front are truly beautiful; from here, the views are heavenly.

Giardini Ravino   BOTANICAL GARDENS

(📞081 99 77 83; www.ravino.it; SS 270, Forio; adult/reduced €9/4; ⏰9am-sunset, closed Tue & Thu, Mar–mid-Nov) The vision of local botanist, Giuseppe D'Ambra, who has travelled collecting plants since the 1960s, this 6000-sq

metre garden pays homage to the not-so-humble cacti. There is a diverse collection here, as well as other succulent plants, many of which apparently have homeopathic qualities.

You can join a guided walk every Sunday at 11am; at other times, you should reserve in advance. The gardens are also the site of concerts, art and craft exhibitions, and there are self-catering apartments to rent.

La Mortella   BOTANICAL GARDENS

(📞081 98 62 20; www.lamortella.it; Via F Calese 39, Forio; adult/reduced €10/5; ⏰9am-7pm Tue, Thu, Sat & Sun Apr-Nov) Designed by Russell Page and inspired by the Moorish gardens of Granada's Alhambra in Spain, La Mortella is recognised as one of Italy's finest botanical gardens and well worth a couple of hours of your time. Stroll among terraces, pools, palms, fountains and more than 1000 rare and exotic plants from all over the world.

These plants include the huge water lily Victoria Amazonica with flowers that turn from white to crimson red. This veritable Eden was established by the late British

DON'T MISS

CASA MUSEO

The good news is that this museum is well signposted and has a car park. The bad news is that it is on a perilous corner on the mountain road between Buonopane and Fontana. Double back if you can because this beguiling museum, Casa Museo (House Museum; ☏349 7198879; SS 270 Serrara Fontana; ⊙10am-7pm) is far more interesting than its name gives on. Tunnelled into the rock face, every room contains extraordinary sculptures and carvings, made out of stone, wood and pebbles; the latter including such quirky exhibits as a life size pig. Other wonderful pieces include a stone head of Neptune, fanciful pebble reptiles, wooden furniture carved out of gnarled tree trunks and intricately patterned pebble mosaics covering the walls, even in the bathroom.... Check out the Alice in Wonderland-style tunnels that lead here, there – and absolutely nowhere! The museum is free, although a donation is appreciated.

composer Sir William Walton and his Argentinian wife, Susana (who died in March 2010, aged 83), who made it their home in 1949, entertaining such venerable house guests as Sir Laurence Olivier, Maria Callas and Charlie Chaplin. His life is commemorated in a small museum and his music wafts over the loudspeakers at the elegant cafe. There are classical music concerts here in the spring and autumn.

Geo-Ausfluge
HIKING
(Geo-Ausfluge; ✎English spoken 081 90 30 58; www.eurogeopark.com) Unlike Capri and Procida, Ischia is not an island that is easily accessible to hikers. If you are interested in exploring the hinterland, Italian geologist Aniello Di Lorio conducts a selection of walks throughout the island ranging from three to five hours, including lunch (€17 to €26), with various collection points in Ischia; pick up in Casamicciola and Panza, costs a further €5.

Note that the walks are primarily conducted in German and Italian, but tours can also be provided in English with advance notice. Even if you do not understand all the explanations, you will still have the opportunity of to explore some beautiful parts of the island that would be difficult to access solo.

La Colombaia
CULTURAL BUILDING
(✎081 333 21 47; www.fondazionelacolombaia.it; Via F Calise 130, Forio; admission €5; ⊙10am-1pm & 4-8pm Tue-Sun) One of the joys of coming here are the untamed rural surroundings; there's also a tangible, lived-in feel about La Colombaia, a handsome neo-Renaissance villa. Little wonder, perhaps, as this is the former bachelor pad of flamboyant Italian film director Luchino Visconti.

Born into one of Milan's wealthiest families in 1906, his 1969 film *The Damned,* about a wealthy German family that turns fascist, received an Academy Award nomination for best screenplay. His aesthetically restored home now houses an arts foundation, which includes a documentary library focussing on Visconti and cinema history, as well as costumes, set pieces and stills from his films. It's also a venue for the Ischia Film Festival and regularly holds edgy exhibitions.

Giardini Poseidon
SPA
(Poseidon Gardens; ✎081 908 71 11; www.giardini poseidon.it; Via Mazzella, Spiaggia di Citara; day pass €30; ⊙9am-6.30pm Apr, 8.30am-7pm May-Oct) South of Forio, spa lovers can enjoy sprawling Giardini Poseidon. There is a wide choice of treatments and facilities available, including massages, saunas, Jacuzzis, various health treatments and terraced pools spilling down the volcanic cliffside. If it's all too stressful, settle for the dazzling private beach below.

SANT'ANGELO & THE SOUTH COAST
Tiny Sant'Angelo attracts a voguish crowd with its chic boutiques, seafront restaurants and great beaches. Quiet lanes spill down the hill to fashionable Piazzetta Ottorino Troia, where tanned Italians sip Campari soda and take in late-night summer music concerts. Keeping an eye on it all is the great hulking *scoglio* (rock), joined to the village by a sandbar sprinkled with fishing boats, beach umbrellas and *bagnini* (lifeguards).

Catch a brightly painted water taxi from the pier to the sandy Spiaggia dei Maronti (one way €5) or the intimate cove of Il Sorgeto (one way €7), with its steamy thermal spring. Sorgeto can also be reached on foot down an albeit poorly signposted path from the village of Panza.

Terme Cavascuro
SPA

(☑081 99 92 42; www.cavascura.it; Via Cavascura 1, Spiaggia dei Maronti, Sant'Angelo; basic thermal bath €12, mud & thermal bath €27; ☺8.30am-1.30pm & 2.30-6pm mid-Apr–mid-Oct) Experience an earthy natural spa by catching a water taxi to Cavascura (one way €3.50) and follow the signs 300m down a rocky gorge to Terme Cavascuro. Wedged between soaring cliffs, this historic no-frills outdoor spa is Ischia's oldest. Soak in old Roman baths hewn into the cliff or sweat it out in a grotto.

For an extra fee top it all off with a mud mask and face massage (€24), manicure (€15) or anti-stress massage (€30). The sulphurous waters are reputedly beneficial for rheumatic, bronchial and skin conditions.

Parco Termale Aphrodite Apollon
SPA

(☑081 99 92 19; www.aphrodite.it; Via Petrelle, Sant'Angelo; admission €40; ☺8am-6pm mid-Apr–Oct) A spectacular, if partly strenuous 2km walk above the coast from Sant'Angelo brings you to this luxurious spa, which is now part of the Miramare Sea Resort. Beyond its ivy-draped entrance is a marble-clad complex of gyms, saunas, lush terraced gardens and 12 differently heated pools, including one for hydro-cycling. The spa offers an extensive range of beauty treatments and therapies.

Orizzonti Blu
DIVING

(☑340 4259162; www.orizzontiblu.net; Via Iasolino 86, Ischia Porto) If diving takes your fancy, this reputable outfit organises open-water dives and courses, including a six-lesson dive master course (€800).

Ischia Diving
DIVING

(☑081 98 18 52; www.ischiadiving.net; Via Iasolino 106, Ischia Porto) This well established diving outfit offers some attractively priced dive packages, like five dives including equipment for €225.

Westcoast
BOAT HIRE

(☑081 90 86 04; www.westcoastischia.it; Porto di Forio; boat hire from €100) Westcoast provides full-day hire of motorised boats and dinghies (with or without a sailor). This is a particularly good idea in August when the more popular beaches are crowded and you are desperate to find a quiet sandy cove.

Festivals & Events
Ischian festivals are all about the good life – food, wine, film and a little laid-back jazz while away those summer evenings.

Ischia Film Festival
FILM FESTIVAL

(www.ischiafilmfestival.it) Serving up free flicks and exhibitions in star locations around the island, including Castello Aragonese, Villa Arbusto and La Colombaia, usually in June.

Vinischia
FOOD FESTIVAL

(www.vinischia.it) Foodies flock to this four-day celebration of regional food and wine, with free tastings and concerts along the Lungomare Aragonese, usually in June and July.

Festa di Sant'Anna
SAINT'S DAY

(www.infoischiaprocida.it; Ischia) The allegorical 'burning of the Castello Aragonese' takes place on the feast day of St Anne on 26 July, with a hypnotic procession of boats and fireworks.

Ischia Jazz Festival
MUSIC FESTIVAL

(www.ischiajazz.com) Ischia's annual jazz festival pumps out five days of smooth Italian sax with a dash of foreign acts, usually in September.

Eating
While seafood is an obvious speciality on the island, Ischia is also famed for its rabbit, bred on inland farms. Another local speciality is *rucolino*, a liquorice-flavoured liqueur made from *rucola* (rocket) leaves.

THE ISLANDS ISCHIA

MONTE EPOMEO

Lace up those hiking boots and set out on a roughly 2.5km (50-minute) uphill walk from the village of Fontana, which will bring you to the top of **Monte Epomeo** (788m). Formed by an underwater eruption, it boasts superlative views of the Bay of Naples. The little church near the top is the 15th-century **Cappella di San Nicola di Bari**, where you can check out the pretty majolica floor. The adjoining hermitage was built in the 18th century by an island governor who, after narrowly escaping death, swapped politics for poverty and spent the rest of his days here in saintly solitude. Have a peek inside then head back down the hill thankful that your saintliness doesn't exclude good wining and dining, Ischia style.

ISCHIA'S BEST BEACHES

Spiaggia dei Maronti (€5 one-way) Long, sandy and very popular, the sand here is warmed by natural steam geysers. Reach it by bus from Barano, by water taxi from Sant'Angelo or on foot along the path leading east from Sant'Angelo.

Il Sorgeto Catch a water taxi (€7 one way; ☺Apr-Oct) from Sant'Angelo or reach it on foot from the town of Panza. Waiting at the bottom is an intimate cove complete with bubbling thermal spring. Perfect for a winter dip.

Spiaggia dei Pescatori Wedged in between Ischia Porto and Ischia Ponte is the island's most atmospheric and popular seaside strip; perfect for families.

Baia di San Montano Due west of Lacco Ameno, this gorgeous bay is the place for warm, shallow, crystal-clear waters. You'll also find the Negombo (p126) spa park here.

Punta Caruso Located on Ischia's northwestern tip, this secluded rocky spot is perfect for a swim in clear, deep water. To get here, follow the walking path that leads off Via Guardiola down to the beach. Not suitable for children or when seas are rough.

Cantine di Pietratorcia WINERY €€
(✆081 90 72 32; www.pietratorcia.it; Via Provinciale Panza 267, Forio; meals €30; ☺Apr-Oct) Enjoying a bucolic setting among tumbling vines, wild fig trees and rosemary bushes, this A-list winery is a foodie's nirvana. Tour the old stone cellars, sip a local drop and eye up the delectable degustation menu. Offerings include fragrant bruschetta and cheeses, hearty Campanian sausages and spicy *salumi* (charcuterie). Full dinners are also available if booked in advance.

Montecorvo ITALIAN €€
(✆081 99 80 29; www.montecorvo.it; Via Montecorvo 33, Forio; meals €30) This is an extraordinary place, with part of the dining room tunnelled into a cave and a terrace which looks like it belongs in a jungle. Owner Giovanni prides himself on the special dishes he makes daily, grilled meat and fish being a specialty, while the menu also includes a good range of pastas and vegetable antipasti.

You will need more than a good compass to find this spot, hidden amidst lush foliage outside Forio. Fortunately, it is well signposted. Fronted by lofty pines, a tumbling waterfall and steep steps, prepare yourself for an exuberant welcome from Giovanni; he's that kind of guy.

Il Focolare TRATTORIA €€
(✆081 90 29 44; Via Creajo al Crocefisso, Barano d'Ischia; meals €25) A good choice for those seeking a little turf instead of surf, this is one of the island's best loved restaurants. Family run, homey and rustic, it has a solidly traditional meat-based menu with steaks, lamb cutlets and specialities, including *coniglio*

all'Ischitana (typical local rabbit dish with tomatoes, garlic and herbs) and *tagliatelle al ragu di cinghiale* (ribbon-shaped pasta with wild boar ragout).

On the sweet front, the desserts are home-made and exquisite. Owner Riccardo D'Ambra (who runs the restaurants together with his son, Agostino), is a leading local advocate of the Slow Food Movement. If you want seafood, coffee or soft drinks, you'll have to go elsewhere, they are not on the menu here.

Ristorante La Pantera Rosa CAMPANIAN €€
(✆081 99 24 83; Via Porto, Riva Destra, Ischia Porto; meals €28) There are some good choices and good prices for those suffering from black-tie burnout at this laid-back restaurant on the port's suppertime strip. The menu has all the traditional pasta and pizza choices, plus specialities like *risotto alla pescatora* (seafood risotto) which comes warmly recommended. Owner Amedeo is something of a linguist and speaks fluent English and French.

La Cantina del Mare CAMPANIAN €€
(✆081 333 03 22; www.lacantinadelmare.it; Corso Angelo Rizzoli 20, Lacco Ameno; meals €25) Tired of sand in your sandwiches? This friendly place is located just across the road from the beach and serves excellent dishes to locals and wised-up tourists; seafood is the speciality. Sit on the pretty terrace or in the moodily-lit interior lined with shelves of wine. The bread is pretty special too, made in the oldest bread oven on the island and delivered here daily. English is spoken.

Da Raffaele
ITALIAN €€

(☑081 99 12 03; www.daraffaele.it; Via Roma 29, Ischia Porto; meals €28; ☺Mar-Nov; 🖶) Handily situated in the middle of Via Roma, this brightly-lit, welcoming place has few surprises on the menu but prepares everything well. Try the *frittura di pesce all'ischitana* (mixed fried fish; €13) or *melanzane a funghetti* (fried aubergine with tomatoes, mushrooms, garlic and basil) and grab a table out front for the best people-watching potential on this pedestrian shopping street.

Ristorante da Ciccio
CAMPANIAN €€

(☑081 99 16 86; Via Luigi Mazzella 32, Ischia Ponte; meals €25; ☺Wed-Mon) Sublime seafood and charming host Carlo make this atmospheric place a winner. Highlights include *tubattone* pasta with clams and pecorino cheese, a zesty mussel soup topped with fried bread and *peperoncino* (chilli), and a delicious chocolate and almond cake. Tables spill out onto the pavement in the summer, from where there are fabulous castle views.

Umberto a Mare
CAMPANIAN €€€

(☑081 99 71 71; Via Soccorso 2, Forio; meals €46; ☺Mar-Dec) In the shadow of the Spanish mission–style Soccorso church, this waterside restaurant has the choice of a low-key cafe-bar for light snacks or the more formal restaurant where the menu changes according to the season. Highlights include long thick tubes of pasta with tuna, fresh tomatoes and *peperoncino*, pennewith lobster and asparagus, and a delicate *al profumo di mare* (lightly grilled freshly caught fish). The orange sorbet dessert comes highly recommended.

Da Ciccio
CAFE €

(☑081 199 13 14; Via Porto 1, Ischia Porto; snacks from €1) Just the spot for ferry-weary arrivals, this much-loved bar does light meals, luscious pastries and dangerously good gelati, including organic strawberry – fabulous! Eat in or take away savoury treats like the *calzone* (pizza folded over to form a pie) stuffed with spinach, pine nuts and raisins (€1.20). At the very least, cool down with an orange and mint *granita*.

Bar de Maio
ICE CREAM €

(☑081 99 18 70; Piazza Antica Reggia 9, Ischia Porto; ice cream €2) This bar has been raising the locals' cholesterol levels since 1930 with a delicious selection of ultracreamy ice creams, as well as coffee, cocktails and snacks. Take a seat in the square with your cone; this central piazza is a prime people-watching spot. According to residents, it's the best ice-cream parlour on the island.

Gran Caffè Vittoria
CAFE €

(☑081 199 16 49; Corso Vittoria Colonna 110, Ischia Porto; pastries €2) At the smarter end of the port, this elegant, wood-panelled cafe has been spoiling customers and waistlines for more than 100 years with its irresistible cakes, pastries, coffees and cocktails, all served by old-school, bow-tied waiters.

Al Pontile
ITALIAN €

(☑081 98 34 92; Via Luigi Mazzella 15, Ischia Ponte) Sit outside, front or back with views of the castle as an evocative backdrop to the shopping street or sea. The reassuringly brief menu includes pasta mainstays like *puttanesca* with capers, tomatoes and olives, as well as reliable meat and fish mains. Smile sweetly and the owner will bring a bottle of *limoncello* along with the bill, allowing you your fill of lemony top ups.

Zi Carmela
CAMPANIAN €

(☑081 99 84 23; Via Schioppa 27, Forio; meals €20; ☺Apr-Oct; 🖶) Dating back several decades, this restaurant has a lovely terrace decorated with copper pans, ceramic mugs and strings of garlic and chillies. Locals in the know come here for seafood dishes such as the *fritturina e pezzogne* (a local white fish baked with potatoes and herbs in the wood-fired pizza oven) or *tartare di palamito al profumo d'arancia* (tartar of local fish with citrus). Undecided taste buds can go for the €28 four-course set menu.

🍸 Drinking & Entertainment

Ischia is not Ibiza. That said, the area around Ischia Porto has the best buzz, with a handful of bars and clubs that stay open way past cocoa time.

Bar Calise
BAR

(☑081 99 12 70; Piazza degli Eroi 69, Ischia Porto; ☺7pm-3am Thu-Sun) One of the oldest bars on the island, located near the harbour, the atmosphere here is one of languid gentility. Waistcoated waiters serve cocktails and coffees to a background of live Latin, swing and folk music.

New Valentino
CLUB

(☑081 98 25 69; www.valentinoischia.eu; Corso Vittoria Colonna 97, Ischia Porto; ☺9pm-late) A rollicking-good time disco with pulsating lights, punchy music and the aesthetic surprise of some pretty, traditional majolica tilework.

THE ISLANDS ISCHIA

ISCHIA ON A FORK

Ischian restaurateur Carlo Buono gives the low-down on his cherished classic island cuisine:

'Fresh, seasonal ingredients are the cornerstone of Ischian cooking, from silky olive oil to plump *pomodorini* (cherry tomatoes). Like Neapolitan cooking, the emphasis is on simple, uncomplicated home cooking using premium produce. Traditionally, there are two types of Ischian cuisine: coastal and mountain. For centuries, the fishermen of Lacco Ameno and Sant'Angelo would barter with the farmers of Barano and Serrara Fontana, who'd offer wine, vegetables, pork and rabbit in exchange for the fishermen's catch.

'Indeed, rabbit is a typical Ischian meat and we're seeing a revival of the traditional *fossa* (pit) breeding method, where rabbits are bred naturally in deep *fosse* instead of in cages. The result is a more tender, flavoursome meat. Leading this renaissance is local Slow Food advocate Riccardo D'Ambra, whose famous trattoria Il Focolare (p130) is well known for its rabbit and rustic mountain dishes. Definitely worth eating on the island is a popular Sunday dish called *coniglio all'ischitana* (Ischia-style rabbit), which is prepared with olive oil, unpeeled garlic, chilli, tomato, basil, thyme and white wine.

'Like the land, the sea is seasonal, so the seafood that we cook depends on the time of year. Typical local fish include *pesce bandiera* (sailfish), the flat *castagna*, *lampuga* and *palamide* (a small tuna). A popular way of cooking it is in *acqua pazza* (crazy water). Traditionally prepared on the fishing boats, it's a delicate sauce made with *pomodorini*, garlic and parsley. Fried fish is also very typical; a fresh serve of *frittura di mare* (mixed fried seafood) drizzled with lemon juice is just superb. May to September is *totano* (squid) season and a great time to try *totani imbotti* (squid stuffed with olives, capers and breadcrumbs, and stewed in wine).

'Equally wonderful is fresh, wood-fired *casareccio* bread. Soft and dense on the inside and crunchy on the outside, it's perfect for doing the *scarpetta* (wiping your plate clean) or for filling with salami or *parmigiano* cheese. If you have any room left, track down a slice of *torta caprese*, a moist chocolate and almond cake. *Buon appetito.*'

Shopping

Ischia's shopping is centred on Via Roma and the web of narrow streets leading to Ischia Ponte. From floss-thin bikinis to decadent jars of *babà* (sponge soaked in rum), there's enough shopping on these cobbled stones to shift your credit card into overdrive. For a more low-key experience, explore the tiny boutiques and art galleries in Sant'Angelo and Forio.

TOP CHOICE **Filippo Cianciarelli** CERAMICS
(www.ceramichecianciarelli.it; Via Luigi Mazzella 113, Ischia Ponte) Filippo is an original artist who creates vividly patterned pieces, including striking, tall pyramid-shaped vases, tiled pictures with abstract themes and smaller easy-to-pack plates, mugs and the like. And there's not a painted lemon in sight (for a change).

Maria Rosaria Ferrara SHOES
(☑081 98 54 18; Via Venanzio Marone 5, Ischia Porto) Get a pedicure and then step out in a pair of these ornate handmade soft gelati-coloured leather sandals decorated with natural shells, shimmering beads and sparkling sequins. Maria will also custom design a pair for you – handy if you want to match an outfit.

Antica Macelleria di Francesco Esposito FOOD
(☑081 98 10 11; Via delle Terme 2, Ischia Porto) This century-old deli is gourmet foodie heaven. Drop in from 8am for fresh mozzarella and wood-fired *casareccio* bread, plus a lip-smacking choice of cheeses, prosciutto, homemade *peperoncino* salami and marinated peppers. In fact, they've got everything you need for a picnic on the beach, including the bottle of obligatory *falanghina* (dry white wine).

Ischia Sapori DRINK
(☑337 972465; Via Luigi Mazzella 5, Ischia Ponte) If you thought rucola was just a tasty green leaf for salads, think again: this savvy little produce shop is the home of *rucolino*, a local, liquorice-flavoured digestive made with none other than the green weed itself (no, not that one). The recipe is a closely

guarded secret but the liquid is yours for the taking.

The shop also sells its own wines, gourmet food stuffs, limoncello-soaked *babà*, olive-oil soaps, and fragrances, all reasonably priced and gorgeously packaged with trademark Italian flair.

Judith Major FASHION

(☑081 98 32 95; Corso Vittoria Colonna 174, Ischia Porte) Despite the headmistressy name, this snazzy boutique is the exclusive stockist of Italian label Brunello Cucinelli. The look here is Polo Ralph Lauren with a sexy Italian twist. Cashmere sweaters, suave shirts, blazers and chic womenswear. Shoes include Prada, Barrett and Alberto Guardiani for men and Stuart Weitzman and Pedro Garcia for women. Everything you'll need for a jaunt on the yacht.

L'Isoletto FOOD

(☑081 99 93 74; Via Chiaia delle Rose 36, Sant'Angelo) Stock up on a mouth-watering selection of local produce, from spicy *peperoncino*, rum-soaked *babà* and lemon-cream *cannoncelli* (pastry filled with lemon cream) to Ischian vino and the ubiquitous *limoncello*. Less tasteful – but deliciously kitsch – is the collection of tourist souvenirs, from seashell placemats to 3D souvenir wall plates.

Percorsi Comunicanti in Galleria CERAMICS

(☑081 90 42 27; Via Sant'Angelo 93, Sant'Angelo) Offering a welcome contemporary ceramic respite from smiling sun platters and souvenir ashtrays, this slick little gallery features bold, contemporary ceramics crafted by Neapolitan artist Massimiliano Santoro. A modest selection of Murano glass jewellery and designer silk kaftans are guaranteed to further loosen the purse strings.

Scaglione Renato JEWELLERY

(☑081 98 45 03; Via Alfredo de Luca 123, Ischia Porto) This small jewellery shop has a small but sparkling range of exquisite jewellery, incorporating turquoise, amethyst, amber and coral. Prices are slightly lower than the glitzier options on nearby Via Roma.

❶ Information

Tourist Office (☑081 507 42 11; www.infoischiaprocida.it; Corso Sogliuzzo 72, Ischia Porto; ⏰9am-2pm & 3-8pm Mon-Sat) A slim selection of maps and brochures.

❶ Getting There & Away

Caremar (☑081 837 07 00; www.caremar.it) operates up to seven daily hydrofoils to/from Naples and Ischia (€17, 30 minutes)

Alilauro (☑081 837 69 95; www.alilauro.it) operates hydrofoils to/from Naples and Ischia (€20, 50 minutes, 10 daily)

SNAV (☑081 837 75 77; www.snav.com) operates hydrofoils to/from Naples and Ischia (€18, one hour, four daily)

For further information on ferries and hydrofoils to the island, see the Transport section (p266) in the Survival Guide.

❶ Getting Around

Ferries and hydrofoils reach Casamicciola Terme and Ischia Porto. The latter is Ischia's major gateway and tourist hub. The island's main bus station is a one-minute walk west of the pier, with buses servicing all other parts of the island. East of the pier, shopping strip Via Roma eventually becomes Corso Vittoria Colonna and heads southeast to Ischia Porto.

Bus

The island's main bus station is located in Ischia Porto. There are two principal lines: the CS (Circolo Sinistro, or Left Circle), which circles the island anticlockwise, and the CD line (Circolo

---

FERRY FACTS

Ferries are the most likely way of getting to the islands. Note that ferries departing from Positano and Amalfi operate solely from Easter to September. At other times of the year, you will have to catch the ferry or hydrofoil from Naples or Sorrento. The information listed in the Getting There & Away sections of this chapter refers to high-season crossings and is not comprehensive; check the respective websites and the Transport section in the Survival Guide in the back of the book for more detailed itineraries. Ferries leave from both the Beverello and adjacent Mergellina ports in Naples; there is a strip of booths with the times, berth numbers and costs clearly displayed. Generally, there is no need to book in advance. Just turn up around 35 minutes before departure in case there is a queue.

Destro, or Right Circle), which travels in a clockwise direction, passing through each town and departing every 30 minutes. Buses pass near all hotels and campsites. A single ticket, valid for 90 minutes, costs €1.40; an all-day, multi-use ticket is €4.50; and a two-day ticket is €7. Taxis and micro-taxis (scooter-engined three-wheelers) are also available.

Car & Scooter

You can do this small island a favour by not bringing your car. If you want to hire a car or a scooter for a day, there are plenty of hire companies. **Balestrieri** (☏ 081 98 56 91; www.autonoleggio balestrieri.it; Via Iasolino 35, Ischia Porto) hires out cars (from €40 per day) and scooters (€30), and they also have mountain bikes (€15 per day). You can't take a hired vehicle off the island.

Parking

If you are hiring a car in high season, parking is going to be a headache. Go for a Smart car if you can, which takes up minimal space. There is a small car park at the entrance of Sant'Angelo (two hours €3) and Ischia Porto and Ponte both have signposted central car parks (per hour €1.50).

Procida

POP 10,700

The Bay of Naples' smallest island is also its best-kept secret. Be sure to dig out your paintbox; this soulful blend of hidden lemon groves, weathered fishermen and pastel-hued houses is memorably picturesque. Mercifully located off the mass-tourist radar, Procida is like the original Portofino proto-type and has the benefit of being refreshingly real. August aside – when beach-bound mainlanders flock to its shores – its narrow sun-bleached streets are the domain of the locals: wiry young boys clutch fishing rods, weary mothers push prams and wizened old seamen swap tales of malaise. Here, the hotels are smaller, fewer waiters speak broken German and the island's welcome is untainted by too much tourism.

At Marina Grande, tumbledown buildings in hues of pinks, whites and yellow crowd the waterfront as an evocative first introduction to the island. Fishermen mend their nets under laundry hung out to dry, while waiters serve the catch of the day in well-worn restaurants.

Even in the height of summer, Procida doesn't attract the number of tourists welcomed by its more famous neighbours. This is a small island, ideal for those seeking to escape the crowds.

◉ Sights & Activities

If you have the time, Procida is an ideal island to explore on foot. The most compelling areas (and where you will also find most of the hotels, bars and restaurants) are Marina Grande, Marina Corricella and Marina di Chiaiolella. Beaches are not plentiful here, apart from the Lido di Procida where, aside from August, you shouldn't have any trouble finding some towel space on the sand.

Abbazia di San Michele Arcangelo MUSEUM
(☑081 896 76 12; Via Terra Murata 89, Terra
Murata; admission €2; ⊙9.45am-12.45pm &
3.30-6pm) Soak in the dizzying bay views
before exploring the adjoining Abbazia di
San Michele Arcangelo. Built in the 11th
century and remodelled between the 17th
and 19th centuries, this one-time Benedictine abbey is a small museum with some
arresting pictures done in gratitude by
shipwrecked sailors, plus a church and
a maze of catacombs that lead to a tiny
secret chapel.

MARINA CORRICELLA
From panoramic Piazza dei Martiri, the village of **Marina Corricella** tumbles down
to its marina in a waterfall of pastel colours: pinks, yellows and whites. Fishing
boats complete the rainbow of colours,
docked alongside piles of fishing nets,
sleek cats and, in the summer, a sprawl
of terrace cafes and restaurants. The
international hit film *Il Postino* was partly
filmed here; it really *is* a magical spot –
don't miss it.

Procida

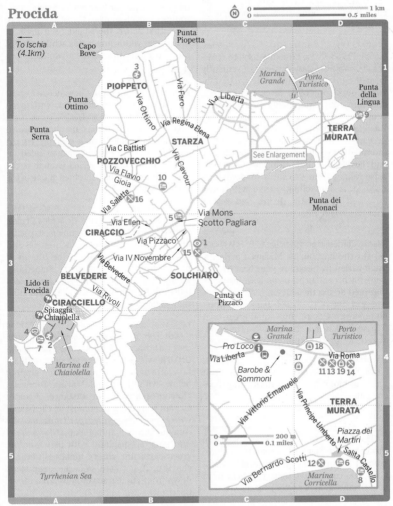

Further south, off Via Pizzaco, a steep flight of steps leads down to sand-brushed Spiaggia di Chiaia, one of the island's most beautiful beaches and home to several good seafood restaurants.

MARINA DI CHIAIOLELLA

All pink, white and blue, crescent-shaped Marina di Chiaiolella was once the crater of a volcano. Today it features a yacht-stocked marina, old-school eateries and a relaxed laid-back charm. From the pier, you can catch a brightly painted water taxi to reach several superb beaches in the surrounding area (from €8). The crystal clear waters around here are perfect for diving too.

Procida Diving Centre DIVING
(☑081 896 83 85; Via Cristoforo Colombo 6, Marina di Chiaiolella; ⊙May-Oct; ⊞) Conveniently located right on the marina, this well-established outfit organises dives and courses, and hires out equipment. Depending on your level, there are four diving sites in Procida: Punta Pizzaco (intermediate to experienced); Secca delle Formiche (beginner-intermediate); Capo Bove (beginner); and Punta Solchiaro (intermediate). The price ranges from €45 for a single dive to €130 for a snorkelling course with more advanced open-water diving and rescue courses also on offer.

Cesare BOAT TOUR
(Marina Corricella; per 2½ hours €26; ⊙May-Oct; ⊞) On the harbour at Marina Corricella, ask for friendly Cesare in your best Italian. Look for his colourful boats with his name blazoned across the side or, if all else fails, check at one of the beach bars – he won't be far away. Cesare runs some great boat trips as well as half-day trips in a traditional galleon for €100 (minimum 25 people).

Barcheggiando BOATING
(☑081 810 19 34; Marina Chiaiolella) This outfit hires out motor boats and *gommoni* (wooden boats) from €100 per day.

**Blue Dream Yacht
Charter Boating** BOAT HIRE
(☑339 5720874, 081 896 05 79; www.bluedream charter.com; Via Ottimo 3, Pioppeto) If you have grander 'champagne on the deck' aspirations, you can always charter a yacht from here (from €1500 per week). Sleeps six.

Barobe & Gommoni BICYCLE HIRE
(☑339 7163303; Via Roma 134, Marina Grande; per day €10; ⊞) The bicycles for hire here are one of the best ways to explore the island. There are small, open micro-taxis that can also be hired for two to three hours for around €35, depending on your bargaining prowess.

★☆ Festivals & Events

Procession of the Misteri RELIGIOUS
Good Friday sees a colourful procession when a wooden statue of Christ and the Madonna Addolarata, along with life-sized tableaux of plaster and papier-mâché illustrating events leading to Christ's crucifixion, are carted across the island. Men dress in blue tunics with white hoods, while many of the young girls dress as the Madonna.

✗ Eating

Prime waterfront dining here needn't equal an overpriced disappointment, with portside trattorias serving fresh classic fare. Several inland trattorias use home-grown produce and game in their cooking. Try the zesty *insalata al limone,*a lemon salad infused with chilli oil. Marina Grande is the place to mix with the fishermen at one of the earthy local bars.

Bar Cavaliere PASTICCERIA €
(☑081 810 10 74; Via Roma 76, Marina Grande; pastries from €1) Procida's prime pastry shop has a delicious range of cakes, pastries and sweet treats. All the rage is the *lingua di bue* (ox tongue), a flaky pastry shaped like a tongue and filled with *crema pasticcera* (custard). It doubles as a cocktail bar if all that sugar builds up a thirst.

La Conchiglia SEAFOOD €€
(☑081 896 76 02; www.laconchigliaristorante. com; Via Pizzaco 10, Solchiaro; meals €25; ⊙Mar-Oct) The views from here are pure holiday-brochure magic: turquoise water lapping below, with the pastel Marina Corricella glowing gently in the distance. A more elegant restaurant than most on the island, with gems such as *spiedini di mazzancolle* (prawn kebabs) and a superb *spaghetti alla povera* (spaghetti with *peperoncino*, green capsicum, cherry tomatoes and anchovies). To get here, take the steep steps down from Via Pizzaco or book a boat from Corricella.

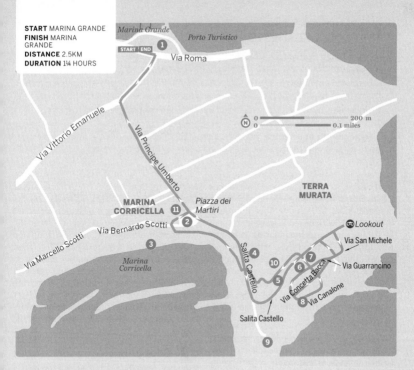

START MARINA GRANDE
FINISH MARINA GRANDE
DISTANCE 2.5KM
DURATION 1¼ HOURS

Marina Grande

Porto Turistico

START | END ① Via Roma

Via Vittorio Emanuele

Via Principe Umberto

0 ──────── 200 m
0 ──────── 0.1 miles

TERRA MURATA

MARINA CORRICELLA ⑪ Piazza dei Martiri

② Via Bernardo Scotti

③ Lookout

Via San Michele

Via Marcello Scotti

Marina Corricella

Salita Castello

④ ⑩ ⑦ Via Guarrancino

⑥ Via Concetta Bacca

⑤ Via Canalone

⑧ Via Canalone

Salita Castello

⑨

Walking Tour
An Evocative Walk

❯ From Marina Grande, turn left past ① **Santa Maria della Pietà** church. Turn right on Via Vittorio Emanuele. After around 200m, turn left at Via Principe Umberto, which gradually climbs. After around 500m you arrive at ② **Piazza dei Martiri**, where you can admire the view of lovely ③ **Marina Corricella** below.

Have a look at the mosaics within the 17th-century church here, then carry on along Salita Castello beside the crumbling 16th-century ④ **Castello d'Avalos**, until you reach the canons. You are now in Procida's ancient Terra Murata district. Walk through the ⑤ **Porta Romantica** tunnel and follow signs to the Belvedere. Turn right on Via San Michele through the ⑥ **Porta di Mezzomo** and stop for an ice cream at hole-in-the-wall ⑦ **Bar del Castello**. Turn left along Borgo San Michele and continue on to the Belvedere to feast your eyes on the spectacular Bay of Naples' view.

Double back 20m and turn left to the ⑧ **Abbazia di San Michele Arcangelo**;

the chapel here dates from the 7th century. Retrace your steps and head for the back of the chapel up Via Concetta Bacca and Via Canalone from where you have a good view of the abandoned church (which is gradually being restored) ⑨ **Santa Margherita Vecchia**. Continue along to the end and turn right through a small tunnel flanked by simple houses. Continue down Via Guarrancino and return via Porta di Mezzomo. Around 50m further on, take the steep steps to your right continuing down to the former moat, flanked by surreal ridged rock. Emerge at the former ⑩ **Penitenziari di Grazia** prison and take the path down to join the road that meets Piazza dei Martiri. Descend the steps to the marina. Walk along this lovely picturesque beach until you reach some steep steps on your right. Take Via Bernado Scotti, flanked by orchards, and turn left at the T-junction past the 18th century ⑪ **Chiesa San Leonardo** to the turn off to Via Principe Umberto and retrace your steps to the marina.

BEST LOCAL FESTIVALS

» **Capri Tango Festival** (www.capritourism.com; Capri) A skirt-swirling combo of music, dancing, exhibitions and tango classes (19 to 22 June).

» **Festa di Sant'Anna** (p129) The allegorical 'burning of the Castello Aragonese' on 26 July, with a hypnotic procession of boats and fireworks.

» **Vinischia** (p129) A four-day regional food and wine celebration in July that brings the foodies out in droves.

» **Settembrata Anacaprese** (www.capritourism.com; Capri) Annual celebration of the grape harvest with gastronomic events and markets (1 to 15 September).

Caracale SEAFOOD €

(☑081 896 91 92; Via Marina Corricella 6, Marina Corricella; meals €20) Along this unpretentious marina, with its old fishing boats, piles of fishing nets and meandering cats, any restaurant will provide you with a memorable dining experience. This place is one of the best. Go for a simple fresh seafood dish, like soup with mussels or grilled swordfish and don't forget to order the tangy fresh lemon salad with fresh mint. Delicious.

Da Giorgio TRATTORIA €

(☑081 896 79 10; Via Roma 36, Marina Grande; meals €18; ☺Mar-Oct; 🖘) These folks try hard to please with a reasonably-priced menu, welcoming window boxes and inexpensive beer. The menu holds few surprises but the ingredients are fresh, zesty and in evidence, like the cherry tomatoes that top the *gnocchi alla sorrentina* (gnocchi in a tomato, basil and pecorino cheese sauce) and the freshly grated Parmesan.

La Lampara SEAFOOD €€

(☑081 896 75 75; Hotel La Corricella, Marina Corricella; meals €25; ☺May-Oct) Enjoy the view of the marina from the restaurant terrace. The dishes of choice are centred on seafood, based on the freshest catch of the day. Get your feet wet with the marinated seafood antipasti before taking the plunge with a hearty plate of *ravioli a'sapore di mare* (seafood ravioli).

Fammivento SEAFOOD €€

(☑081 896 90 20; Via Roma 39, Marina Grande; meals €25; ☺closed Sun night, Mon & Nov-Mar) Get things going with the *frittura di calamari* (fried squid), then try the *fusilli carciofi e calamari* (pasta with artichokes and calamari). For a splurge, go for the house speciality of *zuppa di crostaci e molluschi* (crustacean and mollusc soup). The €14 menu will be sure to put a waddle in your step.

Ristorante Scarabeo CAMPANIAN €€

(☑081 896 99 18; Via Salette 10; meals €28) Behind a veritable jungle of lemon trees lies the venerable kitchen of Signora Battinelli. Along with husband Franco, she whips up classics such as *fritelle di basilico* (fried patties of bread, egg, Parmesan and basil), and homemade aubergine and provola ravioli (€10). They breed their own rabbits, make their own *falanghina* and it's all yours to devour under a pergola of bulbous lemons. Located near the centre of the island.

Shopping

Low-key Procida isn't a shopping heavyweight. Good buys include flouncy beach wear and wine.

Enoteca Borgo Antico DRINK

(☑081 896 96 38; Via Vittorio Emanuele 13, Marina Grande) This slick little bottle shop stocks the best of Campanian vino and a smattering of other Italian drops. The friendly owner will advise you (in Italian) of the best local wines and the best deals. *Limoncello* and a wide choice of traditional and more modern flavoured grappas also available.

Maricella ACCESSORIES

(☑081 896 05 61; www.maricella.it; Via Roma 161, Marina Grande) This is a sweet little boutique which sells brightly coloured accessories, including jewellery that looks good enough to eat: necklaces strung with what resemble M&Ms, brilliant sherbet-yellow earrings, gobstopper sized rings, as well as pretty sandals, raffia bags and totes for the beach.

Mediterraneo FASHION

(☑081 196 69 09; Via Roma 32, Marina Grande) The fashions here are made from wispy fine cotton, perfect for those sizzling summer days. Floaty dresses patterned like a meadow of wild flowers, long light-as-a-feather skirts, snow-drift white transparent shirts and some dressier wear with beautiful colourful designs.

ℹ Information

Tourist Office

Pro Loco (☎081 810 19 68; www.prolocopro cida.it; Via Roma, Stazione Marittima, Marina Grande; ⏱9.30am-6pm) Located at the Ferry & Hydrofoil Ticket Office, this modest office has sparse printed information but should be able to advise on activities and the like.

ℹ Getting There & Away

Bus

Caremar (☎081 837 07 00; www.caremar.it) operates up to 8 daily hydrofoils to/from Naples and Procida (€13, 25 minutes).

SNAV (☎081 837 75 77; www.snav.com) operates hydrofoils to/from Naples and Procida (€18. 25 minutes, four daily)

For more information on ferries to the island, see the Transport section (p266 in the Survival Guide.

ℹ Getting Around

The island measures a mere 3.8 square kilo-metres and can be walked. Apparently, it has been deduced (by an extremely bored person) that no matter where you want to get to on the island, it will only take you a maximum of 6000 steps.

Bus

There is a limited bus service (€1), with four lines radiating from Marina Grande. Bus L1 connects the port and Via Marina di Chiaiolella.

THE ISLANDS PROCIDA

The Amalfi Coast

Best Places to Eat

» Donna Rosa (p157)
» Next 2 (p157)
» Marina Grande (p166)
» L'Antica Trattoria (p147)

Best Places to Stay

» Pensione Maria Luisa (p206)
» Ulisse (p204)
» Hotel Caruso (p209)
» Hotel Lidomare (p208)

Why Go?

Deemed by UNESCO as an outstanding example of a Mediterranean landscape, the Amalfi Coast is a beguiling combination of great beauty and gripping drama: coastal mountains plunge into the sea in a stunning vertical scene of precipitous crags, picturesque towns and lush forests.

Among the glittering string of coastal gems, legendary Positano and Amalfi sparkle the brightest, while mountaintop Ravello has the glossy fame of its grandiose villas and Wagnerian connection. Sorrento and Salerno are the two main entry points to the coast. The former, a cliff-top resort, has miraculously survived the onslaught of package tourism while Salerno is a workaday port with an unhurried charm and vibrant historic centre.

Aside from its sheer beauty, the Amalfi Coast is home to some superb restaurants and hotels. It is also one of Italy's top regions for hiking, with well-marked trails providing a great way of getting away from the clamour on the coast.

Road Distance (KM)

	Sorrento	Amalfi	Positano	Ravello
Amalfi	25			
Positano	13	10		
Ravello	32	03	16	
Minori	30	05	15	06

Getting Around

Consider well-connected Sorrento your base and luxuriate in ferry travel, which connects the major resorts from April to September. Bicycles and scooters can be useful for exploring inland, as can your own two legs with the numerous walking trails in the area. The Circumvesuviana train runs from Naples' Piazza Garibaldi to Sorrento, from where there are regular buses to Positano, Amalfi and Salerno. For ultimate flexibility, consider renting a car in Sorrento and, if you're game, driving along the famous Amalfi Coast road. Overall, although distances between the resorts and towns are not great, congestion in the summer months means car travel can be slow.

THREE PERFECT DAYS

Day 1: Take to the Seas

Wake up in picturesque Positano and head for the Spiaggia Grande, to sip a cappuccino overlooking the bodies-beautiful and bobbing fishing boats. Peruse the fashions, duck into the church and stroll around the cliff to low-key Fornillo for lunch. Catch a ferry to pretty Amalfi and explore the extraordinary cathedral, the museums, the medieval backstreets and the *pasticcerie*. Have dinner in lovely, atmospheric Atrani, a short stroll away.

Day 2: Hike Amid Stunning Scenery

Hiking trails wend their way through compelling coastal routes and countryside. Energetic souls can stride out on the poetically named *Sentiero degli Dei* (Walk of the Gods), high up in the hills. It takes six hours, so it is breathtaking in all senses of the word. If this sounds daunting, there are some delightful shorter walks available; tourist offices and bookshops can provide maps.

Day 3: Head for the Wild West

Rent a car from Sorrento and take in the mountains and seascapes in this little-known corner. Leave town on the minor coastal road, winding through groves of olive and lemon trees. Dip down to the beach at Marina di Puolo, admire the view of Capri from the lookout in Massa Lubrense and head for dramatic Punta della Campanella. Continue to Nerano, and walk to Baia di Leranto beach (the walk takes about an hour), before carrying on to tranquil Sant'Agata sui due Golfi and doubling back to Sorrento.

Accommodation

If you are planning on exploring beyond the coast, Sorrento has the best transport connections and is a good base. Positano, Amalfi and Ravello have some of the classiest accommodation in Italy, ranging from sumptuous *palazzi* to exquisite B&Bs. Book ahead in summer and remember most hotels close over the winter. For more information, see the Accommodation chapter (p194).

DON'T MISS

This is one of the most stunning and accessible regions for exploring on foot. There are numerous well marked trails ranging from straightforward strolls on reasonably level terrain to more taxing puff-you-out hikes.

Best Food Festivals

» Sagra della Salsiccia e Ceppone (Sorrento; p147)

» Gustaminori (Minori; p172)

» Sagra del Tonno (Cetara; p173)

Best Beaches

» Baia de Leranto (p148)

» Spiaggia di Fornillo (p156)

» Marina di Praia (p162)

» Bagni Regina Giovanna (p145)

Resources

» **Positano Online** (www.positanoonline.it) General tourist information about Positano.

» **Sorrento Online** (www.sorrento-online.com) General tourist information about Sorrento.

» **Amalfi Coast Web** (www.amalficoastweb.com) Guide to services throughout the Amalfi Coast.

To Naples

To Naples (21km)

Torre Annunziata

A3

SS

N
0 — 5 km
0 — 2.5 miles

Bay of Naples
(Golfo di Napoli)

Castellammare di Stabia
Stabia

SS145

Marina di Equa

Vico Equense

Massaquano

SS145

Moiano

Santa Maria del Castello

Meta

Positano ❶

Marina di Puolo

Sant'Agnello

Peninsula

SS163

Marina della Lobra

❸ Sorrento

Sorrento

Sant'Agata sui due Golfi

SS145

Massa Lubrense

Termini

Sant'Agata

Mt San Costanzo (497m)

Nerano

Punta Campanella Marine Reserve

Marina del Cantone

Punta Penna

Capri

Capri Town

The Amalfi Coast Highlights

❶ Mixing with the beautiful people on the designer-clad streets of vertiginous **Positano** (p156)

❷ Sitting down to super-fresh seafood at the tiny harbour of **Cetara** (p173)

❸ Going shopping in **Sorrento** (p144) for traditional marquetry pieces

❹ Checking out one of the most stunningly-situated nightclubs in Italy in **Praiano** (p162)

❺ Walking from Amalfi to neighbouring **Atrani** (p164),

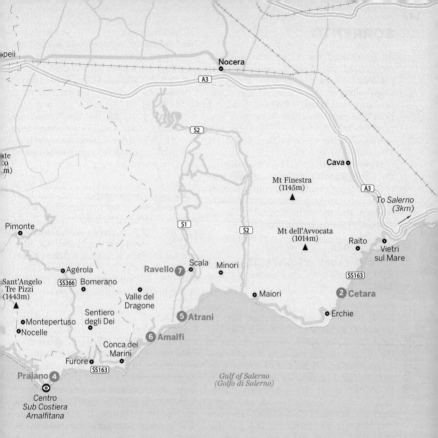

with its ancient piazza, pavement cafes and pretty cove beach

6 Hiring a boat at **Amalfi** (p164) and pootling down the coast in search of the perfect swimming spot

7 Gaping, open-mouthed, at the views from the Belvedere of Infinity in Ravello's **Villa Cimbrone** (p170)

SORRENTO
POP 16,589

An unashamed resort, Sorrento is still a civilized old town. Even the souvenirs are a cut above the norm, with plenty of fine old shops selling ceramics, lacework and *intarsio* (marquetry items) – famously produced here. The main drawback is the lack of a proper beach; the town straddles the cliffs overlooking the water to Naples and Mt Vesuvius.

Sorrento makes a good base for exploring the surrounding area: to the south, the best of the peninsula's unspoilt countryside and; to the east, the Amalfi Coast; to the north, Pompeii and the archaeological sites; offshore, the fabled island of Capri.

◎ Sights

The town centre is compact and all the main sights are within walking distance of Piazza Tasso.

Museo Correale   MUSEUM
(☏081 878 18 46; www.museocorreale.com; Via Correale 50; admission €7; ◷9.30am-6.30pm Tue-Sat, 9.30am-1.30pm Sun) Located to the east of the city centre, this museum is well worth a visit whether you are a clock collector, an archaeological egghead or into embroidery. In addition to the rich assortment of 17th- to 19th-century Neapolitan art and crafts, there are Japanese, Chinese and European ceramics, clocks, furniture and, on the ground floor, Greek and Roman artefacts.

The bulk of the collection, along with the 18th-century villa home, was donated to the city in the 1920s by aristocratic counts Alfredo and Pompeo Correale. Do wander around the gardens with their breathtaking coastal views and rare plants and flowers.

Marina Grande   HARBOUR
(Via Marina Grande) The closest thing to a *spiaggia* (beach) is the pleasant sandy stretch at the harbour at Marina Grande; if you want to just loll in the sun, nearby jetties sport the ubiquitous umbrellas and deckchairs. While it's far smaller than the island of Procida in the Bay of Naples, this former fishing district has a glimmer of similarity with its pastel-coloured houses, brightly painted boats and fishermen mending nets.

There are some earthy seafood restaurants here as well, serving fish from the morning's catch.

Sedile Dominava   HISTORIC BUILDING
(Via San Cesareo) Incongruously wedged between racks of lemon-themed souvenir merchandise, this 15th-century domed *palazzo* has exquisite, albeit faded, original frescoes. Crowned by a cupola, the terrace, open to the street on two sides, was originally a meeting point for the town's medieval aristocracy; today it houses a workingmen's club where local pensioners sit around playing cards, providing a not-to-be-missed photo opportunity.

Centro Storico   HISTORIC CENTRE
(Corso Italia) The bustling old town centres on this street; it's a major hub for shops, restaurants and bars, but duck into the side streets and you will find narrow lanes flanked by traditional green-shuttered buildings, interspersed with the occasional *palazzo,* piazza or church. Souvenir shops, trattorias and some fine old buildings also jostle for space in this tangle of cobbled backstreets.

FREE Duomo   CATHEDRAL
(Corso Italia; free; ◷8am-noon & 4-8pm) To get a feel for Sorrento's history, stroll down Via Pietà from Piazza Tasso and past two medieval palaces en route to the cathedral with its striking exterior fresco, triple-tiered bell tower, four classical columns and elegant *majolica* clock. Take note of the striking marble bishop's throne (1573) and the beautiful wooden choir stalls decorated in the local *intarsio* style.

The cathedral's original structure dates from the 15th century but it has been altered several times, most recently in the early 20th century when the current facade was added.

Museo Bottega della Tarsia Lignea   MUSEUM
(☏081 877 19 42; Via San Nicola 28; admission €8; ◷9.30am-1pm & 4pm-6pm Tue-Sun) Since the 18th century, Sorrento has been famous for its *intarsio* furniture, made with elaborately designed inlaid wood. Some wonderful examples can be found in this museum, housed in an 18th-century palace, complete with beautiful frescoes.

There's also an interesting collection of paintings, prints and photographs depicting the town and surrounding area in the 19th century. If you're interested in purchasing a new intarsio piece, visit Gargiulo & Jannuzzi, one of the longest-established specialist shops in town, who are happy to ship.

FREE **Chiesa di San Francesco** CHURCH
(Via San Francesco; ☺8am-1pm & 2-8pm) Located next to the Villa Communale Park, this is one of Sorrento's most beautiful churches. Surrounded by bougainvillea and birdsong, the evocative cloisters have an Arabic portico and interlaced arches, supported by octagonal pillars. The church is most famous, however, for its summer program of concerts featuring world-class performers from the classical school. If this strikes a chord, check out the schedule at the tourist office. There are also regular art exhibitions.

Il Vallone dei Mulino HISTORIC SITE
(Via Fuorimura, Valley of the Mills) Just behind Piazza Tasso, a stunning natural phenomenon is on view from Via Fuorimura. This deep cleft in the mountain dates from a volcanic eruption 35,000 years ago. Sorrento was once bounded by three gorges, but today this is the only one that remains. It is named after the ancient wheat mills that were once located here, the ruins of which are still clearly visible.

FREE **Basilica di Sant'Antonino** CHURCH
(Piazza Sant'Antonino; ☺9am-noon & 5-7pm) Named after the patron saint of Sorrento, the oldest church in town dates from the 11th century. A few Roman artefacts have ended up here, as well as some dark medieval paintings and the oddity of two whale ribs. Apparently, the much-loved saint performed numerous miracles, including one in which he rescued a child from a whale's stomach. The saint's bones lie beneath the baroque interior in an 18th-century crypt.

🏃 Activities

Hiring a boat is an excellent way to explore this rugged, seemingly inaccessible coastline, while others decide to lace up those hiking boots and stride out.

Bagni Regina Giovanna BEACH
(Pollio Felix; 🚻) Sorrento famously lacks a proper beach, so consider heading to Bagni Regina Giovanna, a rocky beach about 2km west of town, set among the ruins of the Roman Villa Pollio Felix. It's a picturesque spot with clear, clean water and it's possible to walk here (follow Via Capo), although you'll save your swimming (and sunbathing) strength if you get the SITA bus headed for Massa Lubrense.

Villa Comunale Park PARK
(☺8am-midnight) This lushly landscaped park has stunning views across the Bay of Naples, including to Mt Vesuvius. A popular green space to while away the sunset hours, it's a lively spot, with benches, operatic buskers and a small bar.

Sic Sic BOATING
(☎081 807 22 83; www.nauticasicsic.com; Marina Piccola; ☺May-Oct) Seek out the best beaches by rented boat. This outfit rents out a variety of boats, starting at around €40 per hour or €100 per day. They also organise boat excursions, wedding shoots and similar.

🍴 Courses

Sorrento Cooking School COOKING
(☎081 878 35 55; www.sorrentocookingschool.com; Viale dei Pini 52, Sant'Agnello) You can opt for a serious culinary vacation here or one of their popular four-hour classes (€60) learning to make such Italian staples as pizza, ravioli and tiramisu (OK, more a sin than a staple) in a beautiful spot, surrounded by lemon trees. The class ends with a meal of the goodies prepared, accompanied by local wine.

Sant'Anna Institute
Sorrento Lingue LANGUAGE COURSE
(☎081 807 55 99; www.sorrentolingue.com; Via San Francesco 8) There is something very appealing about rattling off your shopping list in faultless Italian. This is one of the longest-established language schools on the Amalfi Coast, attracting students from all over the globe. Prices start at €198 for one week of tuition, plus a €75 enrollment fee.

🎉 Festivals & Events

Sorrento Festival CONCERTS
World-class classical concerts are held in the cloisters of the Chiesa di San Francesco between July and September. Ask at the tourist office.

Sant'Antonino SAINT'S DAY
The city's patron saint, Sant'Antonino, is remembered annually with processions and huge markets. The saint is credited with having saved Sorrento during WWII when Salerno and Naples were heavily bombed; 14 February.

Settimana Santa EASTER WEEK
(Holy Week) Famed throughout Italy; the first procession takes place at midnight on the Thursday preceding Good Friday, with

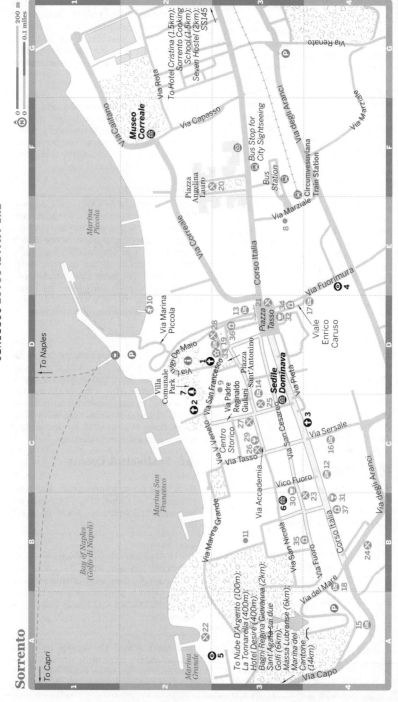

Sorrento

Bay of Naples
(Golfo di Napoli)

To Capri

To Naples

Marina Grande

Marina San Francesco

Marina Piccola

Museo Correale

Villa Comunale Park

Piazza Angelina Lauro

Piazza Tasso

Piazza Sant'Antonino

Piazza Sant'Antonino

Sedile Dominava

Centro Storico

Bus Station

Circumvesuviana Train Station

Bus Stop for City Sightseeing

To Hotel Cristina (1.5km);
Sorrento Cooking
School (1.5km);
Seven Hostel (2km);
SS145

To Nube D'Argento (100m);
La Tonnarella (400m);
Hotel Desirè (400m);
Bagni Regina Giovanna (2km);
Sant'Agata sui due
Golfi (6km);
Massa Lubrense (6km);
Marina del
Cantone
(14km)

Via Califano
Via Rota
Via Capasso
Via Correale
Via Marina Piccola
Via Marina Grande
Via San Francesco
Via San Cesareo
Via degli Aranci
Via Renato
Via Marziale
Via Marziale
Via Fuorimura
Corso Italia
Corso Italia
Viale Enrico Caruso
Via Sersale
Via Pietà
Via Accademia
Via Tasso
Via V Veneto
Via Padre Reginaldo Giuliani
Vico Fuoro
Via San Nicola
Via Fuoro
Via del Mare
Via Capo
Viale Enrico Caruso
Via S/gr De Maio
Via degli Aranci

Sorrento

robed and hooded penitents in white; the second occurs on Good Friday, when participants wear black robes and hoods to commemorate the death of Christ.

Sagra della Salsiccia e Ceppone FOOD FESTIVAL
Sausage lovers can salivate at this annual festival, held on December 13, when hundreds of kilos of sausages are barbecued over a giant bonfire, accompanied by hearty local wine.

 Eating

The centre of town is heaving with bars, cafes, trattorias, restaurants and even the odd kebab takeaway shop. Many of these, particularly those with waistcoated waiters stationed outside (or the ones displaying sun-bleached photos of the dishes) are unashamed tourist traps serving bland food at inflated prices. But this isn't true of all of them and it's perfectly possible to eat well. If you've got your own wheels there are some superb restaurants dotted around the near-

by countryside, including one of Italy's top restaurants in Sant'Agata sui due Golfi.

L'Antica Trattoria CAMPANIAN €€
(☑081 807 10 82; Via Padre Reginaldo Giuliani 33; meals from €40) Head to the upstairs terrace with its flower-filled trellises, traditional tiles and trailing grape vines and you seem a thousand miles away from the pedestrian-choked alleyways outside. With a well-deserved local reputation as being the finest restaurant in town, the menu is mainly traditional, with homemade pasta and a daily fresh fish dish, cooked in salt. There are vegetarian and gluten-free menus, plus a resident mandolin player to ensure a little romance is never too far away.

TOP CHOICE **Aurora Light** CAMPANIAN €€
(☑081 877 26 31; www.auroralight.it; Piazza Tasso 3-4; meals €25) At first glance this menu looks more Californian than Campanian. Predominantly vegetarian, the salads have imaginative combos like spicy chickpeas and spinach, or fennel with beetroot and orange.

HIKING THE PENINSULA

Forming a giant horseshoe between **Punta della Campanella** and **Punta Penna**, the beautiful **Baia de Leranto** is generally regarded as the top swimming spot on the Sorrento Peninsula. To get there you have two alternatives: you can either get a boat or you can walk from the village of Nerano, the steep descent forming part of a longer 6.5km hike from nearby Termini.

This picturesque path is just one of 20 (for a total of 110km) that cover the area. These range from tough all-day treks such as the 14.1km **Alta Via dei Monti Lattari** from the Fontanelle hills near Positano down to the Punta della Campanella, to shorter walks suitable for all the family.

Tourist offices throughout the area can provide maps detailing the colour-coded routes. With the exception of the Alta Via dei Monti Lattari, which is marked in red and white, long routes are shown in red on the map; coast-to-coast trails in blue; paths connecting villages in green; and circular routes in yellow. On the ground, trails are fairly well marked, although you may find some signs have faded to near-indecipherable levels.

Look closer and you'll see that the enthusiastic young owner has tapped into traditional dishes and given them an innovative twist: white bean soup with baby squid, aubergine *parmigiana* with a swordfish sauce, stuffed pepper roulade and so on.

The setting on Piazza Tasso is one of the best for people watching, though one of the worst for exhaust fumes.

🍴 Inn Bufalito
CAMPANIAN €€
(☎081 365 69 75; www.innbufalito.it; Vico 1 Fuoro 21; meals €25; ⊙Apr-Nov) Owner Franco Coppola (no relation to that movie man) exudes a real passion for showcasing local produce – the restaurant is a member of the Slow Food Movement. A mozzarella bar as well as a restaurant, this effortlessly stylish place boasts a menu including delights such as Sorrento-style cheese fondue and buffalo meat *carpaccio*. Cheese tastings are a regular event, along with photography and art exhibitions, and occasional live music.

O'Murzill
NEAPOLITAN €€
(☎081 020 23 71; Via Accademia 17; meals from €20) This restaurant looks as though it belongs in a small rural village, rather than in the heart of tourist-driven Sorrento. There are just six tables in what resembles a homey front room with the kitchen visible beyond. The reassuringly brief menu concentrates on traditional Neapolitan dishes like pasta with lobster, and no-fuss antipasti such as grilled mushrooms with garlic, chilli, parsley and olive oil. There are no complimentary *limoncello* or tomato-topped bruschettas, just well-priced and honest home-style cooking.

Ristorante il Buco
CAMPANIAN €€€
(☎081 878 23 54; Rampa Marina Piccola 5; meals €55; ⊙Thu-Tue Feb-Dec) Housed in a monks' former wine cellar, this dress-for-dinner restaurant offers far from monastic-style cuisine. The emphasis is on innovative regional cooking, so expect modern combos such as pasta with rockfish sauce or *treccia* (local cheese) and prawns served on a bed of capers with tomato and olive sauce. In summer there's outdoor seating near one of the city's ancient gates. Reservations recommended.

Angelina Lauro
CAMPANIAN €
(☎081 807 40 97; Piazza Angelina Lauro 39-40; self-service meal €15; 🍴) Family run since 1980, owner Rafael is a congenial host at this brightly lit, roomy place that has a passing resemblance to a college canteen. No matter – it hits the spot for a filling, inexpensive self-service lunch. Perfect for undecided tastebuds; simply grab a tray and choose from the daily selection of pastas, meats and vegetable side dishes. The owners produce their own wine and olive oil.

Da Emilia
TRATTORIA €
(☎081 807 27 20; Via Marina Grande 62; meals €20; 🍴) Founded in 1947 and still run by the same family, this is an atmospheric, mildly scuffed spot overlooking the fishing boats in Marina Grande. There's a large informal dining room, complete with youthful photos of ex-patron Sophia Loren and a menu of straightforward no-fail dishes like mussels with lemon, and spaghetti with clams.

Refood
CAMPANIAN €€
(☎081 878 14 80; www.refoods.it; Via Accademia 10; meals €35; ⊙5.30pm-midnight) The postmodern

decor with its imaginative lighting, steel exposed pipes and lozenge-coloured seating, is a far cry from Sorrento's traditional trattorias. Go for one of the specialties like large-tube pasta in a fish stew or a classic *chateaubriand*.

La Fenice
CAMPANIAN €€
(☎081 878 16 52; Via degli Aranci 11; meals €24; ☺Tue-Sun) It's too large and bright for a romantic dinner for two but locals continue to recommend this place for its down-to-earth, well-prepared dishes, particularly the seafood, such as mussels with garlic and parsley, and grilled squid.

Drinking & Entertainment

You can do the whole drinking trip in Sorrento: down pints of lager while watching Sky Sports on a big screen, quaff local wines in wood-panelled wine bars, or sip cocktails in swish cafes.

Cafè Latino
CAFE
(☎081 878 37 18; Vico I Fuoro 4A; ☺10am-1am Apr-Sep) Think locked-eyes-over-cocktails time. This is the place to impress your partner with cocktails (from €7) on the terrace, surrounded by orange and lemon trees. Sip a Mary Pickford (rum, pineapple, *grenadino* and maraschino) or a glass of chilled white wine. If you can't drag yourselves away, you can also eat here (meals around €30).

Bollicine
BAR
(☎081 878 46 16; Via Accademia 9; ☺6pm-1am) The wine list at this unpretentious wine bar with a dark, woody interior includes all the big Italian names and a selection of interesting local labels. If you can't decide what to go for, the amiable barman will advise you. There's also a small menu of *panini* (sandwiches), bruschettas and one or two pasta dishes.

English Inn
PUB
(☎081 807 43 57; Corso Italia 55; ☺8am-3am) The vast upstairs garden terrace, with its orange trees and dazzle of bougainvillea, is a delight and attracts a primarily expat crowd who head here for the disco beats and karaoke nights, accompanied by Guinness on tap. The party atmosphere continues late into the night, while the bacon-and-eggs breakfast is a suitable reviver.

Fauno Bar
CAFE
(☎081 878 11 35; Piazza Tasso; ☺8am-midnight Dec-Oct) On Piazza Tasso, this elegant cafe covers half the square and offers the best people-watching in town. It serves stiff drinks at stiff prices – cocktails start around €8.50. Snacks and sandwiches are also available (from €7).

Teatro Tasso
THEATRE
(☎081 807 55 25; www.teatrotasso.com; Piazza Sant'Antonino; admission €25; ☺9.30pm Mon-Sat, Mar-Oct) The southern Italian equivalent of a London old world music hall, Teatro Tasso is home to the *Sorrento Musical*, a sentimental 75-minute revue of Neapolitan classics such as 'O Sole Mio' and 'Trona a Sorrent'.

Shopping

The pedestrian-only *centro storico* (historic centre) is the place to shop. Look out for inlaid wood, Murano glass jewellery and embroidery (including smocked children's dresses).

Unless otherwise stated, the following shops open all day until late in summer and close for lunch in winter.

Gargiulo & Jannuzzi
ARTS & CRAFTS
(☎081 878 10 41; Viale Enrico Caruso 1) Dating from 1863, this old-fashioned warehouse-shop is a classic. Knowledgeable shop assistants will guide you through the three floors

---

MAKE YOUR OWN GELATI

Impress your dinner-party pals with your homemade Italian gelati by taking a course at Gelateria David (☎081 807 36 49; www.gelateriadavidsorrento.it; Via Marziale 19), a cream-of-the-crop gelateria. The third generation in the ice-cream business, David runs classes (€10) that last around an hour and culminate in your very own gelateria certificate. Times vary according to demand, so call or drop by to organise; David speaks excellent English. His specialities include the delicious *profumo de Sorrento*, an orange, lemon and tangerine sorbet, and rum babà. Aside from mango, he only uses fresh fruit, which means his choices vary throughout the season. He also makes all the traditional, more commercial flavours, which are wonderfully creamy and bear little resemblance to that supermarket tub back home.

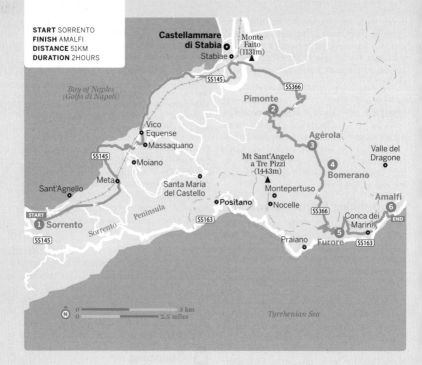

START SORRENTO
FINISH AMALFI
DISTANCE 51KM
DURATION 2HOURS

Driving Tour
Sorrento to Amalfi: The 'Green Ribbon' Route

❯ This drive is an alternative to the infamous Amalfi Coast road (see The Blue Ribbon Drive, p154) and passes through some stunning mountain scenery. From **①** **Sorrento**, hug the coast following signs to Naples on the SS145. Just before Castellammare di Stabia exit, on to the SS366 and head to **②** **Pimonte**. This is a small rural town with tractors trundling through the streets. Stop at the main piazza for the delicious almond-based specialty *torta palummo* at Caffè Palummo. Expect curious stares; tourists are a rarity here. Continue along the SS366, enjoying forests of beech trees and a backdrop of mountains thickly quilted with pines. You are now in the depths of the verdant Parco Regionale dei Monte Lattari.

Next stop is the pretty dairyfood-producing village of **③** **Agérola**. Step into one of numerous delis for local cheeses like *fior di latte* (cows' milk mozzarella) and *caciocavallo* (gourd-shaped traditional curd cheese), produced on the fertile slopes around town. You can also find top quality local salamis

and sausages. The road continues to **④** **Bomerano** (37km), a familiar name to hikers embarking on the Walk of the Gods, p163. Duck into the 16th-century Chiesa San Matteo Apostolo to check out the ceiling frieze, consider the nostalgic treat of poached eggs on toast at Albergo Gentile (geared towards Northern European hikers), then stop by Fusco at Via Principe di Piemonte 3 for a tub of homemade yoghurt.

The road continues winding dramatically down to the sea with some strategically-located lookouts to allow you to gaze at the view with Conca dei Marina twinkling in the distance. At **⑤** **Furore** there is handy parking next to the picturesque Maria SS delle Grazie church, with its adjacent terraced restaurant and small deli. Follow the road round the magnificent Furore fjord (best appreciated from this height), which slices through the mountains all the way to the sea. At km 49.7 the road divides and you can turn off to Positano (16kms) or continue the remaining kilometre or so to **⑥** **Amalfi**.

of locally made goods ranging from ceramic crockery to inlaid *intarsio* wooden pieces, embroidered lace and pottery. The prices are as good as you will get anywhere in town and the choice is certainly superior. Shipping is free for purchases exceeding €220.

La Rapida   SHOES
(☑338 877 705; Via Fuoro 67) There are numerous shops selling leather sandals in the *centro storico* but head to the far end of Via Fuoro and you'll find this tiny cobbler. An old-fashioned shop, it doesn't have a huge range, but the quality's as good as anywhere else and the prices (from €30) are generally better. It also does repairs.

Stinga   ARTS & CRAFTS
(☑081 878 11 30; www.stingatarsia.com; Via Luigi de Maio 16) Well worth seeking out, this place sells distinctive inlaid-wood items made in Sorrento by the same family of craftsmen (and women) for three generations. The pieces are highly original, especially in their use of colour and design, which is often mosaic or geometric. Fine jewellery, including coral pieces, is also on display, made by family member, Amulè.

Venti10   ACCESSORIES
(☑081 180 74 87; Corso Italia 89) Come here for eye catching accessories, including dazzling silk scarves, snazzy jewellery and some classy surprises like genuine Panama hats imported from Ecuador in bright gelati colours (as well as the traditional cream).

❶ Information
Tourist Office (☑081 807 40 33; Via Luigi De Maio 35; ☺8.45am-6.15pm Mon-Sat) In the Circolo dei Forestieri (Foreigners' Club).

❶ Getting There & Around
Car & Motorcycle
Coming from Naples and the north, take the A3 autostrada until Castellammare di Stabia; exit there and follow the SS145 south.

Car Rental
Renting a car provides the optimum flexibility and Sorrento is an excellent base for exploring the Amalfi Coast and beyond. The big international operators are here, as well as some local outfits.

Avis (☑081 878 24 59; www.avisautonoleggio.it; Viale Nizza 53)

Hertz (☑081 807 16 46; www.hertz.it; Via degli Aranci 9)

Autoservizi De Martino (☑081 878 28 01; www.autoservizidemartino.com; Via Parsano 8) Has cars from €58 a day, €280 per week, plus 50cc scooters from €23 for four hours.

Parking
In midsummer, finding a parking spot can be a frustrating business, particularly as much of the parking on the side streets is for residents only and the city centre is closed to traffic for much of the day. There are well-signposted car parks near the ferry terminal, on the corner of Via degli Aranci and Via Renato, and heading west out of town near Via Capo (€2 per hour).

Boat
Sorrento is the main jumping-off point for Capri and also has excellent ferry connections to Ischia, Naples and Amalfi coastal resorts during the summer months.

Gescab (☑081 807 18 12; www.gescab.it) Runs hydrofoils to Naples (€11, 35 minutes, seven daily) and to Capri (€15, 20 minutes, 18 daily), Ischia (€18, one hour, two daily), Positano (€13, 30 minutes, one daily) and Amalfi (€14, 50 minutes, one daily).

Metrò del Mare (☑199 60 07 00; www.metrodelmare.net; ☺Jun-Sep) Runs ferries to Positano (€15, 35 minutes, two daily), Amalfi (€15, one hour, two daily), Naples Beverello (€11, 30 minutes, one daily) and Salerno (€15, 1 hour, 20 minutes, one daily).

Caremar (☑081 807 30 77; www.caremar.it) Runs hydrofoils to Capri (€13, 25 minutes, four daily)

To/From the Airport
Naples' **Capodichino Airport** (www.gesac.it) is the closest airport to Sorrento and the Amalfi Coast.

BUS Curreri (p265) runs eight daily services to Sorrento from Naples Capodichino airport. Buses depart from outside the arrivals hall and arrive in Piazza Angelina Lauro. Buy tickets (€10) for the 75-minute journey on the bus.

CAR Numerous local and international agencies have desks at the airport.

TAXI A taxi from the airport to Sorrento costs around €80.

Bus
SITA (☑199 73 07 49; www.sitabus.it) buses serve Naples, the Amalfi Coast and Sant'Agata, leaving from the bus stop across from the entrance of the Circumvesuviana train station. Buy tickets at the station bar or from shops with the blue SITA sign.

Train
Circumvesuviana (p270) Sorrento is the last stop on the train line from Naples. Trains run every half-hour for Naples (one hour 10

minutes), via Pompeii (30 minutes) and Ercolano (50 minutes). Invest in a *Unico Costiera* card (p152).

West of Sorrento

If you are here in midsummer, consider escaping the crowds by heading to the green hills around Sorrento. Known as the land of the sirens, in honour of the mythical maiden-monsters who were said to live on Li Galli (a tiny archipelago off the peninsula's southern coast), the area to the west of Massa Lubrense is among the least developed and most beautiful in the country.

Tortuous roads wind their way through hills covered in olive trees and lemon groves, passing through sleepy villages and tiny fishing ports. There are magnificent views at every turn, the best from the high points overlooking Punta della Campanella, the westernmost point of the Sorrento Peninsula. Offshore, Capri looks tantalisingly close.

MASSA LUBRENSE

The first town you come to following the coast west from Sorrento is Massa Lubrense. Situated 120m above sea level, it's a disjointed place, comprising a small town centre and 17 *frazioni* (fractions or hamlets) joined by an intricate network of paths and mule tracks. For those without a donkey, there are good road connections and SITA buses regularly run between them.

◉ Sights & Activities

Chiesa di Santa Maria della Grazia   CHURCH
(Largo Vescovado; ⊘7am-noon & 4.30-8pm) Don't forget your camera, as there are fabulous views over Capri from the town's central Largo Vescovado. On its northern flank stands the former cathedral, the 16th-century Chiesa di Santa Maria della Grazia, worth a quick look for the bright majolica-tiled floor, which would look *so* good in your kitchen back home.

Marina della Lobra   HARBOUR
From the square it's a 2km descent to this pretty little marina backed by ramshackle houses and verdant slopes – or, rather, a 40-minute downhill walk, and a wheezing hour-long ascent. The marina is a good place to rent a boat, the best way of reaching the otherwise difficult-to-get-to bays and inlets along the coast.

Coop Marina della Lobra   BOATING
(☑081 808 93 80; www.marinalobra.com; Marina della Lobra; per hr from €30) Operating out of a kiosk by the car park, this boat hire outfit is reliable.

✗ Eating

La Torre   SEAFOOD €€
(☑081 80 89 56; Piazzetta Annunziata 7, Annunziata, Massa Lubrense; meals €42; ⊘Wed-Mon, Apr-Feb) This delightful, laid-back restaurant on a tranquil square serves mouth-watering traditional cuisine with an emphasis on seafood. A member of the Slow Food Movement, the menu changes seasonally, but you can usually depend on classics like *tonani con patate* (tuna with potatoes). Consider the cholesterol-overdose indulgence of a nine-cheese taster (€6), ranging from fresh *caciottina* from Massa Lubrense to *provolone del Monaco* (a seasoned semi-hard cheese made from cows' milk).

Eat alfresco on the terrace, then stroll down to the belvedere for a rare wide-angle shot of Capri, Ischia, Procida, Naples and Vesuvius.

Funiculi Funiculá   SEAFOOD €€
(Via Fontanelle 16, Marina della Lobra; meals €32; ⊘Apr-Oct; ⊞) This great bar-restaurant on the seafront at Marina della Lobra has views of Ischia, Capri and Vesuvius. Unsurprisingly,

---

UNICO COSTIERA

If you plan to do much travelling by SITA bus and/or Circumvesuviana train, then it saves money and hassle to invest in a **Unico Costiera** (www.unicocostiera.it) card, available for durations of 45 minutes (€2.40), 90 minutes (€3.60), 24 hours (€7.20) or 72 hours (€15). Aside from the SITA buses, the 24- and 72-hour tickets also allow you to hop on the City Sightseeing tourist bus, which travels between Amalfi and Ravello and Amalfi and Maiori. Several tickets can be bought at one time for repeat trips. Note that the ticket-use time begins from the time punched on entering the bus or train, not from when the ticket is purchased.

the menu is dominated by seafood, but there are also family friendly meal-in-one salads and the usual array of grilled-meat dishes. Those with expanding midriffs can behave with a fresh fruit salad dessert or misbehave by popping next door to their cafe for a chocolate-filled crêpe or ice cream.

❶ Information

Tourist Office (☑081 533 90 21; www.mas salubrense.it; Viale Filangieri 11; ⊗9.30am-1pm daily & 4.30-8pm Mon, Tue & Thu-Sat) Can provide bus timetables and maps.

❶ Getting There & Around

BUS **SITA** (☑199 73 07 49; www.sitabus.it) Runs hourly buses (7am-9pm) departing from the Circumvesuviana train station in Sorrento.

CAR By car, Massa Lubrense is an easy 20-minute drive from Sorrento.

PARKING A matter of trawling the streets; there are some meters in the centre (€2 per hour).

SANT'AGATA SUI DUE GOLFI

Perched high in the hills above Sorrento, Sant'Agata sui due Golfi is the most famous of Massa Lubrense's 17 *frazioni*. Boasting spectacular views of the Bay of Naples on one side and the Gulf of Salerno on the other (hence its name, 'St Agatha on the two Gulfs'), it's a tranquil place that manages to retain its rustic charm despite a fairly heavy hotel presence. For information on the village and surrounding countryside, stop by the small **Tourist Office** (☑081 533 01 35; www.santagatasuiduegolfi.it; Corso Sant'Agata 25; ⊗9am-1pm & 5.30-9pm) on the main square.

For hikers, this area offers around 22 marked and well-maintained trails, stretching a total length of some 110km (66 miles). The tourist office can provide details. If you fancy a relatively easy stroll which doesn't require a compass or hiking boots, there's a picturesque 3km trail between Sorrento and Sant'Agata. From Piazza Tasso, venture south along Viale Caruso and Via Fuorimura to pick up the Circumpiso footpath, marked in green on the walking maps available from tourist offices. The walk should take approximately one hour.

◉ Sights

Chiesa di Sant'Agata   CHURCH
(Piazza Sant'Agata; ⊗8am-1pm & 5-7pm) Located in the centre of the village, enjoy the cool decorative interior of this 17th-century parish church, famed for its 17th-century polychrome marble altar; an exquisite work of inlaid marble, mother-of-pearl, lapis lazuli and malachite.

Convento del Deserto   CONVENT
(☑081 878 01 99; Via Deserto; ⊗8.30am-12.30pm & 4-9pm) This Carmelite convent is located 1.5km uphill from the village centre, so read on carefully before striding out. It was founded in the 17th century and is still home to a closed community of Benedictine nuns. While of moderate interest (unless you are one of the nuns), it is the 360-degree views that should make that knee-wearying hike worthwhile.

✕ Eating

For such a small place, Sant'Agata offers a surprisingly sophisticated culinary repertoire.

TOP
CHOICE **Ristorante Don Alfonso 1890**   MEDITERRANEAN €€€
(☑081 533 02 26; www.donalfonso.com; Corso Sant'Agata 11; meals €115-125; ⊗closed Mon & Tue, except Tue night Jun-Sep, closed Jan–early Mar & Nov-Dec; ℗) This restaurant with two Michelin stars is generally regarded as one of Italy's finest. Dishes are prepared with produce from the chef's own 6-hectare farm. The dining hall is a picture of refined taste, and the international wine list is one of the country's most extensive and best.

The menu changes seasonally, but hallmark dishes include lightly seared tuna in red-pepper sauce and pasta with clams and courgettes. The restaurant is part of a same name hotel and also organise cooking courses. Reservations essential.

Lo Stuzzichino   NEAPOLITAN €
(☑081 533 00 10; www.ristorantelostuzzichino.it; Via Deserto 1a; meals €18, pizzas from €5; ⊗Feb-Dec) Just down the road from Sant'Agata's church, this Slow Food Movement affiliated restaurant has a gregarious host in owner Paolo de Gregorio. Try the specialities: fish rolls stuffed with smoked cheese or seafood stew with seasonal vegetables. The rare *gamberetti di Crapolla* (prawns) taste a whole lot better than they sound.

❶ Getting There & Around

BUS **SITA** (☑199 73 07 49; www.sitabus.it) Buses depart hourly from Sorrento's Circumvesuviana train station.

CAR By car, follow the SS145 west from Sorrento for about 7km until you see signs off to the right.

THE AMALFI COAST WEST OF SORRENTO

THE BLUE RIBBON DRIVE

Stretching from **Vietri sul Mare** to **Sant'Agata sui due Golfi**, near Sorrento, the **SS163**, nicknamed the *Nastro Azzurro* (Blue Ribbon), remains one of Italy's most stunning and dramatic roads. Commissioned by Bourbon King Ferdinand II and completed in 1853, it wends its way along the Amalfi Coast's entire length, snaking round impossibly tight curves, over deep ravines and through tunnels gouged out of sheer rock. It's a magnificent feat of civil engineering although, as John Steinbeck pointed out in his 1953 essay, *My Positano*, the road is also "carefully designed to be a little narrower than two cars side by side...".

In short, it is a severe test of driving skill and courage, a white-knuckle, 50km ride that will pit you against the extraordinary ability of the local bus drivers. The price for those sublime views is numerous switchbacks and plunging drops to the sea, frequently with only waist-high barriers between you and oblivion.

Originally designed for horse-drawn carriages, the road tends to become even narrower on hairpin bends. To avoid blocking oncoming buses, check the circular mirrors on the roadside and listen for the sound of klaxons – if you hear one, slow right down as it will invariably be followed by a coach. Avoid peak season (July and August) and morning, lunchtime and evening rush hours. The trick to driving the coast is to stay calm, even when your toddler throws up all over the back seat or your partner tells you to look at the view while you're inching around a blind corner.

And never fear, if you are not brave enough to get behind the wheel yourself, you can easily hop on one of the SITA buses that follow this route daily.

PARKING There is generally street parking available, although August can be busy, especially in the evening.

MARINA DEL CANTONE

From Massa Lubrense, follow the coastal road round to **Termini**. Stop a moment to admire the views before continuing on to **Nerano**, from where a beautiful hiking trail leads down to the stunning **Baia de Leranto** and **Marina del Cantone**. This unassuming village with its small pebble beach is not only a lovely, tranquil place to stay but also one of the area's prime dining spots, a magnet for VIPs who regularly boat over from Capri to eat here, like Bill Gates, Michael Caine and Elton John.

Sights & Activities

A popular diving destination, the protected waters here are part of an 11 sq km reserve called the **Punta Campanella**; it supports a healthy marine ecosystem, with flora and fauna flourishing in underwater grottoes.

Nettuno Diving DIVING
(☎081 808 10 51; www.sorrentodiving.com; Via A Vespucci 39; ⊕) Dive the watery depths of this important marine reserve with this PADI-certified outfit which runs various underwater activities for all ages and abilities. These include snorkelling excursions, beginner's courses, cave dives and immersions off Capri and Li Galli islands. Costs start at €25 (children €15) for a day-long outing to the Baia de Leranto. The company can also organise reasonably-priced accommodation and diving packages.

❶ Getting There & Around

SITA (☎199 73 07 49; www.sitabus.it) Runs regular buses between Sorrento and Marina del Cantone from the Circumvesuviana train station in Sorrento.

East of Sorrento

More developed and less appealing than the coast west of Sorrento, the area to the east of town is not totally without interest. There's the district's longest sandy beach, Spiaggia di Alimuri, at Meta di Sorrento and, 12km beyond that, the Roman villas at Castellammare di Stabia.

Rising above Castellammare and accessible by an eight-minute **cable-car ride** (adult/reduced €7/3.50; ⊕about 30 daily Apr-Oct) from the town's Circumvesuviana train station is Monte Faito (1131m), one of the highest peaks in the Lattari mountains. Covered in thick beech forests, the summit offers some fine walks with sensational views.

VICO EQUENSE

Known to the Romans as Aequa, Vico Equense (Vico) is a small cliff-top town about 10km east of Sorrento and just five stops away via the Circumvesuviana train. Largely bypassed by international tourists, it's a laid-back, authentic place worth a quick stopover, if only to sample some of the famous pizza by the metre. General information on the area's attractions is available from the helpful **Tourist Office** (☑081 801 57 52; www.vicoturismo.it; Piazza Umberto I; ☺9am-2pm & 3-8pm Mon-Sat, 9.30am-1.30pm Sun) in the main square.

The town is easy to explore on foot. From Piazza Umberto I, the 19th-century focal point, take Corso Filangieri along to the small *centro storico*. Here, on a small balcony overlooking the village of Marina di Equa, you'll find the **Chiesa dell'Annunziata** (Via Vescovado; ☺10am-noon Sun), Vico's former cathedral and the only Gothic church on the Sorrento Peninsula. Little remains of the original 14th-century structure other than the lateral windows near the main altar and a few arches in the aisles. In fact, most of what you see today, including the chipped pink-and-white facade, is 17th-century baroque. In the sacristy, check out the portraits of Vico's bishops, all of whom are represented here except for the last one, Michele Natale, who was executed for supporting the ill-fated 1799 Parthenopean Republic. His place is taken by an angel with its finger to its lips, an admonishment to the bishop to keep his liberal thoughts to himself.

✖ Eating

Ristorante & Pizzeria da Gigino PIZZA
(☑081 879 83 09; Via Nicotera 15; pizza per metre €12-26; ☺noon-1am; ✚) Run by the five sons of pizza king Gigino Dell'Amura, who was the very first to introduce pizza by the metre to the world, this barn-like pizzeria produces kilometres of pizza each day in three huge ovens to the right of the entrance. There's a large selection of toppings and the quality is a crust above the norm. Although it seats around 200, you may still have to wait for a table. No reservations are taken.

HISTORIC HAMLETS

Dotted around Vico's surrounding hills are a number of ancient hamlets, known as *casali*. Untouched by mass tourism, they offer a glimpse into a rural way of life that has changed little over the centuries. You will, however, need wheels to get to them. From Vico, take Via Roma and follow Via Rafaelle Bosco, which passes through the *casali* before circling back to town. Highlights include **Massaquano** and the **Capella di Santa Lucia** (open on request), famous for its 14th-century frescoes from the school of Giotto di Bondone (recognised as the forerunner of modern Western painting). **Moiano** is also worth checking out; an ancient path from here leads to the summit of **Monte Faito**. And then there is **Santa Maria del Castello**, with its fabulous views towards the southeast.

Three kilometres to the west of Vico, **Marina di Equa** stands on the site of the original Roman settlement, Aequa. Among the bars and restaurants lining the popular pebble beaches you can still see the remains of the 1st century AD Villa Pezzolo, as well as a defensive tower, the Torre di Caporivo, and the Gothic ruins of a medieval limestone quarry.

CELEB-STYLE SEAFOOD

The only one of the marina's restaurants directly accessible from the sea, **Lo Scoglio** (☑081 808 10 26; www.restaurantloscoglio.com; Marina del Cantone; meals €50) attracts a steady ripple of visiting celebs. Johnny Depp, Stephen Spielberg and Sienna Miller are all recent diners, while Elton John, Rod Stewart and Michael Caine have posed for pics (on display) in the past. The locale is certainly memorable – a glass pavilion on a wooden jetty built around a kitsch fountain spurting into a pond full of fish – and the food is top-notch (and priced accordingly). Although you can eat *ravioli alla caprese* and steak here, you'd be sorry to miss the superb seafood. Sample such saltwater specialities as a €30 antipasto of raw seafood on ice, followed by the local classic: *spaghetti al riccio* (spaghetti with sea urchins). Despite the whiff of glamour surrounding the clientele, this is an unpretentious family-run place, complete with grandma keeping a watchful eye on the till.

AMALFI COAST TOWNS

Positano

POP 3882

Positano is the coast's most picturesque and photogenic town, with steeply-stacked houses tumbling down to the sea in a cascade of sun-bleached peach, pink and terracotta colours. No less colourful are its steep streets and steps lined with wisteria-draped hotels, smart restaurants and fashionable boutiques.

Look beyond the facades and the fashion, however, and you will find reassuring signs of everyday reality – crumbling stucco, streaked paintwork and even, on occasion, a faint whiff of drains. There's still a southern Italian holiday feel about the place, with sunbathers eating pizza on the beach, kids pestering parents for gelati and chic women from Milan checking out the boutiques. The fashionista history runs deep – *Moda Positano* was born here in the '60s and the town was the first in Italy to import bikinis from France.

John Steinbeck visited in 1953 and wrote in an article for *Harper's Bazaar*: 'Positano bites deep. It is a dream place that isn't quite real when you are there and becomes beckoningly real after you have gone'.

There certainly is something special about the place and this is reflected, predictably, in the prices, which tend to be higher here than elsewhere on the coast.

◉ Sights & Activities

Positano's most memorable sight is its unforgettable townscape – a vertiginous stack of pastel-coloured houses tumbling down to Spiaggia Grande, the main beach. Although it isn't anyone's dream beach, with greyish sand covered by legions of bright umbrellas, the water's clean and the setting is memorable. Hiring a chair and umbrella on the fenced-off areas costs around €18 per person per day, but the crowded public areas are free.

Getting around town is largely a matter of walking. If your knees can take the slopes, there are dozens of narrow alleys and stairways that make walking relatively easy and joyously traffic-free. Be sure to take the local bus to the top of the town for the best views and wind your way down on foot, via steps and slopes, enjoying the memorable vistas en route.

Chiesa di Santa Maria Assunta CHURCH
(Piazza Flavio Gioia; ⊗8am-noon & 3.30-7pm) This church is the most famous and – let's face it – pretty much the only major sight in Positano. If you are visiting at a weekend you will probably have the added perk of seeing a wedding; it's one of the most popular churches in the area for exchanging vows.

Step inside to see a delightful classical interior, with pillars topped with gilded Ionic capitals and winged cherubs peeking from above every arch. Above the main altar is a 13th-century Byzantine Black Madonna and Child. During restoration works of the square and the crypt, a Roman villa was discovered; still under excavation, it is closed to the public.

Franco Senesi GALLERY
TOP CHOICE
(✆089 87 52 57; www.francosenesifineart.com; Via dei Mulini 19; ⊗10am-midnight Apr-Nov) Nestled between the colourful boutiques and lemon-themed ceramics shops, Franco Senesi is a light and airy exhibition space with several rooms showcasing over 20 Italian modern artists and sculptors. You can walk around here without being hassled, admir-

---

DON'T MISS

A WALK TO FORNILLO

This gentle walk, with (hooray!) an acceptable number of steps, leads from Positano's main Spiaggia Grande to Spiaggia di Fornillo. Toss off the stilettos and don the trainers; Fornillo is more laid back than its swanky *spiaggia* neighbour and is also home to a handful of beach bars, which can get quite spirited post sunset.

To reach here, head for the western end of Spiaggia Grande, by the ferry harbour, and climb the steps. Walk past the Torre Trasita, one of the coast's many medieval watchtowers built to warn inhabitants of pirate raids and now a private residence. Continue on as the path passes dramatic rock formations, tiny inlets of turquoise water and bobbing boats until you reach the appealing Fornillo beach in perfect time for your reward of a long cold drink or multi-scoop ice cream.

AT A SNAIL'S PACE

Positano is one of around 55 towns in Italy to have gained Slow City status (an extension of the Slow Food Movement, established in northern Italy in 1986). In order to be considered, certain criteria must be met: towns need to have fewer than 55,000 inhabitants, no fast food outlets or neon lit hoardings, plenty of cycling and walking paths and neighbourhood restaurants serving traditional cuisine with locally sourced ingredients for example. For more information, check the www.cittaslow.org website.

ing (and buying?) art works that are sufficiently varied to suit most tastes.

The art works range from exquisite life drawings to colourful surrealistic landscapes and edgy abstract sculptures. Shipping can be arranged.

In early 2012, the owners opened a contemporary art gallery, The White Room, a few doors away, which displays some striking cast brass sculptures by Venetian sculptor Gianfranco Meggiato, among other exciting modern works.

Palazzo Murat PALACE
([☏]089 875 51 77; www.palazzomurat.it; Via dei Mulini 23) Just west of the Chiesa di Santa Maria Assunta church, and now a luxury hotel, it may be beyond your budget to stay but you can still visit. Enjoy the stunning flower-filled courtyard, have a drink in the vine-draped patio and contemplate the short, tragic life of flamboyant Joachim Murat, the 18th-century French king of Naples who had the palace built as a summer residence for himself and his wife, Caroline Bonaparte.

Blue Star BOATING
([☏]089 81 18 89; www.bluestarpositano.it; Spiaggia Grande; ⊗9am-8pm Easter-Nov) Operating out of a kiosk on Spiaggia Grande, Blue Star hires out small motorboats for €60 per hour (€200 for four hours). Consider heading for the archipelago of Li Galli, the four small islands where, according to Homer, the sirens lived. At Gullo Lungo you will spy a magnificent villa, the former home of Rudolf Nureyev, now privately owned. The company also organises excursions to Capri and the Grotta dello Smeraldo (€50).

L'Uomo e il Mare BOATING
([☏]089 81 16 13; www.gennaroesalvatore.it; ⊗9am-8pm Easter-Nov) This Italian-English couple offer a range of tours, including Capri and Amalfi day trips (from €50), out of a kiosk near the ferry terminal. They also run a romantic sunset cruise to Li Galli, complete with champagne (€30).

🍴 Eating

Take note that, overall, the nearer you get to the seafront, the more expensive everything becomes. Many places close over winter, making a brief reappearance for Christmas and New Year.

Donna Rosa CAMPANIAN €€
([☏]089 81 18 06; www.drpositano.com; Via Montepertuso 97-99, Montepertuso; meals from €38; ⊗Wed-Mon Apr-Dec) This is one of the Amalfi Coast's most reputable restaurants, located in mountainside Montepertuso, above Positano. Once a humble trattoria and now run by Rosa's daughter Raffaella, the culinary lineage is set to continue with Raffaella's daughter Erika who has studied with Jamie Oliver in London. The celebrity chef has a long connection with the restaurant; after dining here on his honeymoon he declared it to be one of his all-time favourite restaurants.

The menu changes frequently but you can be guaranteed some of the best food – and views – on the coast. Don't miss the hot chocolate soufflé and be sure to book ahead. Future plans include cooking courses; check the website for an update.

Next 2 TOP CHOICE NEAPOLITAN €€
([☏]089 812 35 16; www.next2.it; Viale Pasitea 242; meals €30; ⊗7-11pm) The decor here oozes understated elegance, with its pistachio green-and-cream colour scheme, interior lemon trees and outside terrace with oversized white parasols and dark wicker seating. The mains (a choice of just eight) use organic ingredients as far as possible and include interesting takes on classic Neapolitan dishes such as baked rice with meatballs, salmon and mozzarella, and giant gnocchi with cherry tomatoes, ricotta and smoked cheese. Desserts are wickedly creamy and delicious.

La Cambusa SEAFOOD €€
([☏]089 81 20 51; Piazza A Vespucci 4; meals €40; ⊗Mar-Nov) This restaurant, run by amiable

Positano

G

F

E

D

C

B

A

1   2   3   4

200 m
0.1 miles

To San Pietro
(2km)

SITA Bus
Stop

Via Guglielmo Marconi

Via Cristoforo Colombo

Via Grotte dell'Incanto

☆ 22

Piazza Flavio
Gioia

8

Viale del
Brigantino

☆ 3

Spiaggia
Grande

Piazza A
Vespucci

9

23

↑1

16

15

21
21

19

2

Internal
Bus Stop

Positano
Jet

4

Via dei Mulini

25

Via del
Saracino

ℹ

Via Positanesi d'America

26

P

24

To La Terra (2km); Donna Rosa (2km);
Montepertuso (2km); Nocelle (3.5km);
Praiano (4km)

Via Guglielmo
Marconi

SITA
Bus Stop

2

7

Gulf of Salerno
(Golfo di Salerno)

12

Viale Pasitea

13

14

Viale Pasitea

Spiaggia del
Fornillo

20

17

10

18

11

5

Via Fornillo

P

6

FORNILLO

Via Chiesa Nuova

Positano

THE AMALFI COAST POSITANO

Luigi is on the front line which, given the number of cash-rich tourists in these parts, could equal high prices for less than average food. Happily, that is not the case here. The locals still rate La Cambusa as a top place for seafood.

Go for simple spaghetti with clams, oven baked sea bass or splash out with the Mediterranean lobster. There is a good selection of side dishes, like roasted artichokes, and the position is Positano at its best.

Da Vincenzo
CAMPANIAN €€

(☑089 87 51 28; Viale Pasitea 172-178; meals €35; ☺Apr-Nov, closed lunch Tue Jul & Aug) Superbly prepared dishes are served here by the third generation of restaurateurs. The emphasis is on fish dishes, which range from the adventurous, like grilled octopus tentacles skewered with deep-fried artichokes, to seasonal pasta dishes such as spaghetti with broad beans and fresh ricotta. Enjoy twanging Neapolitan guitarists during the summer months and be sure to try co-owner Marcella's legendary desserts, considered the best in town. Reservations recommended.

La Terra
VEGETARIAN €€

(☑089 81 11 79; Via Tagliata 14, Montepertuso) This superb restaurant on the mountainside above Positano is a world away from the salad and soy penury of some vegetarian eateries. Dishes change according to what is in season but typical plates are pumpkin and provolone cheese risotto and pasta *primavera*, with freshly picked vegetables from the owner's ample adjacent plot. Transport to Positano may be arranged. If you're lucky the waiter may treat you to a tune on his sax while you wait.

Ristorante il Saraceno d'Oro
CAMPANIAN €€

(☑089 81 20 50; Viale Pasitea 254; meals €25, pizzas from €5; ☺Mar-Oct) There is something so typically Italian about the setup of this restaurant, where waiters have to dash to and fro across the road with their dishes. But in the evening the traffic is light and the wacky layout will only add to the delight of eating here. The pizza and pasta choices are good; the *contorni* (vegetables) excellent. Splurge on the legendary profiteroles in chocolate sauce for dessert.

Ristorante Max
CAMPANIAN €€

(☑089 87 50 56; Via dei Mulini 22; meals €40; ☺Mar-Nov) Here you can peruse the artwork (in lieu of a sea view) while choosing your dish. This established restaurant is popular with local ladies who lunch, with a menu including set meals and specials of the day, such as sautéed clams and mussels, and zucchini flowers stuffed with ricotta and salmon. Cooking courses are available in summer.

LOCAL KNOWLEDGE

ZIA LUCY, HIKING GUIDE

Zia Lucy (www.zialucy.it) was born and raised in Positano and organises hikes throughout the region. She is an expert on the local history, flora and wildlife.

Which is your favourite hike on the Amalfi Coast? There are so many wonderful hikes around here but I have to say that the *Walk of the Gods* is still the one I love the most. It has everything: fabulous scenery, beautiful flowers like wild orchids, and is accessible to many, as it is not a tough walk.

Any advice for hikers? It sounds obvious but many people still wear open sandals when they are hiking, which is not just unsafe as they can slip, but also because there are occasionally snakes.

Favourite local restaurant? I love La Terra in Montepertuso; the owners grow all their own produce and the views are fantastic. In town, La Cambusa is where I always head for seafood.

La Brezza   SNACKS €
(☑089 87 58 11; Via R. Giovanna 2; snacks around €5; 🛜) With a steely grey-and-white interior, free internet and wi-fi, and a terrace with views over the beach and quay, this is the best frontline place for a *panini* or snack. There are regular art exhibitions and a daily 'happy hour' (6pm-8pm), with drinks accompanied by complimentary light eats.

 Drinking & Entertainment

Unless the idea of parading up and down town with a cashmere sweater draped over your shoulders turns you on, Positano's nightlife, overall, is not going to do much for you. More piano bar than warehouse, with a handful of exceptions, it's genteel, sophisticated and safe.

TOP CHOICE **La Zagara**   CAFE
(☑089 812 28 92; Via dei Mulini 4; panini €5, cakes €3, cocktails €5) This is the quintessential Italian terrace, draped with foliage and flowers, with an offshoot bar and superb *pasticceria* (pastry shop), elderly red-vested waiters, Neapolitan background music and some great Positano poseur-watching potential. Enjoy sumptuous creamy cakes, as well as savoury snacks. There's live music during the summer.

Music on the Rocks   CLUB
(☑089 87 58 74; www.musicontherocks.it; Via Grotte dell'Incanto 51; admission €10-25; ☺May-Oct) This is one of the town's few genuine nightspots and one of the best clubs on the coast. Music on the Rocks is dramatically carved into the tower at the eastern end of Spiaggia Grande. Join the flirty good-looking crowd and some of region's top DJs spinning mainstream house and reliable disco.

Da Ferdinando   BAR
(☑089 87 53 65; Spiaggia dei Fornillo; ☺10am-3am, May-Oct) This summer-only beach bar rents out sun loungers and serves light snacks, along with drinks. The music is designed to make sure you shift into suitable party mood post sunset.

 Shopping

You can't miss Positano's colourful boutiques – everywhere you look, shop displays scream out at you in a riot of exuberant colour. The humble lemon also enjoys star status; it's not just in *limoncello* and lemon-infused candles, but emblazoned on tea towels, aprons and pottery.

TOP CHOICE **Antonello della Mura**   FASHION
(☑089 87 50 20; Via del Saracino 36) Fashionistas in the know come here for exquisite fashions designed by Antonello himself, who studied at London's prestigious St Martins College of Art and Design. Inspired by Roman frescoes, the printed scarves are stunning enough to frame, as well as being hand finished, pure silk and Hermès quality (at around €100 less). The feather-light women's fashions are similarly irresistible.

La Bottego di Brunella   FASHION
(☑089 87 52 28; www.brunella.it; Viale Pasitea 72) This shop is one of the reasons local women succeed in always looking so effortlessly chic. It is one of just a handful of boutiques here where the clothes are actually designed and made in Positano (most boutiques import despite the sometimes deceptive label-

ling). The garments here are made from pure linen and silks; the colours are earthy shades of cream, ochre, brown and yellow. There are two other branches in town, including a smaller boutique opposite Palazzo Murat.

La Botteguccia de Giovanni SHOES
(☑089 81 18 24; www.labottegucciapositano.it; Via Regina Giovanni 19; ☺May-Oct) A reliable place to come for handmade sandals made by craftsman Giovanni in his small workroom at the back of the shop. Choose the colour leather and any decorative bits and pieces you want (shells are particularly well suited to Positano somehow...), tell him your size and then nip round the corner for a cappuccino while he makes them. Prices start at around €50.

Umberto Carro CERAMICS
(☑089 87 53 52; Viale Pasitea 98; ☺May-Oct) On offer here is a sumptuous display of locally produced ceramics to stress you – and your hand luggage – at check-in time; a better bet is to go for the shipping option. The colours and designs are subtle and classy, and there is a wide range of pieces available, ranging from magnificent urns to minute eggcups and quirky, brightly coloured ceramic animals and ornaments.

ℹ Information

Tourist Office (☑089 87 50 67; Via del Saracino 4; ☺8am-2pm & 3.30-8pm Mon-Sat) Can provide lots of information, although expect to pay for walking maps and similar.

ℹ Getting There & Away

Boat

Positano has excellent ferry connections to the coastal towns and islands from April to October.

Linee Marittime Partenopee (☑081 704 19 11; www.consorziolmp.it) Runs hydrofoils/ferries from Positano to Capri (€16.50/14.50).

Metrò del Mare (☑199 44 66 44; www.metrodelmare.com) Operates summer-only services from Naples Beverello (€17, one hour and 25 minutes, two daily), Amalfi (€8.50, 45 minutes, two daily), Sorrento (€13, 45 minutes, two daily) and Salerno (€11, 45 minutes, two daily).

Positano Jet (☑089 87 50 32) Operates hydrofoils to Capri (€17, 45 minutes, three daily).

Bus

About 16km west of Amalfi and 18km from Sorrento, Positano is on the main SS163 coastal road. There are two main bus stops: coming from Sorrento and the west, it's opposite Bar Internazionale; arriving from Amalfi and the east, it's at the top of Via Cristoforo Colombo. To get into town from the former, follow Viale Pasitea; from the latter (a far shorter route), take Via Cristoforo Colombo. When departing, buy bus tickets at Bar Internazionale or, if headed east, from the *tabaccheria* (tobacconist) at the bottom of Via Cristoforo Colombo.

» **SITA** (☑199 73 07 49; www.sitabus.it) Runs frequent buses to/from Amalfi and Sorrento.

» **Flavia Gioia** (☑089 81 30 77; Via Cristoforo Colombo 49) These local buses follow the lower ring road every half-hour. Stops are clearly marked and you can buy your ticket (€1.20) on board. The Flavia Gioia buses pass by both SITA bus stops. There are also 17 daily buses up to Montepertuso and Nocelle.

Car & Motorcycle

By car, take the A3 autostrada to Vietri sul Mare and then follow the SS163 coastal road. To hire a scooter, try **Positano Rent a Scooter** (☑089 812 20 77; Viale Pasitea 99; per day from €50). Don't forget that you will need to produce a driving licence and passport.

WORTH A TRIP

NOCELLE

A tiny, still relatively isolated mountain village, above Positano and beyond Montepertuso, Nocelle (450m) commands some of the most spectacular views on the entire coast. A world apart from touristy Positano, it's a sleepy, silent place where not much ever happens and where the few residents are happy to keep it that way.

If you want to stay, consider delightful **Villa della Quercia** (☑089 812 34 97; www.villadellaquercia.com; r €70-75; ☏), a former monastery with spectacular views. For food, **Trattoria Santa Croce** (☺Apr-Oct) is a reliable low-key restaurant in the main part of the village.

The easiest way to get to Nocelle is by local bus from Positano (€1.20, 30 minutes, 17 daily). If you're driving, follow the signs from Positano. Hikers tackling the *Sentieri degli Dei* (p163) might want to stop off as they pass through.

THE AMALFI COAST PRAIANO

Parking
Parking here is no fun in summer. There are some blue zone parking areas (€3 per hour) and a handful of expensive private car parks. **Parcheggio da Anna** (Viale Pasitea 173; per day €18) is located just before the Pensione Maria Luisa, at the top of town. Nearer the beach and town centre, **Di Gennaro** (Via Pasitea 1; per day €23) is near the bottom of Via Cristoforo Colombo.

Praiano
POP 1900

An ancient fishing village, a low-key summer resort and, increasingly, a popular centre for the arts, Praiano is a delight. With no centre as such, its whitewashed houses pepper the verdant ridge of Monte Sant'Angelo as it slopes towards Capo Sottile. Formerly an important silk-production centre, it was a favourite of the Amalfi doges (dukes), who made it their summer residence.

Sights & Activities
Praiano is 120m above sea level, and exploring involves lots of steps. There are also several trails that start from town, including a scenic walk – particularly stunning at sunset – that leaves from beside the San Gennaro church due west descending to the **Spiaggia della Gavitelli** beach (via 300 steps!), carrying on to the medieval defensive Torre di Grado.

Marina di Praia   HARBOUR
Located a couple of kilometres east of the centre, this charming small beach and harbour are why most people stop off here. From the SS163 (next to the Hotel Onda Verde) a steep path leads down the cliffs to a tiny inlet with a small stretch of coarse sand

and very tempting water; the best water is actually off the rocks, just before you get to the bottom. In what were once fishermen's houses, there are now four restaurants, including an excellent place for seafood. You can also rent boats here.

Chiesa di San Luca   CHURCH
(Via Oratorio 1) In the upper village, the 16th-century church features an impressive majolica floor, paintings by the 16th-century artist Giovanni Bernardo Lama and a late 17th-century bust of St Luke the Evangelist.

Centro Sub Costiera Amalfitana   DIVING
(☎089 81 21 48; www.centrosub.it; Via Marina di Praia; dives from €80; ☝) Head here if you are into diving. This well-respected local outfit also offers lessons for adults and children over eight years, as well as night dives and full diving days with snacks on board.

Eating

Da Armandino   SEAFOOD €€
(☎089 87 40 87; Via Praia 1, Marina di Praia; meals €35; ⊙Apr-Nov; ☝) If you're a seafood lover, head for this widely acclaimed, no-frills restaurant located in a former boatyard on the beach at Marina di Praia. Da Armandino is great for fish fresh off the boat. There is no menu, just opt for the dish of the day – it's all excellent. The holiday atmosphere and appealing setting – at the foot of sheer cliffs towering up to the main road – round things off nicely.

Onda Verde   CAMPANIAN €€
(☎089 87 41 43; www.hotelondaverde.it; Via Terramare 3; meals €35; ⊙Apr-Nov) Part of a hotel of the same name, this restaurant is located half way down the steep steps leading to the marina (just beyond the defensive tower).

DON'T MISS

ART IN A TOWER

Defensive towers sit all along the Amalfi Coast. They are ironically generally known as Saracen towers, named after the very invaders they were erected to thwart. Although most lie empty, some are privately owned. At Marina di Praia you can combine a visit to one such tower, **Torre a Mare** (☎339 4401008; www.paolosandulli.com; Torre a Mare; ⊙9am-1pm & 3.30-7pm) , all while enjoying the original sculptures and art work of Paolo Sandulli. Most distinctive are his 'heads' with the colourful sea-sponge hair dos (also on sale at Pop Gallery; p119). Check out his sketches and sculptures of the local fishermen where he has totally captured the character of the faces, and his sexy plump women playing tennis in miniskirts. A spiral staircase leads to more works upstairs, including paintings. Paolo's work is on display throughout the Amalfi Coast, including at Positano's prestigious Palazzo Murat.

WALK OF THE GODS

Probably the best-known walk on the Amalfi Coast, the 12km, six-hour **Sentiero degli Dei** (Walk of the Gods) follows the steep paths linking Positano to Praiano. The walk commences at **Via Chiesa Nuova**, just north of the SS163 road, in the northern part of Positano. Head to the right of the church and climb the steps at the end of the narrow road. Cross over and take the steps to your left, where you will see the official beginning of the route marked by red and white stripes; these are repeated along the path, usually daubed on rocks and trees, although some of these have become worn and might be difficult to make out. For a less arduous climb at the beginning of the trail, catch a bus from Positano to **Nocelle** and start from there (the walk is marked).

Not advised for vertigo sufferers, it's a spectacular, meandering trail along the top of the mountains with caves and terraces that plummet dramatically from the cliffs to deep valleys framed by the brilliant blue of the sea. It can sometimes be foggy in the dizzy heights but that somehow adds to the drama, with the cypresses rising through the mist like dark shimmering sword blades.

Don't miss the huge hole in the centre of the cliff at **Montepertuso**, where it looks as if some irate giant has punched through the slab of limestone. The local legend is a holier one: apparently the Virgin Mary, in a contest with the Devil, made the hole by simply touching the rock with her hand. In **Praiano**, you can catch a bus back to Positano but, if you want the more challenging version of this hike, then instead of heading down to the coast and Praiano, turn left to the (signposted) small town of **Bomerano**, near Agerola, in the mountains between Sorrento and Amalfi.

You can pick up a map of this walk at the tourist office. Hiking maps can also be downloaded at www.amalficoastweb.com and www.grottedellangelo.sa.it. Another reliable regional hiking map is the CAI (Club Alpino Italiano; Italian Alpine Club) *Monti Lattari, Peninsola Sorrentina, Costiera Amalfitana: Carta dei Sentieri* (€9) at 1:30,000. If you prefer a guided hike, there are a number of reliable local guides including American **Frank Carpegna** (www.walkingwiththegods.com), a longtime resident here, and **Zia Lucy** (www.zialucy.it).There are also weekly informal hikes throughout the peninsula organised by **Free Ramblers** (www.freeramblers.com), a sociable group of local residents who welcome new walkers on a drop-in basis and generally wind up their weekly walk with a meal somewhere.

Sit outside for the best views of the bay. The food here reflects an innovative take on traditional cuisine and includes a plentiful salad choice – just the thing on a sizzling summer's day.

La Brace CAMPANIAN **€€**
(☎089 87 42 26; www.labracepraiano.com; Via G. Capriglione; meals €25, pizzas from €5) Located on the main street in town, this long-established restaurant is famed for its seafood and pizzas. The dining room has sweeping views over the rooftops to the sea while owner Gianni greets everyone like an old friend – in Italian, naturally; it's a favourite haunt of locals.

★ Entertainment

Africana CLUB
TOP CHOICE
(☎089 81 11 71; www.africanafamousclub.com; near Marina di Praia; ⊗Fri & Sat May-Sep) A night at this extraordinary club may well be on a par with the most memorable boogie of your life. Africana has been going since the '50s when Jackie Kennedy was just one of the famous VIP guests. It has an extraordinary cave setting, complete with natural blowholes and a glass dance floor so you can see confused looking fish swimming under your feet. Shuttle buses run regularly from Positano, Amalfi and Maiori during summer. You can also catch a water taxi (€10) from **Positano Boats** (☎339 2539207; www.positanoboats.info).

🛍 Shopping

Eramos Edone CERAMICS
(☎089 87 40 75; Via Capriglione 140) These original ceramics painted in brilliant colours feature primarily an ocean theme (think fish-shaped plates and the like). Opened in 2012, prices are fair; you can expect to pay

around €25 for an exquisite butter dish that will bring a little bit of Amalfi to your breakfast table every morning.

FURORE

Marina di Furore, a tiny fishing village, was once a busy little commercial centre, although it's difficult to believe that today. In medieval times, its unique natural position freed it from the threat of foreign raids and provided a ready source of water for its flour and paper mills.

Originally founded by Romans seeking sanctuary from barbarian incursions, it sits at the bottom of what's known as the fjord of Furore, a giant cleft that cuts through the Lattari mountains. The main village, however, stands 300m above, in the upper Vallone del Furore. A one-horse place that sees few tourists at any time of the year, it exudes a distinctly rural air despite the colourful murals and unlikely modern sculpture.

To get to upper Furore by car, follow the SS163 and then the SS366 signposts to Agerola. Otherwise, regular SITA buses depart from the bus terminus in Amalfi (€1.20, 30 minutes, 17 daily). It is also one of the stops on the Driving Tour (p149).

Amalfi

POP 5428

It is hard to grasp that pretty little Amalfi, with its sun-filled piazzas and small beach, was once a maritime superpower with a population of more than 70,000. For one thing, it's not a big place – you can easily walk from one end to the other in about 20 minutes. For another, there are very few historical buildings of note. The explanation is chilling – most of the old city, and its populace, simply slid into the sea during an earthquake in 1343.

Today, although the resident population is a fairly modest 5000 or so, the numbers swell significantly during summer, when day trippers pour in by the coachload. Just

around the headland, neighbouring **Atrani** is a picturesque tangle of whitewashed alleys and arches centred on a lively, lived-in piazza and popular beach; don't miss it.

◉ Sights & Activities

First stop is Piazza del Duomo, the town's focalpoint square, with its majestic cathedral. To try and glean a sense of the town's medieval history, be sure to explore the narrow parallel streets with their covered porticos and historic shrine niches. Amalfi also has a beautiful seaside setting; it's the perfect spot for long, lingering lunches.

Cattedrale di Sant'Andrea   CATHEDRAL
(☑089 87 10 59; Piazza del Duomo; ⊙9am-7pm)
You can't miss Amalfi's fabulous cathedral, sitting like a grande dame at the top of a sweeping flight of steps, generally crowded with idle tourists, boisterous students and chattering locals creating a great 'wish-you-were-here' holiday-pic backdrop.

The cathedral dates in part from the early 10th century and its striking stripy facade has been rebuilt twice, most recently at the end of the 19th century. Although the building is a hybrid, the Sicilian Arabic-Norman style predominates, particularly in the two-tone masonry and the 13th-century bell tower. The huge bronze doors also merit a look – the first of their type in Italy, they were commissioned by a local noble and made in Syria before being shipped to Amalfi. Less impressive is the baroque interior, although the altar features some fine statues and there are some interesting 12th- and 13th-century mosaics. In high season, entrance to the cathedral between 10am and 5pm is through the adjacent Chiostro del Paradiso, where you have to pay an entrance fee of €2.50.

Chiostro del Paradiso   CLOISTERS
(☑089 87 13 24; Piazza del Duomo; adult/reduced €2.50/1; ⊙9am-7pm) To the left of Amalfi's cathedral porch, these magnificent Moorish-

---

HIGH DIVING CHAMPIONSHIP

Every July, Furore hosts a high diving competition: The Mediterranean Cup (www. comunefurore.it (in Italian), when fearless (or foolhardy) high divers arrive from all over the world to swan dive off the famous bridge traversing the Furore fjord. The plummeting distance is some 28 metres and the typical speed around 100km per hour. Generally held on a Sunday towards the beginning of the month, it is an annual highlight not to be missed and especially spectacular viewed from a boat.

Amalfi

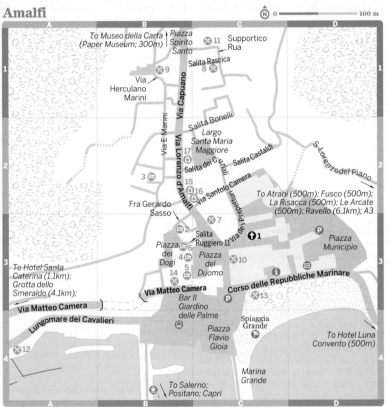

⊙ N   0 ━━━━━━━━ 100 m

Amalfi

style cloisters were built in 1266 to house the tombs of Amalfi's prominent citizens. 120 marble columns support a series of tall, slender Arabic arches around a central garden. From the cloisters, go through to the Basilica del Crocefisso, where you'll find various religious artefacts displayed in glass cabinets and some fading 14th-century frescoes. Beneath lies the 1206 crypt containing the remains of Sant'Andrea.

Grotta dello Smeraldo
GROTTO

(admission €6; ☺9am-4pm; ✦) Four kilometres west of Amalfi, Conca dei Marini is home to one of the coast's most popular sights. Named after the eerie emerald colour that emanates from the water, this grotto is well worth a visit. Stalactites hang down from the 24m-high ceiling, while stalagmites grow up to 10m tall. Each year, on 24 December and 6 January, skin-divers from all over Italy make their traditional pilgrimage to the ceramic *presepe* (nativity scene) submerged beneath the water.

ITA buses regularly pass the car park above the cave entrance (from where you take a lift or stairs down to the rowing boats). Alternatively, Coop Sant'Andrea runs two daily boats from Amalfi (€15 return) at 9am and 3.30pm. Allow 1½ hours for the return trip.

Museo della Carta
MUSEUM

(✆089 830 45 61; www.museodellacarta.it; Via delle Cartiere; admission €4; ☺10am-6.30pm) Amalfi's paper museum is housed in a 13th-century paper mill (the oldest in Europe). It lovingly preserves the original paper presses, which are still in full working order, as you'll see during the 15-minute guided tour (in English) which explains the original cotton-based paper production and the later wood pulp manufacturing. Afterwards you may well be inspired to pick up some of the stationery sold in the gift shop, alongside calligraphy sets and paper pressed with flowers.

Amalfi Marine
BOATING

(✆329 2149811; www.amalfiboats.it; Spiaggia del Porto, Lungomare dei Cavalieri) If you are intent on going for a swim, you're better off hiring a boat and heading out to sea. You'll find a number of operators along Lungomare dei Cavalieri, including this place run by American local resident Rebecca Brooks. You can hire a boat without a skipper from €250 per day (per boat, maximum six passengers). There are also organised daylong excursions along the coast and to the islands (from €45 per person).

✗ Eating & Drinking

Inevitably, most of the restaurants in and around Amalfi's centre cater to the tourist trade. Standards are generally high, however, and it's rare to eat badly. Most places serve pizza and a range of pasta, grilled meat and seafood. The Amalfi drinking scene is fairly subdued, revolving around streetside cafes and bars. It gets a tad more boisterous in Atrani, but is hardly hard-core.

TOP CHOICE Marina Grande
SEAFOOD €€

(✆089 87 11 29; www.ristorantemarinagrande. com; Viale Delle Regioni 4; meals €30; ☺Tue-Sun Mar-Oct) Run by the third generation of the same family, patronised primarily by locals and fronting the beach, this restaurant serves fish so fresh it is almost flapping. Consider the tasting menu (€48) with dishes like warm seafood salad and *linguini alla scoglia* (calamari, prawns, scampi, shellfish and cherry tomatoes). And it gets better... Marina Grande is a member of the Slow Food Movement and uses almost exclusively organic produce. Reservations are recommended.

Dolcería dell' Antíco Portico
PASTICCERIA €

(✆089 87 11 43; Via Supportico Rua 10; cakes from €3) Located under the arches, this place is run by celebrated pastry chef Tiziano Mita, who has worked in Paris and Milan and at the revered Palazzo Sasso in Ravello. Mita applies a contemporary twist to traditional sweet treats, like *sfogliatella* in the form of a *trullo* (conical roofed building unique to Puglia). Olive-oil biscuits, almond pastries and lemon cream cake are similarly delicate and delicious. They also do coffee and have a couple of tables outside.

Ristorante La Caravella
CAMPANIAN €€€

(✆089 87 10 29; www.ristorantelacaravella.it; Via Matteo Camera 12; meals €60, tasting menu €75; ☺Wed-Mon Jan–mid-Nov; ❀) The regional food here has recently earned the restaurant a Michelin star with dishes that offer nouvelle zap – like black ravioli with cuttlefish ink, scampi and ricotta – or that are unabashedly simple, like the catch of the day served grilled on lemon leaves. This is one of the few places in Amalfi where you pay for the food rather than the location, which in this case is far from spectacular, sandwiched between the rushing traffic of the road and the old arsenale. But that doesn't worry the discreet, knowledgeable crowd who eat here. Wine aficionados are likely to find something to try on the 15,000-label list. Reservations essential.

Il Teatro
TRATTORIA €€

(☑089 87 24 73; Via E Marini 19; meals €25; 🔊) This superb no-fuss trattoria is tucked away in the atmospheric backstreets of the *centro storico*. The old-fashioned interior has a series of arches and walls decorated with black-and-white photos and assorted bric-a-brac. Seafood specialities include *pesce spada il teatro* (swordfish in a tomato, caper and olive-oil sauce), plus there are some good vegetarian options, including *scialatielli al teatro* (pasta with tomatoes and aubergines).

La Taverna del Duca
SEAFOOD €€

(☑089 87 27 55; Piazza Spirito Santo 26; pizzas from €7, meals €35; ⊘Fri-Wed) Grab a chair on the square at this popular restaurant complete with its fishy reputation. Specials vary according to the catch of the day but might include *carpaccio di baccalà* (thin strips of raw salted cod) or linguine with scampi. Or go for a pasta dish like *pasta fagioli e cozze* (with mussels and beans). There's an excellent and generous antipasti spread and the interior is elegant, with candles on the tables and tasteful oil paintings on the walls.

Lo Smeraldino
SEAFOOD €€

(☑089 87 10 70; www.ristorantelosmeraldino.it; Piazzale dei Protontini 1, Lungomare dei Cavalieri ; meals €30, pizzas around €9; ⊘Thu-Tue, Mar-Dec) Head eastwards past Marina Grande to reach this inviting blue-and-white beachside restaurant overlooking the fishing boats. As well as crisp-based pizzas, this is a good place for fancy risottos, like smoked salmon and caviar, or simple classics like grilled or poached local fish. Despite the location, this is not a place where you come wrapped in a sarong wearing flip flops; the atmosphere is one of understated elegance. Book ahead at weekends.

Da Maria
CAMPANIAN €€

(☑089 87 18 80; Via Lorenzo d'Amalfi 16; meals €25, pizzas around €6; ⊘Dec-Oct; 🔊) Just off Piazza del Duomo, at the beginning of the main pedestrian thoroughfare, this cavernous place attracts a dedicated crowd ranging from off-the-yacht Neapolitans to coachloads of tourists. But don't be put off as the wood-fired pizzas are excellent, the atmosphere is jolly, and the pastas and main courses are solidly reliable, if a tad overpriced.

Le Arcate
CAMPANIAN €€

(☑089 87 13 67; Largo Orlando Buonocore, Atrani; meals €25, pizzas from €6; ⊘Tue-Sun; ❄) On a sunny day, it's hard to beat the dreamy location – at the far eastern point of the harbour overlooking the beach – with Atrani's ancient rooftops and church tower behind you. Huge white parasols shade the sprawl of tables, while the dining room is a stone-walled natural cave. Pizzas are served at night, while daytime fare includes risotto with seafood and grilled swordfish; the food is good, but it's a step down from the setting.

Fusco
YOGHURT €

(Piazza Umberto 1 4, Atrani; yoghurt €1.50; 🔊) This place specialises in local dairy produce, including wonderful *fior di latte* mozzarella made from cows' milk. The main draw, however, are the decadently creamy and delicious homemade yogurts, with flavours including hazelnut, strawberry, coffee and orange. There is another Fusco branch in Bomerano (see the Green Ribbon Driving Tour boxed text, p149).

La Risacca
BAR

(☑089 87 28 66; www.risacca.com; Piazza Umberto 1 16, Atrani; cocktails €5; ⊘10am-late) This boisterous Atrani bar is about as lively as it gets. Music pumps out over square-side tables as tanned students sip on garish cocktails and bottled beer. Save yourself a euro or two by stocking up during happy hour (between 6pm and 8pm). Pizza and bruschetta are available to ward off hunger pangs.

La Pansa
CAFE €

(☑089 87 10 65; Piazza del Duomo 40; cornetti & pastries from €1.50; ⊘Wed-Mon) A stuck-in-a-time-warp cafe on Piazza del Duomo where black-bow-tied waiters serve a great Italian breakfast: freshly made *cornetti* and deliciously frothy cappuccino.

🛍 Shopping

You'll have no difficulty loading up on souvenirs here – Via Lorenzo d'Amalfi is lined with garish shops selling local ceramic work, artisanal paper gifts and *limoncello*. Prices are set for tourists, so don't expect many bargains.

Il Ninfeo
CERAMICS

(☑089 87 36 353; www.amalficoastceramics.com; Via Lorenzo d'Amalfi 28) Unabashedly tourist-geared, Il Ninfeo has a vast showroom displaying an excellent selection of ceramics, ranging from giant urns to fridge magnets. If they are not too busy, ask whether you can see the fascinating remains of a Roman villa under the showroom. It makes you realise just how much is hidden under this town.

Anastasio Nicola Sas FOOD
(☑089 87 10 07; Via Lorenzo d'Amalfi 32) Unless you're flying long haul, gourmet goodies can make excellent gifts. Here, among the hanging hams, you'll find a full selection, ranging from local cheese and preserves to coffee, chocolate, *limoncello* and every imaginable shape of pasta. There's also a collection of fruit-scented soaps and natural shampoos, perfumes and moisturisers.

L'Arco Antico SOUVENIRS
(☑089 873 63 54; Via Capuano 4) Amalfi's connection with paper-making dates back to the 12th century, when the first mills were set up to supply the republic's small army of bureaucrats. Although little is made here now, you can still buy it and the quality is still good. This attractive shop sells a range of paper products, including beautiful writing paper, leather-bound notebooks and huge photo albums.

ℹ Information

Tourist Office (☑089 87 11 07; www.amalfituristoffice.it; Corso delle Repubbliche Marinare 33; ☺8.30am-1.30pm & 3-7.15pm Mon-Fri, 8.30am-noon Sat) Good for bus and ferry timetables.

ℹ Getting There & Away

Boat

Linee Marittime Partenopee (☑081 704 19 11; www.consorziolmp.it; Via Guglielmo Melisurgo 4, Naples) Runs frequent daily hydrofoils/ferries to and from Capri (return €42/37).

Metrò del Mare (☑199 44 66 44; www.metrodelmare.com) Operates summer-only services between Naples and Amalfi (€18, two hours, two daily), Positano (€8.50, 20 minutes, three daily), Sorrento (€14, one hour, 15 minutes, two daily) and Salerno (€8.59, 50 minutes, one daily).

Bus

SITA (☑199 73 07 49; www.sitabus.it) Located in Piazza Flavio Gioia, SITA runs at least 12 buses a day from the piazza to Sorrento (via Positano), and also to Ravello, Salerno and Naples. You can buy tickets and check current schedules at **Bar Il Giardino delle Palme** (Piazza Flavio Gioia), opposite the bus stop.

Car & Motorcycle

If driving from the north, exit the A3 autostrada at Vietri sul Mare and follow the SS163. From the south, leave the A3 at Salerno and head for Vietri sul Mare and the SS163.

Parking

Parking is a problem in this town, although there are some parking places on Piazza Flavio Gioia near the ferry terminal (€3 per hour), as well as an underground car park accessed from Piazza Municipio with the same hourly rate.

Ravello

POP 2510

Sitting high in the hills above Amalfi, Ravello is a refined, polished town almost entirely dedicated to tourism (and increasingly popular as a wedding venue). Boasting impeccable bohemian credentials – Wagner, DH Lawrence and Virginia Woolf all spent time here – it's today known for its ravishing gardens and stupendous views, the best in the world according to former resident Gore Vidal, and certainly the best on the coast.

Most people visit on a day trip from Amalfi – a nerve-tingling 7km drive up the Valle del Dragone – although, to best enjoy its romantic, otherworldly atmosphere, you'll need to stay here overnight. On Tuesday morning there's a lively street market in Piazza Duomo, where you'll find wine, mozzarella and olive oil, as well as discounted designer clothes.

◉ Sights & Activities

Even if you have absolutely no sense of direction and a penchant for going round in circles, it's difficult to get lost in this town; everything is clearly signposted from the main Piazza Duomo. Explore the narrow backstreets, however, and you will discover glimpses of a quieter, traditional lifestyle: dry stone walls fronting simple homes surrounded by overgrown gardens, neatly planted vegetable plots and basking cats.

Cathedral CATHEDRAL
(Piazza Duomo; museum admission €2; ☺8.30am-1pm & 4.30-8pm) Forming the eastern flank of Piazza Duomo, the cathedral was originally built in 1086 but has since undergone various makeovers. The facade is 16th century, even if the central bronze door, one of only about two dozen in the country, is an 1179

Ravello

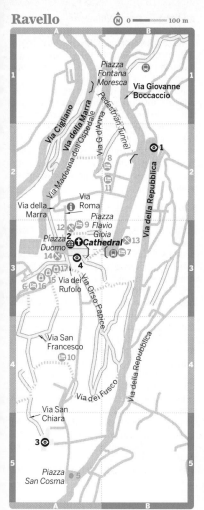

Ⓝ 0 ▬▬▬ 100 m

THE AMALFI COAST RAVELLO

TOP CHOICE **Villa Rufolo** GARDENS

(☎089 85 76 57; Piazza del Vescovado; adult/reduced €5/3; ⊙9am-sunset) To the south of Ravello's cathedral, a 14th-century tower marks the entrance to this villa, famed for its beautiful cascading gardens. Created by a Scotsman, Scott Neville Reid, in 1853, they are truly magnificent, commanding celestial panoramic views packed with exotic colours, artistically crumbling towers and luxurious blooms. On seeing the gardens on 26 May 1880, Wagner was moved to write: 'Finally, the enchanted garden of Klingsor [setting for the second act of the opera *Parsifal*] has been found'.

The villa was built in the 13th century for the wealthy Rufolo dynasty and was home to several popes as well as King Robert of Anjou. Today the gardens are used to stage concerts during the town's classical music festival.

original; the interior is a late 20th-century interpretation of what the original must once have looked like.

Of particular interest is the striking pulpit, supported by six twisting columns set on marble lions and decorated with flamboyant mosaics of peacocks, birds and dancing lions. Note also how the floor is tilted towards the square – a deliberate measure to enhance the perspective effect. To the right of the central nave, stairs lead down to the cathedral museum displaying a modest collection of religious artefacts.

Villa Cimbrone
GARDENS

(☎089 85 80 72; Via Santa Chiara 26; adult/reduced €6/3; ⊙9am-sunset) Some way east of Piazza Duomo, the early 20th-century Villa Cimbrone is worth a wander, if not for the 11th-century villa itself (now an upmarket hotel), then for the fabulous views from the delightful gardens. They're best admired from an awe-inspiring terrace lined with classical-style statues and busts. Something of a bohemian retreat in its early days, the villa was frequented by Greta Garbo and her lover Leopold Stokowski as a secret hideaway. Other illustrious former guests included Virginia Woolf, Winston Churchill, DH Lawrence and Salvador Dalì.

TOP CHOICE Ravello Festival
CLASSICAL MUSIC

(☎089 85 83 60; www.ravellofestival.com) Between June and mid-September, the Ravello Festival turns much of the town centre into a stage. Events range from orchestral concerts and chamber music to ballet performances; film screenings and exhibitions are held in atmospheric outdoor venues, most notably the famous overhanging terrace in the Villa Rufolo gardens.

However, you don't have to come in high summer to catch a concert. Ravello's program of classical music begins in March and continues until late October. It reaches its crescendo in June and September with the International Piano Festival and Chamber Music Weeks. Performances by top Italian and international musicians are world class, and the main venues are unforgettable. Tickets, bookable by phone or online, start at €25 (plus a €2 booking fee). For further information, contact the Ravello Concert Society.

Auditorium Oscar Niemeyer
CONCERT HALL

(☎346 7378561; www.auditoriumoscarniemeyer. it; Via della Repubblica 12) Located just below the main approach to town, this modern building, which follows the natural slope of the hill, has attracted a love-it-or-hate-it controversy in town. Designed by the renowned Brazilian architect, Oscar Niemeyer, it is characterised by the sinuous profile of a wave and approached via a rectangular exterior courtyard, which is typically the site for temporary exhibitions of world class sculpture. The auditorium is a venue for concerts and exhibitions; check the website for an update.

COURSES

Mamma Agata
COOKING COURSE

(☎089 85 70 19; www.mammaagata.com; Piazza San Cosma 9; €180-230) Mamma Agata, together with her daughter Chiara, offers private cooking classes in her home, producing simple, exceptional food using primarily organic ingredients. A one-day demonstration-based cooking class at Mamma Agata culminates with tasting of what you've been taught to make on a lovely sea-view terrace, accompanied by homemade *limoncello*. There is also a cookbook available for purchase.

Apparently Humphrey Bogart made a tradition out of having Mamma Agata's lemon cake (made with *limoncello*) for breakfast when she was cooking for a wealthy American family here back in the '60s. Other guests of this Hollywood-connected couple included Richard Burton, Frank Sinatra and Audrey Hepburn.

The variance in price depends on the time of year.

RAVELLO WALKS

Ravello is the starting point for numerous walks – some of which follow ancient paths through the surrounding Lattari mountains. If you've got the legs for it, you can walk down to **Minori** via an attractive route of steps, hidden alleys and olive groves, passing the picturesque hamlet of Torello en route. This walk kicks off just to the left of Villa Rufolo and should take you no more than 45 minutes. Alternatively, you can head the other way, to Amalfi, via the ancient village of **Scala**. Once a flourishing religious centre with more than a hundred churches, and the oldest settlement on the Amalfi Coast, Scala is now a pocket-sized sleepy place where the wind whistles through empty streets, and gnarled locals go patiently about their daily chores. In the central square, the Romanesque **duomo** (Piazza Municipio; ⊙8am-noon & 5-7pm) retains some of its 12th-century solemnity. Ask at the Ravello tourist office for more information on local walks.

CAMEO MUSEUM

Squeezed between tourist-driven shops and cafes, this very special place, **Camo** (☎089 85 74 61; Piazza Duomo 9, Ravello; ⊙9.30am-noon & 3-5.30pm Mon-Sat), is on the face of it a cameo shop; and exquisite they are too, crafted primarily out of coral and shell. But don't stop here – ask to see the treasure trove of a museum beyond the showroom. Even more of a treat may be in store if cameo creator and shop founder Giorgio Filo-camo is there to explain the background to such gorgeous pieces as a 16th-century crucifix on a crystal cross, a mid-16th-century Madonna, a 3rd-century AD Roman am-phora, gorgeous tortoiseshell combs and some exquisite oil paintings. This shop is the antithesis of the overpriced shops in the centre of Ravello. Giorgio's divine cameos have been commissioned by all kinds of well-known folk, including Hillary Clinton and the American actress Susan Sarandon.

✗ Eating

Surprisingly, Ravello doesn't offer many good eating options. It's easy enough to find a bar or cafe selling overpriced *panini* and pizza but not so simple to find a decent res-taurant or trattoria. There are a few good hotel restaurants, most of which are open to non-guests, and a couple of excellent restaurants, but not much else. The places listed below get very busy in summer, par-ticularly at lunchtime, and prices are uni-versally high.

Da Salvatore   CAMPANIAN €€
(☎089 85 72 27; www.salvatoreravello.co; Via della Republicca 2; meals €28; ⊙Tue-Sun) Located just before the bus stop and the Albergo Ristorante Garden, Da Salvatore is nothing special by way of decor, but the view – from both the dining room and the large terrace – is very special indeed. Dishes include crea-tive options like tender squid on a bed of pureed chickpeas with spicy *peperoncino*. In the evening, part of the restaurant is transformed into an informal pizzeria, serv-ing some of the best wood-fired pizza you will taste anywhere this side of Naples.

Ristorante Pizzeria Vittoria   PIZZA €€
(☎089 85 79 47; www.ristorantepizzeriavittoria. it; Via dei Rufolo 3; meals €30, pizza from €5; ⊕) Come here for exceptional pizza with some 16 choices on the menu, including the Rav-ellese, with cherry tomatoes, mozzarella, basil and courgettes. Other dishes include lasagne with red pumpkin, smoked moz-zarella and porcini mushrooms, and an in-novative chickpea and cod antipasto. The atmosphere is one of subdued elegance, with a small outside terrace and grainy his-torical pics of Ravello on the walls.

Caffe Calce   CAFE €
(☎089 85 71 52; Via Roma 2; ice cream €2) Located just above the Piazza Duomo, this place has a time-tested feel, with its old-fashioned interi-or and crusty local clientele. The coffee is fa-mously the best in town, and the sweet treats of pastries and ice creams are reliably good.

🛍 Shopping

Limoncello and ceramics are the mainstays of the Amalfi Coast souvenir trade and you'll find both sold here.

Profumi della Costiera   DRINK
(☎089 85 81 67; www.profumidellacostiera.it; Via Trin-ità 37) The *limoncello* produced and sold here is made with local lemons; known to experts as *sfusato amalfitano,* they're enormous – about double the size of a standard lemon. The tot is made according to traditional recipes, so there are no preservatives and no colouring. And it's not just the owners who say so – all bottles carry the IGP (*Indicazione Geografica Proteta*; Protected Geographi-cal Indication) quality mark. You may just see the bottling in progress when you visit; t takes place just at the back of the shop.

Wine & Drugs   FOOD
(☎089 85 84 43; Via Trinità 6) Despite the tongue-in-cheek name, no mind-altering substances are sold here, only grappa, or-ganic olive oil, saffron and a good selection of local and international wines. There are also complimentary daily tastings of aged Parmesan dipped into similarly elderly 24-year-old balsamic vinegar. Check out the

PARKING IN RAVELLO

You may want to consider taking a bus from Amalfi to Ravello instead of driving, as the metered parking around the pedestrianised centre of town is obviously geared towards Ferrari owners: a costly €5 an hour and only payable by credit card. Alternatively, head for the underground car park at the Auditorium Oscar Niemeyer (p170). This car park was in the process of being completed at research time but the word at the tourist office was that it promises to be considerably cheaper.

owner's collection of baseball caps (over 400 at last count), sent by appreciative customers from around the world in exchange for a Ravello cap which is routinely included in any shipment.

Cashmere WOMEN'S CLOTHING
(☑089 85 84 67; www.filodautoreravello.it; Via Trinità 8) Although you may associate cashmere with more northern climes, this tiny shop in the Ravello backstreets is worth a visit to view the exceptional quality of the locally produced clothing here, made primarily from pure cashmere, as well as linen.

ⓘ Information
Tourist Office (☑089 85 70 96; www.ravellotime.it; Via Roma 18; ◷9am-7pm) Can assist with accommodation.

ⓘ Getting There & Away
Bus
SITA (☑199 73 07 49; www.sitabus.it) Operates hourly buses from Amalfi departing from the bus stop on the eastern side of Piazza Flavio Gioia.

Car
By car, turn north about 2km east of Amalfi.

Parking
Vehicles are not permitted in Ravello's town centre. See Parking in Ravello boxed text, p172 for more information about parking in town.

Minori
POP 3000
About 3.5km east of Amalfi, or a steep kilometre-long walk down from Ravello, Minori is a small, workaday town, popular with holidaying Italians. Scruffier than its refined coastal cousins Amalfi and Positano, it's no less dependent on tourism, yet seems more genuine, with its festive seafront, pleasant beach, atmospheric pedestrian shopping streets and noisy traffic jams. It is also known for its history of pasta making, dating back to medieval times; the speciality being *scialatielli* (thick ribbons of fresh pasta), featured on many local restaurant menus.

Head for the small **Tourist Office** (☑089 87 70 87; www.proloco.minori.sa.it; Via Roma 30; ◷9am-noon & 5-8pm Mon-Sat, 9-11am Sun) on the seafront for general information and walking maps.

◉ Sights
FREE **Villa Roma Antiquarium** HISTORIC BUILDING
(☑089 85 28 93; Via Capodipiazza 28; ◷9am-7pm) The splendid 1st-century Villa Roma Antiquarium is a typical example of the sort that Roman nobles built as holiday homes in the period before Mt Vesuvius' AD 79 eruption. The best-preserved rooms surround the garden on the lower level.

There's also an interesting two-room museum exhibiting various artifacts, including a collection of 6th-century BC to 6th-century AD amphorae.

🎊 Festivals & Events
Gustaminori FOOD FESTIVAL
Food lovers on the coast gather in Minori in early September for the town's annual food jamboree with pasta stalls (and the like) throughout the town, as well as live music.

✕ Eating
Il Giardiniello CAMPANIAN €€
(☑089 87 70 50; www.ristorantegiardiniello.com; Corso Vittorio Emanuele 17; menu €30, pizza from €8; ◷Thu-Tue) Easy to find, just up from the seafront on a bustling pedestrian street, Giardiniello has been pleasing local palates since 1955. Sit on the outside terrace surrounded by fragrant jasmine and enjoy a 40cm pizza to share (€16) or a girth-expanding menu with the local specialty *scialatielli* followed by local fish and dessert, plus wine.

Gambardella PASTICCERIA €
(☑089 87 72 99; Piazza Cantilena 7; pastries from €1.50) Tucked behind the pretty buttercup-lemon church, this is the place to come

FAVOURITE LOCAL TIPPLE

Wander into a local bar and you may just mistake this for rural France. Cetara locals love to accompany their espressos with a tumbler of Pernod, instead of plain old water. The aniseed-based tipple was introduced to the town by French fishermen several decades ago and the association has continued to the present day. Cetara has recently been twinned with Sète in France and many Italian fishermen have moved there to work in the local fishing industry.

for superb coffee and exemplary pastries – try the *sfogliatella* (ricotta-filled flaky pastry) and *torta di ricotta e pere* (ricotta and pear tart). You can also buy *limoncello* and similar boozy delights made with wild strawberries, bilberries, bay leaves and wild fennel.

Cetara

POP 2400

Just beyond **Erchie** and its pleasant beach, Cetara is a picturesque fishing village with a reputation as a gastronomic hot spot. It has been an important fishing centre since medieval times and today its deep-sea tuna fleet is considered one of the Mediterranean's most important. At night, fishermen set out in small boats armed with powerful lamps to fish for anchovies. Recently, locals have resurrected the production of what is known as *colatura di alici*, a strong anchovy essence believed to be the descendant of *garum*, the Roman fish seasoning. If you want to stay overnight, or for more information, visit the small **Tourist Office** (☑328 0156347; Piazza San Francesco 15; ⊗9am-1pm & 5pm-midnight).

✗ Eating

Al Convento   SEAFOOD €€
(☑089 26 10 39; Piazza San Francesco 16; meals €25) Enjoy the evocative setting of this restaurant located in former church cloisters with its original, albeit faded, 17th-century frescoes. Al Convento is an excellent spot to tuck into some local fish specialities. You can eat *tagliata di tonna alle erbe* (strips of lightly grilled tuna with herbs) as an antipasto, or anchovies prepared in various ways. Particularly delicious is the spaghetti served with anchovies and wild fennel. For dessert, try the deliciously decadent chocolate cake with ricotta and cream.

✿ Festivals & Events

Sagra del Tonno   TUNA FESTIVAL
Each year, in late July or early August, the village celebrates *sagra del tonno,* a festival dedicated to tuna and anchovies. If you can time your visit accordingly, there are plenty of opportunities for tasting, as well as music and other general festivities. Further details are available from the tourist office.

If you miss the festival, no worries, you can pick up a jar (never a tin) of the fishy specialities, preserved in olive oil, at local food shops and delis.

Vietri sul Mare

POP 8600

Marking the end of Amalfi's coastal road, Vietri sul Mare is the ceramics capital of Campania. Production dates back to Roman times but it took off on an industrial scale in the 16th and 17th centuries with the development of high, three-level furnaces. The unmistakable local style – bold brush strokes and strong Mediterranean colours – found favour in the royal court of Naples, which became one of Vietri's major clients. Later, in the 1920s and '30s, an influx of international artists (mainly Germans) led to a shake-up of traditional designs. There's a moderately helpful **Tourist Office** (☑089 21 12 85; Piazza Matteotti; ⊗10am-1pm & 5-8pm Mon-Fri, 10am-1pm Sat) near the entrance to the *centro storico* which is packed with decorative tiled-front shops selling ceramic wares of every description.

 Museo della Ceramica   MUSEUM
(☑089 21 18 35; Villa Guerriglia; ⊗8am-3pm Tue-Sat, 9am-1pm Sun) For more on Vietri's ceramics past, head to this museum in the nearby village of Raito. Housed in a lovely villa surrounded by a park, the museum has a comprehensive collection, including pieces from the so-called 'German period'

(1929-47), when the town attracted an influx of artists, mainly from Germany.

Ceramica Artistica Solimene CERAMICS
(089 21 02 43; www.solimene.com; Via Madonna degli Angeli 7) This vast factory outlet, the most famous ceramics shop in town, sells everything from eggcups to ornamental mermaids, mugs to lamps. Even if you don't go in, it's worth having a look at the shop's extraordinary glass and ceramic facade. It was designed by Italian architect Paoli Soleri, who studied under the famous Californian 'organic' architect Frank Lloyd Wright.

Ceramiche Sara CERAMICS
(089 21 00 53; Via Costiera Amalfitana 14-16) Located at the entrance to town with a convenient car park, the showroom here has a great choice of ceramics, including some reasonably priced and colourful tiles (€8) that make terrific hotplates.

Salerno & the Cilento

Best Places to Eat

» La Cantina del Feudo (p179)
» Vicolo della Neve (p179)
» Anna (p189)
» I Tre Gufi (p191)

Best Places to Stay

» Agriturismo i Moresani (p212)
» Villa Vea (p212)
» Marulivo Hotel (p211)
» Hotel Calypso (p210)

Why Go?

Salerno can be visited on foot, but concentrate on the picturesque *centro storico* (historic centre) with its labyrinth of colourful earthy streets. This is the only area of the city that was miraculously spared during World War II bombing when the city was designated the capital of Allied Italy. Have a look, too, at the splendid waterfront promenade lined with palm trees. Then, allow at least three hours for the fascinating excavations at Paestum, among the best-preserved Greek temples in the world.

And don't miss the Cilento region, one of this area's unsung glories, with a largely undeveloped coastal strip and a beautiful national park. It's a burgeoning region for walkers, too, and *agriturismi* (farm-stay accommodation) make perfect bases. The region has some heavyweight sights as well, including an extraordinary monastery, an evocative archaeological site, and intriguing grottoes and caves.

Road Distance (KM)

	Salerno	Paestum	Agropoli	Castellabate
Paestum	27			
Agropoli	45	17		
Castellabate	58	30	13	
Palinuro	112	69	62	53

DON'T MISS

Ordering the locally produced buffalo-milk mozzarella; soft, creamy and mildly tangy, it is considered to be among the best in the country.

Best Beaches

» Ascea (p191)

» Santa Maria di Castellabate (p190)

» Spiaggia Palinuro (p192)

» Agropoli (p188)

Best Activities

» Wreck diving in Agropoli (p189)

» Moonlit ocean trip on the Cilento Coast (p191)

» Hiking in the Parco Nazionale del Cilento (p182)

» Boat trip to the grottoes in Palinuro (p192)

Resources

» **Salerno City** (www.salernocity.com) Comprehensive city website.

» **Salerno Province** (www.salernomemo.com) Emphasis on sports and activities.

» **Agropoli** (www.commune.agropoli.sa.it) General information and local news.

» **Paestum** (www.infopaestum.it) Information about the town and archaeological site.

» **Cilento** (www.discovercilento.com) General information on the park and coastal resorts.

Getting Around

Salerno is on the ferry route from Naples and Sorrento, and in summer the Amalfi coast resorts and islands. The main Cilento towns can be reached by bus or ferry; however, renting a car will provide the flexibility to explore the smaller villages and the Parco Nazionale del Cilento e Vallo di Diano (Cilento National Park and the Valley of Diano) inland, where the bus service is sporadic, with many villages only accessible by car. Overall the roads are good throughout the Cilento region with well signposted towns and resorts within easy reach.

3 PERFECT DAYS

Day 1 – Culture & Cuisine

Start off in Salerno by checking out the magnificent cathedral (p178), followed by an atmospheric stroll around the narrow backstreets of the city's small *centro storico* (historic centre). Take a cappuccino break in a typical hung-with-washing piazza, then hop on a train or drive to Paestum (p182) for an early lunch and an afternoon visiting its magical temples (p183). In the evening continue south to Agropoli (p188) for an ocean-front dinner.

Day 2 – Coastal Cilento

Stretch your legs with a morning stroll along Agropoli's sweeping promenade. Visit the castle (p188) and historic quarter before continuing south along this dramatic coastline of hidden coves and high cliffs. Stop for a swim, a snack or a stroll at small traditional Italian resorts like Acciaroli (p190), a favourite of Ernest Hemingway's; Pioppi (p191), with its pale pebble beach; and medieval Pisciotta (p191), home to a lovely traditional piazza. Carry on along this unspoiled coastline before ending the day in pretty Palinuro (p192).

Day 3 – Explore hidden caves and grottoes

It's not half as famous as its Capri cousin, but Palinuro's Grotta Azzurra (Blue Grotto; p193) is just as spectacular. Next, head inland into the Parco Nazionale del Cilento (p182) and two otherworldly caves, the Grotta di Castelcivita (p183), one of the largest cave complexes in Europe, and the equally tantalising Grotta dell'Angelo (p183) in Pertosa, where your tour includes the added adventure of a boat ride. Consider staying overnight at one of the park's superb *agriturismi* (farm-stay accommodation).

Accommodation

While Salerno doesn't have a great choice of accommodation, the Cilento coast and park have a diverse range of places to lay your head. Mountaintop discreet *palazzi* (mansions), breezy beachfront hotels and ecofriendly *agriturismi* are here, with prices considerably lower than those on the Amalfi Coast. For more information, see the Accommodation chapter, p194.

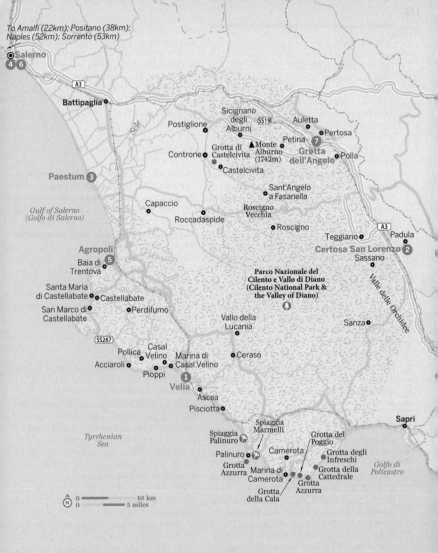

Salerno & the Cilento Coast Highlights

1 Roam the ruins of the Hellenistic town of **Velia** (p191)

2 Wonder at the extraordinary **Certosa di San Lorenzo** (p184) in Padula

3 Explore **Paestum** (p182), one of Europe's most majestic ancient sites

4 Stroll through the fascinating *centro storico* (historic centre) in **Salerno** (p178)

5 Enjoy a sunset stroll along the lovely promenade in **Agropoli** (p188)

6 Marvel at the heady views from Salerno's **castle** (p178)

7 Visit the fascinating **Grotta dell'Angelo** (p183) by boat

Salerno

POP 139,019

Salerno may seem like a bland big city after the Amalfi Coast's glut of postcard-pretty towns, but the place has a charming, if gritty, individuality, especially around its vibrant *centro storico* (historic centre) where medieval churches share space with neighbourhood trattorias, neon-lit wine bars and trendy tattoo parlours. The city recently invested €12.5 million in various urban regeneration programs centred on this historic neighbourhood, under the watchful eye of Oriol Bohigas, who was similarly involved in Barcelona's earlier makeover. A dramatic new ferry terminal designed by the Pritzker Prize–winning architect Zaha Hadid also opened here in 2012, accentuated by a tree-lined seafront promenade widely considered to be one of the most beautiful in Europe.

Originally an Etruscan and later a Roman colony, Salerno flourished with the arrival of the Normans in the 11th century. Robert Guiscard made it the capital of his dukedom in 1076 and, under his patronage, the Scuola Medica Salernitana was renowned as one of medieval Europe's greatest medical institutes. Far later, the city was tragically left in tatters by the heavy fighting that followed the 1943 landings of the American Fifth Army.

Sights

Although Salerno is a sprawling town, you can easily visit it in one day, and on foot, as the main sights are concentrated in and around the historic centre. Don't miss the gracious seafront promenade. For shopping, head for the pedestrian Corso Vittorio Emanuele II, which changes name to Via Mercanti towards the medieval market square of Piazza Sedile del Campo, where there is an eclectic mix of intriguing ceramic stores, boutiques and idiosyncratic small shops.

TOP CHOICE **Cathedral** CHURCH

(Piazza Alfano; ⊙10am-6pm) You can't miss the looming presence of Salerno's impressive cathedral, widely considered to be the most beautiful medieval church in Italy. Built by the Normans in the 11th century and later aesthetically remodelled in the 18th century, it sustained severe damage in the 1980 earthquake. It is dedicated to San Matteo (St Matthew), whose remains were reputedly brought to the city in 954 and now lie beneath the main altar in the vaulted crypt.

Take special note of the magnificent main entrance, the 12th-century **Porta dei Leoni**, named after the marble lions at the foot of the stairway. It leads through to a beautiful harmonious courtyard, surrounded by graceful arches, overlooked by a 12th-century bell tower. Carry on through the huge bronze doors (similarly guarded by lions), that were cast in Constantinople in the 11th century. When you come to the three-aisled interior, you will see that it is largely baroque, with only a few traces of the original church. These include parts of the transept and choir floor and the two raised pulpits in front of the choir stalls. Throughout the church you can see extraordinarily detailed and colourful 13th-century mosaic work.

In the right-hand apse, don't miss the **Cappella delle Crociate** (Chapel of the Crusades), containing stunning frescoes and more wonderful mosaics. It was so named because crusaders' weapons were blessed here. Under the altar stands the tomb of 11th-century pope, Gregory VII.

FREE **Castello di Arechi** CASTLE

(☑089 22 55 78; Via Benedetto Croce; ⊙9am-3.30pm) Hop on bus 19 from Piazza XXIV Maggio to visit Salerno's most famous landmark, the forbidding Castello di Arechi, dramatically positioned 263m above the city. Originally a Byzantine fort, it was built by the Lombard duke of Benevento, Arechi II, in the 8th century and subsequently modified by the Normans and Aragonese, most recently in the 16th century.

The views of the Gulf of Salerno and the city rooftops are spectacular; you can also visit a permanent collection of ceramics, arms and coins. If you are here during the summer, ask the tourist office for a schedule of the annual series of concerts staged here.

FREE **Museo Pinacoteca Provinciale** MUSEUM

(☑089 258 30 73; Via Mercanti 63; ⊙9am-8pm Tue-Sun) Art enthusiasts should seek out the Museo Pinacoteca Provinciale, located deep in the heart of the historic quarter. Spread throughout six galleries, this museum houses an interesting art collection dating from the Renaissance right up to the first half of the 20th century.

SALERNO & THE CILENTO SALERNO

There are some fine canvases on display here by local boy Andrea Sabatini da Salerno, who was notably influenced by Leonardo da Vinci, plus a diverse selection of works by foreign artists who were permanent residents around the Amalfi Coast. These include intricate etchings by the Austrian-born artist Peter Willburger (1942–98) and a colourful embroidered picture of a local market by Polish artist Irene Kowaliska. The museum also hosts free classical concerts during the summer months.

FREE **Museo Didattico della Scuola Medica Salernitana**   MUSEUM
(Medical School of Salerno Museum; ☑089 24 12 92; Via Mercanti 72; ☺9am-1pm Mon-Fri; ⚐) Slap bang in Salerno's historic centre, this engaging museum deploys 3-D and touch screen technology to explore the teachings and wince-inducing procedures of Salerno's once-famous, now-defunct medical institute. Established around the 9th century, the school was the most important centre of medical knowledge in medieval Europe, reaching the height of its prestige in the 11th century. It was closed in the early 19th century.

Museo Archeologico Provinciale   MUSEUM
(☑089 23 11 35; Via San Benedetto 28; ☺closed for restoration) The province's main archaeological museum has been closed for restoration for several years now with no approximate opening date available. Check at the tourist office before turning up here. If it is open, don't miss the highlight: a 1st-century-BC bronze head of Apollo, discovered in the Gulf of Salerno in 1930. One can only wonder what else lies buried in the surrounding seabed.

✕ Eating

Head to Via Roma in the lively medieval centre, where you'll find everything from traditional, family-run trattorias and gelaterias to jazzy wine bars, pubs and expensive restaurants. In summer, the wide seafront promenade is a popular place for the evening *passeggiata* (stroll).

TOP CHOICE **La Cantina del Feudo**   CAMPANIAN €€
(☑089 25 46 96; Via Velia 45; meals €28; ☺Tue-Sun; ⚐) Frequented by locals in the know, this restaurant is tucked up a side street off the pedestrian Corso Vittorio Emanuele II.

Eating here is like eating at your grandma's house when everything was simpler yet the taste was still spot on. The menu changes daily but the emphasis is on vegetable dishes like white beans with chicory, noodles and turnip tops, and ravioli stuffed with cheese and topped with a spinach-pesto sauce. The interior has a rural trattoria feel and there's an outside terrace for al fresco dining.

Vicolo della Neve   CAMPANIAN €
(☑089 22 57 05; Vicolo della Neve 24; meals €20; ☺dinner Thu-Tue) A city institution, located on one of the scruffiest streets in the city, Vicolo della Neve is the archetypal *centro storico* trattoria with brick arches, fake frescoes and walls hung with works by local artists. The menu is, similarly, unwaveringly authentic, with pizzas and *calzones* (pizzas folded over to form a pie), *peperoni ripieni* (stuffed peppers) and a top-notch *parmigiana di melanzane* (baked aubergine with tomatoes and Parmesan). It can get incredibly busy, so reservations are a wise idea.

Pizza Margherita   CAMPANIAN €
(☑089 22 88 80; Corso Garibaldi 201; pizzas/buffet from €5/6.50, lunchtime menu €8.50; ⚐) It looks like a bland, modern canteen but this is, in fact, one of Salerno's most popular lunch spots. Locals regularly queue for the lavish lunchtime buffet that, on any given day, might include buffalo mozzarella, salami, mussels in various guises and a range of salads.

If that doesn't appeal, the daily lunchtime menu (pasta, main course, salad and half a litre of water) is chalked up on a blackboard, or there's the regular menu of pizzas, pastas, salads and main courses.

Ristorante Santa Lucia   SEAFOOD €€
(☑089 22 56 96; Via Roma 182; pizzas from €5, meals €22; ☺Tue-Sun) The surrounding Via

SALERNO & THE CILENTO SALERNO

DON'T MISS

SWEET TREAT

Look for *torta ricotta e pera* (ricotta and pear tart), a speciality in Salerno and sold throughout the Cilento region. Just about every *pasticceria* (pastry shop) sells this delicious sweet and fruity delicacy – although it is the locals' favourite as well, so they tend to sell out fast.

Salerno

N 0 — 400 m
0 — 0.2 miles

Via Torquato Tasso
To Castello di
Arechi (900m)
Piazza Sedile
del Campo

Via del Canali

Via di Porta
Catena
Piazza
Amendola

To Amalfi (40km);
Positano (65km);
Sorrento (65km);
Vietri sul Mare (5km)

Piazza Alfano
Cathedral

Via Duomo
Via Mercanti
Vicolo della
Neve
Via S Michele
Via Genovesi
Via Iannelli
Piazza
Matteotti

Via Velia

Corso Vittorio Emanuele II

Via Roma

Piazza
XXIV
Maggio

Via Nizza

Via Volpe

Via Dalmazia

Via Cilento

Via Diaz

Corso Garibaldi

Piazza
Giuseppe
Mazzini

Train Station
Bus
Station
Piazza
Vittorio
Veneto

Via Torrione

Lungomare Guglielmo Marconi

Piazza
della
Concordia

CSTP Bus
Stop

To A3 (southbound);
Paestum (36km)

Gulf of Salerno
(Golfo di Salerno)

To Capri (45km);
Ischia (68km)

Porto Commerciale
Ferry & Hydrofoil Terminal

Salerno

◎ Top Sights		5 Ostello Ave Gratia Plena........................ B1
Cathedral C1		Sant'Andrea .... (see 11)

◎ Sights		⊗ Eating
1 Museo Archeologico Provinciale C1		**6** Cicirinella... C1
2 Museo Didattico della Scuola		**7** La Cantina del Feudo D2
Medica Salernitana...............................C1		**8** Pasticceria Romolo G3
3 Museo Pinacoteca Provinciale...............C1		**9** Pizza Margherita E3
		10 Ristorante Santa Lucia B1
⊜ Sleeping		**11** Sant'Andrea A1
4 Hotel Montestella...................................D2		**12** Vicolo della Neve B1

Roma area may be one of the city's trendiest, but there's nothing remotely flash about the delicious seafood served up here. Dishes such as *linguine ai frutti di mare* (flat spaghetti with seafood) and chargrilled cuttlefish may not be original but taste quite exceptional – as do the uppercrust wood-fired pizzas.

Pasticceria Romolo   PASTICCERIA €
(☑089 23 26 13; Corso Garibaldi 33; cakes from €1.50) Across from the train station, this sprawling *pasticceria* dates from 1966 and the decor has changed little since. The cakes are similarly legendary in this town, with a mouth-watering display that includes *frollini* (fruit and chocolate tarts), *amaretti* (macaroons) and that all-time irresistible treat *sfogliatelle* (a flaky pastry cake filled with fresh ricotta). Fancy chocolates and a wide range of local and national wine are also on sale.

Sant'Andrea   CAMPANIAN €€
(☑328 727274; www.ristorantesantandrea.it; Piazza Sedile del Campo 58; meals €25) There's an earthy southern Italian atmosphere here, with its outside terrace surrounded by historic houses decorated with washing hung out to dry. Choices are more innovative than you would expect and include seafood dishes, such as squid with porcini mushrooms or cuttlefish accompanied by creamed vegetables. The white-truffle ice cream makes a sexy, sweet finale. The owners run the adjacent B&B.

Cicirinella   CAMPANIAN €€
(☑089 22 65 61; Via Genovesi 28; meals €25) This place has that winning combination of an earthy and inviting atmosphere and unfailingly good, delicately composed dishes. Exposed stone, shelves of wine and an open-plan kitchen set the scene for enjoying traditional Campanian cuisine like pasta

with seafood and chickpeas, or a mussel soup that tastes satisfyingly of the sea.

❶ Information

Tourist Office (☑089 23 14 32; Piazza Vittorio Veneto 1; ☉9am-2pm & 3-8pm Mon-Sat, 9am-12.30pm & 5-7.30pm Sun) Has limited information.

❶ Getting There & Away

Boat

Metrò del Mare (☑199 60 07 00; www.metro delmare.com; ☉Jun-Sep) operates regular ferries to/from Naples (€20, 2½ hours, one daily), Sorrento (€15, one hour, one daily), Amalfi (€8.50, 20 minutes, two daily) and Positano (€11, 50 minutes, two daily).

Linee Marittime Partenopee (☑081 704 19 11; www.consorziolmp.it; Via Guglielmo Melisurgo 4, Naples) runs a daily hydrofoil to/from Capri (€22, 50 minutes)

Alicost (☑089 87 14 83; www.alicost.it; Salita Sopramuro 2, Amalfi) runs several daily hydrofoils to/from Capri (€20.50, 50 minutes), Amalfi (€7, 20 minutes) and Positano (€11, 30 minutes)

Departures are from the Porto Turistico, 200m down the pier from Piazza della Concordia. You can buy tickets from the booths by the embarkation point.

Bus

SITA (☑199 73 07 49; www.sitabus.it) buses for Amalfi depart at least hourly from Piazza Vittorio Veneto, beside the train station, stopping en route at Vietri sul Mare, Cetara, Maiori and Minori. For Pompeii, take **CSTP** (☑089 48 70 01; www.cstp.it) bus 50 from Piazza Vittorio Veneto. There are 15 daily departures. For the south coast and Paestum, take the hourly bus 34 from the CSTP stop on Piazza della Concordia.

Car

Salerno is on the A3 between Naples and Reggio di Calabria; the A3 is toll-free from Salerno south.

Take the Salerno exit and follow signs to the *centro* (city centre). If you want to hire a car, there's a **Europcar** (☏089 258 07 75; www.europcar.com; Via Giacinto Vicinanza) agency not far from the train station.

Parking

Salerno has a reasonable number of car parks. Follow the distinctive blue P sign as you approach the centre of the city. The most convenient car park for the *centro storico* is on Piazza Amendola. Near the train station (and tourist office) other convenient locations are the large car parks on Piazza della Concordia and the adjacent Piazza Giuseppe Mazzini. You can expect to pay around €1.50 an hour for Salerno car parks.

Train

Salerno is a major stop on southbound routes to Calabria, and the Ionian and Adriatic coasts. From the station in Piazza Vittorio Veneto there are regular trains to Naples (€9, 35 minutes, half-hourly) and Rome (Intercity, from €19, three hours, hourly).

Paestum

Paestum, or Poseidonia as the city was originally called (in honour of Poseidon, the Greek god of the sea), was founded in the 6th century BC by Greek settlers and fell under Roman control in 273 BC. Decline later set in following the demise of the Roman Empire. Savage raids by the Saracens and periodic outbreaks of malaria forced the steadily dwindling population to abandon the city altogether.

Although most people visit Paestum for the day, there is a surprising number of good hotels, and this delightful rural area makes a convenient stopover point for travellers heading for the Cilento region. See the Paestum section of the Accommodation chapter (p210) for recommendations.

✖ Eating

Nonna Scepa   CAMPANIAN €€
(☏0828 85 10 64; Via Laura 53; meals €30; ☏) There are various restaurants at the site; however most serve mediocre food at inflated prices. Instead, seek out the superbly prepared, robust dishes at midrange prices at Nonna Scepa, a family friendly restaurant that's rapidly gaining a reputation throughout the region for excellence. Dishes are firmly seasonal and, during the summer, concentrate on fresh seafood like the refreshingly simple grilled fish with lemon.

Other popular choices include risotto with zucchini and artichokes, and spaghetti with lobster.

ⓘ Information

Tourist Office (☏0828 81 10 16; www.infopaestum.it; Via Magna Crecia 887; ☉9am-1.30pm & 2.30-7pm Mon-Sat)

ⓘ Getting There & Away

Bus

CSTP (☏089 48 70 01; www.cstp.it) Bus 34 operates to Paestum from Piazza della Concordia in Salerno (€3.40, one hour 20 minutes, 12 daily).

Parco Nazionale Del Cilento e Vallo Di Diano

Proving the perfect antidote to the holiday mayhem along the coast, the Parco Nazionale del Cilento e Vallo di Diano (Cilento National Park and the Valley of Diano), hereafter referred to as the Parco Nazionale del Cilento, is a compelling combination of dense woods, flowering meadows, dramatic mountains, and water – lots of it – with streams, rivers and waterfalls. A World Heritage Site, it is the second-largest national park in Italy, covering a staggering 1810 sq km, including 80 towns and villages.

Inhabited since prehistoric times, the park's isolation has attracted waves of settlers seeking refuge over the ages. First, the Greeks fled here when the Romans overran the towns of Paestum and Velia. Then, early inhabitants of the coastal cities headed inland to escape piracy and pillaging. Benedictine monks subsequently joined the cultural medley, seeking secluded places of worship. Next up were the wealthy feudal lords who set up house (or rather castle) here, from where they could impose their power.

Centuries later, the park was controlled by the feared *briganti* (bandits), which meant it was a no-go area for Grand Tour visitors. This kept the park out of the tourism loop for decades and helps explain why it remains so pristine today.

⊙ Sights

To get the best out of the park, you will need a car. For a hire company in nearby Agropoli, see p190. Allow yourself a full day to visit the grottoes and more if you're intending to hike.

PAESTUM'S TEMPLES

A Unesco World Heritage site, these **temples** (☑0828 81 10 23; adult/reduced, including museum €10/5; ⊙8.45am-7.45pm, last entry 7pm) are among the best-preserved monuments of Magna Graecia, the Greek colony that once covered much of southern Italy. The temples were rediscovered in the late 18th century, but the site as a whole wasn't unearthed until as late as the 1950s. Lacking the mobs of tourists that can detract from the atmosphere at better-known archaeological sites, there is a wonderful serenity about the place. Take sandwiches and prepare to stay a while. If you are visiting in springtime, the temples are particularly stunning, surrounded by meadows of scarlet poppies and wild flowers.

Buy your tickets in the museum, just east of the site, before entering from the main entrance on the northern end. The first structure to take your breath away is the 6th-century-BC **Tempio di Cerere** (Temple of Ceres). Originally dedicated to Athena, it served as a Christian church in medieval times.

As you head south, you can pick out the basic outline of the large rectangular forum, the heart of the ancient city. Among the partially standing buildings are the vast domestic housing area and, further south, the amphitheatre; both provide evocative glimpses of daily life here in Roman times.

The **Tempio di Nettuno** (Temple of Neptune), dating from about 450 BC, is the largest and best preserved of the three temples at Paestum; only parts of its inside walls and roof are missing. Almost next door, the so-called **basilica** (in fact, a temple to the goddess Hera) is Paestum's oldest surviving monument. Dating from the middle of the 6th century BC, it's a magnificent sight, with nine columns across and 18 along the sides. Ask someone to take your photo next to a column here; it's a good way to appreciate the scale.

Save time for the **museum** (☑0828 81 10 23; adult/reduced €10/4; ⊙8.45am-7.45pm, last entry 7pm, closed 1st & 3rd Mon of month), which covers two floors and houses a collection of fascinating, if weathered, metopes (bas-relief friezes). This collection includes 33 of the original 36 metopes from the Tempio di Argiva Hera (Temple of Argive Hera), situated 9km north of Paestum, of which virtually nothing else remains. The star exhibit is the 5th-century-BC fresco Tomba del Truffatore (Tomb of the Diver), thought to represent the passage from life to death with its depiction of a diver in mid-air (don't try this at home).

TOP CHOICE Grotte di Castelcivita CAVE

(☑0828 77 23 97; www.grottedicastelcivita.com; Piazzale N. Zonzi, Castelcivita; adult/reduced €10/8; ⊙tours 10.30am, 12pm, 1.30pm, 3pm, 4.30pm & 6pm Mar-Sep; P🚺) The grottoes are fascinating other-worldly caves that date from prehistoric times. If you're planning to visit, don't forget a jacket, and leave the high heels at home; the paths are wet and slippery. Located 40km southeast of Salerno, the cave is refreshingly non-commercial.

Excavations have revealed that the caves were inhabited 42,000 years ago, making it the oldest settlement in Europe. Although they extend over 4800m, only around half of the cave complex is open to the public. The standard one-hour tour winds through a route surrounded by extraordinary stalagmites and stalactites, and a mesmerising play of colours, caused by algae, calcium and iron that tint the naturally sculpted rock shapes.

The tour culminates in a cavernous lunar landscape – think California's Death Valley in miniature – called the Caverna di Bertarelli (Bertarelli Cavern). The caves are still inhabited – by bats – and visitors are instructed not to take flash photos for fear of blinding them. There are longer three-hour tours (€18) between May and September when the water deep within the cave complex has dried up. Hard hats, and a certain level of fitness and mobility, are required.

Grotte dell'Angelo CAVE

(☑0975 39 70 37; www.grottedellangelo.sa.it; Pertosa; guided visits adult/reduced €13/10; ⊙9am-7pm; P🚺) Compared to the Grotta di Castelcivita, the Grotta dell'Angelo is a youngster, dating back a mere 35 million years to the Neolithic period and only discovered in

Parco Nazionale del Cilento (Cilento National Park)

1932. Used by the Greeks and Romans as places of worship, the caves burrow through the mountains for some 2500m, with long underground passages and lofty grottoes filled with a mouthful of stalagmites and stalactites.

The first part of the tour takes part as a boat (or raft) ride on the river; you disembark just before the waterfall (phew!) and continue on foot for around 800m, surrounded by marvellous rock formations and luminous crystal accretions. This grotto is more commercial than Castelcivita, with souvenir shops, bars and a €3 parking fee.

Certosa di San Lorenzo　　MONASTERY
(☑0975 77 74 45; Padula; adult/reduced €4/2; ☺9am-7.30pm) One of the largest monasteries in southern Europe, the Certosa di San Lorenzo dates from 1306 and covers 250,000 sq metres. Numerologists can swoon at the following: 320 rooms and halls, 2500m of corridors, galleries and hallways, 300 columns, 500 doors, 550 windows, 13 courtyards, 100 fireplaces, 52 stairways and 41 fountains – in other words, it is *huge*.

As you will unlikely have time to see everything here, be sure to visit the highlights, including the vast central courtyard (a venue for summer classical-music concerts), the magnificent wood-panelled library, frescoed chapels and the kitchen with its grandiose fireplace and famous tale: apparently this is where the legendary 1000-egg omelette was made in 1534 for Charles V. Unfortunately, the historic frying pan is not on view – just how big was it, one wonders?

Within the monastery you can also peruse the modest collection of ancient artefacts at the **Museo Archeologico Provinciale della Lucania Occidentale** (☑0975 7 71 17; ☺8am-1.15pm & 2-3pm Tue-Sat, 9am-1pm Sun).

✈ Activities

There are some excellent *agriturismi* here that offer additional activities, including guided hikes, painting courses and horse riding; see the Accommodation chapter (p212) for more.

Nature Trails
HIKING

The park has 15 well-marked nature trails that vary from relatively easy strolls to serious hikes requiring plenty of stamina and a good set of knees. The countryside in the park is stunning and dramatic and, if you're here in spring, you'll experience real flower power: delicate narcissi, wild orchids and tulips hold their own among blowsier summer drifts of brilliant yellow ox-eye daisies and scarlet poppies.

Thickets of silver firs, wild chestnuts and beech trees add to the sumptuous landscape, as do the dramatic cliffs, pine-clad mountains and fauna, including wild boars, badgers and wolves and, for bird watchers, the increasingly rare golden eagle.

Even during the busier summer season, the sheer size of the park means that hikers are unlikely to meet others on the trail to swap tales and muesli bars – so getting lost could become a lonely, not to mention dangerous experience, if you haven't done some essential planning before striding out. In theory, the tourist offices should be able to supply you with a guide to the trails. In reality, they frequently seem to have run out of copies. Failing this, you can buy the *Parco Nazionale del Cilento e Vallo di Diano: Carta Turistica e dei Sentieri* (Tourist and Footpath Map; €7) or the excellent *Monte Stella: Walks & Rambles in Ancient Cilento* published by the Comunita' Montana Alento Monte Stella (€3). Most of the *agriturismi* in the park can also organise guided treks.

A popular self-guided hike, where you are rewarded with spectacular views, is a climb up Monte Alburno (1742m). There's a choice of two trails, both of which are clearly marked from the centre of the small town of Sicignano degli Alburni and finish at the mountain's peak. Allow approximately four hours for either route. The less experienced may prefer to opt for a guide (see boxed text, p188).

Roscigno Vecchia
GHOST TOWN

Roscigno Vecchia is located in the heart of the national park 28km west of Teggiano. Sudden landslides in the early 20th century caused the population to flee, although most of the original stone houses are still standing, demonstrating the sturdiness of the historic vernacular architecture. These, as well as the church and the central piazza, are all ghostly reminders of a formerly thriving community.

The residents were eventually permanently moved to Roscigno Nuovo (now simply known as Roscigno). There's something about visiting a ghost town that both fires the imagination and is highly contemplative, especially as the history is almost always harrowing.

GOING WILD FOR ORCHIDS

The Parco Nazionale del Cilento is a rich natural environment for fauna and flora and has been declared part of Unesco's Biosphere Preservation program. There are a number of extremely rare plant species here, including the primrose of Palinuro (the symbol of the park). Horticulture enthusiasts will likely trip over their pitchforks when they hear that there are also some 265 varieties of wild orchid that flourish annually in the park (the equivalent of 80% of the total number of wild orchid varieties growing in Europe).

Concentrated in the appropriately named Valle delle Orchidee (Valley of the Orchids), near the picturesque small town of Sassano (9km west of the Certosa di San Lorenzo in Padula), this annual dazzle of sumptuous colour encompasses some 70 orchid species and takes place normally from late April to early May. The surrounding countryside is beautiful, so even if you miss the orchids you can still enjoy the drive and may well catch a glimpse of some other form of wildlife, which includes foxes, badgers, wolves, wild boars and the largest otter population in Italy.

Take the sign marked *percorso turistico* on the left just as you enter Sassano; you will pass the medieval bridge of Peglio and woods of silver birches before this blooming event unfolds in all its glory in the valley beyond. You can also join an organised tour with Gruppo Escursionistico Trekking (p188).

BUFFALA MOZZARELLA

A distant cousin of the North American bison (and no, it is doubtful that cowboys ever topped their T-bone steak with a slice of mozzarella and a couple of basil leaves), the water buffalo was introduced to Italy and, in particular, Cilento by returning Crusaders in the Middle Ages. Today these herds are famed for producing distinctive milk with a far higher fat and protein content than cow's milk. This, in turn, results in that superbly soft and creamy mozzarella that you taste all over the region and which bears little resemblance to the leathery, bland product you find outside Italy.

In Cilento there are several farms producing *buffala*-milk (buffalo being the Italian word for buffalo), but only one organic producer, not just in Cilento, but throughout Italy: **Tenuta Vannulo** (☎0828 72 47 65; www.vannulo.it; Via G Galilei Capaccio Scalo; 1hr tour €4, incl lunch €20) is located a 10-minute drive from Paestum. 'The mozzarella produced here is generally considered to be the best in the region,' says Franco Coppola, owner of Inn Buffalito restaurant in Sorrento, which specialises in local produce. 'The fact that it is organically produced makes all the difference to the quality and taste.'

Tenuta Vannulo makes its mozzarella exclusively from buffalo milk, unlike most producers who combine it with cow's milk. Plus its cheese is unpasteurized. The farm is open to the public for tours (in English and Italian) of the production facilities, buffalo stables and an agricultural museum. Visits culminate in that all-important tasting; lunch is an additional option. Advance reservations are essential.

You can also stop by and buy fresh mozzarella here, though be warned that the demand for the cheese is so high that it generally runs out by early afternoon. And that's despite the considerable daily production of around 408kg of *buffala* mozzarella, enough for several thousand *caprese* salads....

Eating

There remains a lot of poverty in the small villages that dot the park, but that can mean simple, unadulterated food with hearty meat sauces made from mutton and goat. The flat bread, *focaccia*, that you find all over Italy originally came from the Cilento region and the *buffala* mozzarella is similarly famed.

Antichi Feudi
CAMPANIAN €€
(☎0975 58 73 29; Via San Francesco 2, Teggiano; meals €25, pizzas from €3) This gracious restaurant is located within the sumptuous same-name boutique hotel just off Teggiano's elegant main piazza. The menu varies according to what is in season but typical dishes include juicy chargrilled meat, grilled mussels with olive oil and lemon, and seafood soup. The hotel bar-cafe is good for pizza, including the tasty *antichi feudi* with mushrooms, fresh cheese and grilled aubergines (€9). Reservations are recommended.

Faunos Trattoria
CAMPANIAN €
(☎0889 71 24 44; Loc Sastagne delle Carte, Postiglione; meals €15; pizzas from €3; P 🏠) Easy to find, at the crossroad at the main approach to town with a front terrace, plenty of parking and rustic cabin-like dining room with beams. On a budget? You can share a pizza here for just three euros. No wonder this place is always packed. The main menu includes plenty of hearty dishes with *fagioli* (beans) taking centre stage in dishes like *zuppa de fagioli con porcini* (bean and porcini soup).

Pasticceria Mery Diano
GELATERIA €
(☎0975 797 62; Via San Maria, Teggiano; gelato €1.50, cakes from €1.50) Tucked around the corner next to the Chiesa di Santa Maria Maggiore (note the magnificent carved door), this small bar with its couple of outside tables serves the best ice cream in town, as well as drinks and cakes.

Taverna degli Antichi Sapori
CAMPANIAN €
(☎0828 77 25 00; www.tavernadegliantichisapori.it; Via Nazionale 27, Controne; meals from €12) Easy to find on the main road going through town, this bright, spacious restaurant with exposed stone walls has a small front terrace flanked by scarlet geraniums and a firmly traditional menu, which is great if you like *fagioli*, but not so great if you don't. Think *gnocchi e fagioli*, *pasta e fagioli*, *lasagne e fagioli*, *riso* (rice) *e fagioli* and a few grilled meat dishes.

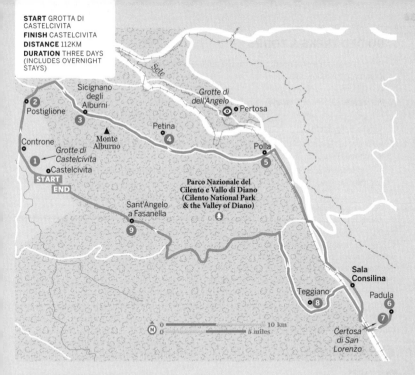

Sele

Sicignano degli Alburni

2 Postiglione

3

Controne
Grotte di dell'Angelo
Pertosa

Petina
4

Grotte di Castelcivita
1

Monte Alburno

Polla
5

Castelcivita

START
END

Parco Nazionale del
Cilento e Vallo di Diano
(Cilento National Park
& the Valley of Diano)

Sant'Angelo
a Fasanella
9

Sala
Consilina

Teggiano
8

Padula
6

7

N   0   10 km
     0   5 miles

Certosa di San Lorenzo

Driving Tour
A Drive in the Park

Start this drive after a visit to the other-worldly **1 Grotta di Castelcivita**. Take the SS488 through Controne continuing on the *strada provinciale* 60 northwards; the road passes soaring cliff faces, ancient dry stone walls and lush, arable countryside with wild cherry and fig trees. Slam on the brakes at **2 Postiglione**, its medieval town centre crowned by an 11th-century Norman castle. Join the locals for a coffee in one of the Piazza Europa bars, before continuing on the SS19 towards Auletta. The countryside here becomes dramatically mountainous, with a wonderful marbled rock face (think rocky road ice cream).

Follow signs eastwards on the SS19 to lovely **3 Sicignano degli Alburni**, taking in its 14th-century castle, baroque churches and historic convent. Sicignano is also the kick-off point for the two hiking trails that ascend Monte Alburno. Stay overnight at the nearby Sicinius *agriturismo*. Next day, continue south on *strada provinciale* 35, passing the village of **4 Petina** dramatically straddling a high ridge. Note that this is a

fairly rough road; if you prefer more reliable tarmac, head north for the SS19, which is similarly scenic and continues southeast, passing the turn-off to the fascinating Grotta dell'Angelo en route.

The next stop is **5 Polla**, a strategic town during Roman times and lovely for a stroll, with its riverfront setting, 12th-century castle and brooding dark-stone houses. Pick up picnic fare here and take the SS19 south (the A3 *autovia* is faster but not as scenic), following signs for **6 Padula**, where you can spend the afternoon exploring the extraordi-nary **7 Certosa di San Lorenzo**. Follow the signs to stunning **8 Teggiano**, around 15km northwest, and bristling with churches and museums, as well as a cathedral and a castle. Stay overnight.

Bright and early on day three, head north until you hit the SS166. Follow the signs to **9 Sant'Angelo a Fasanella**, a 13th-century town with a Roman bridge, medieval con-vents and churches, plus an atmospheric *centro storico*. Continue west some 18km to Castelcivita, your starting point.

GUIDED TREKS & TOURS

Several reputable organisations arrange guided hikes of the Parco Nazionale del Cilento, including the following:

» **Gruppo Escursionistico Trekking** (☑0975 725 86; www.getvallodidiano.it; Via Provinciale 29, Silla di Sassano)

» **Associazione Trekking Cilento** (☑0974 84 33 45; www.trekkingcilento.it; Via Cannetiello 6, Agropoli)

» **Associazione Naturalistica Culturale** (☑0974 82 38 52; http://noitour.it; Via Ianni 16, Agropoli)

» **Trekking Campania** (☑339 7456795; www.trekkingcampania.it; Via Yuri Gagarin 16, Salerno)

Taverna Il Lupo CAMPANIAN €
(☑0975 77 83 76; Via Municipio, Padula; meals from €16; ☑) A hospitable, family-run restaurant with a menu of typical Cilento dishes, including vegetarian choices such as vegetable frittatas, *zeppole di fiori di zucca* (baked courgettes) and homemade pasta with onions and white beans. Consider a slice of the heavenly, moist *torta di cioccolata* (chocolate cake) before you waddle home.

❶ Information

EMERGENCIES
Alpine Rescue (☑338 4351474, 118)

TOURIST INFORMATION
Paestum Tourist Office (☑0828 81 10 16; www.infopaestum.it; Via Magna Crecia 887, Paestum; ☑9am-1.30pm & 2.30-7pm Mon-Sat) Has some information on the Parco Nazionale del Cilento.

Sicignano degli Aburni Tourist Office (☑0828 97 37 55; Piazza Plebiscito 13, Sicignano degle Aburni; ☑9am-1.30pm & 2.30-5pm Mon-Sat)

Vallo della Lucania (☑0974 71 11 11; http://www.parks.it/parco.nazionale.cilento/Eindex.html; Via Polombo 16, Palazzo Mainenti, Vallo della Lucania; ☑9am-1.30pm & 2.30-5pm Mon-Sat) Check out the excellent website.

BOOK AHEAD

Don't just turn up at *agriturismi* or B&Bs in the park; chances are no one will be home, the bell won't work or grandpa won't have the right key. Tourism is recent in these parts – give it time and always reserve in advance.

Agropoli

POP 20.673

Located just south of Paestum, Agropoli is a busy summer resort but otherwise a pleasant, tranquil town that makes a good base for exploring the Cilento coastline and park. While the shell is a fairly faceless grid of shop-lined streets, the kernel, the historic city centre, is a fascinating tangle of narrow cobbled streets with ancient churches, venerable residents and a castle with superb views.

The town has been inhabited since Neolithic times, with subsequent inhabitants including the Greeks, the Romans, the Byzantines and the Saracens. In 915 AD the town fell into the jurisdiction of the bishops and was subsequently ruled by feudal lords. Agropoli was a target of raids from North Africa in the 16th and 17th centuries, when the population dwindled to just a few hundred. Today the residents number closer to 20,000, making it the largest (and the most vibrant) town along the Cilento coast.

◉ Sights & Activities

To reach the *centro storico* of Agropoli, head for the Piazza Veneto Victoria, the pedestrian-only part of the modern town where cafes and gelaterie are interspersed with plenty of shopping choice. Head up Corso Garibaldi and take the wide Ennio Balbo Scaloni steps until you reach the fortified medieval *borgo*. Follow the signs to the castle. The town is famed for its pristine, golden, sandy beaches.

FREE **Il Castello** CASTLE
(☑10am-8pm) Built by the Byzantines in the 5th century, the castle was further strength-

ened during the Algevin period, the time of the Vespro war bloodbath. The castle continued to be modified and only part of the original defensive wall remains. It's an enjoyable walk here through the historic centre, and you can stroll along the ramparts and enjoy magnificent views of the coastline and town below.

Not just a tourist sight, the castle is utilised by the locals, with a permanent art gallery showcasing contemporary local artists and a small open-air auditorium where concerts take place during the summer months.

Cilento Sub Diving Center   DIVING

(☑338 2374603; www.cilentosub.com; Via San Francesco 30; single dives from €25; 🐾) Indulge in your favourite watery pursuit here. Courses include snorkelling for beginners, open-water junior dives (from 12 years) and wreck diving; the latter includes the harrowing (for some) viewing of hulks of ships, tanks and planes that were famously destroyed in the region during WWII.

Diving sites include such tantalising areas as the waters off the coast at Paestum, where – who knows? – you may just come across your very own bronze Apollo.

🍴 Eating & Drinking

TOP CHOICE **Anna**   PIZZA €

(☑0974 82 37 63; Lungomare San Marco 32; meals from €15, pizzas from €3) At the city-centre end of the promenade, this has been a locals' favourite for decades. Family run, with a small B&B upstairs, Anna is best known for its pizzas, especially since a British Sunday broadsheet named Anna's *Sorpresa* the best pizza in Italy back in May 2010. It is certainly well worth the €10 tag, with a seven-slice selection including mussels, aubergines, courgettes, marinated pork, ham, prawns and spicy sausage.

More traditional seafood dishes include grilled swordfish. This is also a good place for an energy-stoking sugar start to the day, with more than eight types of *cornetti* to choose from, including white chocolate.

Bar Gelateria del Corso   BAR €

(Corso Garibaldi 22-24; ice creams from €2, cakes from €1.50, cocktails from €2.50) The most popular spot in town for slurping an ice cream, sipping a cocktail or salivating over a cream cake. Comfortable wicker chairs are ideally positioned for people watching on this pedestrian shopping street. If ice cream is your weakness, there are some unusual flavours, including *marrón glace* (candied chestnut) and *limone sicilia* (Sicilian lemon), plus yoghurt-based choices such as *frutti di bosco* (fruit of the forest).

U'Sghiz   SEAFOOD €

(☑0974 82 93 31; Piazza Umberto 1; meals €15, pizzas from €3) Enjoying a prime *centro storico* position, the rambling dining rooms in this 17th-century building include the upstairs Sala degli Affreschi, complete with mural of jovial owner Antonio (plus family) rendered in Greek mythological style. There is also an alfresco terrace. The house speciality is seafood, with dishes such as *spaghetti a vongole* and an extensive pizza choice.

A quarter carafe of house red wine costs a mere €2 but is better for pickling grandma (sorry, onions); go for one of the marginally more expensive choices instead.

La Brace   CAMPANIAN €

(☑0974 82 16 05; Via A. De Gasperi 60; meals €15, pizzas from €3; ☺Sat-Thu) There's no sea or historic centre view from this simple trattoria on a bustling sidestreet but who cares when the food is this good. It's best for pizza or any of the seafood dishes; eat in the candy-coloured dining room or tranquil back terrace. Very popular with boisterous Italian families at weekends so possibly not the place to whisper sweet nothings to your date.

Il Gambero   SEAFOOD €€

(☑0974 82 28 94; Via Lungomare San Marco 234; meals from €25; ☺Wed-Mon) Located across from Agropoli's long sandy beach, get here early to grab a table out front and enjoy the sun setting over Sorrento with Capri twinkling in the distance. Specialities include seafood mixed salad, pasta with clams and pumpkin, and fried mixed fish. Although there are some non-seafood dishes, it is the fish that, justifiably, enjoys star billing. Reservations are recommended.

ℹ Information

Tourist Office (☑0974 82 74 71; Viale Europa 34; ☺9.30am-2pm) Not a lot of information, but can provide a basic city map.

ℹ Getting There & Around

Boat

Metrò del Mare (☑199 60 07 00; www.metro delmare.com; ☺Jun-Sep) operates daily ferries from Salerno to Palinuro (€7.50, two hours, two daily), San Marco di Castellabate (€6, 50 minutes, two daily) and Acciaroli (€6, one hour 10 minutes, two daily). It also runs weekday ferries from Agropoli to Positano (€9, one hour 10 minutes, one daily), Amalfi (€11, one hour 35 minutes, one daily), San Marco di Castellabate (€4.50, 15 minutes, one daily) and Palinuro (€8.50, one hour, 35 minutes).

Bus

CSTP (☎089 48 70 01; www.cstp.it) operates regular buses from Salerno and Paestum to several Cilento coastal resorts, including Agropoli, Santa Maria di Castellabate, San Marco di Castellabate and Acciaroli.

Curcio Viaggi (☎089 25 40 80; www.curcio viaggi.it) operates a number of routes that cover the coast and park, including a daily bus from Pertosa to Palinuro that stops at Teggiano, Sassano and Padula.

SITA (☎089 22 66 04; www.sitabus.it) has a daily service from Salerno to Castelcivita and Polla.

Car

The coastal towns are well signposted and, in general, good for parking. There are plenty of car-rental outfits here, including **Alba Rent Car** (☎0974 82 80 99; Via A De Gasperi 82, Agropoli; per day from €50) or similarly priced **LT Trasporti** (☎0974 96 13 66; www.ltgroup.it; Via Colombo 11, Santa Maria di Castellabate).

The Parco Nazionale del Cilento is similarly easy to navigate by car, provided you have a detailed map. Relying on public transport can be an incredibly frustrating, not to mention time-consuming, business.

Train

Most destinations on the Cilento coast are served by the main rail route from Naples to Reggio di Calabria. Consult **Trenitalia** (www. trenitalia.it) for fares and information. For Palinuro, the nearest train station is Pisciotta, from where there is regular bus service to the resort.

Cilento Coast

While the Cilento stretch of coastline lacks the gloss and sophistication of the Amalfi Coast, it can afford to have a slight air of superiority when it comes to its beaches: a combination of secluded coves and long stretches of golden sand with a welcome lack of overpriced ice creams and sunbeds. Beyond the options outlined below, the far southeastern stop along the coastline is **Sapri**, which has two pleasant beaches in the centre of town.

AGROPOLI TO CASTELLABATE

Around 14km south of Agropoli is the former fishing village of **Santa Maria di Castellabate**. Head for the southernmost point, which still has a palatable southern Italian feel with dusky pink-and-ochre sun-baked houses blinkered by traditional green shutters. Santa Maria's golden sandy beach stretches for around 4km, which equals plenty of towel space on the sand, even in midsummer.

Medieval Castellabate clings to the side of a mountain 280m above sea level and is one of the most endearing and historic towns on the Cilento coast. Approached from its coastal sidekick Santa Maria de Castellabate, the summit is marked by the broad **Belvedere di San Costabile**, from where there are sweeping coastal views. Flanking this is the shell of a 12th-century castle, with only the defensive walls still standing, and the adjacent art gallery. The surrounding labyrinth of narrow pedestrian streets is punctuated by ancient archways, small piazzas and the occasional *palazzo*. The animated heart and soul of town is the numerological mouthful Piazza 10 Ottobre 1123, with its panoramic valley views of the Valle della Annunziata .

SAN MARCO DI CASTELLABATE TO ACCIAROLI

Heading south from Castellabate, the next stop is the pretty little harbour at **San Marco di Castellabate**, overlooked by the handsome, ivy-clad Approdo hotel. This was once an important Greek and Roman port, and tombs and other relics have been discovered that are now on view in the museum at Paestum. The area between Santa Maria di Castellabate and San Marco is popular for diving; contact **Galatea** (☎334 3485643, 0974 96 67 07; San Marco di Castellabate marina; single dives from €45). San Marco's blue-flag beach is a continuation of the sandy stretch from Santa Maria di Castellabate.

The coastal road heading south lacks the drama (views *and* traffic) of its Amalfi counterpart but is still prettily panoramic. It's an area that Ernest Hemingway apparently rated highly, particularly **Acciaroli** which, despite the disquieting amount of surrounding concrete, has a charming centre. Head for the sea and the peeling facade of the **Parrocchia di Acciaroli** church with its abstract 1920s stained-glass windows. The surrounding streets and piazzas have been tastefully restored using local stone and traditional architecture, and the cafes, bars and restaurants have a buzzing, fashionable appeal.

PIOPPI TO PISCIOTTA

A short 10km hop south of Acciaroli is tiny picturesque **Pioppi** with its pristine, pale pebble beach, and handful of shops and restaurants.

Next stop is **Marina de Casal Velino**, with its small, pretty harbour and family-style stretch of sand, complete with plenty of ice-cream opportunities, plus a playground and pedal boats.

Continuing southeast, **Ascea** is home to some impressive Greek ruins while, further on, lovely **Pisciotta** is a medieval town, piled high above a ridge. Head straight for the central Piazza Raffaele Pinto with its terraced bars and benches occupied by robust elderly locals. There are a couple of excellent restaurants in town and one of the region's top boutique hotels.

Afterwards stop by the **Marina di Pisciotta** lined with seafood restaurants and cafes. Carry on to the far end of the promenade and take a look at the stones and pebbles on the beach, fabulously patterned and in all shades of mauves, greys, creams and ochre – if only you could blitz your hand baggage allowance, they would look *so* good on your driveway back home.

⊙ Sights & Activities

Velia   ARCHAEOLOGICAL SITE
(⌖0974 97 23 96; Ascea; adult/reduced €2/1; ⊙9am until 1hr before sunset Mon-Sat) Founded by the Greeks in the mid-6th century BC, Velia subsequently became a popular resort with wealthy Romans. You can wander around the evocative ruins today, including parts of the original city walls, with traces of one gate and several towers, as well as the ruins of thermal baths, an Ionic temple, a theatre and parts of the original Greek streets, paved in limestone blocks with the original gutters.

The town is best known as being the home of the philosophers Parmenides and Zeno of Elea, as well as of the famous Eleatic School of Philosophy. After all that archaeological academia, reward yourself with a refreshing dip in the sea; the modern town of Ascea is fronted by 5km of glorious sandy beach.

Cilento Explorer   BOAT TOUR
(⌖0974 90 00 50; www.cilentoexplorer.com; Piazza Marconi 79, Marina de Casal Velino; from €28) Travelling with your loved one? Then consider a romantic night cruise, searching for the Milky Way, sipping a cocktail and exchanging sweet nothings under the stars. If this doesn't suit (you're travelling solo or with your in-laws) then Cilento Explorer offers a shoal of other watery activities, including boat trips to surrounding grottoes and fishing trips (local fisher included).

✗ Eating

TOP CHOICE **I Tre Gufi**   CAMPANIAN €€
(⌖0974 97 30 42; Via Roma, Pisciotta; meals €25) Follow the signs from the sweeping main Piazza Raffaele Pinto to this star-setting of a restaurant, its long wide terrace overlooking the pine-forested hillside stretching down to the sea. The menu has plenty of choice, with seafood the speciality.

MEDITERRANEAN DIET

Pioppi has the right to feel smug. It was based on initial observations of this town in the late 1950s that American medical researcher Dr Ancel Keys launched his famous study concerning the health benefits of the Mediterranean diet. Of the residents of Pioppi, Keys famously wrote: "The people were older and vigorous. They were walking up and down the hillside collecting wild grains, and were out fishing before sun up and going out again in the late afternoon and rowing boats." Keys was struck by the low rate of heart disease among poor people here, compared to well-fed northern Europeans and Americans.

Keys also adopted the Mediterranean-style diet and lived to be 101 years old. Ironically, you have to be rich to eat healthy foods like a peasant these days, with virgin olive oil, fresh fish, and organic fruit and vegetables generally costing far more than processed foods.

Join the elderly Pioppi residents today in their more leisurely pursuit of dozing on the shady benches in lovely Piazza de Millenario with its handy central bar. Then, suitably rested, take a healthy Med-diet picnic to the beach a few steps away.

There is also a good choice of salads, plus pastas, *fagiolini*, risotto and specials like sea bass with porcini mushrooms and olives. The interior dining room is lined with jazzy abstract paintings and there's an adjacent cafe and gelateria (they make their own ice cream).

Arlecchino   SEAFOOD €

(☎0974 96 18 89; Via Guglielmini, Santa Maria di Castellabate; meals €20, pizzas from €4; ☺Mar-Nov; ⚑) Located across from the beach in the pretty southernmost part of Santa Maria, popular Arlecchino has picture windows overlooking the small sweep of sand. Packed to the gills with families at weekends, the restaurant offers primarily seafood-based dishes, including a recommended *sepia alla griglia* (grilled cuttlefish). Finish up with the calorific delight of the local speciality *torta ricotta e pera* (ricotta and pear tart).

Cantina Belvedere   CAMPANIAN €€

(☎0974 96 70 30; www.cantinabelvedere.it; Castellabate; meals €30; ☺7.30pm-midnight) Located to the east of the castle, this restaurant clings limpet-like to the vertiginous cliff side guaranteeing uninterrupted sea views. When you are not gazing at the view, you can enjoy dishes like octopus *carpaccio*, peppered fillet steak, and plenty of pasta and pizza choice. This is a popular spot for wedding parties, so be sure to reserve ahead.

Il Capriccio   CAMPANIAN €

(☎0974 84 52 41; Corso da Spiafriddo, Castellabate; meals €18) On the road to Perdifumo, this is a favourite choice of the locals. An unassuming place with an outside terrace, Il Capriccio has a gracious host in owner Enxo. The menu runs the gamut from seafood classics such as *zuppa di cozze* (mussel soup) and *polipetti affogati* (poached octopus) to less fishy options such as *zuppa di ceci* (chickpea soup).

The *crostata della nonna* (grandma's cake) is as promising as it sounds: a delicious confection of puff pastry, almonds and seasonal fruit.

Divino   CAMPANIAN €€

(☎339 8080457; Piazza 10 Ottobre 1123, Castellabate; menus €28-35; meals from €25) Follow the signs to La Piazzetta from the castle, via a short tunnel, and blink hard when you emerge at this movie-set marvel of a piazza with its terraced restaurants, pastel-coloured houses and stunning situation. Divino is fittingly traditional, right down to the chequered tablecloths. Grab the romantic table on the small terrace for the best views.

The menu has local favourites like *pasta e fagioli* (pasta and white beans) and grilled swordfish, plus daily well-priced menus.

Pizza in Piazza   PIZZA €

(☎320 0966325; Piazza Vittorio Emanuele, Acciaroli; pizzas from €4; ☺Apr-Nov; ⚑) An upper-crust pizza place on this pretty piazza with its magnificent rubber trees and wisteria-draped walls. Sit outside or eat on the go. The pizzas include all the standard choices but are excellent, with a crispy base and garden-fresh ingredients. The *caprese* (€7) comes particularly recommended, with its simple topping of cherry tomatoes, *mozzarella di bufala* and basil leaves.

☆ Entertainment

Il Ciclope   CLUB

(☎0974 93 03 18; www.ilciclope.com; Marina di Camerota) While the Cilento region may not be well known to your average tourist, it is definitely on the global hit parade when it comes to DJ hotspots. Pete Tong, Tommy Vee, Marco Carola, David Morales...all the big names are elbowing for the chance to spin discs at Il Ciclope, which occupies four limestone caves and is one of the hippest places to strut your stuff this side of Ibiza.

It's high on the chic-o-meter, look sharp and be the most fashionable cave gal (or guy) since the Flintstones.

Palinuro

POP 4800

Despite being hailed as the Cilento coast's main resort, Palinuro remains relatively low-key (and low-rise), with a tangible fishing-village feel. Located in a picturesque bay sheltered by a promontory, and with superb beaches, it gets crowded with Italian holidaymakers in August. Note that the majority of hotels and restaurants are seasonal and are only open from Easter to October.

◎ Sights & Activities

Aside from the grottoes, Palinuro is famous for its beaches. For a quiet cove, head south of town to Spiaggia Marmelli, surrounded by lush banks of greenery. The beach is approached via steep steps, and there's a small car park at the top. The town's main beach is **Spiaggia Palinuro**, which stretches for around 4km north of the centre. Palinuro's postcard-pretty harbour has colourful fishing boats, several bars and a wide swathe of sand.

The epicentre of town is the Piazza Virgilio, with its modern octagonal church (which looks transplanted from Salt Lake City), and main street Via Indipendenza, which is good for shopping and light eats.

Grotta Azzurra GROTTO

Although it doesn't have the hype of its Capri counterpart, Palinuro's Grotta Azzurra is similarly spectacular, with a technicolour play of light and hue. It owes its name to the extraordinary effect produced by the sunlight that filters inside from an underground passage lying at a depth of about 8m. The best time to visit is the afternoon, due to the position of the sun.

Several boat companies operate out of kiosks on the harbour front, including Da Alessandro (☑347 6540931; www.costieradelcilento.it; trips from €12), which will take you to the Blue Grotto as well as four other caves in the area.

✖ Eating & Drinking

TOP CHOICE Ristorante da Isadora CAMPANIAN €

(☑0974 93 10 43; Via Indipendenza 156; meals €20, pizzas from €3.50; ◉Mar-Oct) One of the consistently good restaurants here, with a large terrace and a down-to-earth interior, complete with TV in the corner. The ample menu includes the highly recommended speciality *vicciatella della nonna* (mixed seasonal vegetables including tomatoes, carrots, aubergine, peppers and green beans, with fried bread and additional options like smoked cheese, eggs or octopus).

There are also good pizzas and risottos. The house wine is perfectly drinkable and, if you're in grappa mode, there is an excellent choice.

Ristorante Miramare SEAFOOD €€

(☑0974 93 09 70; Corso Pisacane 89; meals from €28) Enjoying a supreme position, with a broad terrace overlooking the turquoise sea and small adjacent sandy cove, this place is part of the same-name hotel. The menu is predominantly seafood based and holds few surprises, although there is the odd nod to the international palate, including roast beef (what, no Yorkshire pud!). Otherwise *spaghetti alla vongole* is a safe bet.

Pasticceria Egidio PASTICCERIA €

(☑0974 93 14 60; Via Santa Maria 15; sfogliatelle €1.50) Run by the reassuringly plump Egidio family, this *pasticceria* has a cake display cabinet backed by the large bakery where breads (including *integrale*) arrive steaming hot for picnic time. The cakes really are as good as they look: *sfogliatelle* filled with fresh ricotta, *frollini* (mini fruit and chocolate tarts), and the all-time favourite, crumbly *amaretti* (macaroons).

Bar Da Siena GELATERIA €

(☑0974 93 10 19; Via Indipendenza 53; ice creams from €1.50, cocktails from €3; 🖶) Part of the Albergo Santa Caterina, this L-shaped bar serves the best ice cream in town with *semi freddi* (semi cold) and yoghurt-based ices, as well as enticing flavours such as *ricotta e pistacchio* (ricotta and pistachio) and the possibly less appealing *zuppa inglese* (English trifle). The romantic terrace is a perfect place for a little locked-eyes-over-ice-cream time.

Babylon BAR

(☑0974 93 14 56; Via Porto 47; cocktails €5; ◉8am-midnight) Opened in 2012 as a welcome addition to Palinuro's bar scene, the sprawling terrace with Perspex furniture and palms creates a fashionable space for live music every Saturday in the summer.

ℹ Information

Tourist Office (☑0974 93 81 44; Piazza Virgilio, Palinuro; ◉9.30am-1.30pm & 5-7pm Mon-Sat, 9.30am-1.30pm Sun) Can provide a town map and general information.

Accommodation

Best Luxe Hotels

» Hotel San Francesco al Monte (p199), Naples

» Grand Hotel Vesuvio (p198), Naples

» San Pietro (p206), Praiano

Best Guesthouses

» Casa D'Anna (p199), Naples

» Cerasiello B&B (p199), Naples

» Casale Giancesare (p210), Paestum

Best Agriturismi

» Agriturismo La Tore (p205), Massa Lubrense

» Agriturismo i Moresani (p212), Cilento

» Villa Vea (p212), Cilento

Where to Stay

There is no shortage of satisfying accommodation in Naples and the surrounding region, although the latter and, in particular, the Amalfi Coast and Bay of Naples' islands of Ischia, Capri and Procida, tend towards the high end of the market and are generally seasonal.

In the crumbling historic city of Naples, you can sleep under frescoes in a 16th-century *palazzo* (large building), kick back in a converted candle-lit convent, or share the home of local artists and intellectuals.

Finding somewhere to stay on the high-profile islands of Capri, Ischia and Procida and Amalfi Coast resorts can be more problematic in high season due to the sheer number of visitors, and it is strongly advisable to book ahead as far as possible.

Agriturismi (farm stay accommodation) are increasingly opening up inland from the Costiera Amalfiatana and still more in the Cilento region, particularly in and around the national park. This can be an option to seriously consider if you prefer to holiday away from camera-wielding tourists and stay in a rural environment, with the possibility of activities such as trekking and mountain-bike riding readily accessible. Otherwise, the range of accommodation in these areas is similar to Naples, running the gamut between sumptuous *palazzi* to idiosyncratic B&Bs, with a sprinkling of budget *pensioni* (small guesthouse) and campsites.

Pricing

The price indicators in this book refer to the cost of a double room, including private bathroom and excluding breakfast unless otherwise noted. Price ranges span the low-season price to the high-season price.

» € Budget, less than €80

» €€ Midrange, €80–250

» €€€ Top end, more than €250

HIGH & LOW SEASONS

The high season is July and August, though prices peak again around Easter and Christmas. It's essential to book in advance during these periods. Conversely, prices drop between 30% and 50% in low season. In the winter months (November to Easter) many places, particularly on the coast and islands, completely shut down. In the cities and larger towns accommodation tends to remain open all year. The relative lack of visitors in these down periods means you should have little trouble getting a room in those places that do stay open.

NAPLES

A high-voltage shot of historical sights, buzzing squares and street life, the *centro storico* (historic centre) is Naples' heart and soul and a convenient spot to slumber. Options span secret B&Bs, designer dens and converted baroque *palazzi*.

Closer to the train station, Mercato is awash with budget hotels; the option we've listed was clean and reliable at the time of writing (Hotel Zara), but be warned that the area is bedlam by day and dodgy by night.

Centro Storico & Mercato

TOP
CHOICE Dimora dei Giganti   B&B €€
(Map p40; 338 9264453, 081 033 09 77; www.dimoradeigiganti.it; Vico Giganti 55; s €40-60, d €55-80, tr €70-95, q €85-110, incl breakfast; P❄️🛜; MPiazza Cavour) Run by a warm and personable team, this urbane B&B offers four colour-coordinated bedrooms with specially commissioned sculptural lamps, ethnic-inspired furnishings and designer bathrooms. There's a modern kitchen, cosy lounge and a charming majolica-tiled terrace. Best of all, its quiet side-street location is only steps away from the buzzing heart of the *centro storico*.

Costantinopoli 104   BOUTIQUE HOTEL €€
(Map p40; 081 557 10 35; www.costantinopoli104.it; Via Santa Maria di Costantinopoli 104; s/d/ste €170/220/250; ❄️@🛜♨️; MDante) Chic and tranquil, Costantinopoli 104 is set in a neoclassical villa in the city's bohemian heartland. Although showing a bit of wear in places, rooms remain understatedly elegant, comfortable and spotlessly clean – those on the 1st floor open onto a sun terrace, while ground-floor rooms face the small, palm-fringed pool.

Add tasteful antique furniture, contemporary art and a Liberty-era, stained-glass window, and you have one seriously seductive urban oasis.

Hotel Piazza Bellini   BOUTIQUE HOTEL €€
(Map p40; 081 45 17 32; www.hotelpiazzabellini.com; Via Costantinopoli 101; s €72-142, d €84-154, tr €112-182; ❄️@🛜; MDante) Only steps away from buzzing nightspot Piazza Bellini, this newish art hotel inhabits a 16th-century *palazzo*, its cool white spaces spiked with original majolica tiles and the work of emerging artists. Rooms offer pared-back cool, with designer fittings, chic bathrooms and mirror frames drawn straight on the wall. Rooms on the 5th and 6th floors feature panoramic balconies.

Decumani Hotel
de Charme   BOUTIQUE HOTEL €€
(Map p40; 081 551 81 88; www.decumani.it; Via San Giovanni Maggiore Pignatelli 15; s €89-124, d €89-134, incl breakfast; ❄️@🛜; ☐R2 to Via Mezzocannone) This boutique hotel is fresh, elegant and located in the former *palazzo* of Cardinal Sisto Riario Sforza; the last bishop of the Bourbon Kingdom. The simple,

ONLINE RESOURCES

» **Rent a Bed** (www.rentabed.com) Has an extensive selection of B&Bs and apartments covering Naples, the bay islands and the Amalfi Coast.

» **Agriturismo.it** (www.agriturismo.it) Offers a wide range of *agriturismi* (farm stay accommodation) options with descriptions, reservation details and general information.

» **Sorrento Tourism** (www.sorrentotourism.com) Includes accommodation info on the Sorrentine peninsula.

» **Porta Napoli** (www.hotel.portanapoli.com) Has a comprehensive list of rental apartments, B&Bs and hotels in Naples, Bay of Naples, Amalfi Coast and the Cilento region.

BOOK YOUR STAY ONLINE

For more accommodation reviews by Lonely Planet authors, check out hotels.lonelyplanet.com. You'll find independent reviews, as well as recommendations on the best places to stay. Best of all, you can book online.

stylish rooms feature high ceilings, parquet floors, 19th-century furniture, and modern bathrooms with roomy showers and rustic wooden benchtops. Deluxe rooms boast a Jacuzzi. The piece de resistance, however, is a breathtaking baroque hall.

Hostel of the Sun
HOSTEL €

(Map p40; ☑081 420 63 93; www.hostelnapoli.com; Via G Melisurgo 15; dm €16-18, s €30-35, d €60-70; ✳@☎; ☐R2 to Via Depretis) Recently renovated and constantly winning accolades, HOTS is an ultrafriendly hostel near the port. Located on the 7th floor (have €0.05 for the lift), it's a bright, sociable place with multicoloured dorms, a cute in-house bar (with €3 cocktails between 8pm and 11pm), and – a few floors down – a series of hotel-standard private rooms a couple with private bathroom.

Extras include a laundry service for stays of over four days.

Port Alba Relais
B&B €€

(Map p40; ☑081 564 51 71; www.portalbarelais. com; Via Port'Alba 33; s €65-99, d €80-160, incl breakfast; ✳@; ⓜDante) On a vintage street lined with bookshops, the foyer at this sassy B&B features soaring bookshelves lined with literature, objet d'art and vintage paraphernalia (including a 1745 edition of Dante's *The Divine Comedy*). The six rooms ooze Armani-inspired chic, from muted tones and stainless-steel detailing to mosaiced showers; room 216 comes with a Jacuzzi. While windows look out onto the lively Piazza Dante, double-glazing does a good job of keeping the noise at bay.

DiLetto a Napoli
B&B €

(Map p40; ☑338 9264453, 081 033 09 77; www. dilettoanapoli.it; Vicolo Sedil Capuano 16; s €35-55, d €50-75, tr €65-90, q €80-105, incl breakfast; Ⓟ✳; ⓜPiazza Cavour) In a 15th-century *palazzo*, this savvy B&B features four rooms with vintage *cotto* floor tiles, organza curtains, local artisan lamps and handmade

furniture designed by its architect owners. Bathrooms are equally stylish, while the urbane communal lounge comes with a kitchenette and dining table for convivial noshing and lounging.

Belle Arti Resort
B&B €€

(Map p40; ☑081 557 10 62; www.belleartiresort. com; Via Santa Maria di Constantinopoli 27; s €65-99, d €80-160; ✳@; ⓜDante) More boutique than B&B, this urbane hideaway combines contemporary cool with vintage touches. Four of the impeccable rooms (some as big as small suites) boast ceiling frescoes while all feature marble bathrooms and funky painted bedheads. Languid red drapes in the corridor accentuate the airy, glammed-up vibe.

Caravaggio Hotel
HOTEL €€

(Map p40; ☑081 211 00 66; www.caravaggio hotel. it; Piazza Riario Sforza 157; s €80-140, d €120-190, ste €150-240; ✳@☎; ☐CS5 to Via Duomo) Bold abstract paintings face stone arches, yellow sofas line 300-year-old brick walls and original wood-beamed ceilings cap the comfortable, four-star bedrooms at this hotel. A few rooms boast a Jacuzzi, there's a stylish communal lounge and the breakfast buffet features regional produce.

Hotel Pignatelli Napoli
HOTEL €

(Map p40; ☑081 658 49 50; www.hotelpignatel linapoli.com; Via San Giovanni Maggiore Pignatelli 16; s €45, d €60-80, incl breakfast; @☎; ☐R2 to Via Mezzocannone) Cheap yet chic, Hotel Pignatelli sits pretty in a restored 15th-century house. Rooms are decorated in a rustic Renaissance style, with wrought-iron beds and bronze wall lamps; some rooms also have original wood-beamed ceilings. Best of all, owner Ciro is warm and hospitable.

Mancini Hostel
HOSTEL €

(Map p40; ☑081 553 67 31; www.hostelpensione mancini.com; Via PS Mancini 33 ; dm €15-18, s without bathroom €25-35, d without bathroom €35-45, d €50-60, tr €60-75, incl breakfast; ✳@☎; ⓜGaribaldi) While its gritty address mightn't be perfect, this safe, relaxed hostel more than compensates with its close proximity to Stazione Centrale, friendly staff and modern communal kitchen (perfect after a morning at nearby Porta Nolana market). All four dorms (one of which is female-only) are bright and clean, with modern bathrooms, while a couple of simple double and triple rooms come with private bathroom.

Hotel Zara

HOTEL €

(Map p40; ☑081 28 71 25; www.hotelzara.it; 2nd fl, Via Firenze 81; s €39-45, d €46-62, tr €60-80, s with shared bathroom €30-35, d with shared bathroom €40-50, incl breakfast; ✳@☎; Ⓜ Garibaldi) An easy walk from the main train station, this spotless hotel is a world away from the grungy street below. Rooms are spartan but clean, with functional modern furniture, TV and double-glazed windows. The in-house book exchange is a nice touch. Don't forget €0.05 to use the lift.

Bella Capri Hostel & Hotel

HOSTEL €

(Map p40; ☑081 552 94 94; www.bellacapri.it; Via G Melisurgo 4; dm €16-20, s €50-60, d €60-80, tr €75-95, s with shared bathroom €40-50, d with shared bathroom €50-60, incl breakfast; ✳@☎; ☐R2 to Via Depretis) This central, friendly spot offers hostel and hotel options on two seperate floors. While the hotel rooms could use a bit more attention, all are clean. The hostel is a little funkier, with bright citrus tones, a kitchen, more beds than bunks, and a bathroom in each dorm. Laundry service costs €7 and there is no curfew. Bring €0.05 for the lift.

Toledo & Quartieri Spagnoli

Via Toledo is Naples' main retail strip and a favourite spot for strolling. Directly to the west, the earthy Quartieri Spagnoli (whose reputation for crime is exaggerated) offers an atmospheric mix of razor-thin laneways, lively *trattorie* (informal restaurants) and cosy slumber spots spanning homey hotels to a cosy rooftop B&B.

La Ciliegina
Lifestyle Hotel

BOUTIQUE HOTEL €€

(Map p40; ☑081 1971 8800; www.cilieginahotel. it; Via PE Imbriani 30; d €150-250, junior ste €180-300, incl breakfast; ✳@☎; ☐R2 to Piazza Municipio) Suitably coloured in white, black and grey, this chic, contemporary slumber spot is a hit with fashion-conscious urbanites. All 13 spacious, minimalist rooms feature top-of-the-range Hästens beds, flatscreen TV and marble-clad bathrooms with water-jet Jacuzzi showers (one junior suite has a Jacuzzi tub). Breakfast in bed, or on the rooftop terrace, which comes complete with sunbeds, hot tub and volcano views.

Complimentary iPad use makes for a nice touch.

Nardones 48

APARTMENT €

(Map p56; ☑081 245 14 46, 338 8818998; www.nardones48.it; Via Nardones 48; small apt €30-60, large apt €40-100; ✳☎; ☐R2 to Piazza Trieste e Trento) White-on-white Nardones 48 serves up seven smart mini-apartments in a historic Quartieri Spagnoli building. The five largest apartments, each with mezzanine bedroom, accommodate up to four people. The two smallest, each with sofa bed, accommodate up to two guests. While three apartments also boast a panoramic terrace, all feature a modern kitchenette, flatscreen TV and contemporary bathroom with spacious shower.

Stays of one week or longer enjoy discounted rates and complimentary laundry service.

Sui Tetti di Napoli

B&B €

(Map p50; ☑338 9264453, 081 033 09 77; www. suitettidinapoli.net; Vico Figuerelle a Montecalvario 6; s €35-65, d €45-80, tr €60-95, q €80-115, incl breakfast; ✳☎; Ⓜ Toledo) A block away from Via Toledo, this well-priced B&B is more like four apartments atop a thigh-toning stairwell. While two apartments share a terrace, the rooftop option boasts its own, complete with mesmerising views. All apartments include a kitchenette (the cheapest two share a kitchen), simple-yet-funky furnishings and a homey vibe.

Napolit'amo Hotel Medina

HOTEL €

(Map p40; ☑081 497 71 10; www.napolitamo.it; Via San Tommaso d'Aquino 15; s €55-75, d €65-95, incl breakfast; ✳@☎; ☐R2 to Via Medina) An easy 600m from the ferry terminals, this friendly three-star hotel is looking smart after a recent revamp. While the 5th-floor rooms are comfortable and modern, the 3rd-floor wing has the sleekest rooms, with muted earthy hues and contemporary bathrooms with rainforest showers. Enjoy views of the Castel Nuovo from the silvery-chocolate breakfast room.

Hotel Il Convento

HOTEL €€

(Map p50; ☑081 40 39 77; www.hotelilconvento. com; Via Speranzella 137a; s €50-93, d €65-140; ✳@☎; ☐R2 to Piazza Trieste e Trento) Snugly set in the Quartieri Spagnoli, this lovely hotel this lovely hotel is a soothing blend of antique Tuscan furniture, erudite book shelves and candle-lit stairs. Rooms are cosy and elegant, combining creamy tones and dark woods with patches of 16th-century brickwork. For €80 to €180 you get a room with a private roof garden. The hotel is wheelchair accessible.

La Concordia B&B
B&B €

(Map p50; ☑081 41 23 49; www.laconcordia.it; Piazzetta Concordia 5 ; s/d/tr/q €50/80/90/100, incl breakfast; ❋ 🛜; 🚇Centrale to Corso Vittorio Emanuele) Your host at this personable B&B is retired literature professor Anna Grappone, whose charming abode features ethnic artefacts, antique furniture, and the work of her artist friends. All three guestrooms are clean and comfy, and the communal lounge is peppered with books and a rocking chair. Two of the bedrooms are air-conditioned, and payment is by cash or PayPal only.

Napolit'amo Hotel Toledo
HOTEL €

(Map p50; ☑081 552 36 26; www.napolitamo.it; Via Toledo 148; s €57-67, d €83-103, incl breakfast; ❋ @ 🛜; Ⓜ Toledo) Escape the common hordes and live like nobility in the 16th-century Palazzo Tocco di Montemiletto. Admittedly a little tired in places, there are still enough gilded mirrors and lofty ceilings to satisfy the snob within. Service is courteous and, best of all, its Via Toledo address makes it handy for both the atmospheric *centro storico* and the city's main shopping strips.

Hotel Toledo
HOTEL €

(Map p50; ☑081 40 68 71; www.hoteltoledo.com; Via Montecalvario 15; s/d/ste incl breakfast €50/80/140; ❋ @ 🛜; Ⓜ Toledo) Snugly situated in an old three-storey building, Hotel Toledo offers comfy, smallish rooms with terracotta tiles and mod cons; the rooms are a little on the dark side, however. Suites come with a stovetop, and breakfast is served on the rooftop terrace when the weather warms up.

Santa Lucia & Chiaia

With lavish seaside hotels and sparkling island vistas, Santa Lucia is where presidents and pop stars say goodnight. However, there are still affordable options, some with stunning bay vistas. As a general rule, rooms with water views cost a little more.

A-list Chiaia is *the* place for designer shopping and bar-hopping, so accommodation is chic rather than cheap, though a funky B&B is keeping it real.

🅣🅞🅟 CHOICE Grand Hotel Vesuvio LUXURY HOTEL €€€
(Map p56; ☑081 764 00 44; www.vesuvio.it; Via Partenope 45; s €230-370, d €290-450; ❋ @ 🛜;

🚇154 to Via Santa Lucia) Known for housing legends – past guests include Rita Hayworth and Humphrey Bogart – this five-star heavyweight is a decadent wonderland of dripping chandeliers, period antiques and opulent rooms. Count your lucky stars while drinking a martini at the rooftop restaurant.

B&B Cappella Vecchia
B&B €

(Map p56; ☑081 240 51 17; www.cappellavecchia11.it; Vico Santa Maria a Cappella Vecchia 11; s €50-70, d €75-100; ❋ @ 🛜; 🚇C24 to Piazza dei Martiri) Run by a super-helpful young couple, this B&B is a first-rate choice. Six simple, comfy rooms feature funky bathrooms and different Neapolitan themes, from *mal'occhio* (evil eye) to *peperoncino* (chilli) There's a spacious communal area for breakfast, and free internet available 24/7. Check the website for monthly packages.

Chiaja Hotel de Charme
BOUTIQUE HOTEL €€

(Map p56; ☑081 41 55 55; www.hotelchiaia.it; Via Chiaia 216; s €85-105, d €99-145, superior d €140-165; ❋ @ 🛜; 🚇R2 to Piazza Trieste e Trento) Posh yet personable, this renovated marquis' residence is a soothing blend of pale-lemon walls, gilt-framed portraits, restored original furnishings and elegantly draped curtains. Each room is unique, and those facing boutique-flanked Via Chiaia come with a bubbling Jacuzzi. The breakfast buffet showcases Campanian produce, and it's worth checking the website for the occasional special offer.

Hotel Excelsior
LUXURY HOTEL €€€

(Map p56; ☑081 764 01 11; www.excelsior.it; Via Partenope 48; s/d €270/330; ❋ @ 🛜; 🚇154 to Via Santa Lucia) Facing yacht-packed Borgo Marinaro, the Excelsior sets the scene for your own *Pretty Woman* moment – think marble columns, dark limousines and apartment-sized *fin de siècle* rooms. Jaw-dropping water views provide a suitable love-scene backdrop.

Vomero, Capodimonte & La Sanità

Middle-class Vomero feels a world apart from the seething sprawl below. It's not exactly bursting with sights, but the views are divine, the streets are leafy and that heady Neapolitan chaos is just a funicular ride away. Wedged between the *centro storico* and Capodimonte, La Sanità is pure old-school Naples, with earthy street life, market stalls and a few unexpectantly erudite, artistic slumber surprises.

TOP CHOICE **Casa D'Anna** GUESTHOUSE €€
(Map p62; ☑081 44 66 11; www.casadanna.it; Via Cristallini 138; s €67-102, d €95-145, incl breakfast; ❉⚏; ⓂPiazza Cavour, Museo) Everyone from artists to Parisian fashionistas adore this elegant guesthouse, lavished with antiques, books and original artwork. Run by three charming, erudite gentlemen, its four guestrooms – each with private bathroom – skillfully blend classic and contemporary design features of the highest quality. Breakfast includes home-made baked treats and jams, while the lush communal terrace is perfect for an alfresco *tête-à-tête*.

There is a two-night minimum stay.

TOP CHOICE **Cerasiello B&B** B&B €
(Map p62; ☑338 9264453, 081 033 09 77; www.cerasiello.it; Via Supportico Lopez 20; s €40-60, d €55-80, tr €70-95, q €85-110; ❉⚏; ⓂPiazza Cavour, Museo) This gorgeous B&B consists of four rooms with private bathroom, an enchanting communal terrace and an ethno-chic look melding Neapolitan art with North African furnishings. The stylish communal kitchen offers a fabulous view of the Certosa di San Martino, a view shared by all rooms (or their bathroom) except room Fuoco (Fire), which looks out at a beautiful church cupola. Bring €0.10 for the lift.

Although technically in the Sanità district, the B&B is a short walk from Naples' *centro storico*.

Hotel San Francesco al Monte LUXURY HOTEL €€€
(Map p62; ☑081 423 91 11; www.hotelsanfrancesco.it; Corso Vittorio Emanuele I 328; s €138-253, d €156-266, incl breakfast; Ⓟ❉@⚏≋; 🚋Centrale to Corso Vittorio Emanuele I) Housed in a 16th-century monastery, this hotel is magnificent. The monks' cells are stylish rooms, the ancient cloisters house an open-air bar, and the barrel-vaulted corridors are cool and atmospheric. To top it all off there's a swimming pool on the 7th floor.

Grand Hotel Parker's LUXURY HOTEL €€€
(Map p62; ☑081 761 24 74; www.grandhotelparkers.com; Corso Vittorio Emanuele I 35; s €270, d €350, incl breakfast; Ⓟ❉@⚏; 🚋128 to Via Tasso.) Darling of the Grand Tour set, this stately old pile once hosted the likes of Virginia Woolf and Robert Louis Stevenson. Today Prada-clad guests lounge on Louis XVI armchairs, take *aperitivo* (apéritifs) on the sea-view terrace and nibble by candlelight at the George restaurant. The luxe in-house spa retreat (closed for renovations during our visit) is one of the city's best.

Casa del Monacone B&B
(Map p62; ☑081 744 37 14, 338 9148012; www.catacombedinapoli.it/casaDelMonacone.asp; Via Sanità 124 ; s/d/tr €40/60/80, incl breakfast; ❉@⚏; ⓂPiazza Cavour, Museo) Set in a monastery beside the Basilica di Santa Maria della Sanità, this artful B&B is run by 'La Paranza', the inspiring youth co-op behind the restoration of the Catacomba di San Gennaro. Complete with communal kitchen, lounge, colourful tiled terrace, and artwork by the prolific Riccardo Dalisi, the biggest of its six bright rooms comes with its own kitchenette.

Well-sealed windows block out the noisy traffic, and the junior suite costs the same as a standard – so feel free to request one.

La Controra HOSTEL €
(Map p62; ☑081 549 40 14; www.lacontrora.com; Piazzetta Trinità alla Cesarea 231; dm €15-22, d €60, incl breakfast; ❉@⚏; ⓂSalvator Rosa) Stainless-steel lamps, a sleek bar, blonde-wood bunks, spearmint bathrooms, and a communal kitchen that's very Jamie Oliver: this award-winning hostel melds economy and style. Snooze in a courtyard hammock or surf the net for €2 per hour. Wi-fi access is in communal areas only.

Mergellina & Posillipo

With Liberty *palazzi*, anchored yachts and a buzzing seafront scene, Mergellina is well connected to the city centre and handy for an early-morning hydrofoil out to the bay islands.

Hotel Ausonia HOTEL €€
(Map p71; ☑081 68 22 78; www.hotelausoniapoli.com; Via Francesco Caracciolo 11; s/d/tr incl breakfast €80/100/120; ❉@; ⓂMergellina) This modest and friendly hotel sits opposite the Mergellina marina, a fact not played down in the decor – think portholes, barometers and bedheads in the shape of ships' steering wheels. Corny? A little, but the rooms are clean and comfy, and the few facing the sea won't cost you extra.

THE ISLANDS

Capri

This island is all about lemon trees, pavement cafes, sultry summer evenings and wearing the largest pair of shades you can get your hands on. In other words, accommodation is strictly seasonal, which means bed space is tight and, in general, costly.

TOP CHOICE Hotel Villa Eva   HOTEL €€

(Map p112; ☑081 837 15 49; www.villaeva.com; Via La Fabbrica 8, Anacapri; r €100-120; ☺Mar-Oct; P@☑) A veritable rural retreat, Villa Eva is hidden among fruit and olive trees, which are strung with hammocks. The rooms have lashings of white linen and character, including tiled fireplaces and domed ceilings. Good for families, facilities include a swimming pool and treetop views down to the sea. The only drawback is that it's tricky to get to (take the Grotta Azzurra bus from Anacapri and ask the driver where to get off), or cough up €30 for a port-side taxi.

Hotel La Tosca   HOTEL €€

(Map p114; ☑081 837 09 89; www.latoscahotel.com; Via Dalmazio Birago 5, Capri Town; s €50-100, d €75-160; ☺Apr-Oct; ☀☎) Away from the glitz of the town centre, this charming one-star hotel is hidden down a quiet back lane overlooking the Certosa di San Giacomo and the mountains. The rooms are airy and comfortable with pine furniture, light tiles, striped fabrics and large bathrooms. Several have private terraces, complete with deck chairs and rattan furniture. The owner, a genial, hospitable guy, speaks fluent English (his wife is American).

Casa Mariantonia   BOUTIQUE HOTEL €€

(Map p117; ☑081 837 29 23; www.casamariantonia.com; Via Guiseppe Orlandi 80, Anacapri; r €100-260; P☀☎☑) This fabulous boutique retreat counts Jean-Paul Sartre and Alberto Moravia among its past guests, which may well give you something to muse about while you are enjoying the tranquil beauty of the surroundings. Rooms deliver restrained elegance in soothing hues, and there are private terraces with garden views.

Grand Hotel Quisisana   LUXURY HOTEL €€€

(Map p114; ☑081 837 07 88; www.quisi.com; Via Camerelle 2, Capri Town; r/ste incl breakfast from €300/620; ☺mid-Mar–1st week Nov; ☀☎☑) One of only three hotels here to boast a five-star

L (luxury) rating, the Quisisana is Capri's most prestigious address and, fittingly, a few espadrille steps from the Piazzetta. A hotel since the 19th century, it's a bastion of unapologetic opulence, with two swimming pools, a fitness centre and spa, subtropical gardens, restaurants and bars. Rooms are suitably palatial with cool colour schemes and classy furniture.

Albergo Loreley   HOTEL €€

(Map p117; ☑081 837 14 40; www.loreley.it; Via Giuseppe Orlandi 16, Anacapri; s €60-90, d €95-130, tr €105-150, incl breakfast; ☺Apr-Oct; P☀☎) A welcoming, old-school hotel, the Loreley is surrounded by mature gardens and, despite being located just off the main road into Anacapri, is surprisingly quiet. Rooms are spacious and decorated in styles ranging from granny chintz to Mediterranean classic – cool tiled floors and heavy antique furniture.

Belvedere e Tre Re   HOTEL €€

(Map p112; ☑081 837 03 45; www.belvedere-tre-re.com; Via Marina Grande 264, Marina Grande; s/d incl breakfast €100/120; ☺Apr-Nov; ☀☎) A five-minute walk from the port with superb boat-spotting views, this hotel dates from 1900 and has past: the 'tre re' in the name refers to the three kings (no biblical reference intended) who stayed here in its Grand Tour heyday. A fairly modest two-star today, rooms have been pleasantly modernised and have private covered balconies. There's a sun-bronzing terrace on the top floor.

Capri Palace   LUXURY HOTEL €€€

(Map p117; ☑081 978 01 11; www.capripalace.com; Via Capodimonte 2b, Anacapri; s/d/ste incl breakfast from €195/295/620; ☺Apr-Oct; ☀☎☑) A VIP favourite (Gwyneth Paltrow, Liz Hurley and Naomi Campbell have all languished here), the super-slick Capri Palace is the hotel of the moment. Its stylish Mediterranean interior is enlivened with eye-catching contemporary art and its guest rooms are never less than lavish – some even have their own terraced garden and private plunge pool. For stressed guests, the health spa is said to be the island's best. Note that there's a three-night minimum stay in high season.

Hotel Bellavista   HOTEL €€

(Map p117; ☑081 837 14 63; www.bellavistacapri.com; Via Giuseppe Orlandi 10, Anacapri; s €90-160, d €130-240; ☺Apr-Oct; ☀☎) This hotel is more than 100 years old, so a grand dame among the accommodation here. The rooms are large and have 1960s-style tile floors with enormous flower motifs which you will love (or loathe). On the plus side, it's conveniently positioned near the entrance to Anacapri and has a tennis court, a restaurant with truly beautiful views, and discounted access to a nearby swimming pool. There is a minimum four-day stay in August.

Hotel Gatto Bianco
HOTEL €€

(Map p114; ☑081 837 51 43; www.gattobianco-capri. com; Via Vittoria Emanuele 32, Capri Town; s €100-170, d €150-230, incl breakfast; ⊗Apr-Nov; ❄@☎) This gracious hotel dates from 1953 and boasts leafy courtyards and terraces and a white Persian cat – presumably from a long lineage. The light-filled rooms are decorated in traditional style with stunning blue-and-yellow majolica tiling, a tasteful colour scheme and views of Mt Cesina. The hotel is classily placed for your midmorning coffee, a few minutes' walk from La Piazzetta. It also runs discount deals with the downstairs Dephina health and beauty salon.

Hotel Bussola
HOTEL €€

(Map p112; ☑081 838 20 10; www.bussola.com; Traversa La Vigna 14, Anacapri; s €50-140, d €80-150; ⊗year-round; ❄@☎) The enthusiastic owner, Cristiano, has put some zap into this hotel. The sun-filled rooms have luxurious drapes, majolica tiles and a cheery blue-and-white colour scheme, while the public spaces have a whiff of Pompeii with columns, statues and vaulted ceilings. Snag a room with a sea-view terrace, if you can. To get here take the bus up to Piazza Vittoria and call for the hotel shuttle service.

Hotel Carmencita
HOTEL €€

(Map p117; ☑081 837 13 60; www.hotelcarmencita -capri.com; Via de Tommaso 4, Anacapri; s €69-95, d €110-168; ⊗mid-Mar–mid-Nov; ❄@☎❄) Near the town bus station, the Carmencita is run by a delightful couple who pick you up from the ferry terminal at Marina Grande if you phone ahead with your arrival details. The atmosphere is homey and old fashioned in the public areas, while the rooms are bright – think floral bedspreads and majolica ceramic tiling – big and comfortable. Small terraces overlook the pool and pretty garden.

Hotel Esperia
HOTEL €€

(Map p114; ☑081 837 02 62; www.esperiacapri. eu; Via Sopramonte 41, Capri Town; r incl breakfast €140-190; ⊗Apr-Oct; ❄☎) The peeling facade, handsome columns and giant urns

lend an air of faded elegance to this 19th-century former wealthy private home. A short uphill walk from the centre of town, the rooms are large and airy with modern furniture and a floral theme. The best (and most expensive) have good-sized terraces with sea views.

Hotel Senaria
HOTEL €€

(Map p117; ☑081 837 32 22; www.senaria.it; Via Follicara 6, Anacapri; r incl breakfast €130-160; ⊗Apr-Nov; ❄☎) It's quite a trek to this delightful family-run hotel in Anacapri's original town centre, but worth the effort. Housed in a discreet whitewashed villa, rooms are decorated in a sparse, but elegant, Mediterranean style with terracotta tiles and cooling cream tones, plus the tasteful watercolours of local artist Giovanni Tessitore. It's a very quiet spot and, except for Sunday-morning church bells, you're unlikely to be disturbed by anything other than the breeze.

Hotel Villa Krupp
HOTEL €€

(Map p114; ☑081 837 03 62; www.villakrupp.com; Viale Matteotti 12, Parco Augusto; s €110, d €140-190, incl breakfast; ⊗Apr-Oct; ℗❄☎) Housed in the former residence of Russian author Maxim Gorky, this historic hotel oozes old-school charm, with floral tiling, fading antiques and heavy bedsteads. It also commands some fabulous views over the Giardini di Augusto and beyond to the Isole Faraglioni. If your room doesn't have the view (which costs extra), simply adjourn to the delightful terrace outside reception.

Hotel Villa Sarah
HOTEL €€

(Map p112; ☑081 837 06 89; www.villasarah.it; Via Tiberio 3, Capri Town; s €90-160, d €130-230, incl breakfast; ⊗Easter-Oct; ❄❄) On the road up to Villa Jovis – a 10-minute walk from the centre of Capri Town – Villa Sarah retains a rustic appeal that so many of the island's hotels have long lost. Surrounded by its own fruit-producing gardens and with a small pool, it has 20 airy rooms, all decorated in classical local style with ceramic tiles and old-fashioned furniture. The healthy breakfast includes organic produce.

Relais Maresca
HOTEL €€

(Map p112; ☑081 837 96 19; www.relaismaresca. it; Via Marina Grande 284, Marina Grande; r incl breakfast €140-250; ⊗Mar-Nov; ❄❄) A delightful four-star, this is the top choice in Marina Grande. The look is classic Capri, with acres of gleaming ceramic in turquoise, blue and yellow, and stylish furniture. There is a range of rooms (and corresponding prices); the best have balconies and sea views. There's also a lovely flower-filled 4th-floor terrace. Minimum two-day stay on weekends and four-day minimum in August.

Ischia

Like its classy little sister, most of Ischia's hotels close in winter here and prices drop considerably at those that stay open. In addition to the hotels we've listed, there are the spa hotels, most of which only take half- or full-board bookings. The tourist office can supply you with a list. The largest island of the trio here, an overnight stay here makes good sense.

Mezzatorre Resort & Spa   LUXURY HOTEL €€€
(Map p124; ☑081 98 61 11; www.mezzatorre.it; Via Mezzatorre 23, Lacco Ameno; d €350-480, ste €490-670, incl breakfast; ☺mid-Apr–Oct; P❋@ ☎☀) Perched on a bluff above the sea, this luxurious resort is surrounded by a 2.8-hectare pine wood. An in-house spa centre and tennis courts crank up the spoil factor. The sitting rooms and some guest rooms are located in a 15th-century defensive tower. Rooms are sheathed in sophisticated shades of taupe, peach and ochre, some have private garden and Jacuzzi. Check out the infinity pool above the beach for the ultimate film-star setting. If funds are short, just have a long, slow drink in the adjacent bar.

Albergo il Monastero   HOTEL €€
(Map p124; ☑081 99 24 35; www.albergoilmonastero.it; Castello Aragonese, Rocca del Castello; s €70-85, d €105-125, incl breakfast; ☺Easter-Oct; ❋) The former monks' cells still have a certain appealing sobriety about them with dark-wood furniture, crisp white walls, vintage terracotta tiles and no TV (don't worry – the views are sufficiently prime time). Elsewhere there is a pleasing sense of space and style with vaulted ceilings, chic plush sofas, a sprinkle of antiques, and bold contemporary art by the late owner and artist Gabriele Mattera. The hotel restaurant has an excellent reputation.

Hotel Semiramis   HOTEL €€
(Map p124; ☑081 90 75 11; www.hotelsemiramisischia.it; Spiaggia di Citara, Forio; r incl breakfast €100-120; ☺Apr-Oct; P❋☎☀) A few minutes' walk from the Poseidon spa complex, this bright hotel, run by friendly Giovanni and his German wife, has a tropical oasis feel with its central pool surrounded by lofty palms. Rooms are large and beautifully tiled in the traditional yellow-and-turquoise pattern. The garden is glorious with fig trees, vineyards and distant sea views.

Hotel Norris   HOTEL €
(Map p124; ☑081 99 13 87; www.norishotel.it; Via A Sogliuzzo 2, Ischia Ponte; r incl breakfast €50-80; ❋☎) This place has a great price and a fantastic position within easy strolling distance of the Ponte sights. The decent-sized rooms are comfy and decked out in fresh, good-mood colours with small balconies. Breakfast is the normal, albeit slightly more expansive, continental buffet, and bonus points are due for the special parking deal with the public car park across the way.

Camping Mirage   CAMPGROUND €
(Map p124; ☑081 99 05 51; www campingmirage.it; Via Maronti 37, Spiaggia dei Maronti, Barano d'Ischia; camping 2 people, car & tent €35.50-41.50; ☺year-round; P) On one of Ischia's best beaches within walking distance of Sant'Angelo, this shady campground offers 50 places, showers, laundry facilities, a bar and a restaurant serving great seafood pasta.

Hotel Casa Celestino   HOTEL €€
(Map p124; ☑081 99 92 13; www.casacelestino.it; Via Chiaia di Rose 20, Sant'Angelo; s €80-140, d €100-230, incl breakfast; ☺Jan-Oct; ❋@☎) Hugging the headland, this chic little number is a soothing blend of creamy furnishings, whitewashed walls, contemporary art and bold paintwork. The uncluttered bedrooms sport majolica-tiled floors, modern bathrooms and enviable balconies overlooking the sea. There's a good, unfussy restaurant across the way.

Umberto a Mare   HOTEL €€
(Map p124; ☑081 99 71 71; www.umbertoamare.it; Via Soccorso 2, Forio; s €45-140, d €90-180, incl breakfast; ☺Apr-Oct; ❋☎) Easy to find, right next to Forio's emblematic mission-style church, these 11 quiet rooms ooze understated chic with cool ceramic tiles, modern bathrooms and traditional green shutters. Head out to a sunbed on the terracotta terrace with its holiday-brochure-style sea views. You won't have to stray far to eat well, the hotel is tucked under one of Ischia's finest restaurants.

Hotel La Sirenella   HOTEL €€
(Map p124; ☑081 99 47 43; www.lasirenella.net; Corso Angelo Rizzoli 41, Lacco Ameno; r €110/120, incl breakfast; ☺Apr-Oct; ❋☎) This is a family

owned beachside hotel where you can practically roll out of bed onto the sand. Rooms are bright and colourful with seafront terraces. Sparkling tiled bathrooms and a breezy fun-in-the-sun vibe add to the appeal, as does the downstairs restaurant with its good pizzas.

Procida

The island returns to the locals after the day trippers have gone and takes on a palpable and tranquil Med-island feel. Fittingly, accommodation tends to be of the small-scale variety – think B&Bs and family-run hotels. Many places close over the winter and are booked out in August – so check ahead during these periods.

TOP CHOICE Hotel La Vigna   BOUTIQUE HOTEL €€

(Map p135; ☑081 89 60 69; www.albergolavigna. it; Via Principessa Margherita 46; s €75-150, d €90-180, ste €140-230; ❄@☎) Enjoying a fabulous cliff-side location with a delightful garden and in-house spa, this 18th-century villa is a delight. Five of the spacious, simply furnished rooms offer direct access to the garden. Superior rooms (€110 to €200) feature family friendly mezzanines, while the main perk of the suite is the bedside Jacuzzi; perfect for romancing couples.

Casa Giovanni da Procida   B&B €€

(Map p135; ☑081 896 03 58; www.casagiovanni daprocida.it; Via Giovanni da Procida 3; s €50-80, d €65-100, incl breakfast; ❄closed Feb; P❄☎) This chic converted farmhouse B&B features split-level, minimalist rooms with low-rise beds and contemporary furniture. Bathrooms are small but slick, with mosaic tiling, cube basins, huge showerheads and the occasional vaulted ceiling. In the lush garden, chilled-out guests read and eat peaches under the giant magnolia tree.

Casa Sul Mare   HOTEL €€

(Map p135; ☑081 896 87 99; www.lacasasulmare. it; Salita Castello 13; r incl breakfast €99-170; ❄☎) A fabulous place with the kind of evocative views that helped make *The Talented Mr Ripley* such a memorable film. Overlooking the picturesque Marina Corricella, near the ruined Castello d'Avalos, the rooms are elegant with exquisite tiled floors, wrought-iron bedsteads and a warm Mediterranean colour scheme. During summer there's a boat service to the nearest beaches, the hotel service is great and the morning cappuccino, courtesy of Franco, may well be the best you've ever had.

Hotel Crescenzo   HOTEL €€

(Map p135; ☑081 896 72 55; www.hotelcrescenzo. it; Via Marina di Chiaiolella 33; s €60-120, d €70-120, incl breakfast; ❄year-round; ❄) Just 10 smallish rooms; choose between a bay or balcony with sea view. The decor is a suitably nautical blue and white, with sparkling clean bathrooms. This hotel is fronted by a restaurant, generally bursting with an affable local crowd and where you can enjoy breakfast after a long lie-in as it is, unusually, served until noon. Check the website for good deals on longer stays.

Hotel La Corricella   HOTEL €€

(Map p135; ☑081 896 75 75; www.hotelcorricella. it; Via Marina Corricella 88; s €70-100, d €90-120, incl breakfast; ❄Apr-Oct; ☎) One bookend to Marina Corricella, it's hard to miss this peach-and-yellow candy-cane colour scheme. Low-fuss rooms feature modular-style furniture with fan and TV. The large shared terrace boasts top-notch harbour views, the restaurant serves decent seafood and a boat service reaches the nearby beach.

Le Grand Bleu Guesthouse   APARTMENT €€

(Map p135; ☑081 896 95 94; www.isoladiprocida. it; Via Flavio Gioia 37; apt per week €275-1000; ❄closed mid-Dec–Jan; ❄@☎) Within strolling distance of the beach, these central apartments have bright functional furniture, funky bathrooms, stovetops, internet access, and a cool rooftop terrace with wood-fired oven, barbecue and views of Ischia. Check the web for last-minute deals. Wheelchair access.

THE AMALFI COAST

Sorrento

Accommodation is thick on the ground in this town, although if you're arriving in high summer (July and August), you'll still need to book ahead. Most of the big city-centre hotels are geared towards package tourism and prices are correspondingly high. There are, however, some excellent choices, particularly on Via Capo, the coastal road west of the centre. This area is within walking distance of the city centre, but if you're carrying luggage it's easier to catch a SITA bus for Sant'Agata or Massa Lubrense.

TOP CHOICE Ulisse
HOSTEL €€

(Map p146; ☑081 877 4753; www.ulissedeluxe.com; Via del Mare 22, Sorrento; dm €18-28, d €50-100; [P][✱][@][☎]) Accurately described as a deluxe hostel (in fact there are only two six-person dorms here) the remaining rooms are about as far from a backpackers pad as a hiking boot from a stiletto: they are vast and plush with Regency-style fabrics, marble floors, and large bathrooms with tubs and contemporary colour schemes. Facilities include an adjacent Wellness Centre where guests can use the pool for a paltry €5, as well as enjoy free fitness sessions and reasonably priced treatments.

Grand Hotel Excelsior Vittoria
LUXURY HOTEL €€€

(Map p146; ☑081 807 10 44; www.exvitt.it; Piazza Tasso 34, Sorrento; s/d/ste incl breakfast €350/400/700; ⊙year-round; [P][✱][☎][⊠]) A hotel for over 170 years, the grand old dame of Sorrento oozes belle-epoque elegance. Huge potted palms adorn gilded public rooms awash with sunlight and antique furniture. Guest rooms vary in size and style, ranging from tasteful simplicity to extravagant, frescoed opulence. All, however, have views, either of the hotel's lush gardens dripping with crimson bougainvillea or over the sea to Mt Vesuvius. Past guests have included Pavarotti, Wagner, Goethe, Sophia Loren and British royalty.

Plaza Hotel
HOTEL €€

(Map p146; ☑081 878 28 31; www.plazasorrento.com; Via Fuorimura 3, Sorrento; r incl breakfast €134-200; [P][✱][@][☎]) This is one of the newer hotels in town – and it shows. The whole place sports a bright contemporary look with dazzling white contrasting with earthy parquet floors, accented by splashes of dark pink, blue or yellow. Gennaro Sardella abstracts adorn the walls and the rooftop sky bar (round the corner from the infinity pool) is perfect for a sundowner with its scenic views of rooftops and sea.

Casa Astarita
B&B €€

(Map p146; ☑081 877 49 06; www.casastarita.com; Corso Italia 67, Sorrento; r incl breakfast €80-120; [✱][@]) A pocket-size gem, this B&B is housed in a 16th-century building in the city centre. All six rooms combine original structural elements, like niches and vaulted ceilings, with the modern comforts of flatscreen TV, fridge and excellent water pressure. Brightly painted doors, tasteful art work and an-

tiques complete the eclectic look. Rooms surround a central parlour, where breakfast is served on a large rustic table.

Hotel Astoria
HOTEL €€

(Map p146; ☑081 807 40 30; www.hotelastoriasorrento.com; Via Santa Maria delle Grazie 24, Sorrento; s €60-80, €80-120, incl breakfast; [✱][☎]) This aesthetically renovated classic has the advantage of being located in the heart of the *centro storico* and the disadvantage of no parking. Overall, it's an excellent choice. The interior sparkles with colourful glossy tiles and blue and buttercup-yellow paintwork. The large enclosed back terrace is a delight with seats set under orange and lemon trees and colourful tiled murals lining the back wall.

Hotel Desiré
HOTEL €

(☑081 878 15 63; www.desireehotelsorrento.com; Via Capo 31b, Sorrento; s €47-62, d €57-85, incl breakfast; ⊙Mar-Dec; [P][✱]) One of a cluster of hotels along Via Capo, the Desiré is a top budget choice. It's not so much the simple, sunny rooms (although they're fine) or the facilities (a TV lounge and panoramic roof terrace) as the relaxed atmosphere, friendly owner and beautiful views. The lift down to the rocky beach below is a further plus, even if you still have to pay for the umbrellas and deck chairs.

Mignon
HOTEL €€

(Map p146; ☑081 807 38 24; www.sorrentohotelmignon.com; Via Sersale 9, Sorrento; s €50-85, d €60-105, incl breakfast; ⊙Apr-Oct & Christmas; [✱][☎]) The interior designer here had a serious fit of the blues. From the striking dark-blue-and-white floor tiles, to the pale-blue walls and bedcovers, this is the predominant colour throughout. Contemporary artwork and black-and-white historic photos of Sorrento complete the decor theme. The rooms are spacious and there is a rooftop solarium for catching the rays.

La Tonnarella
LUXURY HOTEL €€

(☑081 878 11 53; www.latonnarella.it; Via Capo 31, Sorrento; d €112-140, ste €240-350, incl breakfast; ⊙Apr-Oct & Christmas; [P][✱][@][☎]) A splendid choice – but not for minimalists – La Tonnarella is a dazzling canvas of blue-and-yellow majolica tiles, antiques, chandeliers and statues. Rooms, most of which have their own balcony or small terrace, continue the sumptuous classical theme with traditional furniture and discreet mod cons. The hotel also has its own private beach, accessible by lift, and a highly regarded terrace restaurant.

Seven Hostel HOSTEL **€**

(☑081 878 67 58; www.sevenhostel.com; Via Iommella Grande 99, Sant'Agnello; dm €20-32, s €55/80, d €60-100; ☺year-round; ✳@☎) The ethos of the young owners here is to offer the best hostel in the world, as well as the first *ostello di design*. Located in an 8th-century former convent setting surrounded by olive and lemon trees, there are chic rooftop terraces, weekend live-music gigs and the more down-to-earth perk of an on-site laundry. The rooms are contemporarily furnished and spacious.

Hotel Cristina HOTEL **€€**

(☑081 878 35 62; www.hotelcristinasorrento.it; Via Privata Rubinacci 6, Sant'Agnello; s €90-135, d €90-200; ☺Apr-Oct; ✳☎☀) Located high above Sant'Agnello, this hotel has superb views, particularly from the swimming pool. The spacious rooms have sea-view balconies and combine inlaid wooden furniture with contemporary flourishes, like Philippe Starck chairs. There's an in-house restaurant and a free shuttle bus to/from Sorrento's Circumvesuviana train station.

Nube d'Argento CAMPGROUND **€**

(☑081 878 13 44; www.nubedargento.com; Via Capo 21, Sorrento; camping 2 people, car & tent €27.50, 2-person bungalows €50-85, 4-person bungalows €65-115; ☺Mar-Dec; @☀) This inviting campground is an easy 1km drive west of the Sorrento city centre. Pitches and wooden chalet-style bungalows are spread out beneath a canopy of olive trees – a source of much-needed summer shade – and the facilities are excellent. Youngsters in particular will enjoy the open-air swimming pool, table-tennis table, slides and swings.

Villa Elisa APARTMENT **€€**

(Map p146; ☑081 878 27 92; www.villaelisasorrento.com; Piazza Sant'Antonino 19, Sorrento; d €70-80, tr €80-90, ste €90-120; ☺year-round; ✳☎) Rooms come with cooking facilities and overlook a central courtyard. Up a steep staircase, the self-contained suite has a pint-sized living room, bathroom, bedroom and kitchen, but the washing machine's a definite plus. Mario will cook for you if you ask nicely and also gives tours (with his daughter) of the region.

Hotel Rivage HOTEL **€**

(Map p146; ☑081 878 18 73; www.hotelrivage.com; Via Capo 11, Sorrento; s €60-70, d €64-80; ☺Mar-Nov; P@☎) A low-rise modern hotel just beyond the shops on the western edge of town, you can lounge on the roof terrace here and there's a reasonable bar and restaurant. The rooms are hotel-style bland but have good-size terraces. This place has a slight tour-group feel but is well located and priced.

Massa Lubrense

Mainly frequented by Italian tourists in the know, pretty Massa Lubrense makes a good base and offers a quieter location than some of its higher-profile Amalfi neighbours.

TOP CHOICE Hotel Ristorante Primavera HOTEL **€€**

(☑081 878 91 25; www.laprimavera.biz; Via IV Novembre 3g; r incl breakfast €75-100; ☺year-round; ✳☎) A welcoming family-run two-star with spacious airy rooms decorated with traditional Vietri tiles, light wood and industrial quantities of white paint. Several rooms have vast terraces with sunbeds, plus tables and chairs (rooms 101 to 103 are good choices). The bathtubs, in most rooms, are an unexpected treat. The bright terrace restaurant, with views stretching over orchards to the sea, serves typical local fare.

Casale Villarena APARTMENT **€€**

(☑081 808 17 79; www.casalevillarena.it; Via Cantone 3, Nerano, Massa Lubrense; 2-/4-person apt from €70/170; P☀) These family friendly apartments have good facilities including a shared pool, playground and a lovely beach within easy strolling distance. There are landscaped terraces with lemon trees, shady pergolas, plus such practical necessities as a laundry. The original property dates from the 18th century, but the apartments are comfortable, spacious and simply, yet elegantly, furnished.

Sant'Agata sui due Golfi

In a superb position overlooking the two gulfs of Salerno and Naples, Sant'Agata is fast gaining a reputation for its *agriturismi* as well as its restaurants. Book ahead if you are planning to visit in high season.

Agriturismo La Tore AGRITURISMO **€**

(☑081 808 06 37; www.letore.com; Via Pontone 43; s €45-55, d €90-110, incl breakfast; ☺Easter-end Oct; P) A working organic farm amid 14 hectares of olive groves, producing olive oil, sun-dried tomatoes (and paste) and marmalade (among other products), La Tore is a wonderful place to stay. Decidedly off the beaten track, it offers seven barnlike rooms with a lovely rustic farmhouse hidden among fruit trees. Terracotta tiles and heavy wooden furniture add to the rural appeal. Children between two and six years of age are offered a 50% discount (30% discount for seven to 10 year olds) if they sleep in their parents' room. During winter there is a self-contained apartment available. Additional meals are available.

Agriturismo Fattoria Terranova
AGRITURISMO €

(☎081 533 02 34; www.fattoriaterranova.it; Via Pontone 10; d incl breakfast €85; ⊘Mar-Dec; P♨) Stone floors, dried flowers hanging from heavy wooden beams and large wine barrels artfully positioned – this great *agriturismo* is the epitome of rural chic. The accommodation is in small apartments spread over the extensively cultivated grounds. The apartments are fairly simple, but the setting is delightful and the swimming pool is a welcome luxury.

Marina del Cantone

A delightful low-key place, you should have little problem finding accommodation here, aside from in August when the tidal wave of Italians swamp the hotels in this holiday hotspot of the Sorrentine peninsula.

Villaggio Residence Nettuno
CAMPGROUND €

(☎081 808 10 51; www.villaggionettuno.it; Via A Vespucci 39; camping 2 people, tent & car per person €16-35, bungalow €35-85; ⊘Mar-early Nov) Marina's campground – in the terraced olive groves by the entrance to the village – offers an array of accommodation options, including campsites, mobile homes, and (best of all) apartments in a 16th-century tower for two to five people. It's a friendly, environmentally sound place with excellent facilities and a comprehensive list of activities.

Positano

Positano is a glorious place to stay, but be aware that prices are, overall, high. Like everywhere on the Amalfi Coast it gets very busy in summer, so book ahead, particularly on weekends and in July and August. Ask at the tourist office about rooms or apartments in private houses.

TOP CHOICE ⧉ **Pensione Maria Luisa**
PENSIONI €

(Map p158; ☎089 87 50 23; www.pensionemaria luisa.com; Via Fornillo 42; r €70-85; ⊘Apr-Oct; ⧉⧉) The best budget choice in town, the Maria Luisa is run by lovely Carlo, a larger-than-life character who will go out of his way to assist and advise. The rooms and bathrooms have been updated with shiny new blue tiles and fittings; those with private terraces are well worth the extra €10 for the view of the bay and visits from the affectionate resident ginger Tom. The sunny communal area (with fridges, coffee machine, books and views) is a major plus. Most rooms also have fridges, complete with complimentary Spumante. Breakfast costs an additional €5.

San Pietro
LUXURY HOTEL €€€

(☎089 87 54 55; www.ilsanpietro.it; Via Laurito 2; r incl breakfast from €420-580; ⊘Apr-Oct; P✱⧉♨) For such a talked-about hotel, the San Pietro is remarkably discreet. Built into a rocky headland 2km east of Positano, it's almost entirely below road level – if driving, look for an ivy clad chapel and a black British telephone box by the side of the road. Once safely ensconced, you probably won't want to leave. All of the individually decorated rooms have spectacular sea views, a private terrace and Jacuzzi. Other facilities include a semicircular swimming pool, Michelin-starred restaurant, and a private beach (accessible by lift) with an adjacent lawn with sunbeds, plus tennis court. The vast lobby is a suitably swish introduction and draped with brilliantly coloured bougainvillea – an unusual decor touch. There's a 24-hour complimentary shuttle service to Positano.

Hotel California
HOTEL €€

(Map p158; ☎089 87 53 82; www.hotelcalifornia positano.com; Via Cristoforo Colombo 141; r incl breakfast €130-160; P✱⧉) This Hotel California is a long way from the West Coast (and the elderly owners don't look like Eagles fans). Housed in a magnificent 18th-century palace with a facade washed in soothing pinks and yellows, the rooms in the older part of the house are magnificent with ceilings painted with original friezes. The new rooms are spacious and luxuriously decorated. Breakfast is served on a leafy front terrace.

Casa Celeste
PENSIONI €

(Map p158; ☎089 87 53 63; Via Fornillo 10; s €42, d €80-90, incl breakfast; ⊘year-round) First of all, a warning: Celeste's home-made *limoncello* (which she will ply you with at any opportunity) has more alcohol in it than most. In her 80s, she's a gem, and also makes all the breakfast preserves and cakes. Son Marco is behind the tasteful restoration of the 17th-century rooms (when he is not running his Fornillo beach bar), which are attractively furnished with bright tile work and dark-wood furniture. Go for room five with its atmospheric vaulted ceiling.

Florida Residence
B&B €€

(Map p158; ☑089 87 58 01; www.floridaresidence. net; Viale Pasitea 171; r €85-110, incl breakfast; ☺Apr-Oct; [P][❄][📶]) There are two rarities here: free parking and boiled eggs for breakfast. This friendly place has good-sized rooms which, although starting to look mildly scuffed, are well equipped with fridge and hairdryer, and several have bathtubs as well as showers. There is plenty of communal kickback space, including a rooftop solarium and garden, complete with gazebo. It's family owned, and the daughter Teresa speaks some English.

Hotel Villa Gabrisa
BOUTIQUE HOTEL €€

(Map p158; ☑089 81 14 98; www.villagabrisa.it; Via Pasitea 223; r €150-220; ☺year-round; [❄][📶]) This historical building dates from the 18th century and has been tastefully restored. Rooms exude Italian style with painted furniture from Tuscany, coupled with traditional wrought-iron beds, Murano glass chandeliers, and majolica and terracotta tiles. Modern perks include Sky TV; some rooms have Jacuzzis, all have fridges, plus balconies with sea views.

Hotel Palazzo Murat
LUXURY HOTEL €€€

(Map p158; ☑089 87 51 77; www.palazzomurat.it; Via dei Mulini 23; r incl breakfast €175-260; ☺May–mid-Jan; [❄][@][📶]) Hidden behind an ancient wall from the surge of tourists who pass this pedestrian thoroughfare daily, the Palazzo Murat is a magnificent hotel. Housed within the 18th-century *palazzo* that the one-time King of Naples used as his summer residence, the lush gardens contain banana trees, bottlebrush, Japanese maple and pine trees. Rooms, five in the original part of the building (more expensive), 25 in the newer section, are decorated with sumptuous antiques, original oil paintings and plenty of glossy marble.

Villa Franco
HOTEL €€€

(Map p158; ☑089 87 56 55; www.villafrancahotel. it; Viale Pasitea 318; r incl breakfast €160-220; ☺Apr–mid-Oct; [P][❄]) This immaculate boutique hotel has a sparkling blue-and-white Mediterranean feel, while the rooftop pool (with its adjacent snack bar) has some of the best views in town. The rooms are white and bright with classical-themed tiled frescoes. Downstairs, there's a small bar, plus a gym with hi-tech machinery (as if you didn't get enough exercise in this town), and a Wellness Centre offering a Turkish bath, massages and various toning treatments (also open to the public). An additional annexe houses nine more rooms with similar decor.

Hostel Brikette
HOSTEL €

(Map p158; ☑089 87 58 57; www.brikette.com; Via Marconi 358; dm €23-25, d €65-85, apt €115-180; ☺late Mar-Nov; [❄][📶]) A short walk from the Bar Internazionale bus stop, this bright and cheerful hostel offers the cheapest accommodation in town. There are various options: six- to eight-person dorms (single sex and mixed), double rooms, and apartments for two to five people. There are also laundry and left-luggage facilities.

Villa Nettuno
HOTEL €

(Map p158; ☑089 87 54 01; www.villanettunoposi tano.it; Viale Pasitea 208; s/d €70/85; ☺year-round) Hidden behind a barrage of perfumed foliage, Villa Nettuno oozes charm. Go for one of the original rooms in the 300-year-old part of the building with frescoed wardrobes, heavy rustic decor and communal terrace. Rooms in the renovated part of the villa obviously lack the same character. That said, you probably won't be thinking of the furniture as you lie in your bed while gazing out to sea.

Positano to Amalfi

One of the most stunning stretches of road on the coast, accommodation here is mostly centred around Praiano.

Agriturismo Serafina
AGRITURISMO €

(☑089 83 03 47; www.agriturismoserafina.it; Via Picola 3, Loc Vigne; s/d incl breakfast €35/70, half-board €50/110; ☺year-round; [❄]) It's difficult to get more off the beaten track than this superb *agriturismo*. But make it up here and you'll find one of the best deals on the coast. Accommodation is in seven spruce, air-conditioned rooms in the main farmhouse, each with its own small balcony and views over the lush green terraces below. The food is quite special, virtually everything made with the farm's own produce (which includes salami, pancetta, wine, olive oil, fruit and veg).

Hotel Onda Verde
HOTEL €€

(☑089 87 41 43; www.hotelondaverde.it; Via Terramare 3, Praiano; r incl breakfast €110; ⊙Apr-Nov; ❄) This hotel enjoys a stunning cliffside position overlooking the picturesque Marina de Praiano. The interior is tunnelled into the stone face, which makes it wonderfully cool in the height of summer. Rooms have lashings of white linen, satin bedheads, elegant Florentine-style furniture and terraces with deckchairs for contemplating that view. The restaurant comes highly recommended.

Hotel Villa Bellavista
HOTEL €€

(☑089 87 40 54; www.villabellavista.it; Via Grado 47, Praiano; r €80-120; ⊙Apr-Oct; ❄🔊🏊) Surrounded by lush gardens with a vegetable plot, this Praiano hotel has an old-fashioned charm with its slightly stuffy furniture in the public areas and large, cool but fairly bare rooms. The appeal lies in the fabulous views from the spacious flower-festooned terrace, the delightful pool surrounded by greenery, the affectionate resident tabby cat (Lily) and the tranquil surroundings, on this narrow lane that leads to the Spiaggia della Gavitelli. The (signposted) hotel is accessed via Via Rezzolo from the SS163 that runs through town.

Amalfi

Despite its reputation as a day-trip destination, Amalfi has plenty of accommodation. It's not especially cheap, though, and most hotels are in the midrange to upper price brackets. Always try to book ahead, as the summer months are very busy and many places close over winter. Note that if you're coming by car, consider a hotel with a car park, as finding on-street parking could lead to an attack of the vapours.

TOP CHOICE ### Hotel Lidomare
HOTEL €€

(Map p165; ☑089 87 13 32; www.lidomare.it; Largo Duchi Piccolomini 9; s/d incl breakfast €50/110; ⊙year-round; ❄@🔊) Family run, this old-fashioned hotel has real character. The spacious rooms have an air of gentility, with their appealingly haphazard decor, vintage tiles and fine antiques. Surprisingly, some, such as room 31, even have Jacuzzi bathtubs; others, room 42 among them, have sea views and a large balcony. Breakfast is laid out, unusually, on top of a grand piano. It's all part of the very special character here. Highly recommended.

Albergo Sant'Andrea
HOTEL €

(Map p165; ☑089 87 11 45; Via Santolo Camera; s/d €50/78; ⊙Mar-Oct; ❄🔊) Enjoy the atmosphere of busy Piazza del Duomo from the comfort of your own room. This modest two-star has basic rooms with brightly coloured tiles that range from purple to baby blue and burgundy – with coordinating fabrics. The recent introduction of double glazing has helped cut down the piazza hubbub, which can reach fever pitch in high season.

Hotel Amalfi
HOTEL €€

(Map p165; ☑089 87 24 40; www.starnet.it/hamalfi; Vico dei Pastai 3; s €60-120, d €80-160, incl breakfast; ℙ❄🔊) Located in the backstreets just off Amalfi's main pedestrian thoroughfare, this family-run three-star is elegant and central. Rooms, some of which have their own balconies, sport pale-yellow walls, majolica-tiled flooring and a deft strip of stencilling. The glossily tiled but, albeit small, bathrooms have a choice of bathtub or shower. Upstairs, the roof garden is a relaxing place to idle over a drink.

Hotel Centrale
HOTEL €€

(Map p165; ☑089 87 26 08; www.hotelcentrale amal fi.it; Largo Piccolomini 1; s €60-120, d €70-140, tr €90-170, q €100-180, incl breakfast; ⊙year-round; ℙ❄@🔊) For the money, this is one of the best-value hotels in Amalfi. The entrance is on a tiny little piazza in the *centro storico* but many rooms actually overlook Piazza del Duomo (rooms 21 to 24 are good choices). The bright-green-and-blue tile work gives the place a vibrant fresh look and the views from the rooftop terrace are magnificent. All rooms have fridges.

Hotel Luna Convento
LUXURY HOTEL €€€

(☑089 87 10 02; www.lunahotel.it; Via Pantaleone Comite 33; s €230-290, d €250-300, incl breakfast; ⊙year-round; ℙ❄🔊🏊) This former convent was founded by St Francis in 1222 and has been a hotel for some 170 years. Rooms in the original building are in the former monks' cells, but there's nothing pokey about the bright tiles, balconies and seamless sea views. The newer wing is equally beguiling, with religious frescoes over the bed (to stop any misbehaving). The cloistered courtyard is magnificent.

Hotel Santa Caterina
HOTEL €€€

(☑089 87 10 12; www.hotelsantacaterina.it; Strada Amalfitana 9; d €290-550, ste from €420; ⊙Mar-Oct; ℙ❄🔊🏊) An Amalfi landmark, the Santa Caterina is one of Italy's most famous hotels. Everything about the place oozes luxury, from the discreet service to the fabulous gardens, the private beach to the opulent rooms. Built in 1880 by the Gambardella family and now run by the third generation, the views are among the best on the coast. For honeymooners, the Romeo and Juliet suite is the one to go for, a private chalet in the colourful grounds – it's a snip at anywhere between €940 and €2800 per night.

Residenza del Duca   HOTEL €€

(Map p165; ☑089 873 63 65; www.residence delduca.it; Via Mastalo 11 Duca 3; s €46-65, d €85-100, incl breakfast; ⊙Mar-Oct; ❀) A family-run small hotel with just six rooms, daughter Daniella speaks excellent English. Call ahead if you are carrying heavy luggage as it's a seriously puff-you-out-climb to reach here and a luggage service is included in the price. The rooms are prettily furnished with antiques, majolica tiles and the odd chintzy cherub, and they are light and sunny; room two is a particular winner with its French windows and stunning views.

Ravello

Ravello is an upmarket town and the accommodation reflects this, both in style and price. There are some superb top-end hotels, several lovely midrange places and a fine *agriturismo* nearby. Book well ahead for summer – especially if you're planning to visit during the music festival.

Agriturismo Monte Busara   AGRITURISMO €

(☑089 85 74 67; www.montebrusara.com; Via Monte Brusara 32; s/d €45/90) An authentic working farm, this mountainside *agriturismo* is located a tough half-hour walk of about 1.5km from Ravello's centre (call ahead and the owners can arrange to pick you up). It is especially suited to families: children can feed the pony while you sit back and admire the views – or for those who simply want to escape the crowds. The three rooms are comfy but basic, the food is fabulous and the owner is a charming, garrulous host. Half-board is also available.

Albergo Ristorante Garden   HOTEL €€

(Map p169; ☑089 85 72 26; www.hotelgarden ravello.it; Via Boccaccio 4; s/d €135/140; ⊙mid-Mar–late Oct; ❀🛜) Take a look at the photos behind reception and you can see current owners Ana and Marco playing with the Jackie Kennedy brood many years ago.

Although no longer the celebrity magnet that it once was, this family-run three-star is still a good bet. The smallish rooms leave little impression (clean with nondescript decor) but the views are superb and fridges are a welcome touch. Apparently Gore Vidal was a regular at its terrace restaurant (meals from around €30).

Hotel Caruso   LUXURY HOTEL €€€

(Map p169; ☑089 85 88 01; www.hotelcaruso.com; Piazza San Giovanni del Toro 2; s €450, d €620-750, incl breakfast; ⊙mid-Mar–Nov; P❀🛜⊜) There can be no better place to swim than the Caruso's sensational infinity pool. Seemingly set on the edge of a precipice, its blue waters merge with sea and sky to magical effect. Inside the sublimely restored 11th-century *palazzo* is no less impressive, with Moorish arches doubling as window frames, 15th-century vaulted ceilings and high-class ceramics. Rooms are suitably mod-conned with a TV/DVD system that slides sexily out of a wooden cabinet at the foot of the bed.

Palazzo Sasso   LUXURY HOTEL €€€

(Map p169; ☑089 81 81 81; www.palazzosasso. com; Via San Giovanni del Toro 28; d incl breakfast €330, with sea view €650; ⊙Mar-Oct; ❀🛜⊜) One of three luxury hotels on Ravello's millionaire row, Palazzo Sasso has been a hotel since 1880, providing refuge for many 20th-century luminaries – General Eisenhower planned the Allied attack on Monte Cassino here while later Roberto Rossellini and Ingrid Bergman flirted over dinner in the hotel restaurant. A stunning pale-pink 12th-century palace, its decor couples tasteful antiques with Moorish colours and modern sculpture. The 20m swimming pool commands great views, and its Michelin-starred restaurant, Rossellinis, has a superb reputation. There is a small spa.

Hotel Toro   BOUTIQUE HOTEL €€

(Map p169; ☑089 85 72 11; www.hoteltoro.it; Via Wagner 3; r incl breakfast €85-118; ⊙Easter-Nov; ❀🛜) A hotel since the late 19th century, the Dutch artist Escher stayed in room six here and was possibly inspired by the dizzily patterned tiles. The rooms are decked out in traditional Amalfi Coast style with terracotta or light marble tiles, soothing cream furnishings and tasteful landscape paintings; several rooms have fridges. Located just off Piazza del Duomo within easy range of the clanging cathedral bells, the walled garden is a delightful place to sip your sundowner.

ACCOMMODATION RAVELLO

Hotel Villa Amore
PENSIONI €

(Map p169; ✆089 85 71 35; www.villaamore.it; Via dei Fusco 5; s €50-60, d €75-100, incl breakfast; ☺year-round; @) A welcoming family-run *pensione*, this is the best budget choice in town. Tucked away down a quiet lane, it has modest, homey rooms and sparkling bathrooms. All rooms have their own balcony and some have bathtubs. The restaurant is a further plus with a terrace with (still more) fabulous views: the food's good, the views are memorable and the prices are right (around €25 for a meal).

Affitacamere Il Roseto
PENSIONI €

(Map p169; ✆089 858 64 92; www.ilroseto.it; Via Trinità 37; r incl breakfast €80; ☺year-round) If you're after a no-frills, clean room within easy walking distance of everything, come here. There are only two rooms, both of which have been decorated in medical white, with white walls, white sheets and white floors. But what they lack in charm they make up for in value, and, if you want colour, you can always sit outside under the lemon trees. No coincidence, perhaps, that the owners also run the Profumi della Costiera *limoncello* shop.

SALERNO & THE CILENTO

Salerno

The little accommodation that Salerno offers is fairly uninspiring, although, conveniently, there are several reasonable hotels in the town centre. Prices tend to be considerably lower than on the Amalfi Coast.

Hotel Montestella
HOTEL €€

(Map p180; ✆089 22 51 22; www.hotelmontestella. it; Corso Vittorio Emanuele II 156; s/d/tr incl breakfast €75/100/110; ✳@☎) Within walking distance of just about anywhere worth going to, the Montestella is on Salerno's main pedestrian thoroughfare, halfway between the *centro storico* and train station. The rooms are spacious and comfortable, with blue carpeting and regency-style wallpaper, while the public spaces have a fresh modern look. This hotel is by far the best midrange option in town. There is a handy underground car park a couple of blocks away (€25 for 24 hours).

Sant' Andrea
B&B €

(Map p180; ✆089 23 40 68; www.ristorantesantan drea.it; Piazza Sedile del Campo; s/d incl breakfast €50/60) Located above an excellent restaurant, the rooms here are compact and comfortable with dark-wood furniture and terraces overlooking the atmospheric piazza.

Ostello Ave Gratia Plena
HOSTEL €

(Map p180; ✆089 23 47 76; www.ostellodisalerno.it; Via dei Canali; dm/s/d €15/33/47; @☎) Housed in a 16th-century convent, Salerno's HI hostel is right in the heart of the *centro storico*. Inside there's a charming central courtyard and a range of bright rooms, from dorms to doubles with private bathroom. The 2am curfew is for dorms only.

Paestum

Despite the fact that most people visit Paestum for one day visit, there is a surprising number of hotels here. Aside from the inevitable modern three-star hotels geared towards coach tours, there are some excellent options.

⬥TOP CHOICE Hotel Calypso
HOTEL €€

(✆0828 81 10 31; www.calypsohotel.com; Via Mantegna 63; s €50-75, d €100-150, incl breakfast; P✳@) This is a top choice for artistically or alternatively inclined folk, with a macrobiotic restaurant (member of the Slow Food Movement) and large tastefully decorated rooms with private balconies and some choice handcrafted decor pieces. Owner Roberto (who made some of the lamps) is a world traveller who can also advise on the local area. Concerts are regularly staged here during summer, ranging from folk to classical, and a sandy beach is a short stroll away. Rooms without TV are available for guests concerned about electromagnetic fields.

Casale Giancesare
B&B €

(✆0828 72 80 61; www.casale-giancesare.it; Via Giancesare 8; s €45-60, d €65-90, incl breakfast; P✳@☎⛱) A 19th-century former farmhouse, this charming stone-clad B&B is run by the delightful Voza family, who will happily ply you with their home-made wine and *limoncello*. Located 2.5km from Paestum and surrounded by vineyards and olive and mulberry trees, the views are stunning, particularly from the swimming pool.

Villaggio dei Pini
CAMPGROUND €

(☑0828 811 030; www.campingvillaggiodeipini.com; camping 2 people, car & tent €40, 2-person cabins per week €350-450; ☎) Paestum has numerous campsites but this is where you should hammer in those tent pegs. Set in a mature landscaped area with lofty pines, facilities include a restaurant, pizzeria, mini market, football pitch, private beach and children's playground. The cabins are simply furnished but have all the essentials.

Agropoli & the Cilento Coast

A popular destination for Italian tourists in the summer months, Agropoli and the main coastal resorts have a good range of accommodation, mainly centred on the seafront resorts.

TOP CHOICE Marulivo Hotel
BOUTIQUE HOTEL €€

(☑0974 973 792; www.marulivohotel.it; Via Castello, Pisciotta; s €70-82, d €80-160, incl breakfast; ❊☎) Whether you are in the mood for romance or just seeking a stress-free break in idyllic surroundings, consider this hotel. Located in the narrow web of lanes behind this medieval town's main piazza, rooms are furnished with earthy colours, antique furnishings, crisp white linen and exposed stone walls. The rooftop terrace with sea views and an adjacent small bar is unbeatable for languishing over a long cold drink.

Albergo il Castello
HOTEL €€

(☑0974 96 71 69; www.hotelcastello.co.uk; Via Amendola, Agropoli; r incl breakfast €80-110; P❊) This ivy clad old-fashioned hotel is housed in an early 19th-century building with large rooms, still with the original floor tiles, plus exposed stone walls and spacious private terraces. The courtyard is a delight with its lemon trees and abundance of plants; the perfect place to enjoy a sundowner at the end of an energetic sightseeing day.

Anna
B&B €

(☑0974 82 37 63; www.bbanna.it; Via S Marco 28-30, Agropoli; s €35-50, d €50-70, incl breakfast; P❊) A great location, across from the town's sweeping sandy beach, this trim budget choice is best known locally for its downstairs restaurant, as you will appreciate while salivating over your home-made morning *cornetti* (Italian-type croissant). The rooms are large and plain with small balconies; specify a sea view to enjoy the sun setting over Sorrento. Sunbeds and bicycles can be hired for a minimal price.

La Lanterna
AGRITURISMO €

(☑089 79 02 51; www.cilento.it/lanterna; Via della Lanterna 8, Agropoli; 2-person cabin €40-50, 4-person cabin €80, d €70-80, dm incl breakfast €17-19; P❊@) Ivo and Tiziana are great hosts at this friendly place, around 1km from the town centre. The homey cabin accommodation is great value, set in the gardens with large terraces, sea views and plenty of storage space. The dorms are straightforward and clean with lockers, while the communal breakfast of rolls with cream cheese or jams and homemade cake is better than most. Internet costs €3 per hour.

La Corallina
HOTEL €€

(☑0974 96 68 61; www.hotellacoralinna.it; Via Porto, San Marco di Castellabate; s €50-75, d €80-120, incl breakfast; P❊☎) This small hotel has a beautiful facade painted in dark ochre with traditional green shutters and flower-filled window boxes. Overlooking the fishing boats in the harbour, the rooms are a dazzle of white tiles with colourful Vietri tile trim, contrasting with dark-blue fabrics.

Albergo Santa Caterina
HOTEL €€

(☑0974 93 10 19; www.albergosantacaterina.com; Via Indipendenza 53, Palinura; r incl breakfast €80-110; P❊@☎) Superb hotel on the main street, with the colour scheme of the rooms varying between brilliant canary yellow to deep Mediterranean blue. All have good-sized bathrooms with tubs, as well as showers, and private terraces. Note that a sea view will cost €20 more. The satellite TV here is a rare treat in these parts, and a major plus if you are suffering from international news withdrawal.

Pensione Anna
PENSIONI €

(☑0974 93 10 59; Piazza Virgilio 22, Palinura; s €25-35, d €40-65, incl breakfast; P) The perks of this family-run place include the position, right on the town's vibrant main square, and the vast old-fashioned front terrace with its plants, vines and congenial granddad, who has his own seat in the corner. The rooms are simply furnished but clean with jaunty red shutters. Prices are very reasonable, even during the silly season (August).

Raggio di Sole
AGRITURISMO €

(☑0974 96 73 56; www.agriturismoraggiodisole.it; Via Terrate, Castellabate; r incl breakfast €80;

Apr-Nov; P✳) Situated on the outskirts of town coming from Santa Maria di Castellabate, this welcoming *agriturismo* is just one mountain peak away from the town, so the views are superb, with the sea and the island of Capri beyond. The main house is surrounded by trees, including lofty eucalyptus, citrus and olive trees, while below there is a small farmyard with goats, geese, ducks and at least one donkey. In a totally refurbished 200-year-old farmhouse, the rooms areplain and modern with balconies. Meals are available.

U'Sghiz
B&B €

(☎0974 82 93 31; Piazza Umberto 8, Palinura; s €45-50, d €55-75, incl breakfast; ✳) In the heart of the *centro storico*, with an excellent restaurant, Antonio (or Antoine – he lived for many years in Quebec) has lovingly restored this 1600 building and offers three atmospheric rooms. Furnished with antiques, they have soothing colour schemes of pale green, peach and cream. Fridges are an agreeable extra.

Villa Sirio
HOTEL €€

(☎0974 96 01 62; www.villasirio.it; Via Lungamare de Simone 15, Santa Maria di Castellabate; s €85-130, d €120-200, incl breakfast; Apr-Nov; P✳) Dating from 1912, this family owned hotel has a classic and elegant facade with its ochre paintwork and traditional green shutters. The rooms are brightly furnished with a yellow, blue and turquoise colour scheme plus shiny marble-clad bathrooms complete with Jacuzzi. The small balconies have forfeited the plastic for tasteful marble tables and have seamless sea views with Capri in the distance.

Parco Nazionale del Cilento

Unsurprisingly, the dramatic and lush scenery in the park makes it an excellent place to stay in an *agriturimso*.

TOP CHOICE Agriturismo i Moresani AGRITURISMO €€

(☎0974 90 20 86; www.imoresani.com; Loc Moresani; s €45-55, d €90-110, incl breakfast; Mar-Oct; ✳✿) If you are seeking utter tranquillity, head here. The setting is bucolic with rolling hills in every direction, interspersed with grape vines, grazing pastures and olive trees. Family run, the 18-hectare farm produces its own *caprino* goat's cheese, wine, olive oil and preserves. The restaurant uses primari-

ly homegrown organic products and has an outside terrace, which fronts onto vineyards. The rooms have cream- and earth-coloured decor and surround a pretty private garden. Horse riding, cooking and painting courses are regularly held; check the website and contact the friendly owners for a schedule.

Villa Vea
AGRITURISMO €

(☎0828 196 22 37; www.agriturismovillavea.it; C da Soubaddei 10, Bellosguardo; r €60-72; ✿✱) Surrounded by olive trees and vines with distant pine-covered mountains, this superb *agriturismo* is run by an American-Italian family. Enjoy distant views of Capri while savouring delicious traditional food prepared by Angela, who also conducts cooking classes. Home-made olive oil, wine and jams are on the menu and breakfasts are a cut above the normal *cornetti*, with cooked breakfasts available on request (a rarity in these parts). The rooms are rustic style with chunky wood furniture and brightly coloured walls. Dating from 1978, this was the first *agriturismo* to open in the area.

Agriturismo Antico Casolare
AGRITURISMO €

(☎339 4572986; www.anticocasolare.com; Contrada Suvero 6; s/d incl breakfast €35/60; Mar-Oct; P✳) On the edge of the park, just 6km inland from the coast, come here for fabulous views and a no-frills rural stay in an 18th-century farmhouse, still in the same Ricciardella family. A large outside terrace is hung with corn cobs and tomatoes and there's an original oven for baking bread. The rooms are pleasant with wrought-iron or dark-wood furnishings and small tiled bathrooms. Various activities, including trekking and horse riding, can be organised.

Agriturismo La Loggia degli Alburni
AGRITURISMO €

(☎334 3204398; Sicignano e'Alburni; s/d incl breakfast €30/40; P✳) More of a country hotel than a true *agriturismo*, but the setting is sublime, high up in a grove of chestnut trees overlooking the magnificent castle. Follow the signs from the village, along a rough track, backed by steep forested slopes. The rooms are large, modern and comfortable. The dining room, complete with colourful hunting mural, serves good traditional fare like home-made *tagliolini* pasta in a ragù sauce (meals €25). Popular with walkers.

Agriturismo Terra Nostra
AGRITURISMO €

(☎333 8069231; www.agriturismoterranostra.it; Contrada Galdo; s/d incl breakfast €20/40; Mar-

Oct; P✳@⌗) Owned by the Salamonte family who lived in England for several years (hence the gnomes in the garden), this folksy place enjoys a lovely pastoral setting, right outside this delightful medieval village. Goats, sheep, ducks and dogs are just part of the menagerie. The rooms are simply furnished with dark-wood furniture, dazzling white walls and terracotta tile floors. The large restaurant dishes up excellent local dishes and has an open fireplace during the winter months. Recent additions include a pool and small fitness centre.

Antichi Feudi BOUTIQUE HOTEL €
(✆0975 58 73 29; www.antichifeudi.com; Via San Francesco 2; s €45-45, d €45-80, incl breakfast; ✳🛜) Located just off the picturesque main Piazza San Cono, this former palace is distinguished by its sumptuous burnt-sienna-coloured exterior. An atmospheric and inexpensive boutique hotel, the rooms are all different, but share a sumptuous attention to detail with decorative painted wardrobes, canopy beds and even the occasional chandelier. The public spaces include a small courtyard with its original well and an excellent restaurant.

Casale San Martino B&B €
(✆0974 83 22 13; www.casalesanmartino.eu; Contrada Vignali 5; r incl breakfast €65-85; ⊘Mar-Oct; P✳) This exquisite B&B has stunning panoramic views of Agropoli and the coast to the west and rolling countryside to the east. Sleep under the beams in the tastefully decorated bedrooms with their stone walls, earth colours and five-star quality bathrooms with mosaic marble tiles. The young family menagerie includes goats and ducks and, if you time your visit right, breakfast will include fresh figs from the pretty garden, complete with wisteria-draped arbour.

Sicinius AGRITURISMO €
(✆330 869287; www.sicinius.com; Contrada Piedi La Serra 22; r incl breakfast €75; ⊘Apr-Oct) A solar-energised 12-hectare farm that is committed to cultivating organic crops, including olives, and offers massages and aromatherapy treatments, plus there's also a small health shop on the premises. The rooms are simple, with superb views of Mt Alburni, and there are mountain bikes available for guests, as well as an excellent restaurant.

Zio Cristoforo AGRITURISMO €€
(✆0974 90 75 52; www.agriturismoziocristoforo.com; Via Chiuse 24; s €80-120, d €90-140, incl breakfast; P✳⌗) If *agriturismi* had stars, this one would have five. That said, it is more like a boutique hotel than a farmstay. No one seems to be trudging around in muddy boots here, although there *is* a surrounding farm and the animals raised do feature in the popular restaurant menu. The rooms are rustic, yet elegant, with wrought-iron bedheads, terracotta tiles and a soothing green-and-white colour scheme. Cooking classes are available during winter (€150 for three days), as well as regular wine-tasting courses.

La Congiura dei Baroni HOTEL €
(✆0975 7 90 44; www.lacongiuradeibaroni.it; Via Castello 16, Teggiano; s/d €30/70) This inviting small hotel has a wonderful position overlooking a castle and moat. Cute comfortable rooms have a reassuring spare-room feel with private terraces, while owner, Anna Maria, will extend a warm welcome (but speaks no English).

ACCOMMODATION PARCO NAZIONALE DEL CILENTO

Understand Naples, Pompeii & the Amalfi Coast

population per sq km

NAPLES   ITALY   NY

≈ 3 people

Naples, Pompeii and the Amalfi Coast Today

A Mayor with Mojo

Beleaguered by years of humiliating headlines involving litter-strewn streets and gun-wielding *camorristi* (members of the Neapolitan mafia), it seems that Naples is finally getting its groove back. In May 2011 the city voted in Luigi de Magistris as mayor. For many disillusioned Neapolitans, electing the youthful ex–public prosecutor was a last-ditch bid to save their city's dignity. As the famous Neapolitan actor Beppe Barra bluntly put it during de Magistris' election campaign, 'Luigi, please don't disappoint me'.

It seems that he hasn't. Since stepping into office, a number of promising initiatives have been implemented. In September 2011 the ZTL (limited traffic zone) was introduced in the Naples' *centro storico* (historic centre) to slash carbon emissions, improve traffic flow and curb the illegal use of traffic lanes reserved for public transport. Naples' liveability was further enhanced by the pedestrianisation of its famous Lungomare (seafront) in time for the World Series of the America's Cup in April/May 2012. The international events continue in April and July 2013, when Naples hosts the Universal Forum of Cultures. Secured by the city's former administration, the Unesco-backed event will see people from across the globe heading to Naples to discuss ideas and promote intercultural understanding.

Despite the progress, not all locals are praising de Magistris' efforts. Among his most vocal critics are traders within the ZTL zone, many of whom argue that limiting traffic into the city centre has negatively affected business. Others sceptics refer back to 1994 and the city's hosting of the G7 summit. A time of significant urban renewal and optimism, it was ironically followed by almost two decades of escalating crime, stop-

» Population: 5,954,882 (2011)

» Area: 13,590 km²

» Unemployment: 31.39% (2012)

» Number of Unesco World Heritage Sites: 5

» Most common surname: Esposito

Faux Pas

» Italians are chic and quick to judge on appearances, so make an effort with your appearance.

» Splitting the bill is deemed the height of *inciviltà* (unsophistication). The person who invites pays, but close friends may split.

» Fondle fruit, vegetables, flowers or clothing in shops and expect to be greeted with a killer glare from the shop assistant. Window displays are especially sacred.

» Take official opening hours with a grain of salt.

Top Movies

» **L'oro di Napoli** (1954) Directed by Vittorio De Sica

» **Passione** (2010) John Turturro

» **Gomorra** (2008) Matteo Garrone

» **Le mani sulla città** (1963) Francesco Rosi

belief systems
(% of population)

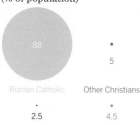

88
Roman Catholic

5
Other Christians

2.5
Muslim

4.5
Other religions

if Naples was 100 people

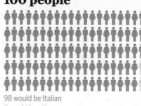

98 would be Italian
2 would be other

start waste disposal crises, and political malaise. Only time will tell if de Magistris will prove his detractors wrong.

People Power

The winds of change are blowing beyond the Municipio. Fed up with years of political inertia and over-stretched services, citizen-based groups are taking matters into their own hands. Grassroots organisation CleaNap is well known for clearing litter and graffiti from Neapolitan streets and squares. Fellow group Friarielli Ribelli ('*friarielli*' is a local type of broccoli and '*ribelli*' means 'rebels') made the headlines with its guerilla gardening, its small army of volunteers pulling out weeds, planting flowers, and giving the city's few pockets of green some much-needed TLC. Online group VANTO. (an acronym for 'pride') is also on board, monitoring and reporting damage to city churches, *palazzi* (large buildings), monuments and gardens, and suggesting low-cost means for their salvage and long-term preservation.

Another inspiring agent of change is Don Antonio Loffredo. Based in La Sanità, an inner-city district long challenged by poverty and organised crime, the bespectacled priest is the force behind 'La Parenza', a social co-operative offering at-risk local youths new opportunities. Among these are the restoration and management of the area's famous catacombs, the running of neighbourhood guided tours, and even the creation and management of a new bed and breakfast. Supported by the likes of prolific Neapolitan artist Riccardo Dalisi, Don Antonio's efforts are slowly reversing the neighbourhood's fortunes. A spirit of civic pride and purpose is on the increase, as are the number of artist residents and curious tourists drawn to its revamped historical treasures.

> While Salerno remains Campania's eco-friendly role model, recycling 71% of its waste, the town of Acerra is quickly catching up, with its recycling rate leaping from 10% in 2011 to 62% in 2012. Much less impressive is Naples, at 17.7%.

Neapolitan Playlist

» **James Senese** (www.jamessenese.it) Jazz icon

» **Enzo Avitabile** (www.enzoavitabile.it) Funk/world artist

» **Letti Sfatti** (www.lettisfatti.com) Pop-rock singer-songwriter

Top Books

» **Capri and No Longer Capri** (Raffaele La Capria) A melancholic vision of modern Capri.

» **Falling Palace: A Romance of Naples** (Dan Hofstadler) Naples' electric streets are brought to life in this evocative love story.

Naples '44: An Intelligence Officer in the Italian Labyrinth (Norman Lewis) An engrossing account of postwar Naples.

» **The Ancient Shore: Dispatches from Naples** (Shirley Hazzard & Francis Steegmuller) Musings on Neapolitan life and history.

History

With almost 3000 candles on its birthday cake, Naples and its sparkling coastline have seen it all, from pleasure-seeking Romans and Spanish conquests to occupying Nazis. Whoever said history was boring has clearly never known this city.

The Early Years

The ancient Greeks were the first major players on the scene, setting up a trading post on Ischia and another settlement at Cumae (Cuma) in the 8th century BC. As their main foothold in Italy, Cumae became the most important city in the Italian peninsula's southwest during the next 200 years, a rich commercial centre whose sibyl was said to be Apollo's mouthpiece.

According to legend, the traders also established Naples on the island of Megaris, current home of the Castel dell'Ovo, in about 680 BC. Christened Parthenope, its namesake was a suicidal siren. Unable to lure the cunning Ulysses with her songs, she drowned herself, washing up on shore.

Failure would also hit the Tuscany-based Etruscans, who twice invaded Cuma and twice failed. After the second of these clashes, in 474 BC, the Cumaeans founded Neapolis (New Town) where Naples' *centro storico* (historic centre) stands.

Despite the Cumaeans' resilience, the Etruscan battles had taken a toll, and in 421 BC the Greeks fell to the Samnites. They, in turn, proved no match for the Romans, who took Neapolis in 326 BC. Not long after, in 273 BC, they added Paestum to their list, a Greek city dating back to the 5th century BC.

Togas, Triumph & Terror

Under the Romans, the Bay of Naples sparkled with lavish villas, thermal spas and cashed-up out-of-towners. Farmland and forests covered

TIMELINE	8th century BC	680 BC	474 BC
	Greeks establish a colony at Cuma in the Campi Flegrei. The area becomes the most important Greek settlement on the Italian mainland and a strategic part of Magna Graecia.	The Cuman Greeks establish Parthenope on the island of Megaris, naming it in honour of a suicidal siren whose song fails to seduce the cunning Ulysses.	The Cumans found Neapolis (New Town) on the site of Naples' *centro storico* (historic centre). The original Greek street plan can still be seen today.

Vesuvius' lower slopes, while VIPs indulged by the coast. Notables holidayed in Stabiae (Castellammare di Stabia), Nero's second wife, Poppea, entertained in upmarket Oplontis and Julius Caesar's father-in-law kept a home at Herculaneum. West of Naples, Puteoli (Pozzuoli) became a major international port, docking everything from Alexandrian grain ships to St Paul, who reputedly stepped on shore in AD 61. Further west, Misenum (Miseno) boasted the ancient world's largest naval fleet.

Despite the Romans' stronghold on the region, the citizens of Neapolis never completely gave in to their foreign occupiers, refusing (among other things) to relinquish their language. While the Romans may have tolerated the linguistic snub, the Neapolitans' opposition to Rome during the Roman Civil War (88–82 BC) was another story, prompting Cornelius Sulla to take the city and slaughter thousands. Equally catastrophic was the unexpected eruption of Mt Vesuvius in AD 79, which drowned nearby Pompeii and Herculaneum in molten lava, mud and ash. Coming just 17 years after a massive earthquake, it was a devastating blow for the rural plebs (plebeians) already struggling in the region.

Inside the city walls, Neapolis was booming: General Lucullus built an enviable villa where the Castel dell'Ovo stands and even Virgil moved to town. Offshore, Capri became the centre of Emperor Tiberius' famously debauched operations.

Yet, as Neapolis' welfare was by now tied to that of the Roman Empire, the death of the last Roman emperor, Romulus Augustus, in AD 476, saw the city pass into barbarian hands.

The Normans & the Angevins

By the beginning of the 11th century, Naples was a prospering duchy. Industry and culture were thriving and Christianity had conquered the masses. Outside the city, however, the situation was more volatile as the

Get to grips with the history, peoples and wars of ancient Greece by logging on to www.ancientgreece.com, which gives compact histories of all the key characters and places. It also has an online bookstore.

AMALFI: THE GOLDEN DAYS

Musing on the fabled town of Amalfi, 19th-century scribe Renato Fucini declared that when the town's inhabitants reach heaven on Judgement Day, it will be just like any other day for them. It must have been a view shared by the Roman patricians shipwrecked on its coast in AD 337. Seduced by the area's beauty, they decided to ditch their long-haul trip to Constantinople and stay put. Despite the fans, Amalfi's golden era would arrive in the 9th century, when centuries of Byzantine rule were ditched for Marine Republic status. Between this time and the ruinous Pisan raids of 1135 and 1137, its ever-expanding fleet brought a little bit of Amalfi to the far reaches of the Mediterranean, from churches named in honour of Sant'Andrea (Amalfi's patron saint) to a 'Little Amalfi' quarter in 10th-century Constantinople, complete with expat shops and schools.

---

326 BC	AD 79
The Romans conquer Neapolis and the city is absorbed into the Roman Empire. Despite this, locals cling to their Greek heritage and language.	At 10am on 24 August, Mt Vesuvius erupts after centuries of slumber, startling the Neapolitans and burying Pompeii, Herculaneum and other towns on the mountain's slopes.

ROGER RESSMEYER/CORBIS ©

» Cast of Pompeiian victim of Mt Vesuvius

Normans began to eye up the Lombard principalities of Salerno, Benevento, Capua and Amalfi.

The Normans had arrived in southern Italy in the 10th century, initially as pilgrims en route from Jerusalem, later as mercenaries attracted by the money to be made fighting for the rival principalities and against the Arab Muslims in Sicily. And it was to just one such mercenary, Rainulfo Drengot, that the duke of Naples, Sergio IV, gave the contract to drive the Lombards out of Capua. Capua duly fell in 1062, followed by Amalfi in 1073 and Salerno four years later. By 1130 most of southern Italy, including Sicily, was in Norman hands and it was only a question of time before Naples gave in to the inevitable. It did so in 1139. The Kingdom of the Two Sicilies was thus complete.

The Normans maintained their capital in Sicily, and Palermo began to outshine Naples. And yet the Neapolitans seemed happy with their lot, but when the last of the Norman kings, Tancred, was succeeded by his enemy Henry Hohenstaufen of Swabia in 1194, the mood turned ugly. The Neapolitans despised their new Swabian rulers and were delighted when Charles I of Anjou defeated them at the battle of Benevento in February 1265.

Under the French Angevins, Naples' artistic and intellectual credentials grew. Charles built the Castel Nuovo in 1279, the port was enlarged, and in the early 14th century Robert of Anjou constructed Castel Sant'Elmo. Alas, nasty politicking between family factions marked the last century of Angevin rule. Queen Joan I was suspected of murdering her husband and fled the city between 1348 and 1352, leaving her vengeful Hungarian in-laws to occupy Naples. Some 70-odd years later her namesake, Queen Joan II, could only stop her husband stealing the crown thanks to substantial popular support.

With the royals tangled up in soap-style angst, the time was ripe for the Spanish Aragonese to launch their attack.

For a wide-ranging general site on Italian history, check out www. arcaini.com. It covers, in potted form, everything from prehistory to the postwar period, and includes a brief chronology.

Aragonese Angst

Taking control of Naples in 1442, Alfonso of Aragon – dubbed Il Magnanimo (The Magnanimous) – did much for Naples, promoting art and science and introducing institutional reforms. What he couldn't do was live down the fact that he'd overthrown the popular Angevins.

In 1485 the city's barons took up arms against Alfonso's successor, Ferdinand I. Within a year, however, the ringleaders had been executed (in the Sala dei Baroni inside Castel Nuovo) and peace restored. In 1495 King Charles VIII of France invaded. Fiercely opposed by the Neapolitan masses, the French monarch was forced out four months later and replaced by Aragonese Ferdinand II.

305	536	1139	1265
San Gennaro, patron saint of Naples, becomes a victim of Emperor Diocletian's anti-Christian campaign. The martyr is arrested and beheaded at the Solfatara Crater in Pozzuoli.	Byzantine chief general Belisarius and his fighters sneak into the city through its ancient aqueduct and lay siege. Conquered, Naples becomes a Byzantine duchy.	Naples joins the Norman-ruled Kingdom of the Two Sicilies after the Norman conquest of Capua, Amalfi and Salerno. The city plays second fiddle to the kingdom's capital, Palermo.	Charles I of Anjou beats Naples' hated Swabian rulers, heralding the city as the capital of the French Anjou dynasty. The port is expanded and Castel Nuovo is built in 1279.

After Ferdinand II's death in 1496, the mutinous barons crowned Ferdinand's uncle, Frederick, as king. This angered everyone: the Neapolitans, the French and the Spanish had all wanted Ferdinand II's widow Joan to succeed him. The upshot was the joint Franco–Spanish invasion of 1501. Frederick tried to hang on to power, but, facing almost total opposition, he skulked off, leaving Naples to the Spanish. Thus King Ferdinand of Spain became King Ferdinand III of Naples.

Don Pedro & the Spanish Years

As part of the cashed-up Spanish empire, 16th-century Naples prospered. By 1600 it was Europe's largest city, with a population of 300,000. The boom heralded urban expansion, with viceroy Don Pedro de Toledo moving the city walls westward and creating the Quartieri Spagnoli (Spanish Quarters). Hundreds of new churches and monasteries sprung up, giving artistic greats like Caravaggio, Giuseppe de Ribera and Luca Giordano the chance to show off their skills. The most prolific of all Naples'

History of the Italian People, by Giuliano Procacci, is one of the best general histories of the country in any language. It covers the period from the early Middle Ages until 1948.

HISTORY DON PEDRO & THE SPANISH YEARS

JOAN II: QUEEN OF LUST

Had tabloids existed in the middle ages, Joan II (1373–1435) would have been a regular fixture. Six centuries after her reign as Queen of Naples, Neapolitans still point out the various settings for her 'man-eating' antics. It was at the Castel Nuovo that she apparently threw her lovers to a hungry crocodile, and at the Palazzo Donn'Anna where she threw them straight off a cliff. One can only assume they had underperformed at the queen's infamous orgies.

While the line separating fact and fiction is a very fine one indeed, it is widely accepted that the daughter of Charles III and Margherita of Durazzo was no stranger to the company of men, many of them power brokers. At the time of her coronation in 1414, she was already the widow of William, Duke of Austria, the rejected fiancé of her cousin, Hedwig of Poland. As queen, Joan wasted little time appointing her lover Pandolfello Alopo Grand Chamberlain, before a short-lived betrothal to John of Aragon in 1415.

Next in line was James II of Bourbon, whom she married that same year. The honeymoon was short-lived, however: refused the title of Prince of Taranto, jealous James II had Alopo murdered and forced Joan to bestow him with the title of King of Naples. As king, James was determined to assume complete power, imprisoning Joan in the royal household. The king's divalike behaviour provoked rioting in Naples in 1416, forcing him to hang up his crown.

If Joan was needing any consolation, she found it in the arms of nobleman Giovanni Caracciolo. Yet even the position of prime minister of Naples wasn't enough for Caracciolo, whose increasingly ruthless ambition drove his royal lover to plot his assassination in 1432. His tomb lies in the Chiesa di San Giovanni a Carbonara, not far from cunning Joan's own resting place, the Basilica della Santissima Annunziata.

1282	1442	1503	1532–53
Resentful of the Angevins' demotion of Palermo as capital city, Sicilian rioters kill 2000 French people on Easter Monday in the former capital.	Alfonso of Aragon drives out René of Anjou to become Naples' new king and a long period of Spanish control begins.	Two years after a Franco–Spanish invasion of Naples, Spanish general Consalvo di Cordoba enters the city and King Ferdinand of Spain becomes King Ferdinand III of Naples.	Don Pedro de Toledo rules as Spanish viceroy, moving the city walls westwards and constructing the Quartieri Spagnoli (Spanish Quarters).

architects was Cosimo Fanzago (1591–1678), whose work on the Certosa di San Martino is a highlight of Neapolitan baroque.

Less welcome were the ever-increasing tax hikes, resulting from the economic depression that descended in the early 17th century. When the Spanish introduced a levy on fresh fruit in January 1647, it was one tax too many and on 7 July violence broke out on Piazza del Mercato. Nine days later, the rebellion's illiterate leader – Amalfi fisherman Tommaso Aniello (aka Masaniello) – was murdered in the Chiesa di Santa Maria del Carmine. The culprits were extremists from within his own camp: they wanted to drive out the Spanish, but their leader had been happy with cheaper fruit. Local lore has it that Masaniello lies buried in an unmarked tomb in the church.

The French then tried to cash in by sending the duke of Giusa to take the city; the duke failed, and on 6 April 1648 was captured by the new Spanish viceroy, the Count of Oñate. Order was soon re-established, the rebel leaders were executed and life in Naples returned to a semblance of normality.

Putting a spanner in the works was the plague of 1656, which wiped out about half of Naples' population and much of the economy. The horror that infected the city's squalid streets is graphically depicted in the paintings that hang in Room 37 of the Certosa di San Martino.

> Between January and August 1656, the bubonic plague wiped out about half of Naples' 300,000-plus inhabitants. The city would take almost two centuries to reach its pre-plague headcount again.

Bourbon Brilliance & Habsburg Cunning

With the death of childless Charles V of Naples (Charles II of Spain) in 1700, Spain's European possessions were up for grabs. Despite Philip, grandson of Charles V's brother-in-law, taking the Spanish throne (and therefore the Neapolitan throne) as King Philip V, Austrian troops nabbed Naples in 1707. Waiting in the wings, however, was King Philip V's Bourbon son Charles, who followed his ambitious mother Elisabetta Farnese's advice to take the city. Between his ascension to the Neapolitan throne in 1734 and Italian unification in 1860, Naples was transformed into Europe's showpiece metropolis. The Palazzo Reale di Capodimonte hit the skyline, central Palazzo Reale was enlarged and the Teatro San Carlo became Europe's grandest opera house.

In 1759 Charles returned to Spain to succeed his father as King Charles III. As European law prohibited the simultaneous holding of three crowns (Naples, Sicily and Spain), Naples was left to Charles' eight-year-old son Ferdinand, though, in effect, power was left to Charles' conscientious prime minister, Bernardo Tanucci.

When in 1768 Austrian Maria Carolina arrived in town to marry Ferdinand, Tanucci's days were numbered. Maria was one of 16 children of the Habsburg Empress of Austria (the very person who Tanucci had opposed in the 1740 crisis of Austrian succession). She was beautiful, clever

PLAGUE

1600	1656	1707	1734
Naples is the biggest city in Europe, boasting a population of more than 300,000. Among its growing number of residents is renegade artist Caravaggio, who arrives in 1606.	A devastating plague hits Naples. Within six months, three-quarters of the city's population is dead and buried in mass graves.	Austrian viceroys rule Naples for 27 years. Tax and university reforms are introduced and coastal roads connecting the city to the slopes of Mt Vesuvius are built.	Encouraged by his ambitious mother and backed by his army, Charles takes control from the Austrians and becomes the first Bourbon king of Naples.

and ruthless; a ready match for Tanucci and an unlikely partner for the famously dim, dialect-speaking Ferdinand.

In accordance with her marriage agreement Maria Carolina joined the Council of State on the birth of her first son in 1777. It was the position she'd been waiting for to oust Tanucci, and into his shoes stepped a French-born English aristocrat, John Acton. Acton had won over Maria with his anti-Bourbon politics and wish to forge closer links with Austria and Britain. But just as things began to go smoothly with the English, France erupted in revolution.

The Parthenopean Republic

While the Neapolitan court naturally disapproved of the 1789 French Revolution, it would take the beheading of Maria Carolina's sister, Marie Antoinette, to prompt Naples to join the anti-French coalition.

Troops from Naples and revolutionary France clashed in French-occupied Rome in 1798. The Neapolitans claimed the city but within 11 days were scurrying back south with the French in hot pursuit. Panicked, Ferdinand and Maria Carolina headed for Palermo, leaving Naples to its own devices.

Bitterly opposed by most of the population, the French were welcomed by the Neapolitan nobility and bourgeoisie, many of whom had adopted fashionable republican ideas. And it was with the full backing of the French that the Parthenopean Republic was declared on 23 January 1799.

But it wasn't a success. The leaders were an ideologically rather than practically minded lot, and were soon in financial straits. Their efforts to democratise the city failed and the army was a shambles.

Over the water in Palermo, the royal exiles had not been sitting idle. Ferdinand and Maria Carolina dispatched Cardinal Fabrizio Ruffo to Calabria to organise an uprising. On 13 June he entered Naples and all hell broke loose as his men turned the city into a slaughterhouse. With a score to settle, Ferdinand and Maria Carolina returned from Sicily on 8 July and embarked on a systematic extermination of republican sympathisers. More than 200 were executed.

Bourbon Decline & Nationalist Fervour

Despite the Parthenopean Republic's failure, French forces marched again into Naples in 1806. The royal family once more fled to Sicily, and in 1808 Joachim Murat, Napoleon's brother-in-law, became king of Naples. Despite his abolishment of feudalism and kick-starting of local industry, Murat could do no right in the eyes of the royalist masses.

With Murat finally ousted in 1815, Ferdinand returned to claim his throne. But the French Revolution had stirred up too many ideas for a

GOETHE

Of Naples, Goethe wrote: 'I can't begin to tell you of the glory of a night by full moon when we strolled through the streets and squares to the endless promenade of the Chiaia, and then walked up and down the seashore. I was quite overwhelmed by a feeling of infinite space'.

1737	1768	1799	1806
The original Teatro San Carlo is built in a swift eight months. Designed by Giovanni Medrano, it is rebuilt in 1816 after a devastating fire.	Marie Antoinette's sister, Maria Carolina, marries the uncouth Ferdinand IV. Nine years later she enters the Council of State and ousts prime minister and enemy Bernardo Tanucci.	The Parthenopean Republic is proclaimed on 23 January. It quickly fails, royal rule is reinstalled and more than 200 republican sympathisers are executed.	Joseph Bonaparte occupies the city and declares himself king of Naples. Two years later Bonaparte is crowned king of Spain.

return to the age of absolutism, and the ruthless Carbonari society forced Ferdinand to grant the city a constitution in 1820. A year later, however, it was abandoned as Ferdinand called in Austrian troops.

Pressured by rising rebellion across Europe, Ferdinand reintroduced a constitution in 1848, only to dissolve the parliament altogether. He was as blind to the changing times as his equally obstinate son, who succeeded him in 1859.

More popular was nationalist fighter Giuseppe Garibaldi, whose goal was a united Italy. Buoyed by the victory of Piedmontese rebels against the Austrian army, he set sail for Sicily in May 1860 with a volunteer army of 1000 Red Shirts. Although Ferdinand's 25,000-strong Neapolitan army was waiting in Sicily, the Bourbons' repression of liberalism was beginning to cost it goodwill. With an army that had swelled to 5000 men, Garibaldi defeated the half-hearted Bourbon forces, declaring himself dictator in the name of King Vittorio Emanuele II.

In a case of too little too late, Ferdinand's son and successor, Francesco II, agreed to a constitution in June 1860 but Garibaldi had crossed over to the Italian mainland and was Naples bound. True to tradition, Francesco fled the city, taking refuge with 4000 loyalists behind the River Volturno, north of Naples. On 7 September Garibaldi marched unopposed into Naples, welcomed as a hero.

A series of last-ditch attacks on the rebels by Bourbon loyalists were defeated at the Battle of Volturno and on 21 October the city voted overwhelmingly to join a united Italy under the Savoy monarchy.

A seasoned royal city, Naples was a serious contender for capital of Italy. But when Rome was wrested from the French in 1870, the newly formed Italian parliament transferred from its temporary home in Florence to the Eternal City. From being the grand capital of a Bourbon kingdom, Naples suddenly became a lowly regional capital – something Naples has never forgotten.

War & Peace

A poorer shadow of its former self, postunification Naples suffered two major blows: mass emigration and a cholera outbreak in 1884. In response to the cholera epidemic, a citywide clean-up was launched. The worst slums near the port were razed, Corso Umberto I was bulldozed through the city centre, and a sparkling new residential quarter appeared on the Vomero.

The fascists continued the building spree: an airport was built in 1936, railway and metro lines were laid, and the Vomero funicular opened for business. No sooner had many of these projects been completed than the strategic port city was hit by the full force of WWII. Savage aerial

> Between 1876 and 1913, 11.1 million Italians left their homeland in search of a better life in the New World. Of these, at least 4 million are believed to have been from Naples and the surrounding area. By 1927, 20% of the Italian population had emigrated.

EMIGRES

» Giuseppe Garibaldi

LEBRECHT MUSIC/ALAMY ©

1860
Garibaldi enters the city to a hero's welcome and Naples votes overwhelmingly to join a united Italy under the Savoy monarchy.

1884
A mass cholera epidemic strikes the city, prompting the closure of Naples' ancient aqueduct system and the launch of a major urban redevelopment project.

1889
Raffaele Esposito invents pizza margherita in honour of Queen Margherita, who takes her first bite of the Neapolitan staple on a royal visit to the city.

bombing by the Allies left over 20,000 people dead and much of the city in tatters.

Although the Nazis took Naples in 1943, they were quickly forced out by a series of popular uprisings between 26 and 30 September, famously known as the Quattro Giornate di Napoli (Four Days of Naples). Led by locals, especially by young *scugnizzi* (Neapolitan for 'street urchins') and ex-soldiers, the street battles paved the way for the Allied 'liberators' to enter the city on 1 October.

Despite setting up a provisional government in Naples, the Allies were confronted with an anarchic mass of troops, German prisoners of war and bands of Italian fascists all competing with the city's starving population for food. Then in 1944, to make matters worse, Mt Vesuvius erupted.

Overwhelmed, the Allied authorities turned to the underworld for assistance. As long as the Allies agreed to turn a blind eye towards their black-market activities, the Mafia was willing to help. And so the dreaded Camorra (p255) began to flourish.

Rocked by Quake & Scandals

The opportunistic Camorra made the most of the devastating earthquake that hit the region in 1980, siphoning off billions of lire poured into the devastated region. Striking on 23 November 1980, the 6.83 Richter scale quake left over 2700 dead and thousands more homeless.

In the decade that followed, *abusivismo* (illegal construction) flourished, profiteering mobsters partied publicly with the city's football icon of Argentine Diego Armando Maradona, and public services virtually ceased to exist. The situation was not unique to Naples – corruption and cronyism were rife across Italy.

It couldn't go on and in 1992 the Mani pulite (Clean Hands) campaign kicked into gear. What had started as an investigation into bribery at a retirement home in Milan quickly grew into a nationwide crusade against corruption. Industry bosses and politicians were investigated, with some imprisoned, and former prime minister Bettino Craxi fled Italy to avoid prosecution.

In Naples, the city voted its approval by electing as mayor former Communist Antonio Bassolino, whose promises to kick-start the city and fight corruption was music to weary Neapolitan ears. In the seven years that followed, a burst of urban regeneration gave Naples a refreshing sense of hope and pride. A-list artists were commissioned to deck out the city's new metro stations, world leaders flew in for the 1994 G7 summit, and arts festival Maggio dei Monumenti spiced up the city's calendar.

Despite winning a second term in 1997, Bassolino couldn't keep up the impressive momentum and in 2000 he was elected president of the

Although much has happened since it was written, Paul Ginsborg's *A History of Contemporary Italy: Society & Politics 1943–1988* remains one of the single most readable and insightful books on postwar Italy.

1934	1943	1980	1987
Screen icon Sophia Loren is born, spending her childhood in the old port town of Pozzuoli, west of Naples.	Allied bombing raids wreak havoc on the city, destroying the 14th-century Basilica di Santa Chiara. A year later, Mt Vesuvius erupts.	At 7.34pm on 23 November, a powerful earthquake rocks Campania, causing widespread damage and killing almost 3000 people.	Under Maradona, Napoli wins both the Serie A championship *(lo scudetto)* and the Coppa Italia. Mass elation sweeps across the city.

Campania region, a move many considered a political fudge to oust him from the day-to-day running of the city.

Into his shoes stepped Rosa Russo Jervolino, a former interior minister and Naples' first female mayor. Elected on a centre-left ticket firstly in 2001, and then for a second term in May 2006, her time in office was not spared of controversy. In April 2002 political chaos ensued after eight policemen were arrested on charges of torturing antiglobalisation protestors arrested at a 2001 government conference. Even more damaging were the waste disposal crises of 2003, 2006 and 2008, which saw images of rubbish-choked streets beamed across the world – a PR disaster for both the city and its administrators.

1992	2003	2004–05	2013
The anticorruption campaign known as Mani Pulite is launched. The following year, Antonio Bassolino is voted mayor and a major city clean-up begins.	The Campanian regional government launches Progetto Vesuvia in an attempt to clear Mt Vesuvius' heavily populated lower slopes. The €30,000 offered to relocate is rejected by most in the danger zone.	Tension between rival Camorra clans explodes on the streets of suburban Scampia and Secondigliano. In only four months, almost 50 people are gunned down in retribution attacks.	Naples plays host to the fourth Universal Forum of Cultures. The 101-day event sees further rejuvenation of the industrial Coroglio area between Naples and Pozzuoli.

The Arts

Dramatic, intense and deliciously contradictory, Naples and its coast have long been a fertile ground for creativity. Caravaggio, Ribera, Scarlatti, Totò, De Sica: the region's list of homegrown and adopted talent spans some of the world's finest painters, composers, playwrights and filmmakers. It's an overwhelming back catalogue, so why not start with the undisputed highlights?

Brush-Clutching Greats

While Naples has produced great paintings throughout the centuries, none compare to the works created in the golden 17th and 18th centuries. High on wealth and power, the booming city had become the New York of its time, a magnet for talented, ambitious artists desperate to put their stamp on Naples' grand new churches and palaces.

The main influence on 17th-century Neapolitan art was Milan-born Michelangelo Merisi da Caravaggio (1573–1610), who fled to the city in 1606 after killing a man in Rome. Although he only stayed for a year, his naturalist style and dramatic depiction of light and shade (termed *chiaroscuro*) in paintings like *Flagellation* (inside the Palazzo Reale di Capodimonte) had an electrifying effect on Naples' younger artists.

Among these was Giuseppe (or Jusepe) de Ribera (1591–1652), an aggressive, bullying Spaniard who arrived in Naples in 1616 after a seven-year stint in Rome. Ribera's combination of shadow, colour and gloomy naturalism proved hugely popular, best captured in his *capo lavoro* (masterpiece), the *Pietà*, inside the Certosa di San Martino.

A fledgling apprentice to Ribera, Naples-born Luca Giordano (1632–1705) found great inspiration in the luminous brushstrokes of Mattia Preti (1613–99), not to mention the pomp of Venetian artist Paolo Veronese and the flounce of Rome-based artist and architect Pietro da Cortona. By the second half of the 17th century, Giordano would become the single most prolific baroque artist in Naples, his many commissions including wall frescoes in the Duomo's nave and a ceiling painting in the adjacent Basilica di Santa Restituta. The Chiesa del Gesù Nuovo boasts several Giordano creations, including vault and wall frescoes in the Cappella della Visitazione and canvases in the Cappella di San Francesco Saverio. Upstaging them all is his *Triumph of Judith*, a ceiling fresco in the treasury of the church of the Certosa di San Martino.

Giordano's contemporary Francesco Solimena (1657–1747) was also influenced by Ribera, although his use of shadow and solid form showed a clearer link with Caravaggio. Solimena would also become an icon of Neapolitan baroque, and his lavish compositions – among them the operatic fresco *Expulsion of Eliodoro from the Temple* in the Chiesa del Gesù Nuovo – represented an accumulation of more than half a century of experimentation and trends, spanning Preti and Giordano himself.

Culture Vulture Musts

» Teatro San Carlo, Naples

» Ravello Festival, Ravello

» Napoli Teatro Festival, Naples

» Centro di Musica Antica Pietà de' Turchini, Naples

» La Mortella, Ischia

O SOLE MIO

The Neapolitan Score

In the 1700s, Naples was the world's opera capital, with industry heavy-weights flocking south to perform at the majestic Teatro San Carlo. Locally trained greats like Francesco Durante (1684–1755), Leonardo Vinci (1690–1730) and Tommaso Traetta (1727–79) wowed conservatories across Europe. Naples' greatest composer, Alessandro Scarlatti (1660–1725), trained at the esteemed conservatory at the Chiesa della Pietà dei Turchini on Via Medina, which also gave birth to the renowned music group Pietà de' Turchini.

Creator of around 100 operatic works, Scarlatti also played a leading role in the development of *opera seria* (serious opera), giving the world the three-part overture and the aria de capo.

Running parallel to the high-brow *opera seria* was *opera buffa* (comic opera). Inspired by the Neapolitan commedia dell'arte, the genre be-gan life as light-hearted, farcical interludes – *intermezzi* – performed between scenes of heavier classical operas. Kick-started by Scarlatti's *Il Trionfe Dell'onore* (The Triumph of Honour) in 1718, the contempo-rary interludes soon developed into a major, crowd-pleasing genre, with homegrown favourites including Giovanni Battista Pergolesi's *La Serva Padrona* (The Maid Mistress), Niccolò Piccinni's *La Cecchina* and Do-menico Cimarosa's *Il Matrimonio Segreto* (The Clandestine Marriage).

The following century saw the rise of the *la canzone napoletana* (Nea-politan song), its roots firmly planted in the annual Festa di Piedigrotta folk song festival. Some tunes celebrated the city, among them the world-famous *Funiculì, Funiculà*, an ode to the funicular that once scaled Mt Vesuvius. Others lamented one's distance from it. Either way, the songs deeply resonated with the locals, especially for the millions who boarded ships in search of a better life abroad.

The arrival of the American Allies in 1943 sparked another one of Nea-politans' musical predilections: jazz, rhythm and blues. As music journal-ist Francesco Calazzo puts it: 'As a port city, Naples has always absorbed foreign influences. Musically, the result is a fusion of styles, from Arab laments and Spanish folk to African percussion and American blues'.

This fusion came to the fore in the late 1970s. A defining moment for Neapolitan music, it saw new-wave pioneers like Eugenio Bennatto, Enzo Avitabile and Pino Daniele revive Neapolitan folk and cross it over with rock, roots and hypnotic African beats. Singing many of his songs in Neapolitan, Daniele's bittersweet lyrics about his beloved hometown – epitomised in songs like *Napule è* (Naples Is) – struck a particular chord with the public.

Naples' rich musical heritage formed the focus of John Turturro's film *Passione* (2010), a self-proclaimed 'cinematic love letter' to the city and its sounds.

The region's diaspora turned Neapolitan tunes into the most internationally recognisable form of Italian music. When the sheet music to the Italian national anthem was lost at the 1920 Olympic Games in Antwerp, the orchestra broke into O Sole Mio instead... It was the only Italian melody that everyone knew.

RIBERA: THE RUTHLESS SPANIARD

Despite becoming the leading light of Naples' mid-17th-century art scene, success did little to brighten Giuseppe de Ribera's dark side. Along with the Greek artist Belisiano Crenzio and local painter Giambattista Caracciolo, Lo Spagnoletto (The Little Spaniard, as Ribera was known) formed a cabal to stamp out any potential competition. Merciless in the extreme, they shied away from nothing to get their way. Ribera reputedly won a commission for the Cappella di San Gennaro in the Duomo by poisoning his rival Do-menichino (1581–1641) and wounding the assistant of a second competitor, Guido Reni (1575–1642). Much to the relief of other nerve-racked artists, the cabal eventually broke up when Caracciolo died in 1642.

Theatrical Legacies

Rivalling Naples' musical prowess is its theatrical tradition, considered one of Italy's oldest. Its most famous contribution to the world stage is the commedia dell'arte, dating back to the 16th century and rooted in the earthy ancient Roman comedy theatre of *Fabula Atellana* (Atellan Farce). Like its ancient inspiration, this highly animated genre featured a set of stock characters in masks acting out a series of semistandard situations. Performances were often used to satirise local situations, and based on a tried-and-tested recipe of adultery, jealousy, old age and love.

Not only did commedia dell'arte give birth to a number of legendary characters, including the Harlequin and Punchinello, it provided fertile ground for the development of popular theatre in Naples and was a tradition in which the great dramatist Raffaele Viviani (1888–1950) was firmly rooted. Viviani's focus on local dialect and the Neapolitan working class won him local success and the enmity of the Mussolini regime.

Despite Viviani's success, the most important figure in modern Neapolitan theatre remains Eduardo de Filippo (1900–84). The son of a famous Neapolitan actor, Eduardo Scarpetta (1853–1925), de Filippo made his stage debut at the age of four and over the next 80 years became a hugely successful actor, impresario and playwright. His body of often bittersweet work, which includes the classics *Il sindaco del Rione Sanità* (The Mayor of the Sanità Quarter) and *Sabato, Domenica e Lunedì* (Saturday, Sunday and Monday), encapsulated struggles well known to Neapolitans, from the injustice of being forced to live beyond the law to the fight for dignity in the face of adversity.

The *furbizia* (cunning) for which Neapolitans are famous is celebrated in de Filippo's play *Filumena Marturano*, in which a clever ex-prostitute gets her common-law husband to marry her by declaring him to be the father of one of her three *bambini*. The film adaptation, *Matrimonio all'italiana* (Marriage, Italian Style; 1964), stars Naples' homegrown siren Sophia Loren (1934–) alongside the great Marcello Mastroianni (1924–96).

Roberto de Simone (1933–) is another great Neapolitan playwright, not to mention a renowned composer and musicologist. While lesser known than de Filippo abroad, his theatrical masterpiece *La Gatta Cenerentola* (The Cat Cinderella) enjoyed a successful run in London in 1999. Artistic director of the Teatro San Carlo in the 1980s and later director of the Naples Conservatory, his extensive research into the city's folkloric tales and tunes has seen him revive rare comic operas and create a cantata for 17th-century Campanian revolutionary, Masaniello, as well as the oratorio *Eleonora*, in honour of the heroine of the Neapolitan revolution of 1799.

The Silver Screen

In this corner of Italy, locations read like a red-carpet roll call: 'la Loren' wiggled her booty through Naples' Sanità district in *Ieri, Oggi, Domani* (Yesterday, Today, Tomorrow; 1963), Julia Roberts did a little soul-searching in its *centro storico* (historic centre) in *Eat Pray Love* (2010), and Matt Damon and Gwyneth Paltrow toasted and tanned on Ischia and Procida in *The Talented Mr Ripley* (1999).

Naples' home-made offerings have often been intense and darkly comic, holding a mirror to the city's harsh realities. Feted for his 1948 neorealist masterpiece *Ladri di Biciclette* (Bicycle Thieves), Vittorio de Sica (1901–74) was a master at depicting the bittersweet struggle at the heart of so much Neapolitan humour. His two Neapolitan classics, *L'Oro di Napoli* (The Gold of Naples; 1954) and *Ieri, Oggi, Domani*, delighted audiences across the world.

RAP

Emerging in the 1990s, Naples' rap scene grew out of deep bitterness towards corruption, the Camorra and social injustices. The most prolific acts to date include hip-hop/reggae hybrids 99 Posse and Almamegretta, hardcore hip-hoppers Co'Sang (With Blood), and rock-crossover group A67. Anti-mafia writer Roberto Saviano collaborated on A67's 2008 album *Suburb*.

A PUPPET WITH PUNCH

His aliases are many, from Punchinello or Mr Punch in Britain to Petruska in Russia. In his home town of Naples, however, he's simply Pulcinella: the best-known character of the commedia dell'arte.

In his white costume and black hook-nosed mask, this squeaky-voiced clown is equally exuberant and lazy, optimistic and cynical, melancholic and vitreously witty. As a street philosopher, he is antiauthoritarian and is often seen beating the local copper with a stick (hence the term slapstick). At home, however, his wife's the beater and he's the victim.

While some trace his creation to a 16th-century actor in the town of Capua, others believe he has been dancing and stirring since the days of togas...or even longer. In fact, his iconic hook-nosed mask appears on frescoed Etruscan tombs in Tarquinia, north of Rome. The mask belongs to Phersu, a vicious Etruscan demon known as the Queen of Hell's servant.

While Naples' contemporary theatre scene remains fairly hit and miss, one of its leading talents is Enzo Moscato (1948–), whose work fuses a vibrant physicality with skilful use of dialect and music. His most famous work is the 1991 multiple-award-winning *Rasoi* (Razors).

Appearing with Loren in both *L'Oro di Napoli* and the slapstick farce *Miseria e Nobilità* (Misery and Nobility; 1954) is the city's other screen deity, Antonio de Curtis (1898–1967), aka Totò. Dubbed the Neapolitan Buster Keaton, Totò depicted Neapolitan cunning like no other. Born in the working-class Sanità district, he appeared in over 100 films, typically playing the part of a hustler living on nothing but his quick wits. It was a role that ensured Totò's cult status in a city where the art of *arrangiarsi* (getting by) is a way of life.

Inheriting Totò's mantle, Massimo Troisi (1953–94) is best known internationally for his role in *Il Postino* (The Postman). In his debut film of 1980, *Ricomincio da Tre* (I'm Starting from Three), he humorously tackles the problems faced by Neapolitans forced to head north for work. Troisi's cameo in the schlock murder mystery *No Frazie, il Caffè mi Rende Nervoso* (No Thanks, Coffee Makes Me Nervous; 1982) – arguably one of his funniest – sees a rambling, pyjama-clad Troisi hopelessly attempting to convince Funiculì, Funiculà (an unseen, helium-pitched psychopath set on sabotaging Naples' new jazz festival) that he is only loyal to the city's traditional cultural offerings.

A new wave of Neapolitan directors, including Antonio Capuano (1945–), Mario Martone (1959–), Pappi Corsicato (1960–) and Antonietta de Lillo (1960–), have also turned their cameras on the city in films such as Capuano's critically acclaimed *Luna Rossa* (Red Moon) of 2001. While Corsicato's queer-centric classics *Libera* (Free; 1993) and *I Bucchi Neri* (The Black Holes; 1995) evoke the ever-present link between the ancient and modern sides of Naples, de Lillo's finest offering to date, *Il Resto di Niente* (The Remains of Nothing; 2003), focuses on the psychological complexities of Eleonora Pimental de Fonesca; it's also the inspiration for De Simone's aforementioned oratorio.

Yet no recent film captures Naples' contemporary struggles as intensely as the multi-award-winning *Gomorra* (Gomorrah; 2008). Directed by Rome's Matteo Garrone (1968–) but based on the explosive book by Neapolitan Roberto Saviano, the film intertwines five stories of characters affected by the ruthless Camorra.

The Neapolitan Way of Life

There is nowhere more theatrical than Naples, a city in which everyday transactions become minor performances and traffic jams give rise to impromptu car-horn concerts. Both literally and metaphorically, locals air their laundry with pride, and the streets and squares are a stage on which to play out life's daily dramas.

Neapolitans know that many of the stereotypes foreigners hold of Italians – noisy, theatrical, food-loving, passionate and proud – refer to them. And they revel in it. Nowhere else in Italy are the people so conscious of their role in the theatre of everyday life and so addicted to its drama and intensity. Everyone has an opinion to give, a line to deliver or a sigh to perform. Eavesdropping is a popular pastime and knowing everyone else's business is a veritable sport. Neapolitans joke that if you were to collapse on the street a local would first want to know all the juicy details, and only after that would they think of calling an ambulance. In a city with a population density of 8566 people per sq km (45 times higher than the national average), this penchant for curiosity is understandable.

Hunting for Work

Naples' scarcity of space is matched by its scarcity of jobs. In mid 2012, overall unemployment in the region of Campania reached a staggering 31.39%, compared to the national average of 10.8%. In the same period, the number of jobless youth in the region reached 43.2%, significantly higher than the record-breaking national figure of 36.2%. These dire statistics are fuelling the country's panic-inducing *fuga dei cervelli* (brain drain), in which an ever-growing number of young university-educated Italians are heading abroad in search of a better future. The statistics are alarming. In a 2012 study of Italians under 30 by Milan's Instituto Toniolo, 48.9% of participants claimed that they were ready and willing to bid their country *'arrivederci'* to improve their job prospects. Of those with both a university degree and a job, only 33% were employed in an area that reflected their formal training.

This mass exodus is well documented in *La Fuga dei Talenti* (Flight of the Talented; www.fugadeitalenti.wordpress.com), a book-turned-blog by Italian journalist Sergio Nava aimed at reversing the trend. As Nava puts it, Italy is a country where 'the value of merit is largely disregarded', where 'it doesn't help to have a good CV, or an international profile: corporative interests and family relations come before anything else'. A recent study backed by Italy's ministry of labour showed that 61% of Italian companies recruit through personal introductions and recommendations. In a landscape so riddled with nepotism, putting in a good word is not simply a thoughtful gesture, it's essential for getting ahead. As the

Over 60% of Neapolitans aged 18 to 34 live at home. This is not because Naples is a city of *mammoni* (mamma's boys) and *figlie dipapa* (daddy's girls) – at least, not entirely. High rents make independent living prohibitively expensive for many young locals.

THE NEAPOLITAN MINDSET

Consummate performers and as *furbo* (cunning) as they come, Neapolitans are famous for their ingenuity. Only in Naples will you hear of vendors flogging T-shirts printed with seat-belt designs to fool short-sighted cops. Tough times have forced Neapolitans to become who they are today. For much of its history, the city was fought over, occupied and invaded by foreign powers that saw the locals as little more than taxable plebs. Consequently the Neapolitans learned early to fend for themselves and to get by on what they had – a situation still all too common.

old Italian adage goes, *Senza angeli non si va in cielo* (Without angels one can't reach heaven).

At the bottom end of the job chain are Italy's migrant communities. While a growing number of Chinese, Sri Lankans and Eastern Europeans are opening their own small businesses – mostly restaurants, grocery shops and cheap clothing outlets – the majority of immigrants in Naples work on construction sites and in private homes. Indeed, around 70% of immigrants in Naples work as housekeepers, babysitters or domestic carers for the elderly. In the 1970s and 1980s, housekeeping was a veritable dream job for the newly arrived. Having a maid was the ultimate status symbol for the city's rich, and as a result many immigrant workers enjoyed long-term job security and friends in high places. Since the 1990s, however, increased demand has come from the time-pressed middle classes. Unlike their upper-class counterparts, many of these more modest clients cannot afford to offer workers the same economic and legal perks. What was once a secure job is also now fraught with insecurity.

Even more precarious is the life of the street sellers, many of whom are *clandestini* (illegal immigrants) from Senegal. Known as *vù cumprà* – named for their trademark catchphrase, 'Do you want to buy?' – they sell counterfeit goods displayed on sheets along the pavement. When the police cruise by, the vendors swoop up their stock and flee, fearing arrest and possible deportation.

Outside the city the situation is worse for *clandestini*, who mostly find short-term seasonal work in the agricultural sector. The work is hard and lowly paid, and some employers are more than happy to exploit their illegal employees' vulnerable position. Many illegal African immigrants are smuggled into Italy by Mafia-run operatives. Once on Italian soil, they are hired out as farmhands, their Mafia handlers demanding a percentage of the labourers' below-minimum wages. Most workers receive no more than €25 for up to two weeks' work on southern Italian farms. Resentment caused by this exploitation exploded in January 2010, when the small Calabrian town of Rosarno became the scene of violent race riots that sent shock waves through Italy and the world.

The North/South Divide

Like New Yorkers, Neapolitans have a very strong sense of their own identity. As homegrown screen diva Sophia Loren once famously quipped, 'I'm not Italian, I am Neapolitan! It's another thing'.

Countless *meridionali* (southern Italians) have left their beloved homeland in search of greener economic pastures. While many have headed abroad, just as many have settled in Italy's wealthier north – a situation comically captured in *Ricomincio da tre* (I'm Starting from Three; 1980), a film starring late Neapolitan actor Massimo Troisi. Punchlines aside, the film reveals Italy's very real north/south divide.

From the Industrial Revolution to the 1960s, millions fled to the industrialised northern cities for factory jobs. As the saying goes, *Ogni vero Milanese ha un nonno Pugliese* (Every true Milanese has a Pugliese grandparent). For many of these in-house migrants, the welcome north of Rome was anything but warm. Disparagingly nicknamed *terroni* (peasants), many faced discrimination on a daily basis, from landlords to *baristi* (people who make coffee at a bar). While such overt discrimination is now practically nonexistent, historical prejudices linger. Many northerners resent their taxes being used to 'subsidise' the 'lazy', 'corrupt' south – a sentiment well exploited by the right-wing, Veneto-based Lega Nord (Northern League) party.

Yet negative attitudes can work both ways. One well-worn southern joke tells how God invented the north of Italy, realised his mistake, and consequently invented its infamous fog.

Family Life & Gender Battles

While Neapolitans pride themselves on their spontaneity and flexibility, Sunday *pranzo* (lunch) with the family is usually non-negotiable. Rain, hail or shine, this time of the week is sacred to Neapolitan families – a time to catch up on each others' lives, pick at the lives of politicians, footballers and celebrities, and eat like royalty. Indeed, the sacred status of Sunday lunch is a reminder that family remains the bedrock of Neapolitan life. Indeed, loyalty to family and friends is deeply engraved in the Neapolitan psyche. As Luigi Barzini (1908–84), author of *The Italians*, noted, 'A happy private life helps tolerate an appalling public life'. This chasm between the private arena and the public one is a noticeable aspect of the southern mentality, and has evolved over years of intrusive foreign domination. Some locals mightn't think twice about littering their street, but step inside their home and you'll get floors clean enough to eat on. After all, you'd never want someone dropping in and thinking you're a *barbone* (tramp), right?

Maintaining a *bella figura* (beautiful image) is very important to the average Neapolitan and how you and your family appear to the outside world is a matter of honour, respectability and pride. To many southern Italians, you are better than your neighbour if you own more and better things. This mentality is rooted in the past, when one really did need to own lots of things to attain certain social roles, and ultimately sustain your family. Yet *fare bella figura* (making a good impression) goes beyond a well-kept house, extending to dressing well, behaving modestly, performing religious and social duties and fulfilling all essential family obligations. In the context of the extended family, where gossip is rife, a good image protects one's privacy.

Neapolitan families are still among Italy's largest; their average size is 2.87, compared to 2.44 in Rome, 2.15 in Milan and 2.19 in Turin. It's still the norm to live at home until you marry and one-third of husbands still visit their mothers every day. While many of these will have a bowl of their favourite pasta waiting for them, some will also have their laundry

Steer clear of chrysanthemums when buying flowers for a local. In Italy they're only used to decorate graves.

FLOWERS

THE OLD PROVERBIAL

They might be old cliches, but proverbs can be quite the cultural revelation. Here are five of Naples' well-worn best:

» *A léngua nun tène òsso ma ròmpe ll'òssa* (The tongue has no bone but it breaks bones.)

» *A mughièra 'e ll'àte é sèmpe cchiù bbòna* (Other people's wives are always more beautiful.)

» *Ògne scarrafóne è bèllo 'a màmma sóia* (Even a beetle is beautiful to its mother.)

» *E pariénte so còmme 'e scàrpe: cchiù so strìtte e cchiù te fànno màle* (Relatives are like shoes: the tighter they are the more they hurt.)

» *L'amico è come l'ombrello, quando piove non lo trovi mai* (The friend is like the umbrella: when it's raining, you never find it.)

IN FOOTBALL WE TRUST

Catholicism may be Italy's official faith, but its true religion is *calcio* (football). On any given weekend from late August to May, you'll find millions of *tifosi* (football fans) at the *stadio* (stadium), glued to the television, or checking the score on their mobile phone. Naples is no exception: the city is home to southern Italy's most successful team (Napoli) and the country's third largest stadium (Stadio San Paolo), not to mention a small shrine dedicated to Napoli's greatest-ever on-field hero, Diego Maradona.

Swooped from Barcelona for a record-breaking €12 million in 1984, the Argentine football star would lead Napoli to its greatest ever glory in the 1986–87 football season, winning both the Serie A title and the Coppa Italia. A first for any mainland southern Italian team, the twin win transformed Maradona into a Neapolitan demi-god.

While captaining Argentina in the 1990 FIFA World Cup, Maradona infamously encouraged the city to cheer on Argentina in the semi-finals against Italy in Naples. Tapping into Italy's north/south tension, Maradona controversially declared: 'I don't like the fact that now everybody is asking Neapolitans to be Italian and to support their national team. Naples has always been marginalised by the rest of Italy. It is a city that suffers the most unfair racism'.

Thankfully, any north/south resentment was relegated to the sidelines in 2006 when Neapolitan pin-up Fabio Cannavaro led Italy to victory in the 2006 World Cup. Nine months after the win, hospitals in northern Italy reported a baby boom.

In interactions with locals, ocus on the positives. Although Neapolitans regularly lament their city's shortcomings, jibes from a *straniero* (foreigner) can cause offence.

freshly washed and ironed. According to a 2009 report by the Uomini Casalinghi (The Italian Association of Househusbands), 95% of Italian men have never turned on a washing machine, and 70% of them have never used a stove. Indeed, a survey released by the Organisation of Economic Co-Operation and Development (OECD) in 2010 found that Italian men enjoy almost 80 more minutes of leisure time daily than their female counterparts. Ironically, a narrow job market has seen women's time in education lengthen. According to figures released by Italy's bureau of statistics, Istat, in 2008, enrolment in tertiary education in Campania was 47.9% for women, and 35.1% for men. Women also out-performed their fellow male students on the graduation front, with 40.6% of university-enrolled females obtaining a basic degree, compared to 29.4% of male students.

Yet, while women are moving forward, obstacles remain. Men continue to receive roughly 10% more in their pay packet than their female colleagues, while some employers still see women as a risk, likely to ditch their jobs to raise a family. Add a largely ineffective childcare system and the juggling of work, and motherhood becomes a rather stressful act for many Neapolitan women.

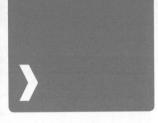

Saints & Superstitions

To call Naples 'magical' verges on the literal. This is Europe's esoteric metropolis par excellence; a Mediterranean New Orleans with less voodoo and more Catholic guilt. Here, miracles pack out cathedrals, dreams channel lottery numbers, and horn-shaped charms ward off the dreaded *mal'occhio* (evil eye). Myths and legends litter the streets, from tales of human sacrifice in the Cappella Sansevero to that of a prophetic egg below the Castel dell'Ovo.

In Naples, it is still possible to see elaborate, coach-style hearses drawn by as many as eight horses. It seems that while people die, the obsession with *fare bella figura* (keeping up appearances) does not.

Friends in High Places

Headlining the city's supernatural scene are the saints. Veritable celebrities, fireworks explode in their honour, fans flock to kiss their marble feet and newborn *bambini* (children) take on their names. That Gennaro is the most common boy's name in Naples is no coincidence; San Gennaro is the city's patron saint. As in much of southern Italy, Neapolitans celebrate their *giorno omastico* (name day) with as much gusto as they do their actual birthdays. Forgetting a friend's name day is a bigger faux pas than forgetting their birthday because everyone knows (or should know) the most important saints' days.

For the religiously inclined, these haloed helpers play a more significant role in their spiritual life than the big 'G' himself. While the Almighty is

---

LOTTERY DREAMS

In every visible aspect the Neapolitan lottery is the same as every other lottery – tickets are bought, numbers marked and the winning numbers pulled out of a closely guarded hat. It differs, however, in the way that Neapolitans select their numbers. They dream them, or rather they interpret their dreams with the aid of *La Smorfia*, a kind of dream dictionary.

According to the good book, if you dream of God or Italy and you should pick number one; for a football player choose number 43 (Maradona, a football-playing god – or *nu dio 'e giocatore* in local parlance – is 43). Other symbols include dancing (37), crying (21), fear (90) and a woman's hair (55).

Some leave the interpreting to the lotto-shop expert by whispering their dreams into the shop owner's ears (no-one wants to share a winning combination) and letting them choose the numbers. According to the locals, the city's luckiest *ricevitoria* (lotto shop) is the one at Porta Capuana. Run by the same family for more than 200 years, the current owner's grandmother was considered a dream-theme expert. To this day, people bring their dreams here from as far afield as the US, Spain and Switzerland.

While *La Smorfia's* origins are obscure, links are often made to the number-word mysticism of the Jewish Kabbalah. The term itself most likely derives from Morpheus, the Greek god of dreams, suggesting that the tradition itself is linked to Naples' ancient Greek origins and to the Hellenic tradition of oneirocriticism (dream interpretation).

VICTORY OF THE SHRINES

It only takes a quick stroll through the *centro storico* (historic centre), Quartieri Spagnoli or Sanità district to work out that small shrines are a big hit in Naples. A kitschy combo of electric votive candles, Catholic iconography and fresh or plastic flowers, they adorn everything from *palazzo* (large building) facades to courtyards and staircases. Most come with an inscription, confirming the shrine as a tribute *per grazie ricevute* (for graces received) or *ex-voto* (in fulfilment of a vow).

The popularity of the shrines can be traced back to the days of Dominican friar Gregorio Maria Rocco (1700–82). Determined to make the city's dark, crime-ridden laneways safer, he convinced the Bourbon monarch to light up the lanes with oil lamps. The lamps were hastily trashed by the city's petty thieves who relied on darkness to trip up their victims with rope. Thankfully, the quick-thinking friar had a better idea. Banking on the city's respect for its saints, he encouraged locals to erect illuminated shrines. The idea worked and the streets did become safer, for even the toughest of petty thieves wouldn't dare upset an adored celestial idol.

seen as stern and distant (just like any old-school Italian papa), the saints enjoy a more familial role as intercessor and confidant. Not everyone is impressed: a sign inside the Santissima Annunziata church reminds the faithful to venerate Christ at the altar before sidling off to the side chapels. Despite the request, many keep marching straight to the saints.

Topping the list of go-betweens is the Virgin Mary, whose status as maternal protector strikes a deep chord in a society where mothers have always fiercely defended the rights of their precious sons. Festival days in honour of the Madonna are known to whip up mass hysteria, best exemplified by the annual Feast of the Madonna dell'Arco. Held on Easter Monday, it sees thousands of pilgrims called *fujenti* (Neapolitan for 'those who run') walk barefoot to the Santuario della Madonna dell'Arco, located near the village of Sant'Anastasia at the foot of Mt Vesuvius. The focus of their devotion is an unusual image of the Virgin Mary, in which her cheek is wounded. According to legend, the wound's origins go back to Easter Monday in 1500, when a disgruntled mallet player hit the Virgin's image with a wooden ball. Miraculously, the image began to bleed, leading to the sour sport's hanging and the construction of the sanctuary on the site of the event. As they approach the sanctuary, the *fujenti* run towards it. Some fall into a trance, with many more shouting, crying and walking on their knees towards the image in what can be described as a collective purging of guilt and pain. In Naples, the lead-up to the festival is an event in itself. From the week following the Epiphany (6 January) to Easter Monday, hundreds of neighbourhood *congreghe* (instrument-playing congregations) parade through the streets, carrying a statue of the Madonna, collecting offerings for the big day and playing an incongruous medley of tunes (think 'Ave Maria' followed by a 1970s Raffaella Carrà pop hit).

Exactly which saint you consult can depend on what you're after. If it's an addition to the family, chances are you'll head straight to the former home of Santa Maria Francesca delle Cinque Piaghe to sit on the saint's miraculous chair. It's the closest thing to a free fertility treatment in Naples.

On the opposite side of Via Toledo, in the Chiesa del Gesù Nuovo, entire rooms are dedicated to Dr Giuseppe Moscati (1880–1927), a much-loved local medic canonised in 1987. Here, body-part-shaped *ex-voti* smother the walls, each one a testament to the MD's celestial intervention.

For centuries, locals believed that a crocodile lurked below the Castel Nuovo. Some said the reptile lunched on Queen Joan II's ex-lovers. Others swore that political prisoners were on the menu. According to writer and intellectual Benedetto Croce, the crocodile was eventually caught using a horse's thigh as bait.

For many, the wish list doesn't stop at good health or the pitter-patter of little feet, with common requests ranging from next week's winning lottery numbers to a decent-looking date.

Despite the Madonna's popularity, the city's ultimate holy superhero is San Gennaro. Every year in May, September and December thousands of Neapolitans cram themselves into the Duomo to pray for a miracle: that the blood of Naples' patron saint, kept here in two phials, will liquefy and save Naples from any potential disaster.

According to scientists, the so-called miracle has a logical explanation. Apparently, it's all to do with thixotrophy; that is, the property of certain compounds to liquefy when shaken and then to return to their original form when left to stand. To verify this, however, scientists would have to analyse the blood, something the Church has effectively blocked by refusing permission to open the phial.

And while many locals acknowledge the scientific line, the fact remains that when the blood liquefies the city breathes a sigh of relief. After all, when the miracle failed in 1944 Mt Vesuvius erupted, and when it failed to happen in 1980, a catastrophic earthquake hit the city the same year.

Beware the Evil Eye

The concept of luck plays a prominent role in the Neapolitan mindset. Curse-deterring amulets are as plentiful as crucifix pendants and the same Neapolitan who makes the sign of the cross when passing a church will make the sign of the horns (by extending their thumb, index finger and little finger and shaking their hand to the ground) to keep the *mal'occhio* (evil eye) at bay.

A common belief throughout Italy, though particularly strong in the country's south, *mal'occhio* refers to misfortune cast upon an individual by a malevolent or envious person. In fact, Neapolitans often refer to this bad luck as *jettatura*, a derivative of the Italian verb *gettare* (to throw or cast).

Ready to deflect the bad energy is the city's most iconic amulet-cum-souvenir: the *corno*. Usually red and shaped liked a single curved horn, its evil-busting powers are said to lie in its representation of the bull and its sexual vigour.

Another traditional, though increasingly rare, deflector of bad luck is the *'o Scartellat*. Usually an elderly man, you'll occasionally spot him burning incense through the city's older neighbourhoods, clearing the streets of bad vibes and inviting good fortune. The title itself is Neapolitan for those suffering from kyphosis (over-curvature of the upper back) as the task was once the domain of posture-challenged figures. According to Neapolitan lore, touching a hunchback's hump brings good luck, as does stepping in dog poop and having wine spilt on you accidentally.

Mythical Hotspots

» Festa di San Gennaro
» Casa e Chiesa di Santa Maria Francesca delle Cinque Piaghe
» Cimitero delle Fontanelle
» Madonna del Carmine
» Complesso Museale di Santa Maria delle Anime del Purguatorio ad Arco

SAINTS & SUPERSTITIONS

A knight who lay down on St Patrizia's tomb was inexplicably cured of all his ills. Seized by religious fervour, he opened her tomb and tore out one of her teeth. Blood flowed miraculously and the knight captured it in two phials, now safely stored in the Chiesa di San Gregorio Armeno.

DEATH & THE CITY

Rattled by earthquakes and the odd volcanic eruption, it makes sense that the Neapolitans are a fatalistic lot. Indeed, the city's intense passion for life is only matched by its curious attachment to death. Here, contemporary culture's death-defying delusions are constantly undermined, whether by death notice–plastered walls, shrines dedicated to the dearly departed or edible treats with names like *torrone dei morti* (nougat of the dead), the latter merrily gobbled on All Saints' Day. Carved skulls adorn churches and cloisters, such as those adorning the Chiostro Grande (Great Cloister) inside the Certosa di San Martino; a constant reminder of one's mortal status.

Scandalous Souls

One figure who could have used some good luck was Donna Maria d'Avalos, who in October 1590 met a gruesome end in the Palazzo dei Di Sangro on Piazza San Domenico Maggiore. Her murderer was Carlo Gesualdo, one of the late Renaissance's most esteemed composers, not to mention d'Avalos' husband. Suspecting her of infidelity, Gesualdo tricked his wife into thinking that he was away on a hunting trip. Instead, Gesualdo was waiting in the wings, ready to catch d'Avalos and her lover, Don Fabrizio Carafa, red-handed. According to eyewitnesses, Gesualdo entered the apartment with three men, shouting 'Kill the scoundrel, along with this harlot!'. Officials investigating the crime scene described finding a mortally wounded Carafa lying on the floor, covered in blood and wearing a woman's nightgown adorned with ruffs of black silk. On the bed was d'Avalos, nightgown drenched in blood and throat slit.

One doubts that Gesualdo's jealous rage was soothed by Carafa's pin-up looks – it's said that the younger nobleman was so devastatingly handsome that he was known around town as *l'angelo* (the Angel). As a nobleman himself, Gesualdo was immune from prosecution, though a fear of retribution for the murders saw him flee to his hometown, Venosa.

In the decades that followed Gesualdo's own death, the Prince of Venosa became a semimythical figure, his name associated with ever more lurid tales of bloody revenge. Some say that 'the Angel's' death wasn't enough for the betrayed husband, who subsequently murdered his own infant son for fear that he belonged to Carafa. According to other accounts, Gesualdo's victims included his father-in-law, who had come seeking his own revenge.

And then there is the beautiful Maria d'Avalos herself, whose scantily dressed ghost is said to still haunt Piazza San Domenico Maggiore when the moon is full, desperately searching for her slaughtered sweetheart.

The Palazzo dei Di Sangro itself was built for the noble Di Sangro family, whose most famous member, Raimondo di Sangro (1710–71), remains one of Naples' most rumour-ridden characters. Inventor, scientist, soldier and alchemist, the Prince of Sansevero came up with some nifty inventions, among them a waterproof cape for Charles III of Bourbon and a mechanical land-and-water carriage 'drawn' by life-size cork horses. He also introduced freemasonry into the Kingdom of Naples, resulting in a temporary excommunication from the Catholic Church.

Yet even a papal rethink couldn't quell the salacious stories surrounding Raimondo, which included castrating promising young sopranos and knocking off seven cardinals to make furniture with their skin and bones. Even fellow Freemason Count Alessandro Cagliostro – who went on trail before the Inquisition court in Rome in 1790 – confessed that everything he knew about alchemy and the dark arts he learned from di Sangro. According to Italian philosopher Benedetto Croce (1866–1952), who wrote about di Sangro in his book *Storie e leggende napoletane* (Neapolitan Stories and Legends), the alchemist held a Faustian fascination for the *centro storico's* masses. To them, his supposed knack for magic saw him master everything from replicating the miracle of San Gennaro's blood to reducing marble to dust with a simple touch.

For centuries rumours surrounded the two perfect anatomical models in the crypt of the di Sangro funerary chapel, the Cappella Sansevero. One popular legend suggested the bodies were those of his defunct domestics. Even taller was the tale that the servants were far from dead when the Prince got started on the embalming. Cruel fiction, undoubtedly, but even today the models' realistic detail leaves many questions unanswered.

So popular was the cult of the *anime pezzentelle* (poor souls) that a special tram ran to the Cimitero delle Fontanelle, packed each Monday with flower-laden locals. Involving the adoption and veneration of skulls (representing a soul trapped in purgatory), the cult was banned by the Church in 1969.

Across from the Solfatara Crater – reputed site of San Gennaro's beheading in 305 – is the Santuario di San Gennaro alla Solfatara, home to the marble slab used for his murder. Legend has it that when the saint's blood liquefies, dark blood stains reappear on the slab.

The Campanian Table

Sampling Campania's larder is an intensely flavoursome experience, reflecting the locals' own infamous seductiveness. Everything seems to taste that little bit better here – the tomatoes are sweeter, the mozzarella is silkier and the *caffè* (coffee) is richer and stronger. Some put it down to the rich volcanic soil, others to the region's sun and water. Complementing these natural perks is the advantage of well-honed traditions, passed down through the generations and still faithfully followed. While LA and London fuss about with fusion, Neapolitan cooks remember what their mammas taught them: keep it simple, seasonal and fresh.

A Historical Melting Pot

The region's culinary line-up is an exotic culmination of foreign influence and local resourcefulness. In its 3000-year history, Naples has played countless roles, from Roman holiday resort and medieval cultural hot spot to glittering European capital. As the foreign rulers have come and gone, they've left their mark – on the art and architecture, on the local dialect and on the food. The ancient Greeks turned up with the olive trees, grapevines and durum wheat. Centuries later, the Byzantines and Arab traders from nearby Sicily brought in the pine nuts, almonds, raisins and honey that they used to stuff their vegetables. They also brought what was to become the mainstay of the Neapolitan diet and, in time, Italy's most famous food – pasta.

Although it was first introduced in the 12th century, pasta really took off in the 17th century when it established itself as the poor man's food of choice. Requiring only a few simple ingredients – just flour and water at its most basic – pasta proved a lifesaver as the city's population exploded in the 17th century. The nobility, however, continued to shun pasta until Gennaro Spadaccini invented the four-pronged fork in the early 18th century.

During Naples' Bourbon period (1734–1860), two parallel gastronomic cultures developed: that of the opulent Spanish monarchy; and that of the streets, the *cucina povera* (cuisine of the poor). As much as the former was elaborate and rich, the latter was simple and healthy.

The food of the poor, the so-called *mangiafoglie* (leaf eaters), was largely based on pasta and vegetables grown on the fertile volcanic plains around Naples. Aubergines (eggplants), artichokes, courgettes (zucchini), tomatoes and peppers were among the staples, while milk from sheep, cows and goats was used to make cheese. Flat breads imported from Greek and Arab lands, the forebear of the pizza, were also popular. Meat and fish were expensive and reserved for special occasions.

Meanwhile, in the court kitchens, the top French cooks of the day were working to feed the insatiable appetites of the Bourbon monarchy.

The excellent food and travel portal www.deliciousitaly.com lists culinary courses and tours. Another useful website for lovers of Italian food and wine is www.gamberorosso.it (mostly in Italian), which offers a plethora of information on Italian food, wine, culinary events and courses.

APPETISING READS

Pique your appetite with the following insightful guides to Campania's culinary riches:

» David Ruggerio's *Italian Kitchen: Family Recipes from the Old Country* (David Ruggerio) Filled with the secrets of a Neapolitan kitchen.

» Guiliano Bugialli's *Food of Naples and Campania* (Guiliano Bugialli) A culinary journey through the region led by a prolific Italian-cookery writer.

» *La Pizza: The True Story from Naples* (Nikko Amandonico and Natalia Borri) Sumptuously illustrated history of pizza, set in Naples' kaleidoscopic streets.

» *Naples at Table: Cooking in Campania* (Arthur Schwartz) Local food trivia and 250 recipes.

» *The Food Lover's Companion to Naples and the Campania* (Carla Capalbo) An encyclopedic guide to Campania's food producers and nosh spots.

The headstrong queen Maria Carolina, wife of King Ferdinand I, was so impressed by her sister Marie Antoinette's court in Versailles that she asked to borrow some chefs. These Gallic imports obviously took to the Neapolitan air, creating among other things highly elaborate *timballi di pasta* (pasta pies), the *gattò di patate* (potato tart) and the iconic *babà*, a mushroom-shaped sponge cake soaked in rum and sugar.

More contentious are the origins of Naples' most famous pastry: the flaky, seashell-shaped *sfogliatella*. Filled with cinnamon-infused ricotta and candied fruit, it was created, some say, by French chefs for the king of Poland in the 18th century. Others say that it was invented by 18th-century nuns in Conca dei Marini, a small village on the Amalfi Coast. Nowadays its two most popular forms are the soft and doughy shortcrust *frolla*, and the crispy, filo-style 'riccia' version.

During spring, summer and early autumn, towns across southern Italy celebrate *sagre*, the festivals of local foods in season. Scan www.prodottitipici.com/sagre (in Italian) for a lip-smacking list.

Enjoy Limoncello?

If so, there is no need to weigh down your luggage with umpteen bottles (with the risk of breakage and booze–soaked clothing), as it is remarkably easy to make. Check the internet for a good recipe (consider following the links on www.jamieoliver.com or www.bbcgoodfood.com) and make sure you use good unwaxed lemons, even if they are *not* the sun-kissed variety from Capri. If you speak Italian, check out the www.limoncellodiprocida.it website where there is a good recipe (and they also ship...).

Campanian Culinary Icons

Pizza

Despite the Bourbons' lavish legacy, Campania's no-nonsense attitude to food – keep it simple, keep it local and keep it coming – remains deeply rooted in the traditions of the poor. This is especially true in its predilection for pizza, a mainstay of *cucina povera* and one of the foundations on which Naples' gastronomic reputation stands.

A derivation of the flat breads of ancient Greece and Egypt, pizza was already a common street snack by the time the city's 16th-century Spanish occupiers introduced the tomato to Italy. The New World topping cemented the pizza's popularity and in 1738 Naples' first pizzeria opened its doors on Port'Alba, where it still stands. Soon after, the city's *pizzaioli* (pizza makers) began to enjoy minor celebrity status.

To this day, the city's most famous dough-kneader remains Raffaelle Esposito, inventor of the classic pizza margherita. As the city's top *pizzaiolo*, Esposito was summoned to fire up a treat for a peckish king Umberto I and his wife Queen Margherita on a royal visit in 1889. Determined to impress the Italian royals, Esposito based his creation of tomato, moz zarella and basil on the red, white and green flag of the newly unified Italy. The resulting topping met with the queen's approval and was subsequently named in her honour.

More than a century later, pizza purists claim that you really can't top Esposito's classic combo when made by a true Neapolitan *pizzaiolo*. Not everyone is in accordance and Italians are often split between those who favour the thin-crust Roman variant, and those who go for the thicker Neapolitan version.

According to the official Associazione Verace Pizza Napoletana (Real Neapolitan Pizza Association), genuine Neapolitan pizza dough must be made using highly refined type 00 wheat flour (a small dash of type 0 flour is permitted), compressed or natural yeast, salt, and water with a pH level between 6 and 7. While a low-speed mixer can be used for kneading the dough, only hands can be used to form the *disco di pasta* (pizza base), which should not be thicker than 3mm. The pizza itself should be cooked at 485°C (905°F) in a doubled-domed, wood-fired oven using oak, ash, beech or maple timber.

Pasta

Pizza's bedfellow, pasta, arrived in Naples via Sicily where it had first been introduced by Arab merchants. The dry, windy Campanian climate was later found to be ideal for drying pasta, and production took off in a big way, especially after the 1840 opening of Italy's first pasta plant in Torre Annunziata.

The staple itself is divided into *pasta fresca* (fresh pasta), devoured within a few days of purchase, and *pasta secca* (dried pasta), handy for long-term storage. One of the top varieties of local *pasta fresca* is Amalfi's own *scialatielli*, a flat noodle both longer and thicker than tagliatelle and often 'pinched' in the middle. With its name stemming from the Neapolitan term *sciglià* (to tousle), it's a perfect match for delicate tomato and seafood *sughi* (sauces).

This said, Naples is more famous for its *pasta secca*, the most obvious examples of which are spaghetti, macaroni, penne (smallish tubes cut at an angle) and rigatoni (similar to penne but with ridges on them). Made from *grano duro* (durum wheat) flour and water, it's often served (al dente, of course) with vegetable-based *sughi*, which are generally less rich than the traditional *pasta fresca* varieties.

The best of the region's artisanal pastas comes from the small town of Gragnano, some 30km southeast of Naples. A pasta-producing hub since the 17th century, its main street was specifically built along the sun's axis so that the pasta put out to dry by the town's *pastifici* (pasta factories) would reap a full day's sunshine.

As for the queen of the region's pasta dishes, it's hard to beat the mouth-watering *pasta al forno* (baked pasta), a decadent combination of

PIZZA

THE CAMPANIAN TABLE

There is no seafood on a Neapolitan pizza marinara – just tomato, garlic, oregano and extra-virgin olive oil. The pizza's name stems from its popularity with local fishermen, who'd take it out to sea for lunch.

TABLE RULES

» Make eye contact when toasting and never clink using plastic cups; it's bad luck!

» Pasta is eaten with a fork only.

» Bread is not eaten with pasta – unless you're cleaning up the sauce afterwards.

» It's fine to eat pizza with your hands.

» If in doubt, dress smart.

» If invited to someone's home, take a tray of *dolci* (sweets) from a *pasticceria* (pastry shop).

macaroni, tomato sauce, mozzarella and, depending on the recipe, hard-boiled egg, meatballs and sausage. No less than a gastronomic 'event', it's often cooked for Sunday lunch and other special occasions.

Vegetables & Fruits

Poverty and sunshine also helped develop Campania's prowess with vegetables. Dishes like *zucchine fritte* (panfried courgettes), *parmigiana di melanzane* (fried aubergines layered with hard-boiled eggs, mozzarella, onion, tomato sauce and basil) and *peperoni sotto aceto* (marinated peppers) are common features of both antipasto buffets and the domestic kitchen table.

The word *melanzana* (aubergine) comes from 'mela insana', meaning crazy apple. In Latin it was called *solanum insanum* as it was thought to cause madness.

Some of the country's finest produce is grown in the mineral-rich volcanic soil of Mt Vesuvius and its surrounding plain, including tender *carciofi* (artichokes) and *cachi* (persimmons), as well as Campania's unique green *friarielli* – a bitter broccoli-like vegetable *saltata in padella* (panfried), spiked with *peperoncino* (red chilli) and often served with diced *salsiccia di maiale* (pork sausage).

In June, slow-food fans should look out for *albicocche vesuviana* (Vesuvian apricots), known locally as *crisommole* and given IGP (Indicazione Geografica Protetta; Protected Denomination of Origin) status.

DOC (Denominazione di Origine; Certified Designation of Origin) status is granted to another lauded local, the *pomodoro San Marzano* (San Marzano plum tomato). Grown near the small Vesuvian town of the same name, it's Italy's most famous and cultivated tomato, best known for its low acidity and intense, sweet flavour. Its sauce, *conserva di pomodoro*, is made from super-ripe tomatoes, cut and left to dry in the sun for at least two days to concentrate the flavour. This is the sauce that adorns so many of Naples' signature pasta dishes, including the colourfully named *spaghetti alla puttanesca* (whore's spaghetti), whose sauce is a lip-smacking blend of tomatoes, black olives, capers, anchovies and (in some cases) a dash of red chilli.

A richer tomato-based classic with aristocratic origins is the Neapolitan *ragù*, whose name stems from the French ragout. A tomato and meat sauce, it is left to simmer for about six hours before being served with *maccheroni* (macaroni-type pasta).

THE CULT OF CAFFÈ

The Neapolitan coffee scene trades hipsters, soy and syphons for retro-vested baristas, chintzy fit-outs and un-hyped java brilliance. Here, velvety, lingering espresso is not a fashion statement – it's a birthright. In most cases, it's also a quick, unceremonious swill standing at local bars. But don't be fooled – the speed with which it's consumed does not diminish the importance of its quality.

According to the Neapolitans, it's the local water that makes their coffee stronger and better than any other in Italy. To drink it like a local, keep milky options like caffè latte and cappuccino for the morning. After 11am, espresso and caffè macchiato (an espresso with a drop of milk) are the norm. For a weaker coffee (shame on you!) ask for a caffè lungo (a watered down espresso in a larger cup) or a caffè americano (an even weaker version of the caffè lungo).

Another ritual is the free *bicchiere d'acqua* (glass of water), offered either *liscia* (uncarbonated) or *frizzante* (sparkling) with your coffee. Drink it before your coffee to cleanse your palate. Just don't be surprised if you're not automatically offered one. After all, what would a heathen *straniero* (foreigner) know about coffee? Don't be shy – smile sweetly and ask for *un bicchiere d'acqua, per favore.*

THE DOLCE VITA

Fragrant *sfogliatelle* (ricotta-filled pastries) and trickling *babà* (sponge cakes) aren't the only *pasticceria* (pastry shop) staples you'll find on a Campanian table. Savour the sweet life with the following local favourites:

» **Cassatina** The Neapolitan version of the Sicilian cassata, this minicake is made with *pan di Spagna* (sponge), ricotta and candied fruit, and covered in glazed sugar.

» **Pastiera** Traditionally baked at Easter (but available year-round), this latticed tart is made of shortcrust pastry and filled with ricotta, cream, candied fruit and cereals flavoured with orange-blossom water.

» **Torta di Ricotta e Pera** A ricotta-and-pear torte that's light, tangy and dangerously moreish.

» **Delizia al Limone** A light, tangy lemon cake made with *limoncello* (lemon liqueur).

» **Paste Reali** Cleverly crafted miniatures of fruit and vegetables, these sweets are made of almond paste and sugar (marzipan) and gobbled up at Christmas.

» **Raffioli** A yuletide biscuit made with sponge and marzipan, and sprinkled with icing sugar.

THE CAMPANIAN TABLE

Mozzarella di Bufala

So you think the cow's milk mozzarella served in Capri's *insalata caprese* (a salad made of mozzarella, tomato, basil and olive oil) is delicious? Taste Campania's *mozzarella di bufala* (buffalo-milk mozzarella) and you'll move onto an entirely different level of deliciousness. Made on the plains surrounding Caserta and Paestum, it's best eaten when freshly made that morning, its rich, sweet flavour and luscious texture nothing short of a revelation. You'll find it served in trattorias (informal restaurants) and restaurants across the region. Sorrento even has a dedicated mozzarella eatery, Sorrento's Inn Bufalito. Bought fresh from *latterie* (dairies), it comes lukewarm in a plastic bag filled with a slightly cloudy liquid: the run-off from the mozzarella making. As for that irresistible taste, it's the high fat content and buffalo milk protein that give the cheese the distinctive, pungent flavour so often absent in the versions sold abroad. Even more decadent is the *burrata*, a mozzarella filled with a wickedly buttery cream. Burrata itself was invented in the neighbouring region of Puglia.

Although some producers find these official Italian classifications unduly costly and creatively constraining, the DOCG (Denominazione di Origine Garantita) and DOC (Denominazione di Origine Controllata) designations are awarded to food and wine that meet regional quality-control standards.

Local Specialities

Campania's regional specialities are testament to the locals' obsession for produce with a postcode. Beyond the STG (Specialità Tradizionale Garantita; Guaranteed Traditional Speciality) protected *pizza napoletana*, surprisingly light *fritture* (fried snacks) and fragrant pastries, Naples' bounty of staples include *pizza di scarole* (escarole pie), 'Napoli' salami, wild fennel sausages, and *sanguinaccio* (a cream of candied fruits and chocolate made during Carnevale).

West of Naples, in the Campi Flegrei, Pozzuoli's lively fish market attests to the town's reputation for superlative seafood. Another Campi Flegrei local is the IGP-status Annurca apple, ripened on a bed of straw to produce the fruit's distinctive stripy red hue.

Seafood revelations are also the norm on the island of Procida, where local concoctions include *volamarina* (moonfish) tripe with tomato and chilli and anchovy-stuffed squid. And while neighbouring Ischia is equally seafood-savvy, the island's agricultural history shines through in classics like *coniglio all'ischitana*, made using locally bred rabbits.

To the southeast of Naples, the Sorrentine peninsula also heaves with local specialities, from the ubiquitous *gnocchi alla sorrentina* to refreshing *limoncello* sorbet. Feast on *burrino incamiciato* (*fior di latte* mozzarella cheese wickedly filled with butter) and pizza-by-the-metre in Vico Equinese, or ricotta-stuffed cannelloni in Sorrento, whose famous walnuts are used to make nocino liqueur. Almonds and chocolate are the key ingredients in the sugar-dusted *torta caprese* (Caprese cake) which alongside seafood dishes like linguine pasta in scorpion-fish sauce, and the refreshing *insalata caprese* (a salad made of mozzarella, tomato, basil and olive oil) call the isle of Capri home.

Predictably, fish features strongly on Amalfi Coast menus, from cod and monkfish to *coccio* (rockfish) and grey mullet. You'll also find two essential larder staples down here – *colatura di alici* (an intense anchovy essence) in Cetara and Colline Salernitane DOP olive oil in Salerno.

Nearby, the Cilento region expresses its earthy tendencies in hearty peasant grub like *cuccia* (a soup of chickpeas, lentils, beans, chickling, maize and wheat) and *pastorelle* (fried puff pastry filled with chestnut custard).

THE CAMPANIAN TABLE

Don't believe the hype about espresso: one diminutive cup packs less of a caffeine wallop than a large cup of French-pressed or American-brewed coffee. It also leaves drinkers less jittery.

Menu Lowdown

» **Menù a la carte** Choose whatever you like from the menu.

» **Menù di degustazione** Degustation menu, usually consisting of six to eight 'tasting size' courses.

» **Menù turistico** The 'tourist menu' usually signals mediocre fare for gullible tourists – steer clear!

» **Piatto del giorno** Dish of the day

» **Antipasto** A hot or cold appetiser. For a tasting plate of different appetisers, request an *antipasto misto* (mixed antipasto).

» **Primo** First course, usually a substantial pasta, rice or *zuppa* (soup) dish.

» **Secondo** Second course, often *pesce* (fish) or *carne* (meat).

» **Contorno** Side dish, usually *verdura* (vegetable).

» **Dolce** Dessert; including *torta* (cake).

» **Frutta** Fruit; usually the epilogue to a meal.

» **Nostra produzione** Made in-house; used to describe anything from bread and pasta to *liquori* (liquers).

» **Surgelato** Frozen; usually used to denote fish or seafood that has not been caught fresh.

The Campanian Vine Revival

Revered by the ancients and snubbed by modern critics, Campanian wine is once again hot property, with a new generation of wine-makers creating some brilliant drops. Producers such as Feudi di San Gregorio, Mastroberardino, Terredora di Paolo and Mustilli have returned to their roots, cultivating ancient grape varieties like the red Aglianico (thought to be the oldest cultivated grape in Italy) and the whites Falanghino, Fiano and Greco (all growing long before Mt Vesuvius erupted in AD 79). Indeed, Feudi di San Gregorio created waves with the release of its delectable red Serpico. It's all a far cry from 1990, when wine critic Burton Anderson humiliatingly wrote that Campania's noteworthy winemakers could be 'counted on one's fingers'.

Campania's three main wine-producing zones are centred around Avellino, Benevento and Caserta. And it's in the high hills east of Avellino that the region's best red is produced. Taurasi, a full-bodied Aglianico wine, sometimes known as the Barolo of the south, is one of southern Italy's finest labels and one of only three in the region to carry Italy's top quality rating, DOCG (Denominazione di Origine Controllata e Garantita; Controlled & Guaranteed Denomination of Origin). The other two

PICK YOUR PLONK

To help you navigate Campania's ever-growing wine list, here are some of the region's top drops:

» **Taurasi** A DOCG since 1991, this dry, intense red goes well with boiled and barbecued meat.

» **Fiano di Avellino** A dry, fresh DOCG white wine, this is one of Campania's historic wines. Ideal with seafood.

» **Greco di Tufo** Another long-standing favourite, this DOCG white comes in both dry and sparkling versions.

» **Falerno del Massico** Its red and white versions originate from the volcanic slopes of Mt Massico in the north of the region.

» **Aglianico del Taburno** Good all-rounded white and rosé from near Benevento.

wines to share this honour are Fiano di Avellino and Greco di Tufo, both whites and both from the Avellino area.

Other vino-producing areas include the Campi Flegrei (home to DOC-labelled Piedirosso and Falanghina vines), Ischia (whose wines were the first to receive DOC-status) and the Cilento region, home to the DOC Cilento bianco (Cilento white) and to the Aglianico Paestum. Mt Vesuvius' most famous drop is the Lacryma Christi (Tears of Christ), a blend of locally grown Falanghina, Piedirosso and Coda di Volpe grapes.

And while vines also lace the Amalfi Coast, the real speciality here are the fruit and herbal liqueurs, with flavours spanning mandarin, myrtle and wild fennel, to the ubiquitous *limoncello* – a simple yet potent concoction of lemon peel, water, sugar and alcohol traditionally served in a frozen glass after dinner. *Limoncello* fans take note: the greener the tinge, the better the drop.

Architecture

Imperial seaside villas, storybook Angevin castles, oversized Bourbon palaces: Campania offers a veritable anthology of architectural classics. It's an overwhelming heap, so why not start with the undisputed highlights?

Graeco-Roman Legacies

Few corners of the world can match the breadth and depth of Campania's ancient architecture. From Greek temples to Roman amphitheatres and villas, the region offers a crash course in classical aesthetics, ambition and ingenuity.

The Greeks invented the Doric architectural order and used it to great effect at the 6th-centuryBC temples of Paestum, confirming not only the ancient Greeks' power, but also their penchant for harmonious proportion. While the temples are the most impressive survivors, they are not Campania's only Hellenic mementos. In Naples, Piazza Bellini reveals remnants of the city's 5th-century-BC walls, while traces of Greek fortifications linger at the acropolis of Cuma.

Having learned a few valuable lessons from the Greeks, the Romans refined architecture to such a degree that their building techniques, designs and mastery of harmonious proportion underpin most of the world's architecture and urban design to this day. The Greeks may have created Naples' first aqueduct, but it was the Romans who extended and improved it. The aqueduct led to the glorious Piscina Mirabilis, a cathedral-like cistern once complete with sophisticated hydraulics.

The space below Pozzuoli's Anfiteatro Flavio also lays testament to Roman ingenuity. Here, an elliptical corridor is flanked by a series of low *cellae* set on two floors and capped by trapdoors that open straight to the arena above. The *cellae* on the upper floor held the caged wild animals used in the stadium games. Hoisted up through the trap doors, the animals could then spring immediately from darkness into the bright light of the arena with rock-star effect.

Across the bay, it's a case of *Vogue Ancient Living* in Pompeii, home to many of Italy's best-preserved classical abodes. Here, buildings like Villa dei Misteri, Villa del Fauno and the Casa del Menandro illustrate the trademarks of classical domestic architecture, from an inward-facing design (for maximum privacy) to the light-filled atrium (the focal point of domestic life) and the ornamental peristyle (colonnaded garden courtyard). The finest villas were adorned with whimsical mythological frescoes, stunningly exemplified at the Villa dei Misteri, as well as at the sprawling Villa Oplontis, located in the nearby town of Torre Annunziata.

Medieval Icons

Following on from the Byzantine style and its mosaic-encrusted churches was Romanesque, a style that found four regional forms in Italy: Lombard, Pisan, Florentine and Sicilian Norman. All displayed an emphasis on width and the horizontal lines of a building rather than height,

Ancient Marvels

» Villa Oplontis, Torre Annunziata

» Villa dei Misteri, Pompeii

» Paestum

» Piscina Mirabilis, Bacoli

» Anfiteatro Flavio, Pozzuoli

and featured church groups with *campanili* (bell towers) and baptisteries that were separate to the church. Surfacing in the 11th century, the Sicilian Norman style encompassed an exotic mix of Norman, Saracen and Byzantine influences, from marble columns to Islamic-inspired pointed arches to glass tesserae detailing. This style is clearly visible in the two-toned masonry and 13th-century belltower of the Cattedrale di Sant'Andrea in Amalfi. It's also echoed in the 12th-century belltower of Salerno's Duomo, not to mention in its bronze, Byzantine-style doors and Arabesque portico arches.

For Naples, its next defining architectural period would arrive with the rule of the French House of Anjou in the 13th century. As the new capital of the Angevin kingdom, suitably ambitious plans were announced for the city. Land was reclaimed, and bold new churches and monasteries built. This was the age of the 'Gothic', a time of flying buttresses and grotesque gargoyles. While enthusiastically embraced by the French, Germans and the Spanish, the Italians preferred a more restrained and sombre interpretation of the style – defined by wide walls, a single nave, trussed ceiling and horizontal bands. One of its finest examples is Naples' Complesso Monumentale di San Lorenzo Maggiore, its bared-back elegance also echoed in the city's Chiesa di San Pietro a Maiella and Basilica di Santa Chiara.

That both the facade of the Basilica di San Lorenzo Maggiore and the coffered ceiling of the Chiesa di San Pietro a Maiella are later baroque add-ons remind us that much of the period's original architecture was altered over successive centuries. A case in point is the Chiesa di San Domenico Maggiore, whose chintzy gilded interior betrays a neo-Gothic makeover. The church's main entrance, in a courtyard off Vico San Domenico, also bears witness to a series of touch-ups. Here, a delicate 14th-century portal is framed by an 18th-century *pronaos* (the space in front of the body of a temple) surmounted by a 19th-century window; and flanked by two Renaissance-era chapels and a baroque belltower. Indeed, even the Angevins' Castel Nuovo wasn't spared, with only a few sections of the original structure surviving, among them the Palatina Chapel. The castle's striking, white triumphal-arch centrepiece – a 15th-century

ARCHITECTURE

Greek geographer, philosopher and historian Strabo (63 BC– AD 24) wrote that the stretch of Italian coast from Capo Miseno (in the Campi Flegrei) to Sorrento resembled a single city, so strewn was it with elegant villas and suburbs sprawling out from central Naples.

ARCHITECTURE SPEAK: 101

Do you know your transept from your triclinium? Demystify some common architectural terms with the following bite-size list:

Apse Usually a large recess or niche built on a semicircular or polygonal ground plan and vaulted with a half dome. In a church or temple, it may include an altar.

Baldachin (Baldacchino) A permanent, often elaborately decorated canopy of wood or stone above an altar, throne, pulpit or statue.

Balustrade A stone railing formed of a row of posts (called balusters) topped by a continuous coping, and commonly flanking baroque stairs, balconies and terraces.

Impluvium A small, ornamental pool, often used as the centrepiece of atriums in ancient Roman houses.

Latrine A Roman-era public convenience, lined with rows of toilet seats and often adorned with frescoes and marble.

Narthex A portico or lobby at the front of an early Christian church or basilica.

Necropolis Burial ground outside the city walls in antiquity and the early Christian era.

Oratory A small room or chapel in a church reserved for private prayer.

Transept A section of a church running at right angles to the main body of the church.

Triclinium The dining room in a Roman house.

THE NOT-SO-BRILLIANT LIFE OF COSIMO FANZAGO

Like many stars of the Neapolitan baroque, Cosimo Fanzago (1591–1678) was not actually Neapolitan by birth. Born in small town Clusone in northern Italy, the budding sculptor-decorator-architect ventured to Naples at the tender age of 17 and quickly earned a reputation for his imaginative way with marble. Alas, it wasn't the only reputation he incurred. According to legal documents, Fanzago was partial to the odd violent outburst, attacking his mason Nicola Botti in 1628 and reputedly knocking him off completely two years later. His alleged involvement in the 1647 Masaniello revolt saw him flee to Rome for a decade to avoid the death sentence on his head.

Yet Fanzago's ultimate downfall would come from his notorious workplace practices, which included missing deadlines, disregarding clients' wishes, and using works created for one client for completing other clients' projects. Responsible for giving him his enviable commissions at the Certosa di San Martino, the Carthusian monks would ultimately learn to loathe the man revamping their hilltop home, suing the artist in a long, arduous legal battle that ultimately affected Fanzago's health and the number of his commissions. By the time of his death in 1678, the greatest baroque master Naples had ever seen cut a poor, neglected figure.

addition – is considered one of Naples' finest early Renaissance creations.

Best Baroque Surprises

» Farmacia Storica, Ospedale degli Incurabili, Naples

» Sacristy, Basilica di San Paolo Maggiore, Naples

» Palazzo dello Spagnuolo, Naples

The Baroque

While the Renaissance all but transformed Italy's north, its impact on southern streetscapes was much less dramatic. In Naples, one of the few buildings to page the Florentine style is the Palazzo Cuomo, now home to the Museo di Filangieri. Featuring typically Tuscan rusticated walls, the late-15th-century building was created for wealthy Florentine merchant Angelo Como ('Cuomo' in Neapolitan) before finding new life as a monastery in 1587. Curiously, the building was taken down in the 1880s and accurately reassembled 20m further west to accommodate the widening of Via Duomo.

Yet, what Naples missed out on during the Renaissance, it more than made up for in the baroque of the 17th and 18th centuries. Finally, the city had found an aesthetic to suit its exhibitionist streak; a style that celebrated the bold, the gold and the over-the-top. Neapolitan baroque rose out of heady times. Under 17th-century Spanish rule, the city became one of Europe's biggest. Swelling crowds and counter-Reformation fervour sparked a building boom, with taller-than-ever *palazzi* (large buildings) mixing it with glittering showcase churches. Ready to lavish the city's new landmarks was a brash, arrogant and fiery league of architects and artists, who brushed aside tradition and rewrote the rulebooks.

A Neapolitan Twist

Like the Neapolitans themselves, the city's baroque architecture is idiosyncratic and independently minded. Architects working in Naples at the time often ignored the trends sweeping through Rome and northern Italy. Pilasters may have been all the rage in late-17th-century Roman churches, but in Naples, architects like Dionisio Lazzari (1617–89) and Giovanni Battista Nauclerio (1666–1739) went against the grain, reasserting the value of the column and effectively paving the way for Luigi Vanvitelli's columnar architecture and the neoclassicism which would sweep Europe in the mid-18th century.

In domestic Neapolitan architecture, a *palazzo*'s *piano nobile* (principal floor) was often on the 2nd floor (not the 1st as was common), encouraging the creation of the epic *porte-cocheres* (coach porticos) that distinguish so many Neapolitan buildings.

Equally grandiose were the city's open staircases, which reached perfection in the hands of Naples-born architect Ferdinando Sanfelice (1675–1748). His double-ramped creations in Palazzo dello Spagnuolo and Palazzo Sanfelice exemplify his ability to transform humble domestic staircases into operatic statements.

Another star on the building scene was Antonio Domenico Vaccaro (1678–1745). Originally having trained as a painter under Francesco Solimena, his architectural legacy would include the redesign of the cloisters at the Basilica di Santa Chiara, the decoration of three chapels of the church inside the Certosa di San Martino, as well as the design of the soaring *guglia* (obelisk) on Piazza San Domenico Maggiore.

With the help of his father, Lorenzo (himself a renowned sculptor), Vaccaro had also contributed a bronze monument dedicated to Philip V of Spain, which topped the Guglia dell'Immacolata on Piazza del Gesù Nuovo. Alas, the work would later be toppled by Charles III and replaced with a much less controversial, and still-standing, Madonna.

For many of Naples' baroque architects, the saying 'It's what's inside that counts' had a particularly strong resonance. Due in part to the city's notorious high density and lack of showcasing piazzas, many invested less time in adorning hard-to-see facades and more on lavishing interiors. The exteriors of churches like the Chiesa del Gesù Vecchio on Via Giovanni Paladino or the Chiesa di San Gregorio Armeno give little indication of the detailed opulence waiting inside, from cheeky cherubs and gilded ceilings to polychromatic marble walls and floors.

In fact, the indulgent deployment of coloured, inlaid marbles is one of the true highlights of Neapolitan baroque design. Used to adorn tombs in the second half of the 16th century, the inlaid look really took off at the beginning of the 17th century, with everything from altars and floors to entire chapels clad in mix-and-match marble concoctions.

The undisputed meister of the form was Cosimo Fanzago. Revered sculptor, decorator and architect, he would cut the stone into the most whimsical of forms, producing luscious, Technicolor spectacles. From early works like the Tomb of Mario Carafa in the Santissima Annunziata and a marble epitaph to Cardinal Ottavio Acquaviva in the Cappella del Monte di Pietà, the fiery Fanzago got his big break in 1623 with a commission to complete and decorate the Chiostro Grande (Great Cloister) in the Certosa di San Martino. To Giovanni Antonio Dosio's original design he added the statues above the portico, the ornate corner portals and the white balustrade around the monks' cemetery.

Impressed, the resident Carthusian monks offered him further work on the Certosa church, a job he continued on and off for 33 years, and one beset with legal dramas. Despite the animosity, Fanzago gave his robe-clad clients one of Italy's greatest baroque creations, designing the church's facade and lavishing its interior with polychrome Sicilian marble. The result would be a mesmerising kaleidoscope of colours and patterns, and the perfect accompaniment to works of other artistic greats, among them painters Giuseppe de Ribera, Massimo Stanzione and Francesco Solimena.

Fanzago took the art of marble inlay to a whole new level of complexity and sophistication, as also seen in the Cappella di Sant'Antonio di Padova and the Cappella Cacace, both inside the Complesso Monumentale di San Lorenzo Maggiore. The latter chapel is considered to be his most lavish expression of the form.

Fanzago's altar designs were equally influential on the era's creative ingénues. Exemplified by his beautiful high altar in the Chiesa di San

ARCHITECTURE

While Greek Doric columns are short and heavy and baseless, with plain, round capitals (tops), Ionic columns are slender and fluted, with a large base and two opposed *volutes* (or scrolls) below the capital. Corinthian columns are fancier still, with ornate capitals featuring scrolls and acanthus leaves.

COLUMNS

Domenico Maggiore, his pieces inspired the work of other sculptors, including Bartolomeo and Pietro Ghetti's altar in the Chiesa di San Pietro a Maiella, Bartolomeo Ghetti and siblings Giuseppe and Bartolomeo Gallo's version in the Chiesa del Gesù Nuovo, and Giuseppe Mozzetti's exquisite choir in the Chiesa di Santa Maria del Carmine.

Another marble maestro was Giuseppe Sanmartino (1720–93). Arguably the finest sculptor of his time, his ability to breathe life into his creations won him a legion of fans, among them the city's Bourbon rulers and the rumour-plagued prince, Raimondo di Sangro. And it's in the di Sangro family chapel, the Cappella Sansevero, that you'll find Sanmartino's astounding *Cristo velato* (Veiled Christ), completed in 1753. Considered the apogee of his technical brilliance, it's quite possibly the greatest sculpture of 18th-century Europe. Even the great neoclassical sculptor Antonio Canova wished it was his own.

End of an Era

Canova may have wished the same of the Reggia di Caserta. Officially known as Caserta's Palazzo Reale, the epic royal residence was one of several grand-scale legacies of the Bourbon years. Designed by late-Baroque architect Luigi Vanvitelli (1700–73), son of Dutch landscape artist Gaspar van Wittel (1653–1736), the Reggia not only outsized Versailles, but it would go down in history as Italy's great baroque epilogue.

Ironically, while it does feature many of the genre's theatrical telltale hallmarks, from acres of inlaid marble to allegorical statues set into wall niches, its late-baroque style echoed a classicising style more indebted to contemporary French and Spanish models and less to the exuberant playfulness of the homegrown brand. According to the Bourbon blue bloods, the over-the-top Neapolitan brand of baroque was *plutôt vulgaire* (rather vulgar). And as the curtain began to draw on Naples' baroque heyday, a more restrained neoclassicism was waiting in the wings.

In *Medieval Naples: An Architectural & Urban History 400–1400*, Caroline Bruzelius, William Tronzo and Ronald G Musto deliver a thoroughly researched review of Naples' architecture and urban development from late antiquity to the high and late Middle Ages. Topics include the Angevins' ambitious reconfiguration of the city.

The Subterranean City

Mysterious shrines, secret passageways, forgotten burial crypts: it might sound like the set of an *Indiana Jones* film, but we're actually talking about what lurks beneath Naples' loud and greasy streets. Subterranean Naples is one of the world's most thrilling urban other-worlds: a silent, mostly undiscovered sprawl of cathedral-like cisterns, pin-sized conduits, catacombs and ancient ruins.

Speleologists (cave specialists) estimate that about 60% of Neapolitans live and work above this network, known in Italian as the *sottosuolo* (underground). Since the end of WWII, some 700 cavities have been discovered, from original Greek-era grottoes to Paleo-Christian burial chambers and royal Bourbon escape routes. According to the experts, this is simply a prelude, with another 2 million sq metres of troglodytic treats to unfurl.

Naples' dedicated caving geeks are quick to tell you that their underworld is one of the largest and oldest on earth. Sure, Paris might claim a catacomb or two, but its subterranean offerings don't come close to this giant's 2500-year history.

And what a history it is: from buried martyrs and foreign invaders to wife-snatching spirits and drug-making mobsters. Naples' most famous saint, San Gennaro, was interred in the Catacomba di San Gennaro in the 5th century BC. A century later, in AD 536, Belisario and his troops caught Naples by surprise by storming the city through its ancient tunnels. According to legend, Alfonso of Aragon used the same trick in 1442, undermining the city walls by using an underground passageway leading into a tailor's shop and straight into town.

Inversely, the 18th-century Bourbons had an escape route built beneath the Palazzo Reale di Capodimonte. A century later they commissioned a tunnel to connect their central Palazzo Reale (Royal Palace) to their barracks in Chiaia: a perfect crowd-free route for troops or a fleeing royal family. Even the city's underworld has got in on the act. In 1992 Naples' dreaded Stolder clan was busted for running a subterranean drug lab, with escape routes heading straight to the clan boss' pad.

From Ancient Aqueduct to Underground Tip

While strategic tunnels and sacred catacombs are important features of Naples' light-deprived other-world, the city's subterranean backbone is its ancient aqueduct system. Naples' first plumbing masterpiece was built by the ancient Greek settlers, who channelled water from the slopes of Mt Vesuvius into the city's cisterns. The cisterns themselves were created as builders dug out the pliable *tufo* sandstone on which the city stands. At street level, well shafts allowed citizens to lower their buckets and quench their thirst.

Not to be outdone, the Romans wowed the plebs (abbreviated term for 'plebeians', common Roman citizens) with their new, improved 70km aqueduct, transporting water from the River Serino near Avellino to Naples, Pozzuoli and Baia, where it filled the enormous Piscina Mirabilis.

The next update came in 1629, with the opening of the Spanish-commissioned 'Carmignano' aqueduct. Expanded in 1770, it finally met its Waterloo in the 1880s, when cholera outbreaks heralded the building of a more modern, pressurised version.

Dried up and defunct, the ancient cisterns went from glorious feats of ancient engineering to handy in-house rubbish tips. As rubbish clogged the well shafts, access into the *sottosuolo* became ever more difficult and within a few generations the subterranean system that had nourished the city was left bloated and forgotten.

**Top Sub-
terranean
Sites**

» Catacomba
di San Gennaro
(p66)

» Napoli Sotter-
ranea (p46)

» Catacomba di
San Gaudioso
(p67)

» Complesso
Monumentale di
San Lorenzo Mag-
giore (p39)

» Tunnel Bor-
bonico (p61)

The WWII Revival

It would take the wail of air-raid sirens to reunite the city's sunlit and subterranean sides once more. With Allied air attacks looming, Mussolini ordered that the ancient cisterns be turned into civilian shelters. The lakes of rubbish were compacted and covered, old passageways were enlarged, toilets were built and new staircases were erected. As bombs showered the city above, tens of thousands took refuge in the dark, damp shelters below.

The fear, frustration and anger of those who took shelter lives on today in the historic graffiti that still covers the walls, from hand-drawn caricatures of Hitler and 'Il Duce' to poignant messages like '*Mamma, non piangere*' (Mum, don't cry). For the many whose homes were destroyed, these subterranean hideouts became semi-permanent dwellings. Entire families cohabited cisterns, partitioning their makeshift abodes with bedsheets and furnishing them with the odd ramshackle bed.

Alas, once rebuilding on the ground began, the aqueducts were once again relegated the role of subterranean dumpsters, with everything from wartime rubble to scooters and Fiats thrown down the shafts. And in a case of history repeating itself, the historic labyrinth and its millennia-old secrets faded from the city's collective memory.

MYTH OF THE LITTLE MONK

It's only natural that a world as old, dark and mysterious as Naples' *sottosuolo* (underground) should breed a few fantastical urban myths. The best-known and most-loved is that of the *municello* (little monk), a Neapolitan leprechaun of sorts known for being both naughty and nice. Said to live in the wine cellar, sightings of the hooded sprite were regularly reported in the 18th and 19th centuries. Some spoke of him as a kindred soul, a bearer of gifts and good fortune. To others, the *municello* spelled trouble – sneaking into homes to misplace objects, steal precious jewels and seduce the odd lonely housewife.

While a handful of Neapolitans still curse the hooded imp whenever the car keys go missing, most now believe that the cheeky *municello* was actually the city's long-gone *pozzari* (aqueduct cleaners). Descending daily down the wells, the small-statured *pozzari* fought off the damp, cool conditions with a heavy, hooded mantel. Naturally, most would pop back up for a breath of fresh air, sometimes finding themselves in people's very homes. For some, the temptation of scouring through drawers in search of valuables was all too tempting. For others, it was a way of making new acquaintances, or a way of bringing a little company to the odd neglected housewife. Whatever the intentions, it quickly becomes clear just how the tale of the 'minimonk' began.

FULVIO SALVI & LUCA CUTTITTA, SPELEOLOGISTS

Dubbed everything from 'the parallel city' to 'the negative city', Neapolitan speleologists Fulvio and Luca prefer to call Naples' subterranean world *la macchina del tempo* (the time machine). As Fulvio explains, 'In 30 to 40 metres you're transported from the 21st century to 2000 BC. Some of the axe pick marks on the *tufo* stone predate Christ himself.'

For Fulvio and Luca, the constant possibility of new discoveries is addictive: 'We can descend into the same cistern 30 times and still find new objects, like oil lamps used by the Greek and Roman excavators'.

One of their most memorable discoveries to date was made after stumbling across an unusual looking staircase behind an old chicken coop in an old *palazzo* (large building) in the district of Arinella.

As Fulvio recalls, 'I headed down the stairs and through a hole in the wall. Reaching the bottom, I switched on my torch and was quickly dumbstruck to find carved columns and frescoes of the ancient Egyptian deities Isis, Osiris and Seth on the walls. We believe we've found part of the Secretorum Naturae Accademia, the laboratory used by scholar, alchemist and playwright Giambattista della Porta (c 1535–1615) after the Inquisition ordered an end to his experiments'.

Speleological associations like NUg (Napoli Underground Group) play a vital role in preserving Naples' collective heritage: 'There are between 10 to 15 NUg members, each with a specific role to play on our expeditions, from photographer or filmmaker to medical support. We're like a well-oiled machine whose role is to sew up the little tears in our city's history. It's a bit like a puzzle and each new passageway or cistern we find is a piece of that puzzle that we're trying to put together. It's too enormous for us to finish in our lifetimes, but at least we will have contributed to what are important scientific, historical and archaeological discoveries'.

Speleologists Fulvio Salvi and Luca Cuttitta prefer dark cisterns to southern sunshine any day.

THE SUBTERRANEAN CITY

Speleological Saviours & Rediscovered Secrets

Thankfully, all is not lost, as a passionate league of professional and volunteer speleologists continues to rediscover and render accessible long-lost sites and secrets – a fact not lost on the likes of National Geographic and the BBC, both of which have documented the work of these subterranean experts. The city's most prolific speleological association today is the aptly named La Macchina del Tempo (The Time Machine). Lead by speleologist Luca Cuttitta, it manages the fascinating Museo del Sottosuolo (Museum of the Underground), a DIY ode to speleologists and the treasures they uncover. Hidden away on Piazza Cavour, its series of restored underground cisterns recreates real-life sites inaccessible to the public, from a phallocentric shrine to the Graeco-Roma god of fertility, Priapus, to a luridly hued Hellenic-era hypogeum (underground chamber). Precious debris that once filled the voids is now displayed, from rare majolica tiles to domestic WWII-era objects. The museum itself was founded by veteran cave crusader Clemente Esposito, lovingly nicknamed *il Papa del sottosuolo* (Pope of the Underground) in local speleological circles.

Even more thrilling are La Macchina del Tempo's speleological tours, which take in unexplored nooks few locals will ever see. On these journeys, surprise discoveries are far from rare, whether it's another secret wartime hideout, an early Christian engraving or an even older Greek urn. A minimum number of six participants is required for these adventures, which run on weekends and last three hours.

Minimum numbers are not an issue for the city's more touristy underground tours, run by Napoli Sotterranea (p46) and Borbonica Sotterranea. While Borbonica Sotterranea's Tunnel Borbonico (p61) conducts tours of the Bourbon tunnel running beneath Mt Echia (home to Naples' earliest settlement), Napoli Sotterranea takes a steady stream of visitors below the *centro storico* for a look at remnants of a Roman theatre frequented by Emperor Nero, as well as to a cistern returned to its original, water-filled splendour.

To dig deeper into the region's subterranean scene, check out the information-packed website www.napoliunderground.org.

Mixed Blessings

And yet, not even the infectious enthusiasm of Naples' speleologists is enough to secure the protection and preservation of the city's *sottosuolo*. The golden era of the 1990s, which saw the city council provide generous funding to speleological research, has since been supplanted by standard Italian bureaucracy and political bickering. As a result, many precious sites uncovered by the city's speleologists remain indefinitely abandoned, with little money to salvage and restore them. As Fulvio Salvi from NUg (Napoli Underground Group) laments: 'The problem with Naples is that it's almost too rich in historical treasure. It creates a certain amount of indifference to such marvels because they are almost a dime a dozen here'.

A more positive outcome involved NUg's discovery of a long, ring-shaped corridor beneath the Quartieri Spagnoli. Part of the ancient Largo Baracche district, the unearthing called for its transformation into a much-needed community centre – a wish that fell on deaf ears at the Municipio. Destined to become a squat, its saving grace was a gung-ho group of young community activists called SABU. Giving the space a mighty scrub, the group opened it as a nonprofit art lab and gallery in 2005, headed by 24-year-old archaeology students Giuseppe Ruffo and Pietro Tatafiore. As Giuseppe explains, 'The gallery is an open space where emerging artists can exhibit their work, amongst them young graduates from Naples' Accademia delle Belle Arti. Unfortunately, such spaces are lacking in Naples'.

Naples' original Graeco-Roman city was covered by a great mudslide in the 6th century. The excavations to open the Roman market beneath the Complesso Monumentale di San Lorenzo Maggiore took 25 years.

MUDSLIDE

The Camorra

Known locally as Il Sistema (The System), Naples' Camorra crime syndicate is Italy's largest. It trafficks drugs, dumps toxic waste, stifles regional development through kickbacks, and makes a bundle along the way. In the past 30 years, the Camorra has claimed more than 3000 lives, more than any other Mafia in the country.

Origins

It is widely believed that the Camorra emerged from the criminal gangs operating among the poor in late-18th-century Naples. The organisation would get its first big break after the failed revolution of 1848. Desperate to overthrow Ferdinand II, pro-constitutional liberals turned to *camorristi* (members of the Neapolitan mafia) to help garner the support of the masses. The Camorra's political influence was sealed. Given a serious blow by Mussolini, the organisation would get its second wind from the invading Allied forces of 1943, which turned to the flourishing underworld as the best way to get things done.

The Value of Vice

Today Italy's Mafia organisations mean serious business: the Camorra's annual profit alone is estimated at €19 billion. This is a far cry from the days of roguish characters bullying shopkeepers into paying the *pizzo* (protection money). As journalist Roberto Saviano writes in his Camorra exposé *Gomorra*: 'Only beggar Camorra clans inept at business and desperate to survive still practice the kind of monthly extortions seen in Nanni Loy's film *Mi manda Picone*'. While small-time extortion still exists, the Mafia big guns are where the serious bucks lie, from the production and sale of counterfeit goods to the construction and waste disposal industries.

One of the Camorra's biggest money spinners is the drug trade. Indeed, the Camorra-ravaged suburbs of Secondigliano and Scampia in northern Naples have the dubious claim of being Europe's largest open-air drug market, supplying addicts from across the country with cheap, low-grade heroin and cocaine. Needless to say, where there is money, there is greed, and disputes between rival clans over this lucrative trade have seen the spilling of much blood.

One of the most serious clan battles in recent history was the so-called 'Scampia Feud', ignited by *camorrista* Cosimo Di Lauro in late 2004. As the newly appointed head of the powerful Di Lauro clan, the 30-year-old decided to centralise the area's drug trade, giving himself more power and the clan's long-respected franchisees much less. This did not go down well with many of Di Lauro's associates. Among them were Raffaele Amato and Cesare Pagano, who broke away to form a rival clan dubbed the Scissionisti (Secessionists). What followed was a long and ruthless series of murders and retributions between the opposing groups, one that would claim over 50 lives in 2004–05 alone.

The Camorra on Screen

» *Gomorra* (Matteo Garrone; 2009)

» *Il camorrista* (The Camorrista; Giuseppe Tornatore; 1986)

» *Mi manda Picone* (Picone Sent Me; Nanni Loy; 1983)

The Greater Naples region is home to over 100 Camorra clans, with an estimated 10,000 immediate associates, and an even larger number of clients, dependents and supporters.

MAFIA TRASH

In early 2012 Italian police arrested 14 people and seized company assets in excess of €8 million in a probe into illegal toxic waste trafficked by the Camorra. This figure is hardly surprising: the Camorra runs a lucrative line in transporting, dumping and burning toxic waste smuggled into Campania from Italy's wealthy, industrial north. In 2004 the medical journal *Lancet Oncology* dubbed an area in Naples' northeast hinterland 'the triangle of death' due to abnormally high cases of liver cancer and congenital malformations of the nervous and urinary systems. The trade's origins are linked to Casalesi clan boss Gaetano Vassallo, who in 2008 confessed to bribing local politicians, farmers and other clan bosses into letting him dump dangerous waste in fields between Naples and Caserta.

Fighting Back

Over the years, the law has captured many Camorra kingpins, among them Cosimo Di Lauro, his father, Paolo, and Giuseppe Dell'Aquila. Yet the war against the Camorra remains an uphill battle. Its presence in Neapolitan society spans centuries, and, for many, the Camorra has provided everything Italy's official avenues have not, from employment and business loans to a sense of order in local communities. The Camorra's weekly drug trade rates range from €100 for lookouts to €1000 for those willing to hide the drugs at home. Driving a shipment of drugs from Milan to Naples can pay as much as €2500.

Italy's recent financial downturn has proven another boon. With liquidity in short supply, hard-pressed companies have become more susceptible to dirty money. Camorra-affiliated loan sharks commonly offer cash with an average interest rate of 10%. An estimated 50% to 70% of shops in Naples are run with dubiously sourced money. Mafia profits are also reinvested in legitimate real estate, credit markets and businesses around the world.

Although too many Neapolitans shrug their shoulders in resignation, others are determined to loosen the Camorra's grip. In the Sanità district, people like parish priest Don Antonio Loffredo and renowned artist Riccardo Dalisi offer youth the opportunity to learn artistic and artisanal skills and help restore local heritage sites, including the Catacomba di San Gennaro.

Across the city in Ercolano, elderly shopkeeper Raffaella Ottaviano made international headlines for her refusal to pay the *pizzo*. Her courage has influenced other local traders to say no, which in turn has led the local council to offer tax breaks to those who report threats of extortion instead of giving in to the Camorra.

Not long ago, this willingness to publicly denounce the Camorra would have been thought impossible, a fact that offers a glimmer of hope in a long, dark battle.

Arrested in 2009, Ugo Gabriele broke the mould like no other. Beefy and cunning, the then 27-year-old would go down in history as Italy's first cross-dressing mobster. In between shaping his eyebrows, dabbing on lipstick and dyeing his hair platinum blonde, 'Kitty' found time to manage prostitution and drug rackets for Naples' Scissionisti clan.

Survival Guide

Directory A–Z

Customs Regulations

Duty-free sales within the EU no longer exist (but goods are sold tax-free in European airports). Visitors coming into Italy from non-EU countries can import the following items duty free:

» **Spirits** 1L (or 2L wine)
» **Perfume** 50g
» **Eau de toilette** 250mL
» **Tobacco** 200 cigarettes
» **Other goods** up to a total of €430

Anything over these limits must be declared on arrival and the appropriate duty paid. On leaving the EU, non-EU citizens can reclaim any Value Added Tax (VAT) on expensive purchases.

Business Hours

Opening times for individual businesses in this guide are only spelled out when they deviate significantly from the standard hours outlined following.

» **Banks** 8.30am-1.30pm & 3-4.30pm Mon-Fri
» **Central post offices** 8am-6pm Mon-Fri, 8.30am-1pm Sat
» **Smaller branch post offices** 8am-1.30pm Mon-Fri, 8.30am-1pm Sat
» **Restaurants** noon-3pm & 7.30-11pm or midnight
» **Cafes & Bars** 7.30am-8pm or later
» **Clubs** 10pm-4am
» **Shops** 9am-1pm & 3.30-7.30pm (or 4-8pm) Mon-Sat some close Mon morning
» The opening hours of museums, galleries and archaeological sites vary enormously. Many museums are closed on either Monday or Tuesday, while some close on Wednesday.
» Currency-exchange offices usually keep longer hours, though these are hard to find outside major cities and tourist areas.

» Restaurant kitchens often shut an hour earlier than final closing time. Most places close at least one day a week; many restaurants take their holidays in August, while those in coastal resort towns usually close in the low season.
» In larger cities, supermarkets may stay open at lunchtime or on Sunday.

Discount Cards

Free admission to many galleries and cultural sites is available to youth under 18 years and seniors over 65 years; in addition, visitors aged between 18 and 25 years often qualify for a 50% discount. In some cases,

PRACTICALITIES

» Use the metric system for weights and measures.

» Smoking in all closed public spaces (from bars to elevators, offices to trains) is banned...even if some locals continue to flout the law.

» If your Italian is up to it, try reading Naples' major daily newspapers *Il Mattino* or *Corriere del Mezzogiorno*. The latter is the southern spin-off of Italy's leading daily, *Corriere della Sera*. The national *La Repubblica* also has a Neapolitan section.

» Tune into state-owned Italian RAI Radio 1, RAI Radio 2 and RAI Radio 3 (www.rai.it), which broadcast all over Italy and abroad. The region's plethora of contemporary music stations includes Radio Kiss Kiss (www.kisskiss.it). Switch on the box to watch the state-run RAI-1, RAI-2 and RAI-3 (www.rai.it) and the main commercial stations (mostly run by Silvio Berlusconi's Mediaset company): Canale 5 (www.canale5.mediaset.it), Italia 1 (www.italia1.mediaset.it), Rete 4 (www.rete4.mediaset.it) and La 7 (www.la7.it).

these discounts only apply to EU citizens.

If travelling to Naples and Campania, consider buying a **Campania artecard** (www.campaniaartecard.it), which offers free public transport and free or reduced admission to many museums and archaeological sites. For more details, see p68.

Embassies & Consulates

For foreign embassies and consulates not listed here, look under 'Ambasciate' or 'Consolati' in the telephone directory. Alternatively, tourist offices generally have a list. The following are located in Naples:

France (☎081 598 07 11; www.ambafrance-it.org; Via Francesco Crispi 86)

Germany (☎081 248 85 11; www.neapel.diplo.de; Via Francesco Crispi 69)

Netherlands (☎081 551 30 03; Via Agostino Depretis 114)

USA (☎081 583 81 11; naples.usconsulate.gov; Piazza della Repubblica)

Electricity

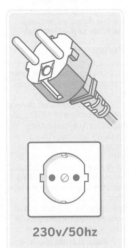

230v/50hz

DIRECTORY A–Z EMBASSIES & CONSULATES

YOUTH, STUDENT & TEACHER CARDS

The European Youth Card offers thousands of discounts on Italian hotels, museums, restaurants, shops and clubs, while a student, teacher or youth travel card can save you money on flights to Italy. All cards listed under 'Discount Cards' (opposite) are available from the **Centro Turistico Studentesco e Giovanile** (CTS; www.cts.it, in Italian), a youth travel agency with branches throughout southern Italy. The final three cards are available worldwide from student unions, hostelling organisations and youth travel agencies such as STA Travel (www.statravel.com).

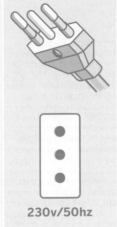

230v/50hz

Food

In restaurant reviews throughout this book, 'meals' denotes the average price for a *primo* (first course), *secondo* (second course), *dolce* (dessert) and house wine for one person. Reviews are listed according to three budget categories as follows:
Meal Price Range
» € Budget, under €20
» €€ Midrange, €20-45
» €€€ Top end, more than €45
For more information on eating in Naples and Campania, see p23 and p239.

Gay & Lesbian Travellers

Homosexuality is legal in Italy and well tolerated in Naples; however, try to avoid overt displays of affection, particularly in smaller towns on the Amalfi Coast. The legal age of consent is 16 years.

Resources include the following:

Arcigay Napoli (www.arcigaynapoli.org, in Italian) Website for Naples' main GLBTI organisation, listing special events as well as gay and gay-friendly venues in town.

Criminal Candy (www.criminalcandy.com, in Italian) Organises one-off queer dance parties in Naples.

Freelovers (www.freelovers.it) Naples-based organisation running one-off GLBT club nights in town.

Gay Friendly Italia.com (www.gayfriendlyitalia.com) English-language site produced by Gay.it, featuring information on everything from hotels to homophobia issues and the law.

Gay.it (www.gay.it, in Italian) Lists gay venues and hotels across the country.

Pride (www.prideonline.it, in Italian) National monthly magazine of art, music, politics and gay culture.

DISCOUNT CARDS

CARD	WEBSITE	COST (€)	ELIGIBILITY
European Youth Card (Carta Giovani)	www.europe anyouthcard. org	11	under 30yr
International Student Identity Card (ISIC)	www.isic.org	10	full-time student
International Teacher Identity Card (ITIC)		10	full-time teacher
International Youth Travel Card (IYTC)		10	under 26yr

Health

Availability of Health Care

» Good health care is available throughout Campania.

» In major centres you will find English-speaking doctors or a translator service available.

» Pharmacists can give you valuable advice and sell over-the-counter medication for minor illnesses. They can also advise when more specialised help is required and point you in the right direction. Pharmacies generally keep the same hours as other shops, closing at night and on Sundays. However, a handful remain open on a rotation basis (farmacie di turno) for emergency purposes. These are usually listed in newspapers. Closed pharmacies display a list of the nearest ones open.

» If you need an ambulance in Italy, call ☑118. For emergency treatment, head to the pronto soccorso (casualty) section of a public hospital, where you can also get emergency dental treatment.

Health Insurance

If you're an EU citizen (or from Switzerland, Norway or Iceland), a European Health Insurance Card (EHIC) covers you for most medical care in public hospitals free of charge, but not for emergency repatriation home or non-emergencies. The card is available from health centres and (in the UK) from post offices. Citizens from other countries should find out if there is a reciprocal arrangement for free medical care between their country and Italy (Australia, for instance, has such an agreement; carry your Medicare card). If you do need health insurance, make sure you get a policy that covers you for the worst possible scenario, such as an accident requiring an emergency flight home. Find out in advance if your insurance plan will make payments directly to providers or reimburse you later for overseas health expenditures.

Recommended Vaccinations

No jabs are required to travel to Italy. The World Health Organization (WHO), however, recommends that all travellers should be covered for diphtheria, tetanus, the measles, mumps, rubella and polio, as well as hepatitis B.

Insurance

A travel-insurance policy to cover theft, loss and medical problems is a good idea. It may also cover you for cancellation or delays to your travel arrangements. Paying for your ticket with a credit card can often provide limited travel accident insurance and you may be able to reclaim the payment if the operator doesn't deliver. Ask your credit-card company what it will cover. Worldwide travel insurance is available at www.lonelyplanet.com/travel-insurance. You can buy, extend and claim online anytime – even if you're already on the road.

Internet Access

Internet access in southern Italy has improved greatly in the past few years, with an increasing number of hotels, B&Bs, hostels and even agriturismi (farm stay accommodation) now offering free wi-fi. On the downside, public wi-fi hot spots and internet cafes remain thin on the ground and signal strength is variable. Internet cafes charge €2 to €6 per hour.

Legal Matters

Despite its mafia notoriety, Campania is relatively safe, and the average tourist will only have a brush with the law if robbed by a bag snatcher or a pickpocket.

Police

Contact details for police stations (questure) are given throughout this book. If you run into trouble in Italy, you're likely to end up dealing with the polizia statale (state police) or the carabinieri (military police). The former wear powder-blue trousers with a fuchsia stripe and a navy blue jacket; the latter wear black uniforms with a red stripe and drive dark blue cars with a red stripe. The following list outlines Italian police organisations and their jurisdictions.

» **Polizia statale** (State Police) Thefts, visa extensions and permits

» **Carabinieri** (Military Police) General crime, public order and drug enforcement (often overlapping with the *polizia statale*)

» **Vigili urbani** (Local Traffic Police) Parking tickets, towed cars

» **Guardia di finanza** Tax evasion, drug smuggling

» **Guardia forestale** (aka Corpo Forestale) Environmental protection

Drugs & Alcohol

Under Italy's tough drug laws, possession of any controlled substances, including cannabis or marijuana, can get you into hot water. Those caught in possession of 5g of cannabis can be considered traffickers and prosecuted as such. The same applies to tiny amounts of other drugs. Those caught with amounts below this threshold can be subject to minor penalties.

The legal limit for blood-alcohol levels is 0.05% and random breath tests do occur.

Your Rights

If detained, you should be given verbal and written notice of the charges laid against you within 24 hours by arresting officers. You have no right to a phone call upon arrest. The prosecutor must apply to a magistrate for you to be held in preventive custody awaiting trial (depending on the seriousness of the offence) within 48 hours of arrest. You have the right not to respond to questions without the presence of a lawyer. If the magistrate orders preventive custody, you have the right to then contest this within the following 10 days.

Money

The euro is Italy's currency. The seven euro notes come in denominations of €500, €200, €100, €50, €20, €10 and €5. The eight euro coins are in denominations of €2

and €1, and €0.50, €0.20, €0.10, five, two and one cents.

For the latest exchange rates, check out www. xe.com.

Credit & Debit Cards

Bancomats (ATMs) are widely available throughout Campania and are the best way to obtain local currency. International credit and debit cards can be used in any Bancomat displaying the appropriate sign. Cards are also good for payment in most hotels, restaurants, shops, supermarkets and tollbooths.

Check any charges with your bank. Most banks now build a fee of around 2.75% into every foreign transaction. In addition, ATM withdrawals can attract a further fee, usually around 1.5%.

If your card is lost, stolen or swallowed by an ATM, you can telephone toll free to have an immediate stop put on its use:

Amex (✆06 7290 0347 or your national call number)

Diners Club (✆800 864064)

MasterCard (✆800 870866)

Visa (✆800 819014)

Moneychangers

You can change money in banks, at the post office or in a *cambio* (currency-exchange bureau). Post offices and banks tend to offer the best rates; currency-exchange bureaus keep longer hours, but watch for high commissions and inferior rates.

Taxes & Refunds

A value-added tax of around 20%, known as Imposta di Valore Aggiunto (IVA), is slapped onto just about everything in Italy. If you are a non-EU resident and spend more than €155 (€154.94, to be more precise!) on a purchase, you can claim a refund when you leave. For information, visit **Tax Refund for Tourists** (www.taxrefund.it) or pick up a pamphlet on the

scheme from participating stores, which usually display a 'Tax Free for Tourists' (or similar) sign.

Tipping

You are not expected to tip on top of restaurant service charges but you can leave a little extra if you feel service warrants it. If there is no service charge, consider leaving a 10% tip, but this is not obligatory. In bars, Italians often leave small change as a tip (usually €0.10 to €0.20). Tipping taxi drivers is not common practice, but you are expected to tip the porter at top-end hotels.

Post

Poste Italiane (www.poste.it), Italy's postal system, is reasonably reliable. For opening hours, see p258.

Francobolli (stamps) are available at *uffici postali* (post offices) and authorised tobacconists (look for the big white-on-black 'T' sign). Since letters often need to be weighed, what you get at the tobacconist for international airmail will occasionally be an approximation of the proper rate. Tobacconists keep regular shop hours.

Naples' main post office is on Piazza Matteotti.

Postal Services Rates

The cost of sending a letter by *via aerea* (airmail) depends on its weight, its size and where it is being sent. Most people use *posta prioritaria* (priority mail), Italy's most efficient mail service, guaranteed to deliver letters sent to Europe within three days and to the rest of the world within four to nine days. Letters up to 20g cost €0.52 within Europe and the Mediterranean basin, and €0.62 to the rest of the world. Packets weighing up to 350g cost €1.86 within Europe and the Mediterranean basin, €4.13 to Africa, Asia and the Americas, and €4.39 to Australia and New Zealand.

Receiving Mail

Poste restante is known as *fermoposta* in Italy. Letters marked thus will be held at the counter of the same name in the main post office in the relevant town. You'll need to pick up your letters in person and you must present your passport as ID.

Public Holidays

Most Italians take their annual holiday in August, with the busiest period occurring around 15 August, known as Ferragosto. As a result, many businesses and shops close for a part of that month.
National public holidays:

» **New Year's Day** (Capodanno) 1 January

» **Epiphany** (Epifania) 6 January

» **Easter Monday** (Pasquetta) March/April

» **Liberation Day** (Giorno della Liberazione) 25 April

» **Labour Day** (Festa del Lavoro) 1 May

» **Republic Day** (Festa della Repubblica) 2 June

» **Feast of the Assumption** (Assunzione or Ferragosto) 15 August

» **All Saints' Day** (Ognisanti) 1 November

» **Feast of the Immaculate Conception** (Festa della Immacolata Concezione) 8 December

» **Christmas Day** (Natale) 25 December

» **Boxing Day** (Festa di Santo Stefano) 26 December

Safe Travel

Naples has an often exaggerated reputation for being unsafe. As is the case in any large city, using common sense should keep problems at bay. The following are some basic safety tips:

» Pickpockets are highly active on crowded transport and in crowds. Avoid keeping money, credit cards and other valuables in easy-to-reach pockets, especially coat and back pockets.

» Never leave your bags unattended – some thieves walk through trains before they depart in search of unattended bags to pinch. At cafes and bars, loop your bag's strap around your leg while seated.

» Be cautious of strangers wanting your attention, especially at train stations.

» Wear bags and cameras across your body and away from the street to avoid scooter-riding petty thieves.

» Be aware of your surroundings, especially at night.

» At archaeological sites, watch out for touts posing as legitimate guides.

Scams

Avoid buying mobile phones and other electrical goods from vendors on Piazza Garibaldi and at street markets. It's not unusual to discover you've bought a box with a brick. At Stazione Centrale in Naples, ignore touts offering taxis; use only registered white taxis with a running meter.

On the Road

Car theft is a problem in Naples, so it pays to leave your car in a supervised car park. If you leave your car on the street, you'll often be approached by an unofficial (illegal) parking attendant asking for money. Clearly you don't have to pay them, but if you refuse, you run the risk of returning to a damaged car. In case of theft or loss, always report the incident to the police within 24 hours, and ask for a statement otherwise your travel-insurance company won't pay out.

Traffic

Neapolitan traffic requires some getting used to. Drivers are not keen to stop for pedestrians, even at pedestrian crossings, and are more likely to swerve. Locals simply step off the footpath and walk through the (swerving) traffic with determination. It is a practice that seems to work, but if you feel uncertain, wait and cross with a local.

In many cities, roads that appear to be for one-way traffic have lanes for buses travelling in the opposite direction – always look both ways before stepping onto the road.

Telephone

Domestic Calls

Telephone area codes begin with 0 and consist of up to four digits – the Naples area code is 081. The area code is followed by a number of anything from four to eight digits. The area code is an integral part of the telephone number and must always be dialled, even when calling from next door. Mobile phone numbers begin with a three-digit prefix such as 330. Toll-free (freephone) numbers are known as *numeri verdi* and usually start with 800. Nongeographical numbers start with 840, 841, 848, 892, 899, 163, 166 or 199. Some six-digit national rate numbers are also in use (such as those for Alitalia, rail and postal information).

Italians choose from lots of providers of phone plans, making it difficult to make generalisations about costs.

International Calls

The cheapest options for calling internationally are free or low-cost computer programs such as Skype, cut-price call centres or an international calling card (*scheda telefonica internazionale*), which are sold at newsstands and tobacconists. Cut-price call centres can be found in the main cities, and rates can be considerably lower than from Telecom payphones for international calls. Place your call from a private booth inside the call centre and pay for it when you've finished. Direct international calls can also easily be made from public telephones with a phonecard. Dial ⏏00 to get out of Italy, then the relevant country and area codes, followed by the telephone number.

To call Italy from abroad, call the international access number (☑011 in the USA, ☑00 from most other countries), Italy's country code (☑39) and then the area code of the location you want, including the leading 0.

To make a reverse-charge (collect) international call, dial ☑170. All operators speak English. Or, use the direct-dialling (Country Direct) service provided by your home-country phone company (such as AT&T in the USA and Telstra in Australia). You simply dial the relevant access number and request a reverse-charge call via the operator in your country. Numbers for this service include the following:

» **Australia** (Telstra) ☑800 172 610
» **Canada** ☑800 172 213
» **New Zealand** ☑800 172 641
» **USA** (AT&T) ☑800 172 444

Directory Enquiries

National and international phone numbers can be requested at ☑1254 (or online at 1254.virgilio.it).

Mobile Phones

Italy uses GSM 900/1800, which is compatible with the rest of Europe and Australia but not with North American GSM 1900 or the totally different Japanese system (though some GSM 1900/900 phones do work here). If you have a GSM phone, check with your service provider about using it in Italy and beware of calls being routed internationally (very expensive for a 'local' call).

Italy has one of the highest levels of mobile phone penetration in Europe, and you can get a temporary or prepaid account from several companies if you already own a GSM, dual- or tri-band phone. You will usually need your passport to open an account. Always check with your service provider in your home country to check whether your handset allows use of another SIM card. If yours does, it can cost as little as €10 to activate a local prepaid SIM card (sometimes with €10 worth of calls on the card). To recharge a card, simply pop into the nearest outlet or buy a charge card (*ricarica*) from a tobacconist. Alternatively, you can buy or lease an inexpensive Italian phone for the duration of your trip.

Of the main mobile phone companies, TIM (Telecom Italia Mobile), Wind and Vodafone have the densest networks of outlets.

Phonecards

You'll find Telecom Italia silver payphones on the streets, in train stations, in some stores and in Telecom offices. Most payphones accept only *carte/schede telefoniche* (telephone cards), although some still accept credit cards and coins.

Phonecards (in denominations of €3 and €5) are available at post offices, tobacconists and newsstands. You must break the top left-hand corner off the card before you can use it.

Time

Italy is one hour ahead of GMT. Daylight saving time, when clocks are moved forward one hour, starts on the last Sunday in March. Clocks are put back an hour on the last Sunday in October. Italy operates on a 24-hour clock.

Toilets

Public toilets are rare in Naples. Bars and cafes usually have toilets, but you may need to buy a coffee first. Public toilets are available at museums and at the main bus and train stations. Several public toilets have attendants, who'll expect a small tip – €0.50 should do.

Tourist Information

The quality of tourist offices varies dramatically. One office might have enthusiastic staff, another might be indifferent. Most offices can offer you a plethora of brochures, maps and leaflets, even if staff are uninterested in helping in any other way.

Campania's **main tourist office** (☑081 410 72 11; www.in-campania.com; Piazza dei Martiri 58; ⊙9am-2pm Mon-Fri) is in the Naples district of Chiaia. It is generally more concerned with planning, budgeting, marketing and promotion than with offering a public information service. However, it still maintains a useful tourist website.

Local & Provincial Tourist Offices

Despite their different (and sometimes confusingly elaborate) names, provincial and local offices offer similar services and are collectively referenced with the generic term 'tourist office' throughout this book. All deal directly with the public, and most will respond to written and telephone requests for information. Staff can usually provide a city map, lists of hotels and information on the major sights. In larger towns and major tourist areas, staff have a working knowledge of at least one other language, usually English but also French and German.

Main offices are generally open Monday to Friday; some also open on weekends, especially in urban areas or during peak summer season. Affiliated information booths (at train stations and airports, for example) may keep slightly different hours.

The main local tourist offices in Naples are listed following.

Piazza Garibaldi (☑081 26 87 79; Piazza Garibaldi, Stazione Centrale; ⊙9am-7pm Mon-Sat)

Piazza del Gesù Nuovo (☑081 552 33 28; Piazza del Gesù Nuovo; ⊙9am-7pm Mon-Sat, 9am-2pm Sun)

Via San Carlo (☑081 40 23 94; Via San Carlo 7; ⊙9.30am-1.30pm & 2.30-6pm Mon-Sat, 9am-1.30pm Sun)

Tourist Offices Abroad

ENIT (Italian National Tourist Office; www.enit.it), the Italian National Tourist Office, maintains offices in over two dozen cities on five continents. Contact information for all offices can be found on its website.

Travellers with Disabilities

Campania is not an easy destination for travellers with disabilities. Cobbled streets, hair-raising traffic, blocked pavements and tiny lifts make life difficult for the wheelchair-bound, and those with sight or hearing difficulties. The uneven surfaces at archaeological sites like Pompeii virtually rule out wheelchairs. However, some city buses, including R2 and R3 in Naples, are set up with access ramps and space for a wheelchair.

The website www.turismo accessibile.it gives a rundown on the disabled facilities at Naples' museums and hotels and on its transport services.

The **ENIT** (Italian National Tourist Office; www.enit.it) office in your country may be able to provide advice on Italian associations for the disabled, and information on what help is available.

Italy's national rail company, **Trenitalia** (www.trenitalia. com) offers a national helpline for disabled passengers at 199 303060 (7am to 9pm daily). To secure assistance at Naples' Stazione Centrale, you should call this number 24 hours prior to your departure.

For more information, try the following organisations:

Accessible Italy (378 94 11 11; www.acessibleitaly.com) A San Marino–based company that specialises in holiday services for the disabled.

Consorzio Cooperative Integrate (COIN; 06 712 90 11; www.coinsociale.it) Situated in Rome, COIN is the best reference point for disabled travellers journeying in Italy, with contact points throughout the country.

Tourism for All (www.tourismforall.org.uk) This group has information on hotels with access for disabled guests, where to hire equipment, and tour oprators dealing with disabled travellers.

Visas & Permits

Italy is one of 25 member countries of the Schengen Convention, under which 22 EU countries (all but Bulgaria, Cyprus, Ireland, Romania and the UK) plus Iceland, Norway and Switzerland have abolished permanent checks at common borders.

Legal residents of one Schengen country do not require a visa for another. Residents of 28 non-EU countries, including Australia, Brazil, Canada, Israel, Japan, New Zealand and the USA, do not require visas for tourist visits of up to 90 days (this list varies for those wanting to travel to the UK and Ireland).

All non-EU and non-Schengen nationals entering Italy for more than 90 days, or for any reason other than tourism (such as study or work) may need a specific visa. For details, visit www. esteri.it/visti/home_eng. asp or contact an Italian consulate. You should also have your passport stamped on entry as, without a stamp, you could encounter problems when trying to obtain a residence permit (permesso di soggiorno). If you enter the EU via another member state, get your passport stamped there.

Study Visas

Non-EU citizens who want to study at a university or language school in Italy must have a study visa. These can be obtained from your nearest Italian embassy or consulate. You will normally require confirmation of your enrolment, and proof of payment of fees and adequate funds to support yourself. The visa covers only the period of the enrolment. This type of visa is renewable within Italy but, again, only with confirmation of ongoing enrolment and proof that you are able to support yourself (bank statements are preferred).

Women Travellers

The most common source of discomfort for solo women in Italy is harassment. Local men are rarely shy about staring at women, especially if the staring is accompanied by the occasional 'ciao bella'. Usually the best response is to ignore them. If that doesn't work, politely say you're waiting for your marito (husband) or fidanzato (boyfriend) and, if necessary, walk away. Avoid becoming aggressive as this may result in an unpleasant confrontation. If all else fails, approach the nearest member of the police.

Watch out for men with wandering hands on crowded buses. Keep your back to the wall or make a loud fuss if someone starts fondling your behind. A loud 'Che schifo!' (How disgusting!) will usually do the trick. If a more serious incident occurs, report it to the police, who are then required to press charges.

Women travelling alone should use their common sense. Avoid solo hitchhiking or walking alone in dark streets, and look for hotels that are central (unsafe areas are noted in this book). In Naples, solo women should be especially vigilant in the Mercato, Quartieri Spagnoli and La Sanità districts after dark.

Work

EU citizens do not require any permits to live or work in Italy but, after three months' residence, are supposed to register themselves at the municipal registry office where they live and offer proof of work or sufficient funds to support themselves. Non-EU foreign citizens with five years' continuous legal residence may apply for permanent residence.

Transport

GETTING THERE & AWAY

A plethora of airlines link Italy to the rest of the world, and numerous airlines fly directly to Naples' international airport, better known as Capodichino. Naples is southern Italy's main transport hub, with excellent rail and bus connections to other parts of Campania and beyond. Naples is also a main port, hosting international cruise ships and operating car and passenger ferries to ports throughout the Mediterranean. Flights, tours and rail tickets can be booked online at lonelyplanet.com/bookings.

Entering the Region

EU and Swiss citizens can travel to Italy with their national identity card alone. All other nationalities must have a valid passport and may be required to fill out a landing card (at airports).

By law you should have your passport or ID card with you at all times. You'll need one of these documents for police registration every time you check into a hotel.

Air

Airports

Capodichino airport (NAP; ☎081 751 54 71; www.gesac.it), 7km northeast of central Naples, is southern Italy's main airport, linking Naples with most Italian and several major European cities, as well as New York.

The **Alibus** (☎800 639525; www.unicocampania.it) airport shuttle (€3, 45 minutes, every 20 to 30 minutes) connects the airport to Piazza Garibaldi (Stazione Centrale) and Molo Beverello (main ferry terminal).

Set taxi fares to the airport are as follows: €23 from a seafront hotel or from Mergellina hydrofoil terminal, €19 from Piazza Municipio and €15.50 from Stazione Centrale.

Curreri (☎081 801 54 20; www.curreriviaggi.it) runs seven services daily between the airport and Sorrento. Journey time is 75 minutes and tickets (available on board) cost €10.

Tickets

The internet is the easiest way of locating and booking reasonably priced seats. Full-time students and those under 26 years may qualify for discounted fares at agencies such as **STA Travel** (www.statravel.com). Many of these fares require a valid International Student Identity Card (ISIC).

Land

Reaching Campania overland involves traversing three-quarters of the entire length of Italy, which can either be an enormous drain on your time or, if you have plenty to spare, a wonderful way of seeing the country. Buses are usually the cheapest option, but services are less frequent and considerably less comfortable than the train.

Bus

Buses are the cheapest overland option to Italy, but services are less frequent, less comfortable and significantly slower than the train.

ONLINE TICKETS

For reasonably priced airfares, check the following online booking websites:

» **Cheap Flights** (www.cheapflights.com)
» **Ebookers.com** (www.ebookers.com)
» **Expedia** (www.expedia.com)
» **Kayak** (www.kayak.com)
» **Last minute** (www.lastminute.com)
» **Orbitz** (www.orbitz.com)
» **Priceline** (www.priceline.com)

Eurolines (www.eurolines.com) A consortium of coach companies with offices throughout Europe. Italy-bound buses head to Milan, Venice, Florence, Siena and Rome, from where Italian train and bus services continue south to Naples.

Miccolis (☑081 20 03 80; www.miccolis-spa.it) Runs several services a day from Naples to Potenza, Taranto, Brindisi and Lecce.

Marino (☑080 311 23 35; www.marinobus.it) Runs daily services from Naples to Bari and Matera.

SAIS (www.saistrasporti.it) Operates long-haul services to Sicily from Naples and Rome.

Car & Motorcycle

If you are planning to drive to Naples, bear in mind the cost of toll roads and the fact that fuel prices in Italy are among the highest in Europe. Most importantly, however, if you are spending time in Naples, it is unlikely you will feel tempted to drive and you will also have to pay for secure parking. Although a definite bonus for visiting more remote areas of Campania, like west of Sorrento and the Parco Nazionale del Cilento, given the cost of driving here, renting a car is a wiser option.

Train

The national rail company, **Trenitalia** (☑892 021; www.trenitalia.com), has a comprehensive network throughout the country, and also operates long-distance trains throughout Europe. Within Italy, direct trains run from Milan, Florence and Rome to Naples. From Naples, trains continue south to Reggio di Calabria and to Messina, Sicily. Naples is served by *regionale* (regional), *diretto* (direct), Intercity and the high-speed Frecciarossa trains. They arrive and depart from **Stazione Centrale** (☑081 554 31 88) or **Stazione Garibaldi** (on the lower level). There are up to 30 trains daily to and from Rome.

GETTING AROUND

Bicycle

Cycling is a dangerous option in Naples – a city where all road rules are seemingly ignored. Most drivers speed, chat on their mobile phones and ignore traffic lights. Bicycle and motorcycle theft is rife.

Bicycle hire is costly in Naples (from €20 per day), so if you are staying for some time and are dead-set on taking to the saddle, it may be cheaper to actually buy a bike. Taking your bicycle to the Amalfi Coast is also a fraught option: think blind corners and sheer, precipitous drops.

Boat

Naples, the bay islands and the Amalfi Coast are served by a comprehensive ferry network. Catch fast ferries and hydrofoils for Capri, Sorrento, Ischia (both Ischia Porto and Forio) and Procida from Molo Beverello in front of Castel Nuovo; hydrofoils for Capri, Ischia and Procida also sail from Mergellina.

Ferries for Sicily, the Aeolian Islands and Sardinia sail from Molo Angioino (right beside Molo Beverello) and neighbouring Calata Porta di Massa. Slow ferries to Ischia and Procida also depart from Calata Porta di Massa.

Ferry services are pared back considerably in winter, and adverse sea conditions may affect sailing schedules.

See the tables (p267, p268) listing hydrofoil and ferry destinations from Naples. The fares, unless otherwise stated, are for a one-way, high-season deck-class single.

Tickets for shorter journeys can be bought at the ticket booths on Molo Beverello and at Mergellina. For longer journeys try the offices of the ferry companies or a travel agent. Following is a list of hydrofoil and ferry companies:

Caremar (Map p56; ☑199 116655; www.caremar.it)

Alilauro (☑081 497 22 22; www.alilauro.it)

Navigazione Libera del Golfo (NLG; Map p56; ☑081 552 07 63; www.navlib.it)

SNAV (Map p56; ☑081 428 55 55; www.snav.it)

Medmar (Map p56; ☑081 333 44 11; www.medmargroup.it)

CLIMATE CHANGE & TRAVEL

Every form of transport that relies on carbon-based fuel generates CO_2, the main cause of human-induced climate change. Modern travel is dependent on aeroplanes, which might use less fuel per kilometre per person than most cars but travel much greater distances. The altitude at which aircraft emit gases (including CO_2) and particles also contributes to their climate change impact. Many websites offer 'carbon calculators' that allow people to estimate the carbon emissions generated by their journey and, for those who wish to do so, to offset the impact of the greenhouse gases emitted with contributions to portfolios of climate-friendly initiatives throughout the world. Lonely Planet offsets the carbon footprint of all staff and author travel.

HYDROFOILS & HIGH-SPEED FERRIES

DESTINATION (FROM NAPLES – MOLO BEVERELLO)	FERRY COMPANY	PRICE (€)	DURATION (MIN)	DAILY FREQUENCY (HIGH SEASON)
Capri	Caremar	19	50	4
Capri	Navigazione Libera del Golfo	20.20	50	9
Capri	SNAV	20.20	50	9
Ischia (Casamicciola Terme)	Caremar	17.50	65	4
Ischia (Forio)	Alilauro	19.80	50-65	7
Ischia (Casamicciola Terme)	SNAV	18.70	55	8
Procida	Caremar	15.70	40	5
Procida	SNAV	13.20	40	4
Sorrento	Alilauro	12.10	45	6
Sorrento	SNAV	13.10	35	7

Siremar (Map p56; ☎199 118866; www.siremar.it)
Tirrenia (Map p56; ☎081 720 11 11; www.tirrenia.it)

Bus

ANM (☎800 639525; www.unicocampania.it) operates city buses in Naples. There's no central bus station but most buses pass through Piazza Garibaldi. Useful routes include the following:

» **140** Santa Lucia to Posillipo via Mergellina

» **154** From Via Volta to Via Vespucci, Via Marina, Via Depretis, Via Acton, Via Morelli, Piazza Vittoria and Via Santa Lucia

» **C24** From Via Mergellina to Corso Vittorio Emanuele, Via Crispi, Via Colonna, Via Carducci, Riviera di Chiaia, Piazza Vittoria, Via Santa Lucia, Via Morelli, Piazza dei Martiri, Via Filangieri, Via dei Mille, Via Colonna, Via Crispi, Corso Vittorio Emanuele, Via Piedigrotta and back to Via Mergellina

» **C55** Circles centro storico (historic centre), travelling from Piazza Cavour to Via Enrico Pessina, Piazza Dante, Via Toledo, Piazza Bovio, Corso Umberto I and Via Duomo

» **R1** From Piazza Medaglie d'Oro to Piazza Carità, Piazza Dante and Piazza Bovio

» **R2** From Stazione Centrale, along Corso Umberto I, to Piazza Bovio, Piazza del Municipio and Piazza Trento e Trieste

» **R4** From Capodimonte down past Via Dante to Piazza Municipio and back again

Hop-on, hop-off tourist bus **City Sightseeing Napoli** (Map p40; ☎081 551 72 79; www.napoli.city-sightseeing.it; adult/child €22/11) operates four routes: Routes A and R cover the centro storico (Route A also reaches Capodimonte); Route B follows the Lungomare seafront and the scenic Posillipo road; and Route C heads up to Vomero. Tickets (adult/child €22/11) are valid for 24 hours.

Regional bus services are operated by a number of companies, the most useful of which is **SITA** (☎199 730749; www.sitasudtrasporti.it), which runs frequent daily services from Sorrento and Salerno to the Amalfi Coast.

Other useful companies include the following:

EAV Bus (www.eavbus.it) Handy for reaching the Campi Flegrei from Naples, with destinations including Lucrino (€2.10, 45 minutes), Bacoli (€2.10, 55 minutes) and Monte di Procida (€2.10, 80 minutes).

Marino (☎080 311 23 35; www.marinobus.it) Destinations include Bari (€19, three hours).

Miccolis (☎081 20 03 80; www.miccolis-spa.it) Runs to Taranto (€22, three to four hours), Brindisi (€29.60, five hours) and Lecce (€32, six hours).

CLP (☎081 531 17 07; www.clpbus.it) Services Foggia (€11, two hours), Perugia (€29.45, 3½ hours) and Assisi (€32, 4½ hours).

Car & Motorcycle

Driving in Naples is not encouraged. The centro storico is off-limits to nonresident vehicles, and anarchic traffic conditions make for highly stressful situations. Parking is also a nightmare. A scooter is quicker and easier to park but is even more nerve-wracking to ride. Car/bike theft is also a major problem.

If you're determined to drive, there are some simple guidelines: get used to tailgaters; worry about what's in front of you, not behind; watch out for scooters; give way to pedestrians no matter where they appear from; approach all junctions and traffic lights with extreme caution; and keep cool.

For more-detailed information, check the website www.comune.napoli.it (in Italian).

Away from the city, a car becomes more practical. However, be aware that driving along the Amalfi Coast can be quite a hair-raising experience as buses careen around impossibly tight hairpin bends and locals brazenly overtake anything in their path. On the bay islands – Capri, Ischia and Procida – hiring a scooter is an excellent way of getting around.

Naples is on the north–south Autostrada del Sole, the A1 (north to Rome and Milan) and the A3 (south to Salerno and Reggio di Calabria). The A30 skirts Naples to the northeast, while the A16 heads across to Bari.

When approaching the city, the motorways meet the Tangenziale di Napoli, a major ring road. The ring road hugs the city's northern fringe, meeting the A1 for Rome and the A2 to Capodichino airport in the east, and continuing towards Campi Flegrei and Pozzuoli in the west.

Automobile Associations

Italy's automobile association, the **Automobile Club d'Italia** (ACI; www.aci.it, in Italian; Piazzale Tecchio 49/d), is the best source of motoring information. It also operates a 24-hour **recovery service** (☎ from landline 803 116, from mobile phone 800 116800).

Bringing Your Own Car

If you are determined to bring your own car to Naples, ensure that all the paperwork is in order and that you carry a hazard triangle and a reflective jacket in your car – and don't forget that Italians drive on the right-hand side! Arriving in Naples, you should be prepared for heavy traffic jams at commuter times and at lunchtime. Familiarise yourself with important road signs like *uscita* (exit) and *raccordo* (ring road surrounding a city).

Driving Licence & Documentation

An EU driving licence is valid for driving in Italy. However, if you've got an old-style green UK licence or a licence issued by a non-EU country, you'll need an International Driving Permit (IDP). Valid for 12 months, these are inexpensive (about US$21 or UK£5.50) and are easily available from your national automobile association – take along a passport photo and your driving licence. When driving you should always carry the IDP with your home licence, as it's not valid on its own.

Fuel & Spare Parts

Petrol stations located along the main highways are open 24 hours. In smaller towns, the opening hours are generally 7am to 7pm Monday to

FERRIES

DESTINATION (FROM NAPLES – CALATA PORTA DI MASSA & MOLO ANGIOINO)	FERRY COMPANY	PRICE (€)	DURATION	FREQUENCY (HIGH SEASON)
Aeolian Islands	SNAV (Jul–Sep only)	from 65	4 to 6 hours	1 daily
Aeolian Islands	Siremar	from 50	30 minutes	2 weekly
Cagliari (Sardinia)	Tirrenia	from 45	16 hours 15 minutes	2 weekly
Capri	Caremar	12.70	80 minutes	3 daily
Ischia	Caremar	11.20	90 minutes	7 daily
Ischia	Medmar	11.35	75 minutes	6 daily
Milazzo (Sicily)	Milazzo (Siremar)	from 50	16 hours	2 weekly
Palermo (Sicily)	SNAV	from 35	10 hours 15 minutes	1-2 daily
Palermo (Sicily)	Tirrenia	from 45	11 hours 45 minutes	1 daily
Procida	Caremar	11.20	60 minutes	7 daily

Saturday with a lunchtime break. At the time of writing the cost of *benzina senza piombo* (unleaded petrol) and *gasoil* (diesel) was €1.825 and €1.725 per litre.

An increasing number of petrol stations are self-service. At these, simply key in the number of the pump, the amount you require and then insert the necessary bill (only acceptable in denominations of €5, €10, €20 and €50).

If you run into mechanical problems, the nearest petrol station should be able to advise a reliable mechanic, although few have workshops on-site and they are, overall, very poor at stocking car parts. If you are driving a hire car and run into any serious problems, your car-hire company will probably have an emergency tow service with a toll-free call. You will need to report which road you are on, which direction you are heading, the make of car and your license plate number (*targa*).

Car Hire

» If hiring a car, expect to pay around €60 per day for an economy car or a scooter. Prebooking via the internet often costs less than hiring a car in Italy.

» Renters must generally be aged 25 years or over, with a credit card and home country driving licence or IDP.

» Consider hiring a small car, which will reduce your fuel expense and help you negotiate narrow city lanes and tight parking spaces.

» Check with your credit-card company to see if it offers a Collision Damage Waiver, which covers you for additional damage if you use that card to pay for the car. Multinational car-hire agencies include the following:

Avis (☎081 28 40 41; www.avisautonoleggio.it; Corso Novara 5 & Capodichino airport)

Europcar (☎081 780 56 43; www.europcar.it; Capodichino airport)

Hertz (☎081 20 62 28; www.hertz.it; Via Giuseppe Ricciardi

5, Capodichino airport & in Mergellina) Also at Via Marina Varco Pisacane Calata Piliero, beside the ferry terminal.

Maggiore (☎081 28 78 58; www.maggiore.it; Stazione Centrale & Capodichino airport)

Rent Sprint (☎081 764 13 33; www.rentsprint.it; Via Santa Lucia 36) Scooter hire only.

Parking

Parking in Naples is no fun. Blue lines by the side of the road denote pay-and-display parking – buy tickets at the meters or from tobacconists – with rates costing €1.50 to €2 per hour. Elsewhere street parking is often overseen by illegal attendants who will expect a €1 to €2 fee for their protection of your car. It's usually easier to bite the bullet and pay them than attempt a moral stance.

East of the city centre, there's a 24-hour car park at Via Brin (€1.30 for the first four hours, and €7.20 for 24 hours). It is also the safer option as thieves often target hired or foreign-registered cars.

Elsewhere in the region, parking can be similarly problematic, especially at the main resorts on the Amalfi Coast and, even more especially, in August.

Road Rules

Contrary to appearances there are road rules in Italy. Here are some of the most essential:

» Cars drive on the right side of the road and overtake on the left.

» Seat belt use (front and rear) is mandatory.

» You must give way to cars entering an intersection from a road on your right, unless otherwise indicated.

» In the event of a breakdown, a warning triangle is compulsory, as is use of an approved yellow or orange safety vest if you leave your vehicle.

» Italy's blood-alcohol limit is 0.05%. Random breath tests

occur and penalties can be severe.

» Speed limits for cars are 130km/h to 150km/h on *autostrade* (freeways); 110km/h on other main highways; 90km/h on minor, non-urban roads; and 50km/h in built-up areas.

» The speed limit for mopeds is 40km/h.

» Helmets are required on all two-wheeled transport.

» Headlights are compulsory day and night for all vehicles on the *autostrade*, and advisable for motorcycles even on smaller roads.

Toll Roads

There are tolls on most motorways, payable by cash or credit card as you exit. For information on traffic conditions, tolls and driving distances, see www.autostrade.it.

Funicular

Three of Naples' four *funiculare* (funicular) railways connect the city centre with Vomero. The fourth, **Funiculare di Mergellina** (7am-10pm), connects the waterfront at Via Mergellina with Via Manzoni. Unico Napoli tickets are valid onboard.

Funiculare Centrale (6.30am-10pm Mon & Tue, to 12.30am Wed-Sun) Ascends from Via Toledo to Piazza Fuga.

Funiculare di Chiaia (7am-10pm Tue & Wed, to 12.30am Thu, Sun & Mon, to 2am Fri & Sat) Travels from Via del Parco Margherita to Via Domenico Cimarosa.

Funiculare di Montesanto (7am-10pm) From Piazza Montesanto to Via Raffaele Morghen.

Local Transport

Metro

Naples' **Metropolitana** (☎800 568866; www.metro.na.it) is, in fact, mostly above ground.

TICKETS, PLEASE

Tickets for public transport in Naples and the surrounding Campania region are managed by the Unico Campania consortium (www.unicocampania.it). There are various plans available, depending on where you are travelling to. The following is a rundown of the various tickets on offer:

» **Unico Napoli** (90 minutes €1.20, 24 hours weekdays/weekends €3.60/3) Unlimited travel by bus, tram, funicular, metro, Ferrovia Cumana or Circumflegrea.

» **Unico Costiera** (45 minutes €2.40, 90 minutes €3.60, 24 hours €7.20, 72 hours €18) A money saver if you plan on much travelling by SITA or EAV bus and/or Circumvesuviana train in the Bay of Naples and Amalfi Coast area. The 24- and 72-hour tickets also cover the City Sightseeing Sorrento tourist bus service between Amalfi and Ravello, and Amalfi and Maiori, which runs from April to October.

» **Unico 3T** (72 hours €20) Unlimited travel through Campania, including the Alibus airport shuttle and transport on the islands of Ischia and Procida.

» **Unico Ischia** (90 minutes €1.40, 24 hours €4.50) Unlimited bus travel on Ischia.

» **Unico Capri** (60 minutes €2.40, 24 hours €8.40) Unlimited bus travel on Capri. The 60-minute ticket also allows a single trip on the funicular connecting Marina Grande to Capri Town; the daily ticket allows for two funicular trips.

Tickets are sold at stations, ANM booths and tobacconists.

» **Line 1** (6am-11pm) At the time this book went to press, the line ran north from Università (for Piazza Bovio), stopping at Toledo (for Via Toledo), Dante (for Piazza Dante), Museo (for Piazza Cavour and Line 2), Materdei, Salvator Rosa, Cilea, Piazza Vanvitelli, Piazza Medaglie D'Oro and seven stops beyond. By late 2013, the line's extension will also see it stop at Municipio (for Piazza Municipio and the ferry terminal), Duomo (for Via Duomo) and Garibaldi (for Stazione Centrale).

» **Line 2** (5.30am-11pm) Runs from Gianturco, just east of Stazione Centrale, with stops at Piazza Garibaldi (for Stazione Centrale), Piazza Cavour, Montesanto, Piazza Amedeo, Mergellina, Piazza Leopardi, Campi Flegrei, Cavalleggeri d'Aosta, Bagnoli and Pozzuoli.

Metro journeys are covered by Unico Napoli tickets.

Taxi

Official taxis are white and metered and bear the Naples symbol, the Pulcinella (with his distinctive white cone-shaped hat and long hooked nose) on their front doors. Always ensure the meter is running.

The minimum starting fare is €3, with a baffling range of additional charges, all of which are listed at www.consorziotaxinapoli.it/who -we-are/rates/. These extras include the following:

» €1 for a radio taxi call

» €2.50 extra on Sundays, holidays and between 10pm and 7am

» €2.60 for an airport run, €4 for trips starting at the airport and €0.50 per piece of luggage in the boot (trunk). Guide dogs for the blind and wheelchairs are carried free of charge.

There are taxi stands at most of the city's main piazzas. Alternatively, call one of the following taxi cooperatives: Consortaxi (☎081 20 20 20) Consorzio Taxi Napoli (☎081 88 88; www.consorzio taxinapoli.it) Radio Taxi Napoli (☎081 556 44 44; www.radiotaxi napoli.it) Radio Taxi La Partenope (☎081 01 01; www.radiotaxila partenope.it)

Train

Circumvesuviana (☎081 772 24 44; wwww.vesuviana. it) trains connect Naples to Sorrento (€4, 65 minutes, around 40 trains daily). Stops along the way include Ercolano (€2.10, 15 minutes) and Pompeii (€2.80, 35 minutes). From Naples, trains depart from Stazione Circumvesuviana (☎081 772 24 44; www.vesuviana.it; Corso Garibaldi), which is attached to Stazione Centrale.

Ferrovia Cumana (www. sepsa.it) train services between Naples and the Campi Flegrei depart from Stazione Cumana di Montesanto on Piazza Montesanto, 500m southwest of Piazza Dante. Stops include Pozzuoli (€1.20, 20 minutes, every 25 minutes).

Trams

The following trams may be useful:

» **Tram 1** Operates from east of Stazione Centrale, through Piazza Garibaldi, the city centre and along the waterfront to Piazza Vittoria.

» **Tram 29** Travels from Piazza Garibaldi to the city centre along Corso Giuseppe Garibaldi.

WANT MORE?

For in-depth language information and handy phrases, check out Lonely Planet's *Italian Phrasebook*. You'll find it at **shop .lonelyplanet.com**, or you can buy Lonely Planet's iPhone phrasebooks at the Apple App Store.

Language

Standard Italian is taught and spoken throughout Italy. Dialects are an important part of regional identity, but you'll have no trouble being understood anywhere if you stick to standard Italian, which we've also used in this chapter.

The sounds used in spoken Italian can all be found in English. If you read our coloured pronunciation guides as if they were English, you'll be understood. The stressed syllables are indicated with italics. Note that ai is pronounced as in 'aisle', ay as in 'say', ow as in 'how', dz as the 'ds' in 'lids', and that r is a strong and rolled sound. Keep in mind that Italian consonants can have a stronger, emphatic pronunciation – if the consonant is written as a double letter, it should be pronounced a little stronger, eg *sonno* son·no (sleep) versus *sono* so·no (I am).

BASICS

Italian has two words for 'you' – use the polite form *Lei* lay if you're talking to strangers, officials or people older than you. With people familiar to you or younger than you, you can use the informal form *tu* too.

In Italian, all nouns and adjectives are either masculine or feminine, and so are the articles *il/la* eel/la (the) and *un/una* oon/oo·na (a) that go with the nouns.

In this chapter the polite/informal and masculine/feminine options are included where necessary, separated with a slash and indicated with 'pol/inf' and 'm/f'.

Hello.	*Buongiorno.*	bwon·*jor*·no
Goodbye.	*Arrivederci.*	a·ree·ve·*der*·chee

Yes.	*Sì.*	see
No.	*No.*	no
Excuse me.	*Mi scusi.* (pol)	mee skoo·zee
	Scusami. (inf)	skoo·za·mee
Sorry.	*Mi dispiace.*	mee dees·*pya*·che
Please.	*Per favore.*	per fa·*vo*·re
Thank you.	*Grazie.*	*gra*·tsye
You're welcome.	*Prego.*	*pre*·go

How are you?
Come sta/stai? (pol/inf)   *ko*·me sta/stai

Fine. And you?
Bene. E Lei/tu? (pol/inf)   *be*·ne e lay/too

What's your name?
Come si chiama? pol   *ko*·me see *kya*·ma
Come ti chiami? inf   *ko*·me tee *kya*·mee

My name is ...
Mi chiamo ...   mee *kya*·mo ...

Do you speak English?
Parla/Parli   *par*·la/*par*·lee
inglese? (pol/inf)   een·*gle*·ze

I don't understand.
Non capisco.   non ka·*pee*·sko

ACCOMMODATION

Do you have a ... room?	*Avete una camera ...?*	a·*ve*·te oo·na *ka*·me·ra ...
double	*doppia con letto matrimoniale*	*do*·pya kon *le*·to ma·tree·mo·*nya*·le
single	*singola*	*seen*·go·la

How much is it per ...?	Quanto costa per ...?	kwan·to kos·ta per ...
night	una notte	oo·na no·te
person	persona	per·so·na

Is breakfast included?
La colazione è compresa? — la ko·la·tsyo·ne e kom·pre·sa

air-con	aria condizionata	a·rya kon·dee·tsyo·na·ta
bathroom	bagno	ba·nyo
campsite	campeggio	kam·pe·jo
guesthouse	pensione	pen·syo·ne
hotel	albergo	al·ber·go
youth hostel	ostello della gioventù	os·te·lo de·la jo·ven·too
window	finestra	fee·nes·tra

DIRECTIONS

Where's ...?
Dov'è ...? — do·ve ...

What's the address?
Qual è l'indirizzo? — kwa·le leen·dee·ree·tso

Could you please write it down?
Può scriverlo, per favore? — pwo skree·ver·lo per fa·vo·re

Can you show me (on the map)?
Può mostrarmi (sulla pianta)? — pwo mos·trar·mee (soo·la pyan·ta)

at the corner	all'angolo	a·lan·go·lo
at the traffic lights	al semaforo	al se·ma·fo·ro
behind	dietro	dye·tro
far	lontano	lon·ta·no
in front of	davanti a	da·van·tee a
left	a sinistra	a see·nee·stra
near	vicino	vee·chee·no
next to	accanto a	a·kan·to a
opposite	di fronte a	dee fron·te a
right	a destra	a de·stra
straight ahead	sempre diritto	sem·pre dee·ree·to

EATING & DRINKING

What would you recommend?
Cosa mi consiglia? — ko·za mee kon·see·lya

What's in that dish?
Quali ingredienti ci sono in questo piatto? — kwa·li een·gre·dyen·tee chee so·no een kwe·sto pya·to

KEY PATTERNS

To get by in Italian, mix and match these simple patterns with words of your choice:

When's (the next flight)?
A che ora è (il prossimo volo)? — a ke o·ra e (eel pro·see·mo vo·lo)

Where's (the station)?
Dov'è (la stazione)? — do·ve (la sta·tsyo·ne)

I'm looking for (a hotel).
Sto cercando (un albergo). — sto cher·kan·do (oon al·ber·go)

Do you have (a map)?
Ha (una pianta)? — a (oo·na pyan·ta)

Is there (a toilet)?
C'è (un gabinetto)? — che (oon ga·bee·ne·to)

I'd like (a coffee).
Vorrei (un caffè). — vo·ray (oon ka·fe)

I'd like to (hire a car).
Vorrei (noleggiare una macchina). — vo·ray (no·le·ja·re oo·na ma·kee·na)

Can I (enter)?
Posso (entrare)? — po·so (en·tra·re)

Could you please (help me)?
Può (aiutarmi), per favore? — pwo (a·yoo·tar·mee) per fa·vo·re

Do I have to (book a seat)?
Devo (prenotare un posto)? — de·vo (pre·no·ta·re oon po·sto)

What's the local speciality?
Qual è la specialità di questa regione? — kwa·le la spe·cha·lee·ta dee kwe·sta re·jo·ne

That was delicious!
Era squisito! — e·ra skwee·zee·to

Cheers!
Salute! — sa·loo·te

Please bring the bill.
Mi porta il conto, per favore? — mee por·ta eel kon·to per fa·vo·re

I'd like to reserve a table for ...	Vorrei prenotare un tavolo per ...	vo·ray pre·no·ta·re oon ta·vo·lo per ...
(two) people	(due) persone	(doo·e) per·so·ne
(eight) o'clock	le (otto)	le (o·to)

I don't eat ...	Non mangio ...	non man·jo ...
eggs	uova	wo·va
fish	pesce	pe·she
nuts	noci	no·chee
(red) meat	carne (rossa)	kar·ne (ro·sa)

Key Words

bar	*locale*	*lo·ka·le*
bottle	*bottiglia*	*bo·tee·lya*
breakfast	*prima colazione*	*pree·ma ko·la·tsyo·ne*
cafe	*bar*	*bar*
cold	*freddo*	*fre·do*
dinner	*cena*	*che·na*
drink list	*lista delle bevande*	*lee·sta de·le be·van·de*
fork	*forchetta*	*for·ke·ta*
glass	*bicchiere*	*bee·kye·re*
grocery store	*alimentari*	*a·lee·men·ta·ree*
hot	*caldo*	*kal·do*
knife	*coltello*	*kol·te·lo*
lunch	*pranzo*	*pran·dzo*
market	*mercato*	*mer·ka·to*
menu	*menù*	*me·noo*
plate	*piatto*	*pya·to*
restaurant	*ristorante*	*ree·sto·ran·te*
spicy	*piccante*	*pee·kan·te*
spoon	*cucchiaio*	*koo·kya·yo*
vegetarian (food)	*vegetariano*	*ve·je·ta·rya·no*
with	*con*	*kon*
without	*senza*	*sen·tsa*

Meat & Fish

beef	*manzo*	*man·dzo*
chicken	*pollo*	*po·lo*
duck	*anatra*	*a·na·tra*
fish	*pesce*	*pe·she*
herring	*aringa*	*a·reen·ga*
lamb	*agnello*	*a·nye·lo*
lobster	*aragosta*	*a·ra·gos·ta*
meat	*carne*	*kar·ne*
mussels	*cozze*	*ko·tse*
oysters	*ostriche*	*o·stree·ke*
pork	*maiale*	*ma·ya·le*
prawn	*gambero*	*gam·be·ro*
salmon	*salmone*	*sal·mo·ne*
scallops	*capasante*	*ka·pa·san·te*
seafood	*frutti di mare*	*froo·tee dee ma·re*
shrimp	*gambero*	*gam·be·ro*
squid	*calamari*	*ka·la·ma·ree*
trout	*trota*	*tro·ta*
tuna	*tonno*	*to·no*
turkey	*tacchino*	*ta·kee·no*
veal	*vitello*	*vee·te·lo*

Fruit & Vegetables

apple	*mela*	*me·la*
beans	*fagioli*	*fa·jo·lee*
cabbage	*cavolo*	*ka·vo·lo*
capsicum	*peperone*	*pe·pe·ro·ne*
carrot	*carota*	*ka·ro·ta*
cauliflower	*cavolfiore*	*ka·vol·fyo·re*
cucumber	*cetriolo*	*che·tree·o·lo*
fruit	*frutta*	*froo·ta*
grapes	*uva*	*oo·va*
lemon	*limone*	*lee·mo·ne*
lentils	*lenticchie*	*len·tee·kye*
mushroom	*funghi*	*foon·gee*
nuts	*noci*	*no·chee*
onions	*cipolle*	*chee·po·le*
orange	*arancia*	*a·ran·cha*
peach	*pesca*	*pe·ska*
peas	*piselli*	*pee·ze·lee*
pineapple	*ananas*	*a·na·nas*
plum	*prugna*	*proo·nya*
potatoes	*patate*	*pa·ta·te*
spinach	*spinaci*	*spee·na·chee*
tomatoes	*pomodori*	*po·mo·do·ree*
vegetables	*verdura*	*ver·doo·ra*

Other

bread	*pane*	*pa·ne*
butter	*burro*	*boo·ro*
cheese	*formaggio*	*for·ma·jo*
eggs	*uova*	*wo·va*
honey	*miele*	*mye·le*

Signs

Entrata/Ingresso	Entrance
Uscita	Exit
Aperto	Open
Chiuso	Closed
Informazioni	Information
Proibito/Vietato	Prohibited
Gabinetti/Servizi	Toilets
Uomini	Men
Donne	Women

ice	ghiaccio	gya·cho
jam	marmellata	mar·me·la·ta
noodles	pasta	pas·ta
oil	olio	o·lyo
pepper	pepe	pe·pe
rice	riso	ree·zo
salt	sale	sa·le
soup	minestra	mee·nes·tra
soy sauce	salsa di soia	sal·sa dee so·ya
sugar	zucchero	tsoo·ke·ro
vinegar	aceto	a·che·to

Drinks

beer	birra	bee·ra
coffee	caffè	ka·fe
(orange) juice	succo (d'arancia)	soo·ko (da·ran·cha)
milk	latte	la·te
red wine	vino rosso	vee·no ro·so
soft drink	bibita	bee·bee·ta
tea	tè	te
(mineral) water	acqua (minerale)	a·kwa (mee·ne·ra·le)
white wine	vino bianco	vee·no byan·ko

EMERGENCIES

Help!
Aiuto! a·yoo·to

Leave me alone!
Lasciami in pace! la·sha·mee een pa·che

I'm lost.
Mi sono perso/a. (m/f) mee so·no per·so/a

There's been an accident.
C'è stato un incidente. che sta·to oon een·chee·den·te

Call the police!
Chiami la polizia! kya·mee la po·lee·tsee·a

Call a doctor!
Chiami un medico! kya·mee oon me·dee·ko

Where are the toilets?
Dove sono i gabinetti? do·ve so·no ee ga·bee·ne·tee

Question Words

How?	Come?	ko·me
What?	Che cosa?	ke ko·za
When?	Quando?	kwan·do
Where?	Dove?	do·ve
Who?	Chi?	kee
Why?	Perché?	per·ke

I'm sick.
Mi sento male. mee sen·to ma·le

It hurts here.
Mi fa male qui. mee fa ma·le kwee

I'm allergic to ...
Sono allergico/a a ... (m/f) so·no a·ler·jee·ko/a a ...

SHOPPING & SERVICES

I'd like to buy ...
Vorrei comprare ... vo·ray kom·pra·re ...

I'm just looking.
Sto solo guardando. sto so·lo gwar·dan·do

Can I look at it?
Posso dare un'occhiata? po·so da·re oo·no·kya·ta

How much is this?
Quanto costa questo? kwan·to kos·ta kwe·sto

It's too expensive.
È troppo caro/a. (m/f) e tro·po ka·ro/a

Can you lower the price?
Può farmi lo sconto? pwo far·mee lo skon·to

There's a mistake in the bill.
C'è un errore nel conto. che oo·ne·ro·re nel kon·to

ATM	Bancomat	ban·ko·mat
post office	ufficio postale	oo·fee·cho pos·ta·le
tourist office	ufficio del turismo	oo·fee·cho del too·reez·mo

TIME & DATES

What time is it?	Che ora è?	ke o·ra e
It's one o'clock.	È l'una.	e loo·na
It's (two) o'clock.	Sono le (due).	so·no le (doo·e)
Half past (one).	(L'una) e mezza.	(loo·na) e me·dza

in the morning	di mattina	dee ma·tee·na
in the afternoon	di pomeriggio	dee po·me·ree·jo
in the evening	di sera	dee se·ra

yesterday	ieri	ye·ree
today	oggi	o·jee
tomorrow	domani	do·ma·nee

Monday	lunedì	loo·ne·dee
Tuesday	martedì	mar·te·dee
Wednesday	mercoledì	mer·ko·le·dee
Thursday	giovedì	jo·ve·dee
Friday	venerdì	ve·ner·dee
Saturday	sabato	sa·ba·to
Sunday	domenica	do·me·nee·ka

Numbers

1	uno	oo·no
2	due	doo·e
3	tre	tre
4	quattro	kwa·tro
5	cinque	cheen·kwe
6	sei	say
7	sette	se·te
8	otto	o·to
9	nove	no·ve
10	dieci	dye·chee
20	venti	ven·tee
30	trenta	tren·ta
40	quaranta	kwa·ran·ta
50	cinquanta	cheen·kwan·ta
60	sessanta	se·san·ta
70	settanta	se·tan·ta
80	ottanta	o·tan·ta
90	novanta	no·van·ta
100	cento	chen·to
1000	mille	mee·lel

January	gennaio	je·na·yo
February	febbraio	fe·bra·yo
March	marzo	mar·tso
April	aprile	a·pree·le
May	maggio	ma·jo
June	giugno	joo·nyo
July	luglio	loo·lyo
August	agosto	a·gos·to
September	settembre	se·tem·bre
October	ottobre	o·to·bre
November	novembre	no·vem·bre
December	dicembre	dee·chem·bre

TRANSPORT

Public Transport

At what time does the ... leave/arrive?	A che ora parte/ arriva ...?	a ke o·ra par·te/ a·ree·va ...
boat	la nave	la na·ve
bus	l'autobus	low·to·boos
ferry	il traghetto	eel tra·ge·to
metro	la metro-politana	la me·tro-po·lee·ta·na
plane	l'aereo	la·e·re·o
train	il treno	eel tre·no

... ticket	un biglietto ...	oon bee·lye·to
one-way	di sola andata	dee so·la an·da·ta
return	di andata e ritorno	dee an·da·ta e ree·tor·no

bus stop	fermata dell'autobus	fer·ma·ta del ow·to·boos
platform	binario	bee·na·ryo
ticket office	biglietteria	bee·lye·te·ree·a
timetable	orario	o·ra·ryo
train station	stazione ferroviaria	sta·tsyo·ne fe·ro·vyar·ya

Does it stop at ...?
Si ferma a ...?   see fer·ma a ...

Please tell me when we get to ...
Mi dica per favore   mee dee·ka per fa·vo·re
quando arriviamo a ...   kwan·do a·ree·vya·mo a ...

I want to get off here.
Voglio scendere qui.   vo·lyo shen·de·re kwee

Driving & Cycling

I'd like to hire a/an ...	Vorrei noleggiare un/una ... (m/f)	vo·ray no·le·ja·re oon/oo·na ...
4WD	fuoristrada (m)	fwo·ree·stra·da
bicycle	bicicletta (f)	bee·chee·kle·ta
car	macchina (f)	ma·kee·na
motorbike	moto (f)	mo·to

bicycle pump	pompa della bicicletta	pom·pa de·la bee·chee·kle·ta
child seat	seggiolino	se·jo·lee·no
helmet	casco	kas·ko
mechanic	meccanico	me·ka·nee·ko
petrol/gas	benzina	ben·dzee·na
service station	stazione di servizio	sta·tsyo·ne dee ser·vee·tsyo

Is this the road to ...?
Questa strada porta a ...? kwe·sta stra·da por·ta a ...

(How long) Can I park here?
(Per quanto tempo)   (per kwan·to tem·po)
Posso parcheggiare qui? po·so par·ke·ja·re kwee

The car/motorbike has broken down (at ...).
La macchina/moto si è   la ma·kee·na/mo·to see e
guastata (a ...).   gwas·ta·ta (a ...)

I have a flat tyre.
Ho una gomma bucata.   o oo·na go·ma boo·ka·ta

I've run out of petrol.
Ho esaurito la   o e·zow·ree·to la
benzina.   ben·dzee·na

GLOSSARY

Albergo (alberghi) – hotel (hotels)

alimentari – grocery shop

allergia – allergy

archeologica – archaeology

autostrada (autostrade) – motorway, highway (motorways, highways)

bagno – bathroom; also toilet

bancomat – Automated teller machine (ATM)

bassi – one-room, ground-floor apartments mostly found in the traditionally poorer areas of Naples

benzina – petrol

biblioteca (biblioteche) – library (libraries)

biglietto – ticket

biglietto giornaliero – daily ticket

caffettiera – Italian coffee percolator

calcio – football (soccer)

camera – room

cambio – currency-exchange bureau

canzone (canzoni) – song (songs)

cappella – chapel

carabinieri – police with military and civil duties

carta d'identità – identity card

carta telefonica – phonecard

casa – house; home

casareccio – home style

castello – castle

catacomba – underground tomb complex

centro – city centre

centro storico – historic centre; old city

chiesa (chiese) – church (churches)

chiostro – cloister

cimitero – cemetery

colle/collina – hill

colonna – column

commissariato – local police station

comune – equivalent to a municipality or county; town or city council; historically,

a commune (self-governing town or city)

concerto – concert

corso – main street

cripta – crypt

cupola – dome

Dio (Dei) – God (Gods)

faraglione (faraglioni) – rock tower; rock pinnacle (rock towers; rock pinnacles)

farmacia – pharmacy

ferrovia – train station

festa – feast day; holiday

fiume – river

fontana – fountain

forno – bakery

forte/fortezza – fort

forum (fora) – (Latin) public square (public squares)

francobollo (francobolli) – stamp (stamps)

gabinetto – toilet; WC

gasolio – diesel

gelateria – ice-cream parlour

giardino (giardini) – garden (gardens)

golfo – gulf

gratis – free (no cost)

isola – island

lago – lake

largo – small square

lavanderia – laundrette

libreria – bookshop

lido – beach

lungomare – seafront; esplanade

mare – sea

medicina (medicine) – medicine (medicines)

mercato – market

monte – mountain

mura – city wall

museo – museum

nazionale – national

nuovo/a – new (m/f)

orto botanico – botanical gardens

ospedale – hospital

ostello – hostel

palazzo (palazzi) – mansion; palace; large building of any type (including an apartment block)

panetteria – bakery

panino (panini) – sandwich (sandwiches)

parcheggio – car park

parco – park

passeggiata – a stroll

pasticceria – cake shop

pastificio – pasta-making factory

pensione – small hotel or guesthouse, often offering board

pescheria – fish shop

piazza (piazze) – square (squares)

pinacoteca – art gallery

piscina – pool

polizia – police

ponte – bridge

porta – city gate

porto – port

presepe (presepi) – nativity scene (nativity scenes)

questura – police station

reale – royal

ruota – wheel

sala – room in a museum or a gallery

salumeria – delicatessen

santuario – sanctuary

scavi – archaeological ruins

scheda telefonica – phone-card

sedia a rotelle – wheelchair

sentiero – path; trail; track

servizio – service charge in restaurants

sole – sun

sottosuolo – underground

spiaggia – beach

statua – statue

stazione – station

strada – street; road

tabaccheria – tobacconist's shop

teatro – theatre

tempio – temple

terme – baths

torre – tower

treno – train

via – street, road

vecchio – old

vicolo – alley, alleyway

MENU DECODER

Places To Eat & Drink

enoteca – wine bar
friggitoria – fried-food kiosk
osteria – informal restaurant
pasticceria – patisserie/ pastry shop
ristorante – restaurant
trattoria – informal restaurant

At the Table

cameriere/a – waiter (m/f)
carta dei vini – wine list
conto – bill/cheque
spuntini – snacks
tovagliolo – napkin/serviette
vegetaliano/a – vegan (m/f)
vegetariano/a – vegetarian (m/f)

Staples

aglio – garlic
fior di latte – cow-milk mozzarella
insalata – salad
limone – lemon
mozzarella di bufala – buffalo-milk mozzarella
oliva – olive
panna – cream
peperoncino – chilli
pizza margherita – pizza topped with tomato, mozzarella and basil
pizza marinara – pizza topped with tomato, garlic, oregano and olive oil
rucola – rocket

Fish & Seafood

acciughe – anchovies
carpaccio – thin slices of raw fish (or meat)
granchio – crab
merluzzo – cod
pesce spada – swordfish
polpi – octopus
sarde – sardines
seppia – cuttlefish
sgombro – mackerel
vongole – clams

Meat

bistecca – steak
capretto – kid (goat)
coniglio – rabbit
fegato – liver
prosciutto cotto – cooked ham
prosciutto crudo – cured ham
salsiccia – sausage
vitello – veal

Cooking Methods

arrosto/a – roasted
bollito/a – boiled
cotto/a – cooked
crudo/a – raw
fritto/a – fried
alla griglia – grilled (broiled)

Fruit

ciliegia – cherry
fragole – strawberries
melone – cantaloupe; musk melon; rockmelon
pera – pear

Vegetables

asparagi – asparagus
carciofi – artichokes
fagiolini – green beans
finocchio – fennel
friarielli – Neapolitan broccoletti
melanzane – aubergine/ eggplant
peperoni – capsicums; peppers
tartufo – truffle

Gelato Flavours

Amarena – wild cherry
bacio – chocolate and hazelnuts
cioccolata – chocolate
cono – cone
coppa – cup
crema – cream
frutta di bosco – fruit of the forest (wild berries)
nocciola – hazelnut
vaniglia – vanilla
zuppa inglese – 'English soup', trifle

Drinks

amaretto – almond-flavoured liqueur
amaro – a dark liqueur prepared from herbs
espresso – short black coffee

Behind the Scenes

SEND US YOUR FEEDBACK

We love to hear from travellers – your comments keep us on our toes and help make our books better. Our well-travelled team reads every word on what you loved or loathed about this book. Although we cannot reply individually to postal submissions, we always guarantee that your feedback goes straight to the appropriate authors, in time for the next edition. Each person who sends us information is thanked in the next edition – the most useful submissions are rewarded with a selection of digital PDF chapters.

Visit **lonelyplanet.com/contact** to submit your updates and suggestions or to ask for help. Our award-winning website also features inspirational travel stories, news and discussions.

Note: We may edit, reproduce and incorporate your comments in Lonely Planet products such as guidebooks, websites and digital products, so let us know if you don't want your comments reproduced or your name acknowledged. For a copy of our privacy policy visit lonelyplanet.com/privacy.

OUR READERS

Many thanks to the travellers who used the last edition and wrote to us with helpful hints, useful advice and interesting anecdotes:
Jenny Arkell, Annukka Asikainen, Laura Braslins, Hendon Chubb, Steven Cook, Katie Dokshina, Henning Ericson, Tim Jerram, Erica Johnson, Raquel Miguel, Sheila Miller, Joe Parlavecchio, Katherine Tildesley

AUTHOR THANKS
Cristian Bonetto

As always, a heartfelt *grazie* to the generous, insightful Neapolitan friends who enriched this guide: my 'Re e Regina di Napoli', Valentina Vellusi, Alfonso Sperandeo, Giancarlo Di Maio, Claudio Cornia, Susy Galeone, Raffaele Scuotto, Guglielmo Muoio, Agostino Riitano and the dashing Vincenzo Mattiucci. Special thanks also to Clelia Santoro, Antonio Emanuele Piedimonte, the team at the Complesso degli Incurabili and Elena Vellusi. At Lonely Planet, sincere thanks to Joe Bindloss for the commission and to my ever-diligent coauthor, Josephine Quintero.

Josephine Quintero

Firstly many thanks to Robin Chapman for a great sense of humour, map-reading skills and for sharing hardwon expertise on hunting down the ultimate slice of pizza perfection, along with the best wines. Also a mega thank you to my daughter Isabel for the crash course in Italian and some insider tips. Thanks to the staff of all the tourist offices, particularly Fabiola Fasulo in Sorrento who went out of her way to decipher complex ferry schedules. Thanks also to Joe Bindloss and Cristian Bonetto for their troop-rallying emails during research.

ACKNOWLEDGMENTS

Climate map data adapted from Peel MC, Finlayson BL & McMahon TA (2007) 'Updated World Map of the Köppen-Geiger Climate Classification', Hydrology and Earth System Sciences, 11, 163344.
Illustrations pp94-95 by by Javier Zarracina.
Cover photograph: Atrani Amalfi Coastline, Campania, Italy, Rissell Kord/Alamy ©

This Book

This 4th edition of Lonely Planet's Naples, Pompeii & the Amalfi Coast guidebook was researched and written by Cristian Bonetto and Josephine Quintero. The previous two editions were written by Cristian Bonetto, Josephine Quintero and Duncan Garwood. This guidebook was commissioned in Lonely Planet's London office, and produced by the following:

Commissioning Editor
Joe Bindloss
Coordinating Editor
Jeanette Wall
Coordinating Cartographer Hunor Csutoros
Coordinating Layout Designer Joseph Spanti
Managing Editors Brigitte Ellemor, Bruce Evans
Managing Cartographers Shahara Ahmed, Anita Banh, Amanda Sierp
Managing Layout Designer Chris Girdler
Assisting Editors Elizabeth Anglin, Pat Kinsella, Joanne Newell, Kristin Odijk, Sam Trafford

Assisting Cartographers
Chris Tsismetzis, Sam Tyson
Cover Research
Naomi Parker
Internal Image Research
Frank Deim, Barbara Di Castro
Illustrator Javier Zarracina
Language Content
Branislava Vladislavljevic
Thanks to Laura Crawford, Ryan Evans, Larissa Frost, Jouve India, Kate McDonell, Annelies Mertens, Trent Paton, Raphael Richards, Dianne Schallmeiner, Gerard Walker

index

how to use this book

These symbols will help you find the listings you want:

- ◉ Sights
- 🐟 Beaches
- 🏃 Activities
- 🎓 Courses
- 👉 Tours
- 🎊 Festivals & Events
- 🛏 Sleeping
- 🍴 Eating
- 🍷 Drinking
- ⭐ Entertainment
- 🛍 Shopping
- ℹ Information/Transport

Look out for these icons:

- **TOP CHOICE** Our author's recommendation
- **FREE** No payment required
- 🍃 A green or sustainable option

Our authors have nominated these places as demonstrating a strong commitment to sustainability – for example by supporting local communities and producers, operating in an environmentally friendly way, or supporting conservation projects.

These symbols give you the vital information for each listing:

- ☎ Telephone Numbers
- ☺ Opening Hours
- Ⓟ Parking
- ☺ Nonsmoking
- ❄ Air-Conditioning
- @ Internet Access
- 📶 Wi-Fi Access
- 🏊 Swimming Pool
- 🥗 Vegetarian Selection
- 📖 English-Language Menu
- 👪 Family-Friendly
- 🐾 Pet-Friendly
- 🚌 Bus
- ⛴ Ferry
- Ⓜ Metro
- Ⓢ Subway
- 🚋 Tram
- 🚆 Train

Reviews are organised by author preference.

Map Legend

Sights
- 🏖 Beach
- 🅑 Buddhist
- 🏰 Castle
- ✝ Christian
- 🕉 Hindu
- ☪ Islamic
- ✡ Jewish
- ▮ Monument
- 🏛 Museum/Gallery
- 🏚 Ruin
- 🍷 Winery/Vineyard
- 🐾 Zoo
- ⦿ Other Sight

Activities, Courses & Tours
- 🤿 Diving/Snorkelling
- 🛶 Canoeing/Kayaking
- ⛷ Skiing
- 🏄 Surfing
- 🏊 Swimming/Pool
- 🚶 Walking
- 🏄 Windsurfing
- ⦿ Other Activity/Course/Tour

Sleeping
- 🛏 Sleeping
- ⛺ Camping

Eating
- 🍴 Eating

Drinking
- ☕ Drinking
- ☕ Cafe

Entertainment
- 🎭 Entertainment

Shopping
- 🛍 Shopping

Information
- 🏦 Bank
- 🏛 Embassy/Consulate
- ➕ Hospital/Medical
- @ Internet
- 👮 Police
- ✉ Post Office
- 📞 Telephone
- 🚻 Toilet
- ℹ Tourist Information
- • Other Information

Transport
- ✈ Airport
- ⊗ Border Crossing
- 🚌 Bus
- Cable Car/Funicular
- Cycling
- Ferry
- Monorail
- Ⓟ Parking
- ⛽ Petrol Station
- 🚕 Taxi
- Train/Railway
- Tram
- Ⓜ Underground Train Station
- • Other Transport

Routes
- Tollway
- Freeway
- Primary
- Secondary
- Tertiary
- Lane
- Unsealed Road
- Plaza/Mall
- Steps
-)= =(Tunnel
- Pedestrian Overpass
- Walking Tour
- Walking Tour Detour
- Path

Geographic
- 🛖 Hut/Shelter
- 🗼 Lighthouse
- 🔭 Lookout
- ▲ Mountain/Volcano
- 🌴 Oasis
-)(Park
-)(Pass
- 🧺 Picnic Area
- 💧 Waterfall

Population
- ✪ Capital (National)
- ◉ Capital (State/Province)
- ● City/Large Town
- ○ Town/Village

Boundaries
- — — - International
- - - - - State/Province
- - - - Disputed
- — - - Regional/Suburb
- Marine Park
- Cliff
- Wall

Hydrography
- River, Creek
- Intermittent River
- Swamp/Mangrove
- Reef
- Canal
- Water
- Dry/Salt/Intermittent Lake
- Glacier

Areas
- Beach/Desert
- + + + Cemetery (Christian)
- × × × Cemetery (Other)
- Park/Forest
- Sportsground
- Sight (Building)
- Top Sight (Building)

Note: not all symbols displayed above appear in this book

OUR STORY

A beat-up old car, a few dollars in the pocket and a sense of adventure. In 1972 that's all Tony and Maureen Wheeler needed for the trip of a lifetime – across Europe and Asia overland to Australia. It took several months, and at the end – broke but inspired – they sat at their kitchen table writing and stapling together their first travel guide, *Across Asia on the Cheap*. Within a week they'd sold 1500 copies. Lonely Planet was born.

Today, Lonely Planet has offices in Melbourne, London and Oakland, with more than 600 staff and writers. We share Tony's belief that 'a great guidebook should do three things: inform, educate and amuse'.

OUR WRITERS

Cristian Bonetto

Coordinating Author, Naples As an ex-writer of farce and TV soap, it's not surprising that Cristian clicks with Campania. The Italo-Australian scribe has been hooked on the region for years, returning regularly to compromise his waistline and take his favourite ride in the world – the chairlift from Anacapri to Monte Solaro. According to Cristian, few cities are as richly layered as Naples, and his musings on the city's complexities have appeared in print (and on screen) from London to Sydney. His Naples-based play *Il Cortile* (The Courtyard) toured a number of Italian cities in 2003 with the support of the prestigious Australia Council. To date, Cristian has contributed to over a dozen Lonely Planet guides, including *Italy, New York City, Denmark* and *Singapore*.

Read more about Cristian at:
lonelyplanet.com/members/cristianbonetto

Josephine Quintero

The Islands, the Amalfi Coast, Salerno & the Cilento Originally from England and a UC Berkeley graduate, Josephine's first encounters with Italy were visiting her daughter who lived and worked there for several years. The country continues to impress and inspire and she has contributed to several *Italy* guidebooks, including two editions of *Naples & the Amalfi Coast*. Josephine considers this a job made in heaven, such is the beauty, culture and, of course, the cuisine in this deservedly famous region. Highlights during this trip included discovering a Roman villa concealed under an Amalfi ceramics shop and managing to perfect her *limoncello* (lemon liquer) recipe – with plenty of tasting opportunities along the way.

Read more about Josephine at:
lonelyplanet.com/members/josephinequintero

Published by Lonely Planet Publications Pty Ltd
ABN 36 005 607 983
4th edition – Jan 2013
ISBN 978 1 74179 917 0
© Lonely Planet 2013   Photographs © as indicated 2013
10 9 8 7 6 5 4 3 2 1
Printed in China

Although the authors and Lonely Planet have taken all reasonable care in preparing this book, we make no warranty about the accuracy or completeness of its content and, to the maximum extent permitted, disclaim all liability arising from its use.

All rights reserved. No part of this publication may be copied, stored in a retrieval system, or transmitted in any form by any means, electronic, mechanical, recording or otherwise, except brief extracts for the purpose of review, and no part of this publication may be sold or hired, without the written permission of the publisher. Lonely Planet and the Lonely Planet logo are trademarks of Lonely Planet and are registered in the US Patent and Trademark Office and in other countries. Lonely Planet does not allow its name or logo to be appropriated by commercial establishments, such as retailers, restaurants or hotels. Please let us know of any misuses: lonelyplanet.com/ip.